# American
## Gold and Silver

Young Mark Twain was lured to Nevada during the silver- and gold-mining craze of the early 1860s; he failed as a miner but earned a living as a writer. In 1981 Twain would be honored on an American Arts gold medallion.

# AMERICAN
# GOLD AND SILVER

## U.S. MINT COLLECTOR AND
## INVESTOR COINS AND MEDALS,
## BICENTENNIAL TO DATE

## Dennis Tucker

*Foreword by Q. David Bowers*

Whitman
Publishing, LLC
PUBLISHING SINCE 1934

Whitman.com

# AMERICAN
## GOLD AND SILVER
U.S. MINT COLLECTOR AND INVESTOR COINS
AND MEDALS, BICENTENNIAL TO DATE

© 2016 Whitman Publishing, LLC
3101 Clairmont Road • Suite G • Atlanta, GA 30329

ISBN: 0794842372
Printed in China

Correspondence concerning this book may be directed to Whitman Publishing, Attn: American Gold and Silver, at the address above.

*Disclaimer:* Expert opinion should be sought in any significant numismatic purchase. This book is presented as a guide only. No warranty or representation of any kind is made concerning the completeness of the information presented. The author, a professional numismatist, regularly buys, sells, and sometimes holds certain of the items discussed in this book.

*Caveat:* The value estimates given are subject to variation and differences of opinion. Certain rare coins and medals trade infrequently, and an estimate or past auction price may have little relevance to future transactions. Before making decisions to buy or sell, consult the latest information. Past performance of the rare-coin market or any coin, medal, or series within that market is not necessarily an indication of future performance, as the future is unknown. Such factors as changing demand, popularity, grading interpretations, emergence of hoards, new discoveries, strength of the overall market, and economic conditions will continue to be influences.

*About the coins on the cover:* The 1984 John Steinbeck gold medallion is among the scarcest in the U.S. Mint's American Arts program. The "Bald Eagle" silver medal is part of the 2003 National Wildlife Refuge System series. American Buffalo gold coins, recreating the design of the famous Buffalo nickel, have been minted since 2006. The 9/11 national medal honors the fallen of September 11, 2001. The 2015 Jackie Kennedy First Spouse gold coin was one of the most popular in that series; collectors bought more than 10,000 pieces in the first day of sales. All of these and more are among the hundreds of outstanding and highly collectible gold and silver coins and medals crafted by the U.S. Mint in recent years—and they all await you within this book.

For a complete catalog of numismatic reference books, supplies, and storage
and display products, visit Whitman Publishing online at www.whitman.com.

# CONTENTS

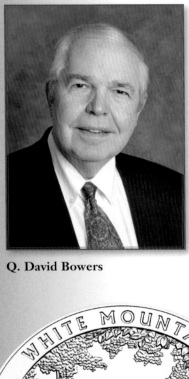

**Q. David Bowers**

# FOREWORD

**I**magine if a coin collector had visited the Philadelphia Mint in the 1790s and had seen engraver Robert Scot working on dies, had watched copper, silver, and gold coins being struck on presses, had seen newly minted "pennies" packed in wooden casks and shipped by horse wagon, and had taken notes and asked questions. How much more we would know now!

This book, *American Gold and Silver*, reflects the work of a modern-day equivalent of that fictitious visitor. Author Dennis Tucker, through the office of Mint Director of Corporate Communications Tom Jurkowsky and his staff, has had the opportunity in recent years to visit and go behind the scenes at all four operating mints: Philadelphia, Denver, San Francisco, and West Point. I had the honor of accompanying him, Tom, and on occasion some other researchers. At the Philadelphia Mint he visited with the artist-sculptors in the Engraving Department, viewed sketches and models, and learned many details of their work. At West Point he saw gold bullion-related coins being struck. Examining coinage dies under microscopes, witnessing a huge Gräbener press stamping out five-ounce silver discs, watching limited-edition collector coins being carefully packaged, observing circulation coins being put in huge sacks and handled by forklifts—Dennis experienced it all.

The result is this numismatic study, a *tour de force*, and for you the reader an "I was there" experience. In this book there are no untested theories, no questions left unanswered! Deputy Mint Director Dick Peterson shared information, as did the superintendents (today called plant managers) of Philadelphia, Denver, San Francisco, and West Point, and mint employees involved in all aspects from planchet preparation to coinage to shipping. This level of first-person experience is at once exciting, informative, and in the annals of numismatic research unique.

While we know much about how copper, silver, and gold coins were made at the Philadelphia Mint in the 1790s, much more about that era is still conjecture. There was no Dennis Tucker present. So far as I have been able to determine, no dedicated researcher or journalist ever visited to take detailed notes.

**White Mountain National Forest: the famous New Hampshire park, and the silver bullion coin that honors it. In *American Gold and Silver*, Dennis Tucker studies this modern U.S. Mint coin and hundreds of others.**

Absent that type of first-hand experience, traditional research still is fascinating. The standard methodology in research (which I know well from having written quite a few books) is to visit libraries, consult works already in print, write letters, explore old newspapers, and in modern times look on the Internet. Numismatic information has been gathered in similar ways since the first money-related book was published in America in 1839: the impressive 248-page *An Historical Account of Massachusetts Currency*. Author Joseph Felt dealt with Massachusetts coins and other money dating back to 1652—money made and spent by generations who had long since passed.

Today the U.S. Mint—the Treasury agency headquartered in Washington, DC—is the center for supervising the nation's four mint facilities plus the Fort Knox bullion depository, keeping records, implementing coin programs (with themes mandated by Congress), releasing news to keep the public informed, and many other activities. The Mint often has displays at leading coin conventions, where officials and employees are on hand to meet and greet visitors. It is a new era of information and communication.

The above said, the book you are reading is the first in numismatics to have been produced with the collaboration of those actively involved, day to day, in American coinage—artists, assayers, historians, factory workers, technicians, managers, and other Mint staff and workers.

In my own world of research, writing, buying, and selling, I concentrate mainly on older coins (although I do have a collection of modern dollars). As I read the advance proofs of this book I learned many things that for me were new and even amazing. I was quite surprised to learn that one of the First Spouse gold coins, a series honoring presidential wives, depicts and names a lady who, for all I know, was never in the White House! In fact, her cause was anathema to President Woodrow Wilson, who might have had her tossed in jail (as he did with others of her persuasion). Her name is Alice Paul. (If you can't wait, fast-forward to chapter 6.)

Much other information—some familiar, some new—awaits you, compiled, distilled, and analyzed in *American Gold and Silver*. Beyond the interesting text the book will serve permanently as *the* source for facts on the U.S. Mint's modern gold and silver coins and medals.

Enjoy the experience!

**Q. David Bowers**
**Wolfeboro, New Hampshire**

Q. David Bowers is chairman emeritus of Stack's Bowers Galleries and numismatic director of Whitman Publishing. He served as president of the American Numismatic Association (1983–1985) and president of the Professional Numismatists Guild (1977–1979). Bowers is the author of more than 50 books and several thousand articles, including columns in *Coin World* and *The Numismatist*. His books have earned more "Book of the Year Award" honors bestowed by the Numismatic Literary Guild than have those of any other author.

Bowers is a trustee of the New Hampshire Historical Society and a fellow of the American Antiquarian Society, the American Numismatic Society, and the Massachusetts Historical Society. In Wolfeboro, New Hampshire, he serves on the board of selectmen and is the town historian. He has been a consultant for the Smithsonian Institution, the Treasury Department, and the U.S. Mint, and is research editor of the *Guide Book of United States Coins* (the hobby's best-selling "Red Book").

# PREFACE

**Various U.S. Assay Commission medals from the 1800s and 1900s.**

This book is the third in a trilogy of Whitman Publishing volumes exploring the modern silver, gold, and platinum coins and medals of the U.S. Mint. The first was *American Silver Eagles*, coauthored by retired Mint chief engraver John M. Mercanti and numismatist Michael Standish. The second was *American Gold and Platinum Eagles*, by retired Mint director Edmund C. Moy.

Those two books covered the ins and outs of our nation's most popular and successful bullion coins: the American Eagles. This volume, *American Gold and Silver*, covers "everything else"—focusing first on the American Arts Commemorative Series of the early 1980s, which laid the foundation for the successes that followed (including the American Eagles).

Until now the American Arts gold medallion program has never been fully examined in a book-length study. While conventional wisdom dismisses the program as a complete failure, this book seeks to examine it in a new light, as a transition in what was a turbulent period for gold in the United States. In the 1970s and early 1980s, Congress, the nation's executive branch (including the Treasury Department), and the country as a whole were struggling to understand the best role for our stockpiles of gold. As I explain in chapter 3, "the American Arts medals were a crucial part of the nation's learning curve, and seen in this light the program was if not entirely *successful*, certainly *important*."

America's relationship with silver and gold didn't start in the 1980s, of course. Chapter 1 of this book sets the stage with a brief history of Man's ancient fascination with the precious metals. This leads into the British colonial era, wherein mercantilism and other economic and legal forces affected (and largely restricted) the circulation of gold and silver in America. A discussion of the coinage of the U.S. Mint starts in the 1790s and leads to the mandated end of circulating gold in 1933. The "villain" in this scenario (or hero, depending on your viewpoint) is President Franklin Roosevelt, with his famous Executive Order 6102, under which millions of dollars' worth of gold coins were surrendered to the Federal Reserve. The 30-plus-years stretch of gold being illegal was finally broken in 1974, when President Gerald Ford retracted Roosevelt's orders and made gold legal to own again. From this came a period of robust debate and study on the federal level—leading, as noted above, to the American Arts gold medal experiment and, ultimately, to the birth of today's hugely successful American Eagles. Not long before that, silver went through its own turbulent period, rising in value worldwide until the United States was forced to remove it from all circulating coinage.

As I note in chapter 2, it's interesting that gold and silver have left the realm of day-to-day *money*, but gold is now more readily and legally accessible to the average American than ever in the past. In recent years the U.S. Mint has continued to innovate and develop new bullion programs. They are part of America's rich heritage. They occupy the final pages of a national story still being written, and they deserve our study—hence this book. The country's first 24-karat gold coins, in the American Buffalo series, are herded together in chapter 5. The beautiful First Spouses, which include some of the rarest of modern U.S. coins, are assembled in chapter 6. Silver is given the spotlight in chapter 7, with the massive five-ounce coins of the America the Beautiful series. Other chapters focus on other silver and gold coins and medals, mostly dating from the 1976 national Bicentennial to today.

The American Eagles are without a doubt the most popular of U.S. bullion coins. Collectors and investors have bought more than 350 million one-ounce American Silver Eagles since the modern bullion program started in 1986, and more than 43 million gold and platinum Eagle coins in various sizes and formats.

However, the U.S. Mint's other silver and gold programs—those explored in this book—have also made their mark and won their share of enthusiasts. Each series has its own special charm, and it's notable that six of the coins cataloged in this volume have been ranked among the "100 Greatest U.S. Modern Coins."[1] Since 2006 collectors and investors have bought nearly 3 million gold coins of the American Buffalo series; a testament, in part, to the uniquely American artistry of their design. Other programs that might not sell in the millions hold the potential for hidden gems—"sleepers" of low mintage and high aesthetic appeal, waiting to be discovered by the mainstream of the hobby. The entire mintage of First Spouse bullion coins sold since 2007—accounting for some 175,000 ounces of gold—is eclipsed by the output *of any single year*, even the least active, in the American Gold Eagle program. And yet, for collectors, their very scarcity makes them far more desirable than their more common cousins. American Arts gold medallions, honoring some of the nation's most popular artists, have seen attrition over the years that makes even the most common pieces much scarcer than their mintages suggest. And the Mint's other silver and gold medals and coins celebrate great Americans (Martha Washington, Benjamin Franklin, Teddy Roosevelt), historic places (Gettysburg, Mount Rushmore), significant events (the Bicentennial of Independence, 9/11), and other national subjects that make their appeal and their importance timeless.

*American Gold and Silver* is the first book to systematically study each of the Mint's recent bullion-related coinage and medallic programs. It was written to be an overview for the newcomer to these series—the collector who wants a detailed but engagingly readable education in history, rarity levels, popular varieties, and market values. It's also a book for the longtime collector who wants a single-source reference: a guide not to be read once and then shelved, but to be kept handy for frequent visits and consultations. It's a textbook for the serious numismatist who wants a behind-the-scenes view of the intricacies of design, production, distribution, and other technical and artistic factors. And for the investor this book introduces and explains the lure of numismatics— the art and science of the hobby of collecting coins—adding another aspect to the desirability of these interesting bullion issues.

**Dennis Tucker**
**Atlanta, Georgia**

# 1
# Silver and Gold in Human Civilization

Gold is the most legendary and coveted of the precious metals—more valuable than silver, more useful than platinum. We humans have been intrigued by it since time immemorial. Gold has launched more ships than Helen of Troy; it has sparked wars, built empires, doomed civilizations, fueled religions, and inspired wild-goose chases. It has entered the languages of mankind as a profound and metaphorical concept that embodies brilliance (the Golden Age), goodness (the Golden Rule, a "heart of gold"), truth and authenticity ("good as gold"), value ("worth its weight in gold"), immutability (the "gold standard"), and longevity (golden anniversaries).

A Hungarian proverb encourages hard work by invoking the metal: "He who wakes up early finds gold." A Chinese metaphor uses it to extol courage: "True gold does not fear the furnace." Children are entertained with tales of a pot of gold at the end of the rainbow (a legendary and tantalizing goal). In days past, the loyalty of longtime employees traditionally was rewarded, upon retirement, with a gold watch.

Man's love of gold is so powerful that the metal can also inspire fear, greed, and other dark feelings. The fourth-century Roman poet Prudentius warned that "Hunger for gold is made greater as more gold is acquired." A Latin proverb made note of gold's ability to tempt and corrupt: "Even the just may sin with an open chest of gold before them." The Syrian wit Publilius Syrus noted its overpowering ability to persuade and influence: "When gold argues the cause, eloquence is impotent."

Silver, too, has a long history of human fascination, going back thousands of years. The precious metal can symbolize optimism ("Every cloud has a silver lining," or,

"Gold fever" has been around since humans discovered the precious metal. In 1925 Charlie Chaplin's Little Tramp character would head to the Klondike in the Yukon Territory to strike it rich.

as P.T. Barnum quipped, "Every *crowd* has a silver lining"). A quick, fail-safe solution to a problem is a "silver bullet." A person with family connections and wealth is said to have been born with a silver spoon in his mouth. Valuable things presented with ease and in a grand manner are handed to you on a silver platter. A smooth talker is said to be silver-tongued. The 25th wedding anniversary is silver.

As might be expected, in proverbs and popular culture silver often takes a back seat to its more valuable cousin. We're told to "Make new friends, but keep the old; one is silver, the other is gold." Many cultures have a saying along the lines of "If speaking is silver, silence [or listening] is golden." An English saying tells us that "Butter is gold in the morning, silver at noon, and lead at night."

> The sweat of the sun; the tears of the moon.
> —*Inca descriptions for gold and silver*

> "Says the boaster: 'All of my goods are of silver and gold, even my copper kettles.'"
> —*Dutch proverb*

Silver and gold are classified as two of the "Seven Metals of Antiquity" (along with copper, lead, tin, iron, and mercury). Gold was first worked by Man at the end of the Stone Age, around 6000 BC, and silver around 4000 BC, so both were known to ancient Mesopotamia, Egypt, Greece, and Rome. The two precious metals together made up the first coins—in ancient Lydia (today part of Turkey), a gold/silver alloy called *electrum* was their source material.

**Abraham Lincoln used gold as a metaphor, lamenting that greed could blind a person from seeing simple reason and recognizing injustice. Speaking of slavery and its firmly entrenched financial interests, he said that "The plainest print cannot be read through a gold eagle [$10 coin]."**

**Electrum is an alloy of silver and gold that occurs naturally, as well as being blended by metalworkers. The tiny electrum coins pictured here are from ancient Ionia, in present-day Turkey. They are among the earliest coins ever made.**

**A mineral collector might assemble a "thumbnail" collection of gold. Thumbnail specimens typically are fastened into individual boxes with hinged tops. The box protects smaller samples while the collector handles and examines them. The small size of a thumbnail collection makes it convenient for those with limited storage and display space. A desk drawer or a single small display case can hold dozens of specimens.**

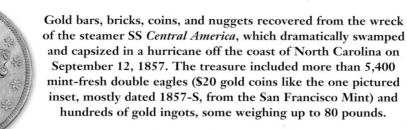

Gold bars, bricks, coins, and nuggets recovered from the wreck of the steamer SS *Central America*, which dramatically swamped and capsized in a hurricane off the coast of North Carolina on September 12, 1857. The treasure included more than 5,400 mint-fresh double eagles ($20 gold coins like the one pictured inset, mostly dated 1857-S, from the San Francisco Mint) and hundreds of gold ingots, some weighing up to 80 pounds.

# GOLD THROUGHOUT HISTORY

The value of gold comes from its unique combination of aesthetic and useful qualities, as well as its rarity. It is both warmly beautiful as an ornamental metal, and remarkably diverse in its utility in scientific and industrial applications. It's malleable—it can be hammered thin enough to cover the dome of Georgia's State Capitol building with a sparkling brilliant skin. A mere 43 ounces of Dahlonega-mined metal will layer the entire expanse of the "Gold Dome" (75 feet in diameter) to make it shine in Atlanta's summer sun. That same golden lump of 43 ounces could be finely drawn into a wire long enough to be wrapped *twice* around the Earth, with plenty to spare. (That's not an intellectual exercise along the lines of "How many angels can dance on the head of a pin?"—gold wire really does get stretched that thin, for use in electrical contacts and bonding wire.) In addition to this extraordinary ductility, gold is highly resistant to corrosion. Gold coins from the 1857 shipwreck of the SS *Central America* were brought up from the bottom of the ocean after 130 years, some looking as bright and crisp as the day they were minted. Gold's value as a conductor of electricity is exceeded by few other metals, making it a high-demand resource for industry and science. It is flexible enough to fill a cavity in a tooth, and strong enough to last a lifetime once the filling is set. In jewelry and other artistic uses gold has no equal. It decorates royal crowns. It's wrought into wedding rings that bind souls together. To "gild the lily" means to take a perfect creation and try to make it even more so.

Today a huge quantity of gold is used in jewelry (in 2010 amounting to 2,017 tons, valued at $79 billion, according to the World Gold Council). For jewelry, gold's purity is measured in karats. "Pure gold" (defined as having 0.3% or less impurities) is rated as 24 karat (24k). Silver added to it will make it paler, reducing its yellow color and moving it toward greenish-gold as more is added. Mixing copper with pure gold makes a redder alloy. These metals and others (such as nickel, palladium, and zinc) are added because pure gold is too soft to use in jewelry. In the United States, 10k fineness (41.7% purity) is the minimum at which an alloy can be advertised as "gold."

**Various samples of natural, unwrought gold.**

*Chemical symbol:* **Au**
*Atomic number:* **79**
*Density:* **19.3 times the weight of water, by volume.**
*Environment:* **Quartz veins and alluvial deposits.**
*Color:* **Yellow, pale yellow, orange, yellow white, reddish white.**
*Habit:* **Massive (having no particular shape); granular (fracturing into separate grains); dendritic (exhibiting branching tree-like growths).**
*Locality:* **Many places worldwide, including the United States, Siberia (Russia), South Africa, and Canada. In 2013 China was the world's top producer of gold (accounting for about 15 percent of the world supply), followed by Australia, the United States, and Russia. In the United States, gold is found in all of the western states as well as in Georgia, Maryland, Michigan, New Hampshire, North Carolina, Pennsylvania, South Carolina, South Dakota, Tennessee, Texas, and Virginia. Georgia was the site of the first U.S. gold rush, in the region of Dahlonega (which eventually would be home to a federal mint). California and Alaska are also famous for their gold rushes. Today more than three-quarters of all gold mined in the United States comes from Nevada.**

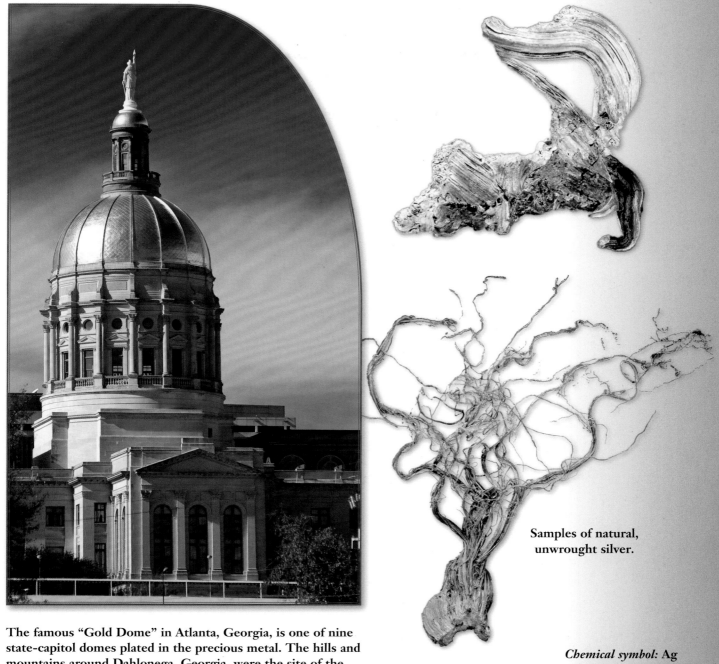

Samples of natural, unwrought silver.

The famous "Gold Dome" in Atlanta, Georgia, is one of nine state-capitol domes plated in the precious metal. The hills and mountains around Dahlonega, Georgia, were the site of the first significant gold rush in the United States, predating California's by 20 years.

*Chemical symbol:* Ag
*Atomic number:* 47
*Density:* 10.5 times the weight of water, by volume.
*Environment:* Sulfide ore veins.
*Color:* Silver white, gray white, gray.
*Habit:* Arborescent, dendritic (exhibiting branching tree-like growths).
*Locality:* Many places worldwide, including the United States, Canada, Mexico, Australia, and Russia. According to the British Geological Survey, in 2013 Mexico was the world's top producer of mined silver (accounting for more than 20 percent of the world supply), followed by Peru and China, each of which mined about two-thirds of Mexico's output. In the United States, silver has been mined extensively in Alaska (recently the nation's leading silver-producing state), Arizona, California, Colorado (a major producer in the 1800s), Idaho (home of the Coeur d'Alene silver district, the nation's top producer of all time), Missouri, Montana, Nevada (where the discovery of the Comstock Lode in 1858 gave birth to large-scale silver mining in the United States), New Hampshire, New Mexico, Oregon, Pennsylvania, Texas, Utah, and Washington. In many states silver production is a by-product of copper mining.

## Table 1: Karat Rating of Gold Alloys

| Karat | Composition | Percentage of Gold |
|-------|-------------|--------------------|
| 24k | Pure gold | Greater than 99.7% gold |
| 18k | 18 parts gold, 6 parts other metal(s) | 75% gold |
| 14k | 14 parts gold, 10 parts other metal(s) | 58.3% gold |
| 12k | 12 parts gold, 12 parts other metal(s) | 50% gold |
| 10k | 10 parts gold, 14 parts other metal(s) | 41.7% gold |

## Table 2: Chemical Composition of Gold Alloys With Color and Karat Rating[1]

| Color of Gold | Karat | Alloy Composition |
|---------------|-------|-------------------|
| Yellow gold | 22k | Gold 91.67%<br>Silver 5.00%<br>Copper 2.00%<br>Zinc 1.33% |
| Red gold | 18k | Gold 75%<br>Copper 25% |
| Rose gold | 18k | Gold 75%<br>Copper 22.25%<br>Silver 2.75% |
| Pink gold | 18k | Gold 75%<br>Copper 20%<br>Silver 5% |
| White gold* | 18k | Gold 75%<br>Platinum or palladium 25% |
| White gold* | 18k | Gold 75%<br>Palladium 10%<br>Nickel 10%<br>Zinc 5% |
| Gray-white gold | 18k | Gold 75%<br>Iron 17%<br>Copper 8% |
| Soft-green gold | 18k | Gold 75%<br>Silver 25% |
| Light-green gold | 18k | Gold 75%<br>Copper 23%<br>Cadmium 2% |
| Green gold | 18k | Gold 75%<br>Silver 20%<br>Copper 5% |
| Deep-green gold | 18k | Gold 75%<br>Silver 15%<br>Copper 6%<br>Cadmium 4% |
| Blue-white or blue gold | 18k | Gold 75%<br>Iron 25% |
| Purple gold | 18k | Gold 80%<br>Aluminum 20% |

* Also known as *jeweler's gold*.

Jewelry today accounts for about 60% of gold use. In addition, the precious metal is used in technology (for mobile phones, laptop computers, space travel, and other high tech) and in medicine (for example, in dentistry, cancer treatments, and bacteria-resistant implants). Those and similar industrial uses account for about 10% of *gold* consumption. For the purposes of this book, we focus on another important use of gold: the remaining 30% of the world supply that goes to investment, hoarding, and speculation. This includes coins and investment-grade bullion.

Gold has been used in coins since the first coins were struck—tiny electrum (gold-and-silver-alloy) pieces made in ancient Lydia around 700 BC. By 600 BC the Lydians and others were making coins of unalloyed gold. Philip II of Macedon, who would "divide and rule" quite a bit of territory in the fourth century BC, minted coins of gold, as did his son, the celebrated Alexander the Great. Their coins circulated widely throughout the civilized world. Rome existed for about 500 years before the Romans began making coins; the Republic's first gold pieces were struck to help finance its wars. Gold coins called *aurei* were minted for circulation in the time of Julius Caesar, a half century preceding Christ's birth, and continued for the next 500 years. The far-reaching Romans extracted their gold from Spain, central Europe, and southern Europe. After Rome's imperial power collapsed, gold's circulation in the West slowed down. To the east, the Byzantine Empire had numerous mints that produced gold coins. In chapter 3 ("Coins of the Middle Ages") of *Money of the World: Coins That Made History*, Robert Wilson Hoge gives a beautifully illustrated tour-de-force study of gold (as well as silver) coins minted as Rome was in its decline, plus coins of Persia, the Aksumite Kingdom, and other medieval issuers. The circulation of gold coins picked up during the High and Late Middle Ages, during the Crusades, and later when various German, Italian, French, and other European powers and potentates started significant coinage. Venice introduced the gold ducat in 1284—it would be hugely popular as a trade coin for hundreds of years, its mintage ending only when Napoleon Bonaparte dismantled the Republic of Venice in 1797. England's first significant gold coins, the florin and the noble, came out in 1343 and 1344, respectively. These were followed by various other English gold pieces, with the milled (machine-made) guinea introduced in 1663. The Coinage Act of 1816 was part of Britain's planned economic stabilization after the expensive Napoleonic Wars. A new British gold sovereign debuted in 1817.

This 14-karat gold Waltham pocket watch from the late 1890s, with its elaborately engraved scene of a hunter and two hound dogs, sold for more than $5,300 in November 2014. Jewelry today accounts for 60% of gold use.

An ancient Greek distater minted in the name of Alexander the Great. This gold coin features the goddess Athena wearing a crested helmet in the Corinthian style and, on the reverse, Nike holding a victory wreath. (shown 3x actual size)

After the New World was "discovered" and colonized, Spain exploded into production of massive amounts of gold and silver coins from American-mined metal.

# SILVER THROUGHOUT HISTORY

As with gold, silver's value derives from a rare combination of beauty, usefulness, and scarcity. It is extremely malleable and ductile (second only to gold in those features) and highly resistant to corrosion. It conducts heat and electricity better than any other metal. Silver is harder than gold, making it useful in decoration and jewelry, and like gold it has numerous applications in science and high-tech, medicine, and other important industries.

The ancient Greeks used silver in coinage issued by various city-states over many centuries. The earliest silver coins were not the perfectly round, machine-produced disks we use today, but simpler lumps of metal fashioned to a specified weight and stamped with designs. Over time they became more and more artful and sophisticated. Greek merchants carried these coins throughout the Mediterranean in the course of their trade. For their issuers, coins had the added bonus of educational, political, and propaganda value; they spread messages through their portraits, religious symbols, and allegorical designs.

Alexander the Great, the most powerful king of Macedonia, dominated the Greek world in the fourth century BC. He federated the Greek states and conquered other lands, including the kingdom of the Persians. His coinage circulated far and wide. After Alexander's death his empire was broken up into kingdoms that continued to mint silver (as well as gold and copper) coins of their own account.

Silver was one of the first coinage materials of the ancient Roman Republic, along with subsidiary bronze pieces, starting in the early third century BC. The silver denarius was the principal Roman Imperial coin for several centuries. As the Empire grew, its conquests (including acquisition of large silver mines in Macedonia) led to more and more silver currency. Imperial as well as local silver coinage increased. Over time, extravagant Rome declined in power, with taxation meeting less and less of the imperial expenses and coinage of freshly mined metal filling in the gap—in other words, inflation of the money supply. Various rulers felt pressure to debase their silver coinage until some denominations ended up as simply silver-washed copper.

Other authorities minted silver coins in ancient times, including in Carthage, Phoenicia, Persia, and the Sasanian Empire, and among the Celtic, Jewish, and Arab cultures.

**The turtle on this silver stater (circa 480–457 BC) of Aegina was sacred to Aphrodite, the Greek goddess of love and beauty. The owl on the silver tetradrachm (circa 449–420 BC) of Athens was a symbol of Athena, goddess of wisdom, courage, and civilization. These coins, colloquially known as "turtles" and "owls," circulated throughout the civilized world. (shown 3x actual size)**

In the Byzantine Empire—basically what remained of conquered Rome's eastern civilization after the barbarian invasions of the 400s AD—coinage was centered more on gold and copper, rather than silver. Medieval England and Europe, meanwhile, had their silver pennies, pfennigs, pennings, deniers, and similar small-sized coins, minted in small quantities mostly for local or regional use. As had happened in imperial Rome, economic pressure forced the debasement of many silver coinages until they were ghosts of their earlier selves—sometimes alloyed as 95 parts of base metal for every 5 parts of silver.

This situation began to change by the late 1400s and early 1500s. The discovery and subsequent mining of great amounts of silver in central Europe led to a broad expansion of silver coinage. In the German Tyrol region, large-sized coins minted in the 1480s quickly became popular. Around Bohemia's Joachimsthal (the *Thal*, or valley, of St. Joachim, now in the Czech Republic), so much silver was mined and minted that the resulting large silver coins, called *joachimsthalers*, became an international standard. With their German name shortened to *thaler* and then translated into local languages, their style was adapted as the Dutch *rijksdaalder* ("national thaler"), the Danish *rigsdaler*, the Italian *tallero*, and the Polish *talar*, among others.

Discoveries of enormous silver deposits in Mexico and South America in the 1540s (and later) would change the equation even further. With its New World empire, Spain would become the world's largest producer of silver coins, as well as gold, quickly dwarfing even the massive coinages of the Joachimsthal region. This would trigger inflation in Europe, reorganize the global economy, and confirm Spain as the richest empire on Earth. The Spanish dollar (or 8-reales coin) would become an early North American unit of account, and from there the fledgling United States would authorize its own silver dollar in 1785.

# SILVER AND GOLD IN MONETARY SYSTEMS

It was natural that silver and gold grew into important forms of money in ancient times, and that their status continued into the modern era. These are rare metals, but not so rare (like platinum) that a significant amount of coinage is impossible. They're soft enough to hammer into small, standardized shapes and weights. This makes them a more logical measure of value than, say, a bag of wheat or a horse. Silver and gold coins easily meet the requirements of *money*:

> they are a universally recognized medium of exchange (an intermediary used in trade to avoid the inconveniences of pure barter);
>
> they are a unit of account (a means of valuing goods, services, assets, liabilities, income, and expenses);
>
> they are a store of value (an asset that can be saved, retrieved, and exchanged at a later time); and
>
> they can be a standard of deferred payment (a way to pay debts).

This 15th-century silver taler (or *guldiner*) of Archduke Sigismund, Austria, was minted from locally mined metal. It was the first dollar-sized coin to use an Arabic-numeral date (1486). (shown 1.5x actual size)

By the 1500s, private-citizen Europeans who had accumulated a store of gold and silver often would entrust their coins to the safekeeping of a goldsmith. Such arrangements gave birth to modern banking and checking and bank notes. In medieval and early Renaissance Italy and elsewhere, wealthy citizens of prosperous cities such as Florence, Venice, and Genoa would use their gold as a convenient tool for transacting business. A merchant, instead of physically moving gold coins himself to make a purchase, could send an order to the goldsmith who stored his gold. The goldsmith would either pay out the ordered quantity, or, if the receiver was agreeable, would issue a receipt for the amount of gold. This receipt—a form of paper money—could then be used to settle other payments or debts. The gold itself, meanwhile, would stay safe and secure in the goldsmith's vault.

A goldsmith of solid stability and reputation might feel confident to issue more paper money than could be redeemed by the gold held in his vaults. Normal market forces of money supply and demand would come into play. A healthy amount of inflation—paper money pumped into circulation—would encourage commerce; on the other hand, if people felt too much paper money was being issued, cheapening it compared to gold, they would return it to its issuer for redemption in coins. With trade booming, and thus keeping paper money in circulation, there was little risk for the goldsmiths that everyone would cash in all their paper at any given time. Markets would fluctuate, but a collapse would be rare because gold was always backing up the system.

As trade flourished between nations, governments naturally looked to gold as the means of controlling their economies. The economic theory and practice of mercantilism (see chapter 2) was predominant in the 1500s and into the 1700s as the great powers built up their overseas colonies. With mercantilism (basically a form of bullionism), governments sought to hoard as much gold and silver as possible in the mother country, while limiting its export (but still encouraging commerce by maintaining a positive balance of trade, and circulating other kinds of money). Through commerce Great Britain built up a huge store of gold and silver, despite the fact that practically no precious metal was mined from its own soil.

It was Britain that established the first formal gold standard, in 1821, four years after it introduced its new gold sovereign coin. Under this system the British government

**"Il Cambiavalute" ("The Money-Changer"), a modern stained-glass panel in the National Roman Museum, Rome, Italy. Based on an anonymous 15th-century miniature in the Biblioteca Estense (Modena, Italy), it shows a money-changer in his shop, with account books and coins on the counter.**

issued paper money backed by its gold reserves. British paper currency could be redeemed ("converted") on demand into British gold coins. The gold standard was built to foster certainty in the marketplace and stabilize the nation's paper currency, discouraging inflation. Most countries followed suit and by the 1870s held their own money supplies to the gold standard. The United States was on a silver standard, originally inspired by the Spanish silver dollar, but would switch to a gold-dollar unit of account in 1900. Globally the gold-coin supply increased by more than 50% from the early 1890s to 1914 thanks to new discoveries of ore in Colorado, Nevada, northwestern Canada, and South Africa, and advances in extraction technology.

World War I (1914–1918) brought an end, or at least a decline, to many old institutions. The gold standard, which had served European and global commerce for nearly 100 years, was one of them. The huge expenses of the war led to inflationary pressures that couldn't be resisted. Great Britain in particular shipped much of its gold to the United States to pay for military materiel and to finance its war effort. For many governments it was impossible to limit the paper-money supply to the amount of gold held in their reserves, and they suspended their reliance on the gold standard. The United States profited, and actually became a net creditor by 1919. After the war, half of the world's gold was held by the United States and much of the rest had been converted from paper money and tucked away by private citizens. Inflation (and in some places hyperinflation—in particular in Germany, which was forced to pay out much of its gold in war reparations) was the norm.

The United Kingdom and many other countries tried to stabilize their economies by following the British Gold Standard Act of 1925. This kept gold *bullion* as a standard, but relieved some pressure by repealing convertibility. Certain governments would be required to sell gold bullion (mostly in 12-kilogram, or roughly 400-ounce, bars) on demand at a fixed price, but would not be required to redeem paper money with gold coins.

This new economic system brought deflation and provided some stability, but the Great Depression finally forced an end to the gold standard. Runs on the British pound drained the United Kingdom of gold and in September 1931 it went off the gold standard officially. Australia and New Zealand were already off the standard by then, and Canada followed suit. Austria and Germany had collapsed financially earlier in the year. In 1934 the United States passed the Gold Reserve Act. This ended America's gold standard, nationalizing much gold and stopping convertibility.

Nearly all gold would remain illegal for the average private U.S. citizen to own from the early 1930s to the early 1970s. Chapters 2 and 3 discuss this in more detail.

**World War I brought the end to many old monarchies, including those of the German Empire. Kaiser Wilhelm II, seen here in happier times, would exile himself to the Netherlands in November 1918. Most of Germany's gold supply would be used to pay for the war. Internationally, the gold standard itself would be dethroned by the conflict's economic turmoil. (Prussian 20-mark coin shown 2x actual size)**

# SILVER AND GOLD TODAY: MINING, COINAGE, AND BULLION

For coinage and bullion purposes, gold and silver purity is measured as fineness in parts of 1,000. For many years the standard fineness for precious-metal U.S. coins was .900—that is, 90% silver (for dimes, quarters, half dollars, and silver dollars) or 90% gold (for gold dollars and $2.50, $3, $5, $10, and $20 coins). Metals typically alloyed with silver for coinage include copper and nickel. A gold coin's alloy often includes silver and/or copper to make it harder and more durable.

Today silver and gold are no longer used in circulating coinage, but many nations mint official bullion coins. These are primarily for investment, though some are specially made with attractive finishes and limited editions, as numismatic collectibles. Typically today's bullion coins are of high purity—up to 24 karats for gold and .9999 fineness for silver.

The top 20 producers of mined silver in 2013 were as follows.[2]

## Table 3: The Top 20 Silver-Mining Countries

| Rank | Country | Production in kilograms (silver metal content) |
|---|---|---|
| 1st | Mexico | 5,821,001 |
| 2nd | Peru | 3,674,283 |
| 3rd | China | 3,670,210 |
| 4th | Australia | 1,840,000 |
| 5th | Russia | 1,412,100 |
| 6th | Bolivia | 1,288,000 |
| 7th | Chile | 1,173,845 |
| 8th | Poland | 1,100,000 |
| 9th | USA | 1,090,000 |
| 10th | Kazakhstan | 963,580 |
| 11th | Argentina | 682,600 |
| 12th | Canada | 645,976 |
| 13th | India | 349,774 |
| 14th | Sweden | 341,346 |
| 15th | Guatemala | 265,943 |
| 16th | Morocco | 255,000 |
| 17th | Indonesia | 200,000 (estimated) |
| 18th | Turkey | 186,621 |
| 19th | Finland | 100,890 |
| 20th | Papua New Guinea | 89,666 |

The top 20 producers of mined gold in 2013 were as follows.[3]

**Table 4: The Top 20 Gold-Mining Countries**

| Rank | Country | Production in kilograms (gold metal content) |
|------|---------|----------------------------------------------|
| 1st | China | 428,000 |
| 2nd | Australia | 265,000 |
| 3rd | USA | 228,000 |
| 4th | Russia | 213,977 |
| 5th | South Africa | 159,724 |
| 6th | Peru | 151,486 |
| 7th | Canada | 124,054 |
| 8th | Mexico | 117,848 |
| 9th | Ghana | 90,510 |
| 10th | Brazil | 79,563 |
| 11th | Uzbekistan | 73,000 (estimated) |
| 12th | Indonesia | 59,066 |
| 13th | Papua New Guinea | 56,035 |
| 14th | Colombia | 55,745 |
| 15th | Argentina | 52,486 |
| 16th | Chile | 51,309 |
| 17th | Kazakhstan | 43,470 (estimated) |
| 18th | Tanzania | 43,390 |
| 19th | Mali | 41,751 |
| 20th | Burkina Faso | 32,613 |

Not surprisingly, many of the top silver- and gold-mining countries are also the top producers of bullion coins for investment and collecting. China, Australia, the United States, South Africa, Canada, and Mexico all boast robust bullion-coinage programs.

Since 1986 Americans have had access to silver and gold American Eagle bullion coins, struck by the U.S. Mint. These are legal tender, with their weight, content, and purity guaranteed by the federal government. The Mint offers a variety of other silver and gold bullion coins, including 24-karat gold pieces, as cataloged within this book. Collectors and investors buy millions of these coins every year, from a global network of distributors and retailers as well as directly from the U.S. Mint. Ordering the coins is easy and convenient. But America's relationship with silver and gold hasn't always been as rosy as it is today. In chapter 2 we look at the precious metals and their place in the history of American money.

"**Gold has worked down from Alexander's time. . . . When something holds good for two thousand years I do not believe it can be so because of prejudice or mistaken theory.**"

—**American financier and philanthropist Bernard M. Baruch**

After gold was discovered in California in 1848, Americans rushed west by hook or by crook to cash in on the craze. In the oil painting *Old Whaler—A Forty-Niner*, American artist Milton James Burns (1853–1933) showed an old whaling boat that was pressed into service transporting hopeful miners to California's gold fields in 1849.

# 2

# Silver and Gold and the History of Money in America

"There are three faithful friends," Benjamin Franklin wrote. "An old wife, an old dog, and ready money." For many decades, Americans considered the best kinds of ready money to be *silver* and *gold*, prized above copper, paper currency, credit, and other financial instruments. As treasured as they were, in many periods of our nation's history silver and gold coins were the most difficult to obtain and keep. In recent years, within the memory of living generations, gold has even gone through a period of government recall (termed "seizure" or "confiscation" by critics) and for a time was illegal for most Americans to own; and silver, for many years a staple of U.S. money, was officially removed from our circulating coinage and quickly disappeared from our pocket change. Today silver and gold are the bailiwick of rare-coin collectors, hard-money advocates, gift-givers, and bullion investors. Ironically, though the precious metals have left the realm of day-to-day *money*, they are now more readily accessible than in many parts of our past.

In seeking to understand the role and significance of gold and silver in the United States, we benefit from an exploration of American money in general.

## AMERICAN MONEY: THE EARLY YEARS

If you transported some money of the modern United States back in time to the 1600s, it would seem strange but not entirely alien to a British-American colonist. He would recognize our round and metallic coins as coins, and our Federal Reserve Bank Notes, with their legends and symbols of government, he would identify as paper money.

Compared to what was most often used as money in colonial times, though, they would be very unusual. There simply wasn't much coinage and paper currency circulating in those early days. The colonists used *other* kinds of money.

In the colony of Virginia, named after England's "Virgin Queen" Elizabeth I, the settlement of Jamestown was started in 1607. Some 13 years later (and some 600 miles to the north) Plymouth was established, in what would become the Massachusetts Bay Colony. As years passed and more settlers made the journey over the Atlantic, other communities sprung up along the coast. From these early settlements the original 13 British North American colonies grew.

For the colonists, money in the traditional European sense was hard to come by. Coins were few and far between. Various forms of paper money would become more common by the early 1700s, but earlier on the commercial order of the day was barter, or "country pay"—a farmer trading corn for tools, a cobbler exchanging boots for bread. This system worked, but it only went so far. Financial historian Robert E. Wright notes that, for example, Pennsylvania's early colonists (like many others in British North America) quickly realized that barter was inefficient.

> "Bartering one species of property for another," they realized, "would be endless labour." "For some years after the settling of this colony," a Pennsylvanian wrote in 1768, "we had but little specie, and trade was carried on chiefly by truck or barter." "Under such inconveniences," the aged man correctly noted, "it was found impossible for a colony to flourish, or the inhabitants to make any considerable progress in their improvements." The legal monetization of country produce, like wheat and beef, helped but was not as efficient as the use of coins, which finally began to circulate after about 1700.[1]

The early colonists also used local forms of money adopted from the sacred customs of the Native Americans. Wampum (shortened from the Algonquin *wampumpeage*, or "white beads") consisted of cylindrical beads made from local quahog, periwinkle, and other shells, pierced and strung together. It didn't take long for Dutch settlers to recognize wampum's cultural value among the Indians local to Long Island, where much of it was produced. For the newcomers it evolved into a medium of exchange in the European sense—a type of money. Numismatic historian Kenneth Bressett describes wampum and its monetary evolution:

> The nature of wampum is one of the most complex and misunderstood aspects of North American native culture. Most confounding is that its form and use were often quite different among different nations (or tribes) and it was apt to be used differently at different times. Beyond that it often had not only different uses but also different forms and functions within each society.
>
> The most frequent misstatement is that it was "Indian money" (wrong on all counts), or that it served a widespread use as circulating currency.

Beads of all sorts, whether native-made or imported, were considered important and desirable items for use as personal or dress adornments. They were not unlike gold and silver jewelry of today. And as such they had a special value and could be easily bought, sold, and traded. In early times wampum and other beads were most often used as hair and clothing adornments and as strands that could be traded with others. Belts made of native wampum were an essential part of any major land exchange or treaty. They represented not *payment* but a binding and sacred contract.

European settlers observed wampum being used as part of a trade agreement and thought it was payment of some sort. Actually it was part of the agreement—a sales receipt, you might say—in a culture that had no complex written language. When merchants began receiving and giving beads in their transactions it eventually morphed into a form of currency that was for a period recognized by some local authorities as a special form of money.[2]

In 1626 Peter Minuit, the third director general of the Dutch settlement of New Netherland, "bought" the island of Manhattan from a native chief for various trade articles valued at 60 Dutch guilders. The trade likely included some wampum. (Over centuries of retelling, the transaction would be immortalized as "$24 worth of beads, buttons, and trinkets.")

In the New World the Pilgrims—seen here embarking on the *Speedwell*—would have for their commerce not coins and paper currency, but barter and wampum. "The Indians on the sea shore were the first to manufacture [wampum]," writes Henry Phillips in *Historical Sketches of the Paper Currency of the American Colonies* (1865), "and the inland tribes afterwards learnt it from them. The English learnt to trade in it from the Dutch."

In 1627 merchant Isaac de Razier carried 50 English pounds' worth of wampum from New Netherland to Plymouth Plantation to trade for corn for the Dutch colony. The concept of accepting the small white beads (as well as their more valuable black or dark-purple varieties) as money spread through the New England colonies, and further south.

Ten years later, in November 1637, the Massachusetts General Court officially valued wampum beads at six to an English copper penny, making them legal for payment in sums up to twelve pence. Connecticut accepted wampum as payment for taxes, valuing one bead the same as a copper farthing (four to the penny).

Ratios of exchange varied over the years and across colonies, for individual beads and for standardized strands—and problems with quality, oversupply, and even counterfeiting plagued the system—but wampum served its commercial purpose. Colonists in New England, New York, New Jersey, Pennsylvania, Virginia, and elsewhere knew the little hand-tooled shell fragments as a form of money.

**Wampum. The string of white beads to the right is attributed to the Algonquin Indian tribe.**

**This illustration from the magazine *Puck*, 1913, lampoons the popular concept of early European settlers using trinkets and brightly colored cloth to bargain with Native Americans.**

Meanwhile, coins from abroad, when they were available, were readily accepted for purchases. The French louis d'or, German thalers, Dutch and Venetian ducats, and others were welcome in commerce. The most popular and widespread coins were Spanish and Spanish-American pieces including the gold doubloon and the silver 8-reales coin (called a milled dollar or piece of eight). The latter sometimes was cut into two, four, or eight sections, with one real (12-1/2 cents) called a *bit*. Spain also minted silver coins of those smaller denominations.

In addition to drilled clams and foreign coins, the colonists used various commodities as legal tender—things that seem as strange to today's observer as a roll of perfectly engineered, machine-made Jefferson nickels would have been in the early 1600s. Political scientist Jesse Macy, whose textbooks educated American lawyers and historians in the early 1900s, described the situation thus:

> The first English colonists in America were obliged to live in that rude, primitive condition, in which some more bulky form of property is better suited for a medium of exchange than are gold and silver. Tobacco, furs, wampum, salt, codfish, cattle, and other things were at different times and in different places used as money: and these various kinds of extemporized currency were recognized by the colonial governments.[3]

Kansas newspaper editor and Populist senator William A. Peffer wrote:

> Early in the eighteenth century Virginia adopted tobacco as a currency. It was deposited in warehouses, and the receipts for it passed as currency. Prof. Sumner [*History of American Currency*] says: "It was a true money."[4]

Numismatic historian Q. David Bowers observes:

> From time to time, such diverse goods and commodities as grain, cows, corn, tobacco, and musket balls had a legal-tender basis in some areas. As an example, on March 27, 1694, the Massachusetts General Court set exchange rates for corn, wheat, rye, barley malt, oaks, and peas for use as currency.[5]

Lumber in New England, tobacco in Virginia, fish in Massachusetts—these are all examples of local or regional commodities that developed special commercial value. Another especially significant trade item was the beaver pelt. From the mid-1500s, gentlemen's felt hats were high fashion in Europe, and British and French North America became the prime source of the finest felt made from beaver fur. "By the end of the century," writes James A. Haxby, "the beaver had become virtually extinct in Britain and Western Europe and was greatly endangered in Russia and Scandinavia."[6] The European colonies in North America, meanwhile, had what appeared to be a never-ending supply of the rodents, just waiting to be trapped and their hides processed into luxurious felt. A "made" beaver was the fur of a prime adult animal, worn for several months so the long outer hairs wore off, making the pelt easier to process. "Though its value fluctuated over the years (as with most currency), the made beaver had a fixed rate of exchange in trade goods over much of its history and range. In 1733, at the Hudson's Bay Co. Albany fort in Ontario, a made beaver

could be exchanged for a pair of shoes, a blanket, 20 fishhooks, or a gallon of brandy. A rifle could be obtained for a dozen made beavers, or 10 if the trapper was an especially skilled bargainer."[7]

Deerskins, too, were used as a type of currency and a measure of value. They were popularly referred to as "bucks." An early example of the term comes from the journal of Conrad Weiser, a German-born American settler. In 1748, traveling through Indian territory in what is now Ohio, Weiser referred to a man "robbed of the value of 300 Bucks" and, later, a cask of whiskey sold for "5 Bucks."[8] The American dollar that would debut some decades later naturally inherited the nickname.

A mixed bag of neighborly trading, foreign coins, and locally convenient commodities: thus was facilitated the bulk of early American commerce in the absence of a standard, widespread, native coinage.

## MERCANTILISM AND THE DRAIN OF COINAGE

Back in Britain, politicians and merchants who subscribed to the politico-economic system known as *mercantilism* did everything they could to discourage colonists from benefiting from a hard-cash economy. Britain's global power, in their understanding, would see healthy growth from an imbalance of trade with the colonies. They sought to maximize British exports, while minimizing any imports, in order to build the kingdom's store of gold, silver, and trade value.

Dr. Richard Doty, senior curator of the National Numismatic Collection, Smithsonian Institution, discussed mercantilism in *America's Money, America's Story* (2008):

> Simply stated, mercantilism viewed a colony and its mother country in a fixed, monopolistic trading relationship, in which almost everything of value found in the ground or grown on the land was sent home. Furthermore, anything needed by the colonists that they could not produce themselves, or were not allowed to produce (e.g., for centuries, Latin Americans were

A Warm Springs Apache Indian known as Chah, posing with a rifle and a beaver, circa 1885. The pelt of the beaver was a valuable form of currency in colonial North America and during the early days of the United States. The North West Company, founded in 1779 and headquartered in Montreal, issued an 1820-dated token (shown here enlarged) worth one beaver pelt. These were circulated in the West.

Spanish-American silver coins of the late 1500s and early 1600s, such as this Mexican 8-reales cob of King Philip III, were far from elegant. Still, they served as a means of transporting and accounting for the Spanish king's colonial silver. "Their place in lore and history, their rustic charm, and their appeal to treasure hunters far overshadow their crudeness," writes numismatic historian Kenneth Bressett.[9]

discouraged from growing grapes because of complaints from vintners in Spain), had to be sent from the mother country, in ships of the mother country, and paid for in currency of the mother country. In other words, any coins that the colonies managed to accumulate should be remitted to the metropolis in payment for goods received under the closed economic arrangement.

A central goal for any nation with the wherewithal was to *sell* more than it *bought*, thereby accumulating bullion and the power it represented. Concentrating gold and silver in the homeland gave Europeans the ability to finance their wars of expansion and maintain their armies, their governments, and their standards of living.[10] Governments would promote their own interests by monitoring and influencing the shipment of raw resources and the manufacture of goods. This might be accomplished by raising or lowering duties, levies, taxes, and tariffs. Corporations and trading companies were formed and grew with government encouragement. Governments and monarchs arranged treaties, granted trading rights, and used colonies and trading posts to further their aims.

Over time, the quality and consistency of Spain's dollars increased, as seen in these pieces from 1732 and 1772. If a smaller-denomination coin was unavailable to make change, an 8-reales coin could be cut into two, four, or eight pieces. One quarter of a Spanish dollar, valued at two reales, was called "two bits." In later years the U.S. quarter dollar would inherit this nickname.

Britain's colonies in North America, unlike most of Spain's in Mexico and Central and South America, never were significant sources of native gold and silver. The British would have to mine their New World treasure not with pick axes and shovels, but with trade and commercial policy. Tariffs and other regulations were designed to give every advantage to British producers, and America's colonists were forced into the dependent status of consumers. The effect was a draining of capital, and in particular silver and gold coins, from the New World back to the Old. In addition, for years the Crown jealously restricted the colonies' authority to strike their own coins. Minting was a royal prerogative, a right reserved for those with political sovereignty—which the colonies, for the most part, lacked. All of these market and legal forces combined to discourage the rise of local silver and gold coinage.

The American colonists used coins from Europe and Latin America, whenever they were available. Pictured are an English 1701 gold 2-guinea coin of King William III and a rare 1684 Dutch 3-gulden silver coin.

# INITIAL STEPS TOWARD A LOCAL COINAGE

Starting in the mid-1600s, England's rulers began to grant some rights of coinage to their American colonies—and in some cases the colonists took that right upon themselves, in defiance of higher authority.

From 1652 to 1682, the Massachusetts Bay Colony issued silver coins ranging in denomination from twopence to one shilling, following the English system. They were made by John Hull and Robert Sanderson, operating a mint in Boston, as authorized by the colony's General Court in 1652. For their labor the minters received a portion of the coins struck. Their first products were simple little affairs, with no dates, stamped NE on one side (for "New England"). The other side bore Roman numerals: III on the threepence, VI on the sixpence, XII on the shilling. Soon thereafter, the coins' designs were elaborated. Types known as Willow Tree, Oak Tree, and Pine Tree coins were struck, all in silver and all bearing the date 1652 (except for a twopence dated 1662). The coins were all about 20 percent lighter than their British counterparts.

**Massachusetts' NE or "New England" coinage of threepence, sixpence, and shillings was marked by its simplicity. The minters, Hull and Sanderson, received one shilling threepence for every 20 shillings they coined; this compensation rate was adjusted several times during their contract. (These and the following colonial-era coins and tokens are shown at 1.5x actual size.)**

**Some contemporary accounts referred to the coins of Massachusetts as *Boston money*, so called for the city they were minted in, or as *Bay shillings* or *Tree coins*. Shown are silver shillings of the designs long known to collectors as Willow Tree, Oak Tree, and Pine Tree.**

Meanwhile, Maryland's proprietor, Cecil Calvert, the second Lord Baltimore, arranged to have his own coins minted in London. His colony needed hard money to stabilize its largely agricultural and barter-based economy, wherein tobacco, gunpowder, and such were pressed into service as money in the absence of gold, silver, or even copper coins. Calvert believed that his royal charter granted him the right of coinage. (It didn't, not in so many words; but it was similar to other charters that did explicitly grant that right.) The coins (which bore no dates) were struck in the winter that bridged 1658 and 1659, during the waning weeks of Oliver Cromwell's English Commonwealth. Calvert's money included silver shillings, sixpence, and fourpence (the latter called "groats"), along with a pattern "denarium" or copper penny (known today by only a handful of surviving examples). Calvert was arrested by British authorities later in 1659 and had to explain his coinage activities; apparently he was able to reason his way out of any charges, including the serious offense of exporting silver out of England (a violation of the goals of mercantilism). The British government finally recognized Calvert's right to strike the Maryland coins. Those that had already been made continued to circulate, to the colony's advantage, until about 1700. It is likely that no more were struck, though, and Calvert's plans to establish an active local mint in Maryland never came to fruition.

# OTHER EARLY ATTEMPTS AT AMERICAN COINAGE

Late in 1681 a Quaker named Mark Newby arrived in the New World from Ireland, bringing with him copper pieces that were probably struck in Dublin several decades earlier. Newby's cargo included thousands of the coins, in two sizes, of roughly farthing and half-penny diameters. In May 1682, the New Jersey General Assembly made a ruling on these interesting coppers—they would pass as legal tender, valued at two for a penny. The coins feature a crowned king kneeling and playing a harp, with the legend FLOREAT REX—"May the King Prosper." On the back of the larger piece, St. Patrick appears holding a bishop's crosier and a trefoil, surrounded by the faithful and the legend ECCE GREX ("Behold the Flock"). The smaller coin shows the saint holding a staff, driving serpents and a winged dragon from Ireland; its legend reads QUIESCAT PLEBS ("May the People Be at Ease").

**The Latin legend on Cecil Calvert's coinage declares him "Lord of Mary's Land." "The charter of this Colony passed the great seal of England June 20th, 1632," said speaker Henry Chapman at the Annual Dinner of the Rochester Numismatic Association in 1916, "and though it conferred sovereign powers on Cecil Calvert, the second Lord Baltimore, it did not specifically refer to coinage, and it was not until 1659 that he had dies made and coins struck, samples of which he sent to his brother, Philip Calvert . . . with a letter requesting him to endeavor to get the Colonists to use them, but not to compel or make it compulsory unless they passed a law in the General Assembly."**

**Although not denominated as such, the St. Patrick coins are traditionally known as "farthings" and "halfpennies." In *America's Money, America's Story*, Richard Doty described these coppers: "They are handsome, their attractive appearance augmented by a bit of yellow metal (brass, meant to resemble gold), apparently splashed onto the copper during the minting process and positioned so that the king would appear to be receiving a golden crown. This care suggests a limited mintage, a suggestion belied by the known number of die combinations—more than 120 for the farthings alone."[11]**

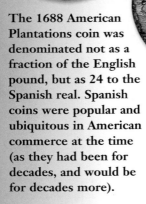

**The 1688 American Plantations coin was denominated not as a fraction of the English pound, but as 24 to the Spanish real. Spanish coins were popular and ubiquitous in American commerce at the time (as they had been for decades, and would be for decades more).**

In that same decade a royal patent authorized Richard Holt (an agent for Cornish tin-mining interests) to make coins for the American Plantations. The coins, dated 1688 and struck in nearly pure tin, were denominated in the Spanish style, as 1/24th part of a real (eight of which made up a Spanish silver dollar). On the obverse is a dramatic horseback portrait of King James II, and the reverse features the royal arms. (Unfortunately for coin collectors, tin proved to be a poor choice for the coins; they were prone to oxidation, and today most surviving pieces are found with black spots called *tin pest*.)

In 1694 or thereabouts copper halfpenny-sized tokens were struck, probably in England, with an elephant on one side and, on the other, the legend GOD PRESERVE CAROLINA AND THE LORDS PROPRIETORS. Similar tokens were made with the legend GOD PRESERVE NEW ENGLAND. These may have served as advertisements for the New World colonies, in addition to passing as money. Other theories opine that they might have been advertising tokens for the "New England Coffee-House" and the "London Coffee-House," both on Threadneedle Street in London. Or they might have referred to two commercial sections of the Royal Exchange, known as "Carolina" and "New England."[12] The coppers are reminiscent of other Elephant tokens, undated, reading GOD PRESERVE LONDON. These all are mysterious coins; tantalizingly little is known about them for certain. Historians generally agree that they were *not* struck specifically for the colonies, and probably did not circulate widely in America. Still, they are attractive in their own unique way, with their amazing tusk-to-tail standing portrait of a fierce-looking pachyderm, and their apparent references (however circuitous) to America.

In the early 1720s, an English entrepreneur named William Wood struck coins for use in Ireland and the American colonies. His right of coinage was granted by a patent from King George I. (Legend has it Wood had to bribe the king's mistress, the duchess of Kendal, with a £10,000 payoff to secure the favor.) In 1722 and 1723 Wood produced several clever coins that likened America to a beautiful flower. Called *Rosa Americana* coinage from their legends (ROSA AMERICANA / UTILE DULCE; or "The American Rose, Useful and Sweet"), the American pieces were struck as halfpence, pennies, and twopence. Some Rosa Americana coins were also struck dated 1724 and 1733, possibly as patterns. Other Wood coins—farthings and halfpence intended for Ireland, with a symbolic representation of Hibernia—may also have circulated in America.

Researchers have cataloged a large number of die varieties, which suggests that the mintage of Rosa Americana coins was substantial. Each coin, however, was only about half the size and weight of its English counterpart. For this reason they were unpopular in American commerce, and did not circulate widely. Many are thought to have been returned to England, where they did pass as small change—though at less than their intended values. Had they been larger and heftier, Wood's coppers might have spread through America like hardy wild roses: his royal patent granted him the right to strike up to 300 tons of coins over a 14-year period.

Elephant tokens of the London and Carolina varieties. Their connection to America is uncertain.

UTILE DULCI: To King George I, the American rose must have seemed "useful and sweet" indeed.

Certain Rosa Americana coins of 1724 and 1733 are thought to be patterns. One 1724 penny labeled the American flower "Rosa Sine Spina"—a rose without thorns. Wishful thinking for Britain's kings! This conceit would be proved false a couple generations later, by George Washington and other Revolutionaries born around the time these coins were struck.

In the late 1730s, near Granby, Connecticut, the Higley family used local copper to mint their own threepence coins. It was a private undertaking; no official license was granted for their coinage. Dr. Samuel Higley had earlier purchased a copper mine, which he worked himself, smelting his own ore, crafting his own dies, and striking pure-copper coins of his own design. After he died in 1737, his brother John took over the operation with some business partners. Numismatist Sylvester S. Crosby described the local environment in *The Early Coins of America* (1875). According to Crosby, Higley paid his local tavern bills with the coppers—a drink at the time cost threepence—and the bartender "soon became overburdened with this kind of cash." Legend has it that Samuel Higley's neighbors complained about the coins: they were the same size as a halfpenny, and therefore not really worth threepence (despite their bold inscription to that effect). Accordingly, he changed the design to read VALUE ME AS YOU PLEASE.[13]

**Samuel Higley's privately issued coppers were worth threepence—or were they? Users were eventually urged to value the coins as they pleased. "Although some merchants disliked Higley's coins, others were eager to get them as a handy source of nearly pure copper," notes Kenneth Bressett. "Many of them were melted for that reason and today all survivors are considered to be great rarities."[14]**

The suction caused by mercantilism, then, pulled the bulk of gold and silver toward Britain but was not powerful enough to keep small change out of the colonists' hands. More copper tokens that circulated as cash in America include several varieties of "Voce Populi" coins, struck in Dublin, Ireland; so-called Pitt tokens or medalets, made to honor the English statesman and friend of America; and others. Nearly any small copper coin or token, regardless of size or stated denomination, would be used to make change in simple transactions, just to even out the trade.[15]

**Farthing- and halfpenny-sized Voce Populi tokens were made by the Irish firm of Roche, at that time (1760) a manufacturer of buttons for the army. Although the tokens had nothing to do with America, their legend might have been popular among colonists increasingly dissatisfied with British rule. The "Voice of the People" would be heard.**

**William Pitt the Elder endeared himself to America by opposing the unpopular Stamp Act of 1765—and was thanked as a "Friend of Liberty and Trade" on these 1766 commemorative medalets. They found their way into the colonial money supply. Ten years later the colonies would declare independence.**

**Various copper and low-grade-silver colonial coins were struck in mints in Paris, Metz, Lyon, Rouen, and other French cities, then shipped across the Atlantic to be used in New France, Louisiana, and the French West Indies. Some were popular and saw wide circulation; others were rejected in favor of other money.**

While these coins and coin substitutes made the rounds, another form of American money developed as the 17th century drew to a close: paper currency.

# PAPER MONEY OF THE COLONIES

It was not only "country pay," copper, and low-grade silver that oiled the commercial engine in colonial America. In the cities, by the 1700s bills of credit and receipt were common, especially for large transactions. By the early 1800s many storekeepers kept ledgers showing debits and payments for their local customers, with accounts balanced by "cash on the barrel head" perhaps once or twice a year.[16] And with increasing frequency from the late 1600s through to the colonies' official split from Britain in 1776, legal-tender *paper* money emerged as a staple of day-to-day business.

Eric P. Newman, in his magisterial *Early Paper Money of America* (2008), describes the British Crown's instructions to its colonial governors. Generally, approval was to be denied any American requests to authorize paper money—except in situations of military emergency. The Crown could also disallow (except in Maryland, Connecticut, and Rhode Island) any law passed with a governor's consent. As Newman observes, "[Such action] was of little practical value if the paper money had already been put into circulation by the time the matter was being reviewed in England."

As for special dispensation in times of military emergency, Newman notes:

> During the eighteenth century the situation was complicated by an almost continuous military conflict in America between the English on one side and the French, Spanish, or Native Americans on the other. The English needed military support from the American colonists and this required prompt payment for expeditions, supplies, salaries, bounties, and fortifications. Since the money in colonial treasuries was barely sufficient to meet normal current expenses, a resort to paper money issues to meet military needs became a necessity. England naturally preferred to permit colonial issues of paper money to be redeemable by the issuing colony out of future taxes rather than for England to make a direct outlay of funds for military expenses.

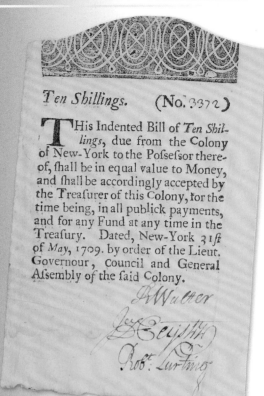

Indented notes had a scalloped edge whose corresponding indentation was kept in a receipt file.

For the average American colonist in the 1700s, most "money" was paper. Massachusetts issued the first American paper currency in 1690. South Carolina followed in 1703; Connecticut, New Hampshire, and New Jersey in 1709. By the 1750s all of the original 13 colonies were issuing paper cash. With their economies slowly growing, and their populations on the rise as well, "folding money" served the colonies in the absence of gold and silver. It was accepted in payment of taxes and in private transactions. Paper, in the words of Richard Doty, "was a godsend."[17]

Most colonial paper money was denominated in traditional English values: pounds, shillings, and pence. Naturally gold and silver were preferred—and a colony's bills spent in a distant region were likely to be accepted only at a discount (or even outright refused)—but paper helped fill a substantial need. "Every one of the colonies," wrote William Peffer in *The Farmer's Side*, "at one time or other during the first one hundred years of their existence, used paper money, to the general good of the people."

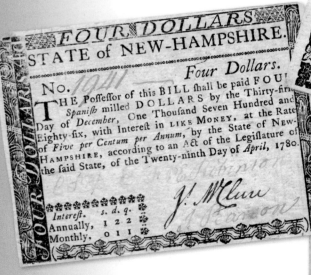

A sampling of colonial currency. Massachusetts issued paper money from 1690 to 1781; South Carolina from 1703 to 1788; Connecticut and New Hampshire, both, from 1709 to 1780; New Jersey from 1709 to 1786; New York from 1709 to 1788; Rhode Island from 1710 to 1786; North Carolina from 1712 to 1785; Pennsylvania from 1723 to 1785; Delaware from 1723 to 1777; Maryland from 1733 to 1781; Georgia from 1735 to 1786; Virginia from 1755 to 1781; and Vermont (not one of the original 13 colonies) in 1781.

Typically prices, currency legislation, and contracts in the colonies were also set in English pounds, or in Spanish dollars. (It was Maryland that first issued paper money denominated in *dollars*, in 1767.) But those denominations weren't the only ones that circulated. Historian Robert E. Wright in *The First Wall Street* quotes colonial sources describing various robberies in the 1700s. A thief in 1755 "managed to lay his hands on 'about Seventy Pounds,' fifty of it in bills of credit and the balance in foreign coins. In 1764 a mugger made off with 'in Paper Money two Five Pounds Bills, and three Twenty Shilling Bills, and other small Money, which amounted to £17 5 s. 6 d., 4 Dollars, some English shillings, and £45 in Gold, chiefly English Guineas, some Moidores and Doubloons.' Similarly, in 1772 a thief stole 'about 190 Half Joes, about 30 Pistoles, 8 Moidores, 4 Guineas, 60 Pieces of Eight, and 48 Pounds in Jersey Six Pound bills'. . . ."

This was an unavoidable complexity of doing business at the time. Books and periodicals were published that offered conversion tables to translate the various currencies into those of each colony or state.

During and after the Revolution, the leaders of the emerging United States would seek to tame and homogenize this turbulent mix of currencies.

# PAPER MONEY OF THE CONTINENTAL CONGRESS

On May 10, 1775, the Continental Congress—the body that would eventually declare independence and forge a preliminary national constitution in the Articles of Confederation—authorized the issuance of paper money. The first bills, denominated in "Spanish milled dollars, or the value thereof in gold or silver," were issued in the name of the United Colonies. They were followed by additional issues, none of them truly backed by sufficient amounts of precious metal.[18]

Over the next few years, well into the war, the Continental Congress issued paper bills from 1/6 of a dollar to $80—the higher denominations made necessary as the currency dropped in value. Starting with the authorization of May 20, 1777, the notes' imprint was changed from *United Colonies* to *United States*. As the months passed, their wording reflected the movement of the government's headquarters—Philadelphia, Baltimore, York—as necessitated by the war, with all of the currency printed in Philadelphia by Hall and Sellers, a firm that also produced paper money for various states. Throughout this period of tumult and uncertainty, silver and gold became more and more valuable relative to paper money. By the issue of January 14, 1779, Continental Currency had been depreciating in value for two years. In that month it took $742 in paper money to purchase $100 in Spanish silver coins. The depreciation continued; two years later it required ten times as much!

After the war, in the early 1790s, an act of Congress would authorize the government to buy back Continental bills at the rate of one silver dollar for each $100 of paper turned in to the Treasury. The debased currency had earned its tin-plated reputation and the derogatory insult, "Not worth a Continental."[19]

Continental Currency notes offered inspirational mottoes (many of them suggested by Benjamin Franklin) and symbols meant to strengthen their readers' resolve. In their day-to-day transactions, Revolutionaries such as these artillerymen would have spent mostly paper money (including Continental Currency and notes of various states), rather than silver or gold coins.

# AN EXPLOSION OF SMALL CHANGE—BUT STILL LITTLE SILVER OR GOLD

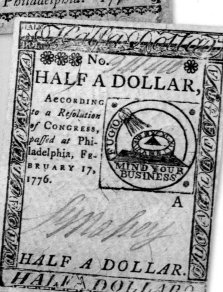

After the Declaration of Independence made the case for American freedom from British rule, the first of the emerging states to consider the subject of coinage was New Hampshire. The State House of Representatives authorized a limited quantity of pure-copper coins. Silversmith William Moulton was empowered to make them; he prepared cast patterns featuring a pine tree and a harp, and the date 1776. Historians believe these patterns were not accepted by the public, and few of them entered circulation. Still, they marked the beginning of a new period in American money.

New Hampshire's House of Representatives recommended that 108 of the state's coppers be equal to a Spanish milled dollar. Each weighed the same as an English halfpenny.

In October 1786, after the war had ended, the Massachusetts General Court would authorize an "Act for establishing a mint for the coinage of gold, silver and copper."

War or no war, the commercial need for hard cash continued, and private citizens and organizations experimented to solve its scarcity. In 1783 a silversmith named John Chalmers struck silver threepence, sixpence, and shilling tokens in Annapolis, Maryland. These coins, of his own design, were a response to popular refusal of underweight cut-down Spanish coins then in circulation.

Private or unofficial coppers with the legend IMMUNE (or IMMUNIS) COLUMBIA were struck in the mid-1780s. There is no record of these coins being authorized by legislation, although one variety, with the legend E PLURIBUS UNUM and a heraldic eagle, may have been a prototype for later federal coinage. Some of these copper pieces even featured a portrait of King George III, the ruler whose colonies had united to fight for and maintain their freedom.

Other pattern or experimental pieces, called Confederatio coppers, were made in the mid-1780s. These used about a dozen different obverses combined with a common reverse design of encircled stars with the word CONFEDERATIO.

In 1785, the Bar copper—undated, and of uncertain origin, though perhaps made in England—started to circulate in New York. The *New Jersey Gazette* of November 12, 1785, describes the piece: "A new and curious kind of coppers have lately made their appearance in New York. The novelty and bright gloss of which keeps them in circulation. These coppers are in fact similar to Continental buttons without eyes; on the one side are thirteen stripes and on the other U.S.A., as was usual on the soldiers' buttons."

John Chalmers's silver tokens, from dies engraved by fellow silversmith Thomas Sparrow, were heavy with political symbolism. On one side, hands are clasped in friendly cooperation. On the other, two birds squabble over a worm, while a snake approaches them unnoticed behind a hedge.

Some of these 1787-dated "Immunis Columbia" coppers, with the E PLURIBUS UNUM reverse, were actually coined after that date.

The Confederatio coppers were made with about a dozen different dies in various combinations. There are two reverse varieties: one with stars contained within a small circle, and the other with larger stars in a larger circle.

Thirteen bars, separate but merged to form a whole circle, decorate one side of the Bar copper. Further symbolizing the unity of the new states, the letters U, S, and A are interlocked in a coherent whole.

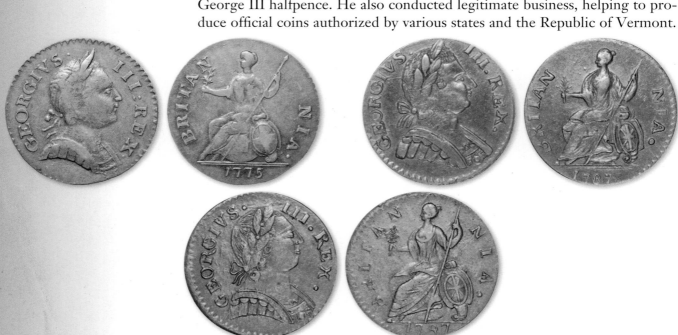

Kenneth Bressett describes the Brasher gold doubloons: "Ephraim Brasher was commissioned to test foreign gold and adjust it to a weight that was familiar to U.S. trade. He and his partner John Bailey wanted to get rights to coin New York coppers, and likely produced the famous doubloons as a demonstration of their ability to make suitable dies and coins."[20]

Meanwhile the firm of Constable, Rucker & Co., undertook a private coinage endeavor, and had a large quantity of copper pieces struck in Birmingham, England, beginning in 1785. These so-called Nova Constellatio coppers were shipped to New York City and entered circulation there.

Many other copper coins and tokens used as money in the colonial and postcolonial years could be added to this overview. While the coppers were in use, there also were scattered pockets of silver and gold mintage during this era, although these precious metals remained scarce and the activity was mainly experimental and speculative as opposed to large-scale official coinage. In New York, in 1787, a goldsmith named Ephraim Brasher struck gold coins valued at one Spanish doubloon (16 dollars) apiece. (He and his partner, John Bailey, also made various copper coins, including imitation British halfpence, to circulate in New York and New Jersey.) In 1790 in Baltimore, 27-year-old clockmaker and engraver Standish Barry made a silver threepence token bearing the patriotic date of July 4. Around the same time he is believed to have cast gold imitation doubloons hallmarked with his own initials.

New York City and its environs seem to have been the center of a demimonde of counterfeiters minting imitation British halfpence. Britain's copper halfpenny was the coin of choice for most small transactions, widely accepted though not officially legal tender. In the 1780s private individuals took it upon themselves to strike unauthorized (and lightweight) reproductions of these coins, sometimes casting them or using other crude production methods. Circulating their handiwork at full value would bring the greatest profit to their creators. Many were made by Machin's Mills, a firm organized and operated in secrecy by Thomas Machin, near Newburgh, New York. With various partners Machin minted several varieties of imitation George III halfpence. He also conducted legitimate business, helping to produce official coins authorized by various states and the Republic of Vermont.

These imitation British halfpence struck by Machin's Mills and other private minters show a portrait of King George III, and Britannia—imprecise replicas, but similar to the authentic coins they copied.[21]

Through the 1780s and 1790s, and into the new century, fascinating and diverse copper (and some silver) coins of private manufacture circulated through the states. Many were actually made to order in England, for entrepreneurial Americans who saw the need for circulating coinage and a chance to make a profit. (The difference between the cost of manufacturing and transporting the coins, and the face value they were passed at, represented their proceeds.) It was a time of turmoil, with America working through a postwar economic depression, continuing shortage of currency (including small change), high taxes, and many bankruptcies and foreclosures. Any hard cash—whether an English merchant's advertising token, a church's private offering-plate coin, or a fake British halfpenny—was welcome (for the most part) and made its way into day-to-day transactions.

Eventually, though, the individual states—and then the united nation itself—would enter the business of making money.

**In the late 1780s the elders of the First Presbyterian Church of Albany, New York, found that many parishioners had either no small change at all, or only worn-out (undervalue) coppers to drop into the offering plate on Sunday. Some churchgoers even donated counterfeit coins, which circulated quite freely in the absence of other small change. "In order to add respect to the weekly collections," the elders resolved, one thousand coppers would be "placed with the treasurer to exchange with members of the congregation, at the rate of twelve for one shilling." The Albany church pennies were made in two varieties, one with a large D (for the Latin "denarium," or *penny*) and one without.**

# COINAGE OF THE EMERGING STATES

The Articles of Confederation in early 1781 had granted Congress the sole right to regulate the alloy and value of coins struck under its own authority or by the various states. No longer was the sovereign right of coinage reserved by a distant monarch; each state now held that privilege, with Congress regulating. From 1785 to 1788, several states allowed individuals and companies to strike their coins, in exchange for a portion of the face value produced. Massachusetts established its own mint.

In 1785 Connecticut authorized Samuel Bishop, Joseph Hopkins, James Hillhouse, and John Goodrich to set up a mint near New Haven. This they did, subcontracting the work and turning out many varieties of small copper coins. The state treasury received a five percent commission on their output.

**AUCTORI: CONNEC indicates that the Connecticut coppers were coined by the state's authority. INDE ET LIB abbreviated the Latin for "Independence and Liberty." Both legends were specified by law. Today's collectors know various Connecticut coppers by engaging nicknames: the Muttonhead and the Laughing Head (pictured), the Horned Bust, the Hercules Head, and others.**

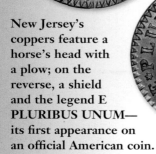

**The state mint in Massachusetts was shut down in early 1789, after its production ceased to be profitable.**

**New Jersey's coppers feature a horse's head with a plow; on the reverse, a shield and the legend E PLURIBUS UNUM— its first appearance on an official American coin.**

The Massachusetts legislature in 1786 authorized the establishment of a state mint for coining gold, silver, and copper. This went against the wishes of the governor, who preferred to wait and see what would come of the federal government's discussions of a *national* coinage. The coins, the legislature directed, would bear "the figure of an Indian with a bow and arrow and a star on one side, with the word COMMONWEALTH, and on the reverse a spread eagle with the words MASSACHUSETTS 1787." They would be the first official coins bearing the denomination *cent* (Congress established the term in 1786 when it approved a decimal coinage system). Many varieties were struck.

In New York in 1787 several individuals petitioned the Legislature for the right to coin copper for the state. A law was passed regulating the copper coins already in circulation, but no official coinage was authorized.

New Jersey, however, did authorize an official state coinage. On June 1, 1786, its legislature granted Thomas Goadsby, Albion Cox, and Walter Mould the right to coin some three million coppers, not later than June 1788. The coins were to weigh six pennyweight and six grains apiece, and pass current at 15 to the shilling. The state treasury would take ten percent of the coins struck as its commission. After that deduction, the minters would make any profit by subtracting their expenses (including raw copper, machinery, and labor) from the face value of the coins. The legislature later allowed Goadsby and Cox to coin two thirds of the three million coins on their own, in Rahway, while Mould operated in Morristown. The coins were also minted in Elizabethtown and New York City.

During this time the Republic of Vermont desired to become a state, but it did not enter the Union as one of the original states because of a border dispute with New York. (It would finally join as the 14th, in 1791.) Vermont's first officially authorized coins were the Landscape coppers, so called for their scenic view of pine trees lining a mountaintop, with an anthropomorphic sun rising in the background. Later Vermont coinage would more closely (and deliberately) mimic the regal copper coins of Britain. These showed a male portrait (anonymous, but resembling King George II) and a seated Goddess of Independence and Liberty, similar in appearance to Britannia. Later issues would feature a bust of King George III, one of which identifies him as such in the coin's legend.

**Vermont's "Landscape" copper coinage was unusual in design— perhaps too much so for popular taste. Later issues featured motifs based on Britain's coinage, which was already well known in commerce and widely accepted.**

Within a few years the states that had started coinage endeavors abandoned them. Over time the average weight of authentic copper coins had decreased, while in circulation their ratio to counterfeits and underweight imitations plummeted. This led to public skepticism, and widespread devaluation of all coppers, in what historians call the "copper panic" of 1789. By that year distrust drove copper pieces to a fraction of their former values, across the board, making continued production unprofitable. Eventually the panic subsided, and the coins did remain in circulation for many more years—but the era's state and private copper coinage had come to an end.

# NEW MONEY FOR THE YOUNG SOVEREIGN NATION

In regard to America's money there came a time of long-range planning, during the Revolutionary War and for several years thereafter—a period of experimentation and development. The Continental Congress authorized an issue of paper currency, as mentioned above; it also looked into the possibility of a dollar-sized silver coin. Such a coin would be a tangible symbol of America's hard-won freedom as well as hard-money backing for the nation's cash supply. The resolution of July 22, 1776, did not authorize a paper dollar. In its place was a coin whose design would be engraved by New York artist Elisha Gallaudet. These "dollars" were struck mostly in pewter, with some in brass, and others in silver. Congress had expected a loan of French silver to provide metal for more bountiful coinage, but the deal was never finalized.

The failure of the Continental Congress's paper currency in the late 1770s and 1780s led to brainstorming among those who sought to develop the emerging nation's money system. In 1782 Robert Morris, the Confederation's superintendent of finance, proposed to Congress a curious money system of 1,440 "units" making up a dollar. This was calculated to figure (to the smallest fraction) into the many different valuations of the Spanish dollar, which varied throughout the states. Thomas Jefferson favored a simpler dollar unit and a decimal system. "The most easy ratio of multiplication and division is that of ten," he noted in 1784. "George Washington referred to it as 'a measure, which in my opinion, has become indispensably necessary.'"[22]

Varieties of the Continental coins exist—some with the legend spelled CURENCY, some CURRENCY, some CURRENCEY; some bearing the credit line EG FECIT ("E.G. Made It"). The coins were struck in pewter, brass, and silver.

In 1783 Morris submitted to Congress a series of patterns, designed by Benjamin Dudley, as a proposal along the decimal line. The largest piece, with a denomination of 1,000 "units" (each unit being a quarter grain of silver), he called a *mark*. The 500-unit piece was a *quint*, and the 100-unit a *bit*. These silver patterns were proposed along with a copper 5-unit piece. The system never went beyond the experimental stage. (However, it did inspire another speculative issue—that of the Nova Constellatio coppers dated 1783, 1785, and 1786, with their mintage starting in the middle year. These pieces were made in Birmingham, England, for a trading firm that Morris started with some partners.)

In August 1786 Congress formally approved the dollar as the basic unit of the nation's monetary system, which would be decimal in format. Further action on the national currency, mint, and coinage system commenced with the Constitutional Convention, held in Philadelphia from May 25 to September 17, 1787.

Alexander Hamilton—later the first secretary of the U.S. Treasury—was among those who distrusted paper money and insisted on a firmer financial foundation. A standard federal coinage would symbolize the United States' strength and authority as a sovereign power, the equal to any European kingdom. By the late 1780s the individual states had ceased to issue their own coins and paper money. When coins were available in commerce, they tended to be Spanish dollars and their parts, Portuguese gold, British halfpence, and a mishmash of lightweight and counterfeit coppers. Hamilton agreed fundamentally with the decimal concept and urged that gold and silver be used in the nation's standard money.

Finally, on March 3, 1791—midway through George Washington's first presidential term—Congress resolved to establish a federal mint, authorizing the president to hire artists and acquire machinery for coinage. Some initial steps were taken, but that October, in his annual address, Washington emphasized that the mint continued to be an urgent concern. "The disorders in the existing currency," he told the houses of Congress, "and especially the scarcity of small change, a scarcity so peculiarly distressing to the poorer classes, strongly recommend the carrying into immediate effect the resolution already entered into concerning the establishment of a mint."

**Robert Morris's proposed Nova Constellatio patterns did not gain congressional approval for coinage. (All shown at actual size.)**

THE CONSTITUTIONAL CONVENTION · 1787

**On July 6, 1787, during the Constitutional Convention in Philadelphia, Congress set the designs for "three hundred tons of copper coin of the federal standard" that it had authorized earlier in the year. The coins are called *Fugio coppers*, after their inscription FUGIO (meaning, when combined with the sundial, "Time Flies"), or sometimes *Franklin cents*, as Benjamin Franklin was credited with their legends. They were privately struck under government contract in New Haven, Connecticut, from scrap copper. The Fugio coppers circulated widely; many varieties exist, and new variations are still being discovered.**

Five months later, Congress passed a bill of lasting significance. The Mint Act of April 2, 1792, provided that "the money of account of the United States should be expressed in dollars or units, dismes or tenths, cents or hundredths, and milles or thousandths; a disme being the tenth part of a dollar, a cent the hundredth part of a dollar, a mille the thousandth part of a dollar. . . ." Beyond establishing this decimal relationship, the Mint Act also set the metal content of the coins, and their imagery; identified the "seat of government," Philadelphia, as the site of the new mint; and guaranteed that silver and gold would be coined free of charge to those who brought the metal in. The latter provision would save the Mint from having to source its own raw gold and silver. It also offered banks, merchants, and others a way to transform bullion and miscellaneous foreign specie into official, spendable U.S. coins, and thereby inject larger-denomination coins into commerce. (The conversion, while convenient, was not automatic; refining and coining took time. Alternately, one could deliver bullion to the Mint and exchange it immediately for equivalent U.S. coins, with one-half of 1 percent deducted for expenses.) The act also provided for a token coinage of copper small-change coins.

George Washington.

**Progress toward a national currency and a federal mint began before the Constitution was signed in 1787, and would continue for several years thereafter.**

Alexander Hamilton.

The coins specified in the Mint Act of 1792 included these:

| Denomination | Value | Fineness |
|---|---|---|
| eagle | $10.00 | 91.7% pure gold (22k) |
| half eagle | $5.00 | 91.7% pure gold (22k) |
| quarter eagle | $2.50 | 91.7% pure gold (22k) |
| dollar | $1.00 | 89.2% pure silver |
| half dollar | $0.50 | 89.2% pure silver |
| quarter dollar | $0.25 | 89.2% pure silver |
| disme | $0.10 | 89.2% pure silver |
| half disme | $0.05 | 89.2% pure silver |
| cent | $0.01 | 100% pure copper |
| half cent | $0.005 | 100% pure copper |

Copper cents and half cents comprised the entire production of the Mint in 1793. The Mint purchased copper for its own account, and retained the profits from this coinage. The coins' Liberty Cap design was based on the obverse of the Libertas Americana medal of 1782, whose dies were engraved in Paris from concepts and mottoes proposed by Benjamin Franklin.

Benjamin Franklin was U.S. commissioner to France when the Libertas Americana medals were struck in 1782. "I have presented one to the King," Franklin wrote to the American secretary of foreign affairs, "and another to the Queen, both in gold, and one in silver to each of the ministers, as a monumental acknowledgment, which may go down to future ages, of the obligations we are under to this nation." The reverse featured an allegory of France protecting the infant United States from a British lion. On the obverse, the rod and cap behind Miss Liberty, in the words of numismatist Robert Morris in the *American Journal of Numismatics*, no. 13 (1879), are "the *rudis* and *pileus*, the 'rod of touch,' and the 'cap of announcement' connected with the ancient forms of freeing a slave."

As Franklin recounted, two noble metals—gold and silver—were deemed precious enough for court presentation of these important pieces: gold for the French royalty, and silver for powerful government leaders. From gold and silver the symbolic design flowed downward, infusing even the humble copper coinage of the new United States with its significance. The influence of the Libertas Americana medal on the Liberty Cap cents and half cents, shown here, is obvious.

The earliest circulating-coin designs of the new Mint featured Miss Liberty and a bare-breasted, spread-winged eagle. Illustrated are the half dime, dime, quarter dollar, half dollar, and dollar in silver; and the half eagle and eagle in gold. The quarter eagle would debut in 1796 with a heraldic-eagle design. (All shown at 1.5x actual size)

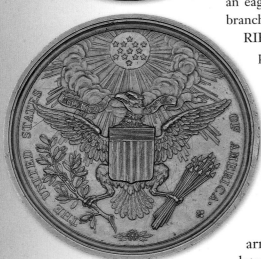

A new heraldic eagle took its place on the reverse of American coinage in the late 1790s and early 1800s. In *Numismatic Art in America*, Cornelius Vermeule traces the motif back through the coinages of the newly independent states to a 1791 commemorative medal designed by French artist Augustin Dupré (who had earlier designed the Libertas Americana medal). "This creation was termed the Diplomatic medal," writes Vermeule, "since it was conceived of as a work of art suitable in the precious metals for the presentation to foreign statesmen who had aided the colonies in their struggle for freedom."

Numismatist William Sumner Appleton describes the Diplomatic medal in the 1875 *American Journal of Numismatics* (no. 9):

[The obverse consists of] THE UNITED STATES OF AMERICA; an eagle displayed, on his breast a shield . . . in his right claw an olive branch, in his left thirteen arrows, in his mouth a ribbon inscribed E PLURIBUS UNUM; above a sun of thirteen stars, from which issues rays, passing through a circle of clouds, and extending below the wings of the eagle. [The reverse consists of] TO PEACE AND COMMERCE.; in exergue, IV JUL. MDCCLXXVI, DUPRÉ. F.; at the left an Indian Queen, personifying America, is seated, holding in her left hand a horn containing fruits and grains; by her side are bales, a barrel and an anchor, to which she points with her right hand; at the right Mercury just alighted extends toward her his right hand; behind him is the ocean, on which at the extreme right is the forepart of a ship, and beyond this is the land.

The Diplomatic medal of the United States, 1791, commissioned by Secretary of State Thomas Jefferson.

Many of these elements—in particular the eagle with a clutch of arrows, an olive branch, and a shield—are precursors to the nation's later numismatic iconography. The silver and gold coinage of the United States would return again and again to these motifs.

Despite the U.S. Mint's best efforts in its early years, its coinage remained scarce in circulation. Gold and silver in particular were rarely seen in commerce, but the problem extended to small change, as well. By 1799 only about $50,000 worth of copper Liberty Head cents and

The heraldic American eagle, seen on the silver dollar and gold $2.50 and $10 pieces. (All shown at 1.5x actual size)

half cents had been pumped into the economy—roughly one coin for every citizen, not nearly enough for the nation's day-to-day business. Helping to fill the void, earlier tokens and coins of the colonies and states continued to circulate, as did foreign coins, some of which (including Spain's silver and gold) Congress granted legal-tender status, which continued in effect until 1857.

The scarcity of circulating U.S. gold and silver coins wasn't from a lack of gumption at the Mint or a dearth of good intentions in Congress. The precious-metal content of the coins was the problem. They had full intrinsic value—a silver U.S. dollar contained $1 worth of silver—but they were tied together on the old pre-1792 ratio of 15 units of silver being equivalent to 1 unit of gold. In Europe the ratio favored gold more heavily, making U.S. silver coins more valuable on the world market. With such economic forces in play, the Treasury and many banks chose to hoard their specie reserves (gold and silver coins) rather than pay them out, leading copper and (increasingly) paper currency to populate the marketplace.[23] According to numismatic lore, a speculator in the late 1700s or early 1800s could take U.S. silver dollars to the Caribbean, exchange them at par for heavier Spanish-American silver dollars, and return the latter to the Philadelphia Mint to be melted and recoined into U.S. dollars, with the leftover silver representing his profit.[24] Congress would tinker with the weights and fineness of U.S. gold and silver coins well into the 1800s, in an attempt to control the situation and keep coins flowing in the channels of commerce.

In 1807 John Reich was hired to assist Mint chief engraver Robert Scot, whose early Flowing Hair, Draped Bust, and Turban designs were, over time, replaced with others, including Reich's depictions of Miss Liberty wearing a soft cap. It was Reich who designed the various heraldic eagles carrying both olive branches and arrows—symbolic of a nation hopeful for peace but ready, if necessary, for war. Reich would leave the Mint in 1817, but his artistry would grace American coins into the 1830s.

William A. Kneass (an experienced engraver, including of bank-note plates, who took over as engraver after Scot died in 1824) and Christian Gobrecht (a talented contractor later hired as "second engraver" when Kneass suffered a stroke) both contributed their skills to early coinage designs, as well.

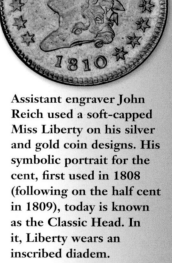

**Assistant engraver John Reich used a soft-capped Miss Liberty on his silver and gold coin designs. His symbolic portrait for the cent, first used in 1808 (following on the half cent in 1809), today is known as the Classic Head. In it, Liberty wears an inscribed diadem.**

**Christian Gobrecht's half cent and half dollar; and William Kneass's quarter dollar, quarter eagle, and half eagle.**

The normal ups and downs of bullion and international markets affected U.S. coinage, and Congress enacted legislation to try to keep things under control. For example, in 1853 fractional silver coins (smaller than $1 in denomination) had their weights reduced so their face value would exceed their silver value. This protected them from simply being melted down for a profit, and kept them in circulation. It also effectively put the United States on a gold standard, demonetizing silver. The weights of silver coins would be modified again in 1873.

The Coinage Act of February 21, 1857, reformed America's copper coinage, abolishing the old half cents and large cents (which had become unprofitable to produce, given the rising cost of their metal) and introducing a new smaller-sized copper-nickel cent. The act also ended the legal-tender status of Spanish-American and other foreign coins, in an attempt to retire them from circulation.

For decades, starting in the late 1830s and running through the early 1890s, it was Christian Gobrecht's Liberty Seated design that would embody American silver coinage. Cornelius Vermeule, in *Numismatic Art in America*, describes an era of mediocrity in U.S. coinage before the Civil War. About the long-running Liberty Seated series, he writes, "Quaint and dated though the entire ensemble may seem in the light of later coin design, the seated Liberty symbolizes American numismatic art during the generations of westward expansion, the Civil War, the centennial of the young republic, and commercial expansion that was to propel the United States into the role of a worldwide power."

United States gold coins, too, would see the generations-long run of a dominant theme. Gobrecht's Liberty Head design would be minted from the late 1830s to the early 1900s, being replaced on most denominations in 1907 and the half eagle in 1908.

These staples of antebellum American coinage continued through the Civil War years and emerged largely unchanged on the other side. Like much in the nation, however, other aspects of American money would be dramatically and irrevocably transformed by the conflict.

Christian Gobrecht's Liberty Seated silver coinage, and his Liberty Head gold, would be staples of American money for decades before and after the Civil War.

## Gold in the Old West

The January 1848 discovery of gold at Sutter's Mill on the American River, and the resulting California Gold Rush, soon brought significant changes to U.S. coinage. Two new federal coins would debut: the gold dollar, first released for circulation in May 1849, and the $20 double eagle, the largest denomination of regular-issue U.S. coinage, which followed in early 1850.

The little gold dollars—smaller in size than a cent—were very popular when they first came on the American scene. Gold bullion was pouring from the West to the U.S. Mint's facilities back east. Millions of gold dollars would be minted in Philadelphia, with smaller quantities made in Charlotte (North Carolina), Dahlonega (Georgia), New Orleans, and, starting in 1854, San Francisco. From 1850 through 1853 they were plentiful enough to take the place of silver dollars and half dollars in day-to-day commerce. (Silver became "scarce" in relation to the flood of gold.) After those peak years of the early 1850s, gold dollars continued to be minted in good numbers, sometimes exceeding one million coins per year into the early 1860s.

The double eagle, too, would become a popular coin, as well as a heavily minted one.[25] James Longacre's Liberty Head design might not have been universally beloved when the coin first came out, but, aesthetics aside, the new high-value denomination was welcomed. Individuals and firms depositing gold at the Mint could have the precious metal coined into any federal denomination they chose, and the large $20 pieces, containing almost an ounce of pure gold apiece, were most convenient for accounting, handling, and large transactions. Beginning in 1854 many of the coins would be produced right in California, at the newly opened San Francisco Mint. Loads of California gold continued to be shipped east, too, mainly for the Philadelphia Mint's massive output of coins. Interestingly, some years saw the federal mint in Dahlonega using more *California* gold than metal from its native Georgia! Through the 1850s and up to 1861, double eagles were commonly used in banking and commerce on the West Coast and in the lands west of the Mississippi. Many were also shipped overseas, in particular to London.

In the East and Midwest, the Civil War changed the scenario of readily available gold. Worried citizens hoarded all the gold coins they could, fearing that the federal government's new "greenbacks" (paper

Federal gold $1 and $20 coins, shown here at actual size, were born in the California Gold Rush.

A promotional poster beckoning miners and traders toward the golden West.

Some California entrepreneurs privately issued their own small-denomination gold coins.

Larger gold pieces were also issued by various private and semi-official Western interests, before the federal government asserted its right to control all coinage. Pictured are a "half eagle" of Norris, Gregg & Norris, of San Francisco (1849); a $20 gold piece of Augustus Humbert, U.S. Assayer of Gold (1852); and a "Vaquero" $10 gold piece by Baldwin & Co., San Francisco, 1850.

currency) would be devaluated by wartime inflation. A shopper with a paper dollar in one pocket and a gold dollar in the other would spend the paper first, and keep the gold as long as possible. By the end of 1861 Eastern banks stopped paying gold coins at par in exchange for paper money, and the Treasury threw its newly minted gold coins into storage instead of distributing them. Silver met a similar fate, disappearing from circulation, and by mid-July of 1862 even copper-nickel cents were being hoarded. In the East, a person could buy gold coins with paper money only by paying a high premium over face value. Paper currency became the day-to-day money, and gold coins would not begin to circulate again until December 1878. In the South, which did not mint its own gold coins, Confederate paper currency became virtually worthless; by January 1865 it required $5,882 in CSA cash to purchase $100 in federal gold coins on the London market. All the way across the country, meanwhile, on the West Coast, silver and gold coins continued to circulate at face value and it was paper money that was uncommon. In fact, paper currency was illegal under California law.

Ironically, considering the outpouring of metal during the California Gold Rush, there was a scarcity of small-change gold coins in the region for many years. Starting in 1852 private minters stepped in to fill the demand, making their own quarter dollar, half dollar, and dollar coins from locally mined gold. These were tiny pieces, even smaller than the federal government's 13-mm gold dollars. They typically were underweight, containing 85% or less of their face value in gold—with that percentage decreasing over time until some of the coins were only gold-plated base metal. In 1864 Congress passed the Coinage Act of April 22, which outlawed private-sector making of coins, but public demand kept the law from being fully enforced until 1883. Jewelers, dentists, and others experienced in working with small quantities of gold continued to make the little "coins" (sometimes without denominations, to try to get around the law, and sometimes back-dated to the 1850s or 1860s to "grandfather" them in). Numismatists have identified nearly 600 different varieties.

In addition to these tiny issues, the late 1840s to early 1860s were a golden age for larger-sized private gold coins in the West. Like earlier private coiners in the Southern states (Templeton Reid in Gainesville, Georgia, and the Bechtler family in North Carolina being notable), enterprising businessmen set up shop in various California cities, in Colorado, in Oregon, and elsewhere. In Salt Lake City, Utah, the Mormons minted their own gold coins, decorating them with religious messages. Today all of these privately produced issues are studied and collected by enthusiasts who prize them for their historical connections. In their time, they were simply a convenient way to transform raw Western gold into spendable currency for local use. By the mid-1860s, American money had largely moved on: the federal government affirmed that it would be the only issuer of legal tender, and the era of the privately produced gold coin drew to a close.

# COINAGE FROM THE CIVIL WAR TO THE GREAT WAR

America's money was fundamentally altered by the Civil War. The federal mints in North Carolina, Georgia, and Louisiana—all member states of the Confederacy—were closed by the spring of 1861. The Confederates made an attempt at a sovereign coinage, but didn't get beyond the striking of a handful of trial cents and half dollars. After the New Orleans Mint was seized, its federal workers were invited to stay as employees of the state of Louisiana. They used its remaining silver bullion (and federal coinage dies) to strike about $500,000 face value of half dollars for the state and then some $620,000 for the new Confederacy. That took less than a month to accomplish. In Dahlonega, Georgia, the state and, later, the Confederacy struck approximately 1,250 gold dollars and an estimated 1,000 to 2,000 half eagles before the gold supply ran out.

The North, meanwhile, did have enough copper, silver, and gold on hand to continue striking coins in quantity—but the coins didn't circulate for long.

By the end of 1862, a year and a half into the war, the U.S. Mint had struck 95 million–plus Indian Head cents—more than four of the coins for every man, woman, and child in the Union. And yet, by Christmas that year you would have been lucky to receive one in change when you went to pay for a newspaper, a loaf of bread, or a mug of holiday cheer. Hardly a "penny" was in sight in American commerce.

Where were the Mint's 980,000 pounds of Indian Head cents hiding? They were squirreled away with the rest of the nation's coinage, hoarded by nervous citizens and speculators. Long before New Year's Eve was observed and 1862 marched into 1863, Northerners had lost any childlike illusion of a short and successful tussle with the Confederacy. Dramatic changes and uncertainty in banking and the economy increased the public's anxiety. How would a protracted and expensive war be paid for? From April to December 1861 alone the Union spent $50 million just to feed its troops—before the war, that budget would have funded the entire federal government for nearly a year. Within weeks of the opening of hostilities, the United States was spending $1.5 million every day.[26] (By 1865, that rate would more than double.) To keep the wartime economy going, the federal government crafted an intricate financial system that included new taxes, increased borrowing (through bond sales), and innovative currencies.

Down on Main Street, in those anxious times especially, average Americans wanted to protect their financial future. One way to do that was to hold onto valuables like gold and silver—including coins. By the end of 1861 gold coins were practically gone from day-to-day circulation. Silver coins dried up in the spring of 1862. Congress got creative, voting to allow ordinary postage stamps to be used to pay certain debts up to $5. By the second week of July 1862, Americans were hoarding even the Mint's Indian Head cents; speculators packed them away, paying (with paper money) a premium of $4 over face value for every $100 worth of coins. That premium would increase to $20 over time! The Treasury Department, with its finger on the nation's pulse, knew that silver and gold coins would be hoarded; it stopped paying out new precious-metal

**Americans hoarded coins during the Civil War—gold coins, silver coins, even the humble copper-nickel cent. (shown enlarged)**

coins at face value and either stored the Mint's output in vaults or sold it to speculators at a premium, for export. Used in their place was a smorgasbord of new federal paper currency; privately issued coupons, tickets, and scrip notes with small-change denominations; and good old-fashioned barter.

Beginning in July 1862 and continuing into 1863 American business was essentially coinless. All gold and silver coins were being hoarded. The two-cent piece, the nickel three-cent piece, and the nickel five-cent coin hadn't been invented yet. Indian Head cents were being held near and dear. Neil Carothers, writing in his 1930 study *Fractional Money*, quoted Philadelphia's *Public Ledger* on the "difficulty among small shopkeepers, provision dealers in the markets and in the city generally, in making change" and the "extraordinary demand for cents." An editorial cartoon from *Frank Leslie's Illustrated Newspaper* portrayed "The Currency Question" with an embarrassed storekeeper begging a disgruntled customer, "I've no pennies; would you mind taking a ticket for the Broadway 'Free and Easy' instead?" As the Philadelphia Mint churned out its cents, citizens "stood in line for hours, waiting for an opportunity to get into the Mint," and "they had to go home without them, as the supply on hand was exhausted before half the applicants were accommodated."[27]

Of course, as the old saying goes, "necessity is the mother of invention." The need was there (for small-change coins), and Americans are nothing if not inventive. To meet the public demand, private firms and merchants started minting their own small, bronze, cent-sized tokens. Though they lacked the government-backed status of official federal coins, these tokens at least looked like currency (round and metallic, and many featured patriotic designs). Manufacturers would typically charge $7 to $9 for 1,000 bronze or copper tokens, using stock dies or preparing custom dies to advertise a particular merchant. The buyer would then distribute the tokens through his grocery store, restaurant, or other business. Everybody won: the minter made a profit over his costs and labor; the merchant essentially bought $10 worth of small change (and free advertising) for $7 to $9; and the public finally had convenient "coins" for making change in everyday transactions. An estimated 50 million or more Civil War tokens were minted over time, mostly in 1863 and into mid-1864, to help fuel small business.

**Privately minted tokens of the Civil War era. These served as small change in an era when gold and silver had disappeared from circulation. (shown enlarged)**

U.S. Mint Director James Pollock felt the privately issued tokens were fundamentally illegal, despite there being no law forbidding tradesmen's tokens or private coins that didn't imitate official U.S. coinage. Legislation in 1864 changed that. The Coinage Act of April 22, 1864, made it a misdemeanor to privately mint any one- or two-cent tokens to pass as money. That put an official end to the creation of *new* Civil War tokens.[28] On June 8 a new section to the U.S. code made it illegal to use the millions of tokens already in circulation. The punishment of a fine and/or imprisonment up to five years applied to the use of *any* privately made tokens or coins. The Mint introduced its own new bronze Indian Head cent in 1864, producing nearly 40 million in that year alone to pump into circulation.

As for gold and silver coins, it would be many years after the war before they started circulating freely again in different regions of the country.

In 1873 the United States issued a new kind of silver coin called a *trade dollar*. These coins were legal tender domestically until 1876, but they were really intended for circulation in Asia, to compete commercially with other nations' coinage. Each was slightly heavier (by about 2%) than a standard U.S. silver dollar. Chinese merchants in particular preferred silver to gold, and avoided paper currency of all kinds. The U.S. trade dollar was a popular success in Asia and it circulated by the millions.

The Mint stopped making trade dollars for commerce after 1878. In that year the Bland-Allison Act required the federal government to buy two to four millions of ounces of silver every month and use it to produce standard silver dollars (which had not been minted since 1873). Political "Silverites" thought that a growing number of dollars in circulation would increase wages and raise the average worker's quality of living. Business interests preferred the gold standard and argued that a flood of silver would simply bring inflation. The dollar coins were unpopular in commerce, and millions of them were thrown into Treasury storage vaults as backing for Silver Certificates.

In 1890 the Sherman Silver Purchase Act took the place of Bland-Allison. It allowed 4,500,000 ounces of silver per month to be paid for with Treasury Notes, which were legal-tender paper currency redeemable in gold or silver dollars made from the bullion purchased. This was a boondoggle—a political gift handed to influential American silver miners. The Treasury Notes were mainly redeemed for gold, which was then exported. Combined, the acts of 1878 and 1890 added some 570 million silver dollars to the nation's coinage.

American gold and silver were further affected by the Gold Standard Act of 1900 ("An Act to define and fix the standard of value, to maintain the parity of all forms of money issued or coined by the United States, to refund the public debt, and for other purposes"). This put the United States on a single standard whereby paper notes could be redeemed at par for gold coins, but not silver. The earlier-enacted Coinage Act of 1873 had been symptomatic of a national political and monetary struggle between pro-silver interests (which supported bimetallism) and pro-gold interests. With the Gold Standard Act of 1900, the "gold bugs" won out over the "silver menace." Silver coins would still be legal tender, but all of them, including the silver dollar, would be worth more in *face value* than in real meltdown or exchange value, similar to the copper-nickel coins of today.

Minting of silver dollars stopped after 1904, due to a shortage of silver. That shortage would be remedied by the Pittman Act of April 23, 1918, which was both a wartime deal with Great Britain and a federal subsidy to encourage American silver miners. Under this act, more than 270 million of

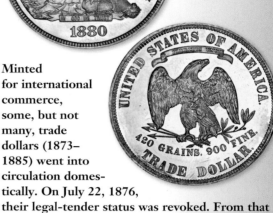

Minted for international commerce, some, but not many, trade dollars (1873–1885) went into circulation domestically. On July 22, 1876, their legal-tender status was revoked. From that point they traded widely in the United States based on their *silver content*, not their ostensible face value. Thus an American shopkeeper might accept a trade dollar at only $0.90, even though it contained more silver than a Liberty Seated dollar. The latter was legal tender and thus accepted at $1.00. Pictured is a Proof trade dollar minted in Philadelphia in 1880. (shown enlarged)

The Morgan silver dollar, named after its designer, U.S. Mint engraver George T. Morgan, was struck from 1878 to 1904, with a final coinage in 1921.

The Peace dollar was designed as a tribute to the end of World War I and the return (more or less) of global accord.

the Treasury's stored-away silver dollars were melted into bullion. The equivalent of roughly 259 million of the coins was slated for sale to Britain at the rate of $1.00 per fine ounce plus expenses, and the other 11 million were recoined into smaller denominations. Between 1920 and 1933, the federal government bought that same quantity of silver (209 million ounces all together) from U.S. mines, at the subsidized above-market price of $1.00 per ounce. (During that time the metal saw a market high of only $0.69 per ounce in 1924 and 1925 and a low of $0.25 in 1932.)

Meanwhile, the U.S. Mint continued to strike gold coins by the millions from 1900 to 1933. In 1907 a new gold $20 piece debuted, featuring a striding figure of Miss Liberty and a soaring American eagle. This was part of the Renaissance of American coinage brought about by the collaboration of President Theodore Roosevelt and sculptor Augustus Saint-Gaudens, who also redesigned the $10 gold coin. The Mint also made bullion bars of gold, held by the Treasury as backing for its paper money.

President Theodore Roosevelt felt the United States was the greatest nation on Earth—and that Americans deserved the greatest coinage. He commissioned Augustus Saint-Gaudens to redesign the gold double eagle and other U.S. coins.

# THE GREAT DEPRESSION AND BEYOND: MODERN SILVER AND GOLD

After the Great War ended in 1918 the United States seemed flush with new prosperity, but the economy of the Roaring Twenties wasn't as solid as it appeared. The illusory boom was fueled in part by exuberant overspending on credit, from Main Street to Wall Street. The inevitable crash of the stock market in October 1929 and a crop-killing drought in the early 1930s brought a general collapse of the American economy in the Great Depression. Its extent was dramatic, severe, and countrywide. About half of the nation's banks failed, and 86,000 businesses closed. Industrial output slowed and commodity prices dropped. By 1933 one out of every four Americans was unemployed; if you were fortunate enough to have a paying job, you were likely making less than $30 per week in wages. The national average wage was about $1,500 per year. A textile worker would expect to earn about $450, a farm hand, only $225.

In an attempt to strengthen the economy, on April 5, 1933, newly elected president Franklin D. Roosevelt issued Executive Order 6102. This prohibited banks from paying out gold coins or Gold Certificates.

**President Franklin Roosevelt.**

It was an effort to keep nervous depositors from withdrawing all the hard money from the banks that were still open. (Few if any banks would have held enough gold in their vaults to pay off all of their cash deposits.)

Executive Order 6102 furthermore required citizens and corporations to deliver, by May 1, 1933, their gold coins, gold bullion, and Gold Certificates to the Federal Reserve or a member bank, to be exchanged for an equivalent amount of other coins or paper currency.[29] Roosevelt's intent was to relieve the national banking emergency by keeping money circulating in the "recognized and customary channels of trade." Gold sitting in a box under Grandpa's bed, or hoarded in a company's office safe, was not being spent on goods and services. Paper cash such as Federal Reserve Notes and Silver Certificates was more likely to be spent, greasing the wheels of commerce and getting the economy back on track. Tens of millions of dollars in gold was shipped to the Treasury, eventually ending up in federal storage at Fort Knox. The Gold Reserve Act of January 1934 demonetized Gold Certificates and made U.S. currency "redeemable in lawful money"—not necessarily in silver or gold coins. The government raised the official value of gold from $20.67 per ounce to $35.00, immediately

**Roosevelt's executive order of April 1933 made it illegal to hoard gold.**

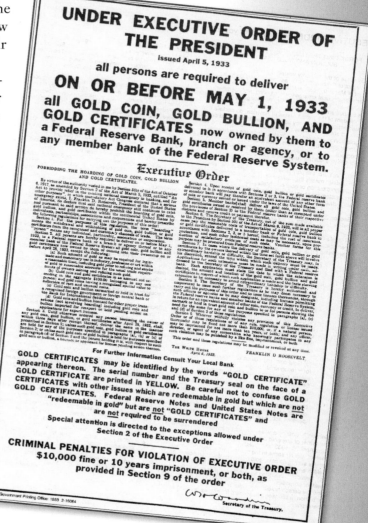

creating a $2.8 billion paper profit that was partially used to fund the nation's economic recovery. These federal actions, plus the Federal Reserve System's ability to manage and manipulate the currency supply (expanding it in depression and contracting it in inflation), effectively spelled the end of the gold standard in the United States.

Roosevelt's economic policies and the industrial mobilization of World War II helped bring the United States out of the Great Depression. Silver stayed at its market value of $1.27 per ounce and could be bought or sold at that price in nearly unlimited quantities; another executive order (no. 6814, signed August 9, 1934) sought to prevent hoarding of huge amounts of silver, but did not affect coins, silver less than .800 fine, or Silver Certificates, and had nowhere near the effect of Executive Order 6102. Newly mined gold had to be sold to the government.

In the 1944 Bretton Woods monetary conference, the Allies met to plan a new postwar exchange-rate that pegged international currencies to the U.S. dollar, which officially, if not in practice, was still based on the gold standard.

In the early 1960s silver's value started to rise due to demand, and by 1965 it cost the U.S. Mint more than face value to make dimes, quarters, and half dollars. Responding to this pressure, Congress passed the Coinage Act of 1965, which eliminated silver from the dime and quarter (replacing it with a copper-nickel composition) and reduced the half dollar's silver content from .900 fineness to .400. Silver's spot price continued to rise, and Americans quickly pulled pre-1965 silver coins from circulation, to be sold at a profit and melted. Bags of common silver coins (including dollars) became commodities, and there was even a market in Silver Certificates, which could be exchanged for their equivalent in precious metal from the Treasury Department. One-ounce silver "art bars" and rounds became popular collectibles and a means of investing in the metal.

The gold prohibitions of the 1930s would be repealed by congressional legislation and executive orders during the administration of President Gerald Ford.

In 1971, to strengthen the U.S. dollar, President Richard Nixon signed executive order 11615, which temporarily removed the United States from its Bretton Woods participation: the nation would no longer convert international obligations from U.S. dollars to gold at a fixed rate. In 1973 the United States increased the official value of gold to $42.22 per ounce. In 1977 Nixon's executive order was made permanent; the U.S. dollar lost the last of its gold-standard vestiges and became a fiat currency. Gold prices became officially free-floating, as they remain today, open to the forces and interpretations of the free market.

With gold being uncoupled from monetary policy, it became apparent that the Great Depression–era prohibition of gold ownership no longer served its original purposes. Congress passed Public Law 93-373. On December 31, 1974, this law removed the restrictions on U.S. citizens purchasing, holding, selling, or otherwise dealing with gold. President Gerald Ford then issued Executive Order 11825, which cancelled President Roosevelt's earlier orders.

In the late 1970s Nelson and Bunker Hunt, Texas oil-billionaire brothers, tried to corner the silver market, driving the spot price to skyrocket from $6.00 per ounce to a peak of $48.70 in January 1980. The Hunts' efforts failed later in 1980 when they couldn't honor the calling-in of huge payments made on margin. Silver nose-dived to half its high value and then spiraled downward until it was trading around $4.00 an ounce in 1990. After 2001 its price started to climb back up, finally averaging above $10.00 in 2006.

After more than 200 years of independence, the United States in the late 1970s and early 1980s found itself back to numismatic square one, in terms of silver and gold coinage. The precious metals were legal to own, but rarely if ever seen in circulation. The country was about to begin several experiments that would finally put silver and gold coins back within convenient reach of the average American.

**Louisville, Kentucky, early 1980: people line up outside a coin shop to sell their silver and gold coins for record prices.**

Legendary actress Helen Hayes was one of 10 creative Americans honored by the American Arts program of gold medallions in the early 1980s.

# 3

# The American Arts Commemorative Series Gold Medallions (1980–1984)

**T**he American Arts Commemorative Series gold-medallion program (1980 to 1984) was a step in the direction toward widespread personal ownership of gold by U.S. citizens. Today we see the program as a bridge: Left behind was the era of federally outlawed gold (from the early 1930s to the early 1970s). Waiting in the future was the robust, dynamic, and popular U.S. bullion market that would debut in 1986 and continue to the present day.

In hindsight, it might be tempting to label the American Arts initiative a complete failure. The medals themselves certainly failed to capture the average American's attention—and checkbook. Their marketing and distribution were largely inept. Potential buyers who *were* interested in the gold pieces were frustrated by a complicated multiple-step ordering system. In its final year, 1984, the program sold fewer than 50,000 net ounces of gold bullion. This is a drop in the bucket compared to the 2,381,492 ounces of American Gold Eagles the U.S. Mint would sell just two years later in 1986. But the American Arts medals were a crucial part of the nation's learning curve, and seen in this light the program was if not entirely *successful*, certainly *important*. Congress and the Treasury Department were feeling their way toward what would become the world's best-selling gold-bullion series.

President Gerald Ford's signature of Executive Order 11825 in December 1974 had revoked certain executive orders of the 1930s and their amendments, thus allowing average Americans to once again legally buy and own gold. The nation's leaders recognized the grassroots demand for this kind of private investment. The laws of economics being what they are, that demand was being met—but from outside the United States. Countries such as South Africa were supplying, in coin and bar form, the gold bullion that Americans wanted to buy. Did this present a political embarrassment or, even worse, a national-security risk? Was the United States even capable of competing in the international bullion market? Would a U.S. gold-coin program undermine faith in the soundness of the nation's financial system? All of these questions and more faced the administration of President Jimmy Carter, the U.S. Treasury Department, and Congress in the 1970s. Against this backdrop, on Friday, August 25, 1978, the Senate Committee on Banking, Housing, and Urban Affairs convened to hear opinions on a proposed new gold-bullion program.

The minutes of the committee meeting run more than 100 pages long.[1] The cast of participants included many who would later continue to be involved in national economic and numismatic affairs. William Proxmire of Wisconsin was the committee chair. Other members included senators John Sparkman of Alabama; Harrison Williams Jr. of New Jersey; Thomas McIntyre of New Hampshire; Alan Cranston of California; Adlai Stevenson of Illinois; Robert Morgan of North Carolina; Donald Riegle Jr. of Michigan; Paul Sarbanes of Maryland; Edward Brooke of Massachusetts; John Tower of Texas; Jake Garn of Utah; H. John Heinz III of Pennsylvania; Richard Lugar of Indiana; and Harrison Schmitt of New Mexico. Witnesses at the hearing included several of the committee members, plus other senators; Treasury and General

**Senator William Proxmire of Wisconsin chaired the Committee on Banking, Housing, and Urban Affairs in August 1978. Dating back to 1913 (when it was the "Committee on Banking and Currency"), the Senate committee's bailiwick includes banks and financial institutions, national monetary policy, the Federal Reserve, money and credit (including coinage and paper currency), export and foreign trade, and related areas. The House of Representatives has a similar committee with jurisdiction over banking and finance, which in the 1970s included a subcommittee on historic preservation and coinage.**

Services Administration officials; bankers and academics; and representatives of the American Numismatic Association. Additional statements and data were supplied by consultants, elected officials and government administrators, and media sources. Eighteen charts, tables, and other exhibits were submitted for the record. These ranged from studies of different methods of pricing and selling gold to analysis of national and global gold markets.

Present at the 10 a.m. convening of the hearing were senators Proxmire, Stevenson, Garn, and Lugar of the committee; and senators Jesse Helms of North Carolina, Orrin Hatch of Utah, and S.I. Hayakawa of California.

Chairman Proxmire brought the committee to order. The hearing concerned Treasury sales of U.S. gold—in particular it focused on bill S. 2843, the Gold Medallion Act of 1978, introduced by Senator Helms, which would require that a portion of any gold sold by the Treasury be in the form of 90% pure gold one-ounce and half-ounce medallions.[2] Proxmire remarked on the significance of the moment: "This is the committee's first oversight hearing on Treasury gold sales and it comes at an important juncture for U.S. policy."

Ultimately it would be *other* legislation, signed into law less than three months later, that would authorize the American Arts gold medals. But the conversations surrounding the Gold Medallion Act of 1978 richly illustrate the important questions and concerns of the day, and so are worth studying in the broader context of the United States' bullion programs.

# THE TREASURY DEPARTMENT'S GOLD SALES

By the time of the Senate hearing the U.S. Treasury was already selling from its bullion stockpile, and had been since 1975. Since May 1978 the government had been auctioning off gold at a rate established at 300,000 ounces per month (in minimum bids of 400 ounces, in ingot form, each brick costing about $80,000). That monthly rate was scheduled to be increased in November to 750,000 ounces. (Grover C. Criswell Jr., president of the American Numismatic Association, would testify during the hearing. He would note, quoting a *New York Times* report, that nearly all of the Treasury's auctioned gold to that point had been bought by corporations—some of them foreign, including the Dresdener Bank [641,600 ounces], the Union Bank of Switzerland [128,000 ounces], and the Bank of Oman [100,000 ounces]. A mere 800 ounces had been purchased by a private American citizen, oilman Morris Cannan of San Antonio, Texas.[3]) Much of this gold went to the arts (mainly for jewelry and gold chains) and dentistry, electronics, and other industries. Some was bought for hoarding, investment, and speculation.

This sale of precious metal supported the Carter administration's goals, shared by earlier administrations, of reducing (and eliminating) the

Key players in the 1978 discussions of Treasury gold sales included U.S. senators Richard Lugar, Jake Garn (shown walking with President Ronald Reagan), and Adlai Stevenson III.

**Retired chairman of the Federal Reserve, Arthur F. Burns: "Treasury should have started selling the gold sooner and in larger quantities."**

national and international role of gold in the monetary system, and to help ameliorate U.S. demand for imported gold.

The United States was plagued by inflation in the 1970s. In theory, government gold sold into the market would soak up extra dollars in circulation and return them to the Treasury. But fighting inflation and strengthening the dollar were *not* substantial Treasury goals for its sale of gold. "Obviously," Chairman Proxmire said, "to do anything significant about the dollar we have to cope with the inflation problem. That's the heart of it and if we don't adopt fiscal policies and monetary policies which are prudent and careful and inspire the confidence of investors here and abroad the dollar is going to continue to fall no matter what we do with gold."

Proxmire definitely did *not* see a return to the gold standard as a solution to the nation's economic woes. "Gold is a commodity," he stated, "like copper, zinc, wheat, and sugar—it is not money." Getting gold out of the U.S. monetary system with the Gold Reserve Act of 1934 and subsequent actions had been "the right step," he opined. Gold had stopped playing a major role in the international monetary system with the advent of floating exchange rates in 1973. The global community formalized the bullion/currency divorce by ratifying certain amendments to the International Monetary Fund's articles of agreement earlier in 1978. Proxmire expressed national financial-security concerns when he noted that the world's gold supply was largely controlled by the Soviet Union and South Africa. "An increase in the role of gold in the monetary system would run the risk of putting those two countries in a position to manipulate the world's money supply." Reducing gold's role in the monetary system would temper that risk.

Given the administration's goals, Proxmire raised a question: Why did the federal government continue to stockpile gold at all, paying for storage and security, if the bullion was completely unnecessary for monetary purposes? He invoked a famous economist (and retired chairman of the Federal Reserve): "Arthur Burns has said that Treasury should have started selling the gold sooner and in larger quantities. It has been suggested by others that the American taxpayer would be well served if Treasury were to announce its intention to sell off all the gold within a few years to anyone who wants to buy it at the best price that can be obtained." Curiously, in spite of the huge federal gold stockpile, the United States was at the time a net *importer* of gold. Despite the beginning of public gold auctions in April, there was "a net deficit this year just as large as last year, when there were no gold sales." Why, Proxmire asked the assembled senators, had the Treasury's bullion sales failed to reduce this imbalance in the gold trade?

Clearly Congress and the Treasury were in uncharted territory.

Proxmire made another observation: the nation's imports of gold *bullion* (bars, ingots, and the like) were down, but imports of gold *coins* were up. "Would the sale of gold medallions reduce gold coin imports and thereby be more effective than bullion sales [in 400-ounce lots] in reducing the U.S. trade deficit in gold?" Americans were buying foreign gold coins, mainly South African Krugerrands, at a rate of 1.6 million ounces per year. (This was among a total 9.5 million net ounces imported in 1977; however, most of the non-coin "imports" were actually balance-of-trade bank transactions on paper, as opposed to physical movement of precious metal.)

Chairman Proxmire raised five more questions that he hoped the hearing's witnesses would address:

1. What effect would the government's production and sales of gold medallions have on private producers and sellers of gold medallions and other gold objects?

2. How would the medallions be minted and marketed, and at what cost?

3. Would the Treasury's sale of gold *medallions* be significantly greater than its ongoing sale of gold *bars*?

4. Would average Americans "of limited means" be able to buy the medallions conveniently, without paying a large markup?

5. Would the sale of the U.S. gold medallions significantly reduce the importation of Krugerrands and other gold?

**The administration of President Jimmy Carter opposed the sale of Treasury gold in medallion form.**

# JESSE HELMS AND THE PROPOSED GOLD MEDALLION ACT OF 1978

Senator Jesse Helms, who had introduced the Gold Medallion Act of 1978, began his remarks by noting that in general he opposed the sale of the nation's "ultimate assets," including gold. He quoted Robert Roosa, the Treasury's undersecretary for monetary affairs under presidents Kennedy and Johnson: "It's the storm cellar we should retain in case the system breaks down."[4] Beyond that philosophical foundation, the matter came down to freedom—if the U.S. government did decide to sell the nation's gold, the American people should enjoy the freedom and opportunity to purchase some of it. "Why should we ship it overseas for sale," he asked, "when our own people here at home would like to buy it in small quantities?"

**Senator Jesse Helms of North Carolina was one of the leaders of the push for gold-medallion sales.**

In a printed statement to the committee, Helms noted that the gold-medallion bill "was drafted in a manner which would not affect the Treasury's authority to sell gold. If Treasury sells gold, however, this bill would require that some of it be sold in the form demanded by the American people—one-ounce and one-half-ounce pieces." In the first year after the bill's enactment, it would require that the first 1.5 million ounces of gold sold be in the form of medallions. (Any quantity above that could be in whatever form the Treasury secretary deemed appropriate.) With the Treasury's monthly release of gold scheduled to increase in November, 1.5 million ounces would be two months' worth of gold sales— about equal to the nation's importation of foreign gold coins in 1977. After that, production of the medallions would be to demand.

Helms's vision of the gold medallions was patriotic and rich in American symbolism: "The one-ounce medallion would have on one side the head of the statue of *Freedom* atop the Capitol, and it would be marked with the words ONE OUNCE FINE GOLD and the word FREEDOM. The reverse of the piece would be the Great Seal of the United States and the words UNITED STATES OF AMERICA, and the year in which it was produced. The one-half-ounce medallion would have on one side some representation of the rights of individuals and the words HUMAN RIGHTS, and ONE-HALF OUNCE FINE GOLD. The reverse would be similar to the back side of the 'Freedom' medallion, with the Great Seal."

Conspicuously missing from these proposed designs: any indication of face value. The medallions were specifically intended to be bullion pieces, not legal-tender coins.

Senator Helms envisioned patriotic design elements on his proposed gold medallions, including *Freedom* (the statue surmounting the U.S. Capitol Building) and the Great Seal of the United States. *Freedom* would eventually be featured on a 1989 silver dollar commemorating the bicentennial of Congress. The statue is pictured here during its 1993 renovation.

# THE TREASURY'S OBJECTIONS TO THE GOLD MEDALLION BILL

Several months before the August 1978 Senate hearing, Helms had expressed to the Treasury Department that he was open to making changes to the gold-medallion bill if desirable. In response he had received no suggestions—"merely a statement of opposition."

In various venues and through various official spokespeople, the Carter administration voiced its objections to the bill. Helms and his supporters sought to dismantle their arguments in the Senate banking committee's hearing.

## The "Weakened Dollar" Argument

In his remarks before the committee, Helms specifically addressed the Treasury's objection that the gold program would adversely affect the exchange rate of the U.S. dollar. "This is perhaps the most intimidating of arguments," he said, "because no one understands international monetary markets. I am quick to admit that I do not. I fear sometimes, in view of the tragic decline of the dollar in these markets, that perhaps our officials of the Treasury have trouble understanding them as well."

To counter the "weakened dollar" argument, Helms quoted various authorities he'd consulted. William Simon, former secretary of the Treasury, said that "the gold medallions proposed in S. 2843 should have no impact on either inflation or the value of the dollar in world markets." Simon further had told Helms that if reducing the imbalance of gold trade had *any* effect on the dollar's exchange rate, it would be positive. The former Treasury chief saw the out-of-control federal deficit and the too-rapid growth of the money supply as being more salient threats. "Gold medallions will have no effect on inflation or exchange rates," Simon stated, "but indeed are consistent with the freedom to own gold."

Senator Helms had also consulted with one of the largest American banks, which dealt daily with millions of dollars in foreign currencies. The bank's economists, he reported, "could not fathom the Treasury Department's view that the Gold Medallion Act would adversely affect exchange rates."

It wasn't only domestic experts that Helms had conferred with. At his informal request, Dr. Rudolf Geisler, a senior economist with Germany's Bundesbank, reviewed the gold proposal and discussed it with colleagues in the German Central Bank and the German Finance Ministry. Their unofficial response was that they could not see "in any way how the selling of gold medallions in the amount called for could adversely affect the dollar exchange rate."

"In other words," Helms summarized in plain language, "the Treasury's arguments about exchange rates are so much smoke-screen."

Jesse Helms consulted many experts in his bid to dismantle the Treasury's objections to gold-medallion sales. Among them: former secretary of the Treasury William E. Simon, who maintained that selling federal gold in medallion form would have no effect on inflation or exchange rates.

## The Anti-Inflation Argument

Helms objected, too, to the argument that the Treasury sale of gold would undermine President Jimmy Carter's ongoing anti-inflation programs. "There is a credibility gap there that no amount of gold medallions could fill," he said. "Selling gold to sop up excess dollars is a little like attacking a flood with a sponge." (On the latter point Helms and the Treasury Department agreed.)

Speaking in support of the Gold Medallion Act, Elizabeth B. Currier, executive vice president of the nonprofit Committee for Monetary Research & Education, called the Treasury's argument against undermining President Carter's anti-inflation programs "irrelevant." U.S. Representative Steven D. Symms of Idaho, sponsor of the House bill that mirrored Helms's in the Senate, was more scathing: "If the Treasury Department construes the production and sale of one-ounce gold medallions as undermining their anti-inflation rhetoric, then it would logically follow that the sale of the 400-ounce bars would also undermine the effort. After all, the only difference is the unit quantity being sold. Is the Treasury implying that it is acceptable to encourage the very rich to protect themselves from inflation by buying 400-ounce bars at some $80,000 but unacceptable to sell the gold in such a manner that allows the middle-income people to participate? Do they think that the middle-income people are too stupid to realize that the government really has no program underway to curtail inflation, and can be manipulated by rhetoric?"

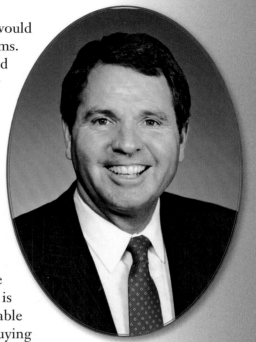

U.S. Representative Steve Symms: "Do [Treasury officials] think that the middle-income people . . . can be manipulated by rhetoric?"

## The "Official Endorsement of Gold" Argument

Related to the inflation argument, the Treasury Department further worried that the proposed gold medallions, bearing the words UNITED STATES OF AMERICA and the Great Seal of the United States, would imply an official U.S. "stamp of approval" of gold as an investment, which would weaken the government's fiscal strategies to strengthen the dollar. Treasury Secretary W. Michael Blumenthal was on record stating "I do not believe the U.S. government should permit the erroneous impression to be created that it cannot or will not take the necessary steps to combat inflation and that the public therefore needs to buy gold as a hedge against inflation." Helms waved this away. "If people see the dollar going down," he said, "they will try to save themselves. In some minds, a gold piece is one way to do this." For the senator and his supporters, the important principle was *freedom*—the freedom of Americans to buy U.S. gold if they wanted it. The Treasury's objection was "the kind of paternalism that is just not becoming of the government of what we like to call 'the land of the free.' Treasury should be less concerned with what was economic policy in the Depression and [more with] what the wishes of the American people are today." He pointed out that the bill was drafted so that if demand was insufficient, the gold medallions could be phased out. The American people—not the government—would decide one way or the other.

**Treasury Secretary W. Michael Blumenthal supported the Carter administration's objection to gold as a hedge against inflation.**

"So," Chairman Proxmire asked Helms, "the purpose isn't to persuade them to hold gold as a hedge against inflation; the purpose is to give them the freedom to do so if they wish to?" Helms replied in the affirmative. Later in the hearing he would colorfully call the Treasury objections "as silly as a ten-cent watch."

Senator Richard Lugar of Indiana, also strongly in support of the Gold Medallion Act, was equally forceful in tearing down the Treasury's objection. If Americans sought gold as a hedge against inflation, he argued, it wasn't their fault and they shouldn't be prevented from exercising that freedom. "I can understand why the Treasury is embarrassed that the subject even arises," he said, "but I'm not sympathetic to that embarrassment. My guess is that the Treasury has brought it upon themselves, and aided and abetted by a good number of members in the Congress of the United States."

## The "Legal Tender" Argument

Some objecting economists and politicians were concerned that gold medallions might be used as a quasi–legal tender. The Treasury's assistant secretary for international affairs, C. Fred Bergsten, protested that "The very existence of the U.S. Seal on the gold medallion would be an invitation to those who favor the remonetization of gold to press for designation of the medallions as legal tender—if not now, then at some subsequent date. Foreign governments might well question whether passage of this legislation meant that the U.S. government was reconsidering its policy with respect to gold."

Senator Jake Garn of Utah downplayed this worry. "It would not be very common for people to be floating medallions worth 200-and-some-odd dollars," Garn said. "I don't think that's a very realistic point—that because they resembled a coin, even if they were not intended to be, that they would be used."

Helms agreed with Garn that this was "a rather impractical possibility" and "exceedingly unlikely." First of all, he noted, "there would be no denomination on the one-ounce or half-ounce medallion. I don't see how they could use it as a coin of the realm." Furthermore: "It would be exceedingly risky and I just don't think it will happen and I think that any suggestion along that line is just obfuscation of the issue."[5]

Among the arguments advanced by Treasury assistant secretary C. Fred Bergsten: "official" symbols such as the Great Seal of the United States would make the gold medallions wrongly appear to be legal tender.

Senator S.I. Hayakawa of California noted that Canada, a staunch U.S. ally, had no fear that its own soon-to-launch gold bullion coins would ever circulate as cash.

Senator S.I. Hayakawa of California observed that Canada's government, which was as committed to demonetizing gold as was the United States, would soon be introducing its own gold-bullion coins complete with face values. "That [Canada] is willing to produce what is, at least officially, a gold coin, without fear that that coin would ever circulate as money, is an indication that perhaps the U.S. Treasury should reconsider its position regarding U.S.–minted gold medallions."

## The "Merchant Government" Argument

The hearing included some discussion of whether it was appropriate for the federal government to sell gold like a business. Proxmire asked Helms, "Why should the U.S. government inject itself further in the private gold market by minting gold medallions—a private market which includes such institutions as U.S. banks, gold dealers, and so forth?" Helms insisted it would have no effect on private producers, and reiterated his position that the real issue was the freedom of American citizens to buy gold that the government was going to sell in one form or another anyway. "No one in the bullion coin market has protested insofar as I know," he said.

Proxmire pressed Helms on how the government could effectively compete against the Krugerrand when large and specialized private firms found it to be impossible. He specifically cited Engelhard Minerals & Chemicals Corporation, producer of a one-ounce .9995 fine "American Prospector" gold round. Engelhard had bankrolled large-scale production and marketing of this private bullion medal, but the sliver-thin markup on the Krugerrand made competition

Private-issue "Prospector" gold rounds were marketed by Engelhard Corporation.

unrealistic. "South African gold producers effectively subsidize Krugerrands, as I understand it," Proxmire said. "They don't care about a profit over the bullion content. How could the U.S. government produce a medallion which matched the Krugerrand in price without subsidizing such sales?" Helms hemmed and hawed over this question, but finally insisted he didn't think a taxpayer subsidy would be necessary. He further remarked that the intent of the proposed program wasn't to get into a "selling contest" with the Krugerrand, but to make American gold available to Americans who couldn't afford a 400-ounce ingot.

Senator Orrin Hatch of Utah submitted his statement for the record, basically emphasizing that American citizens, after having their gold taken away in the 1930s, deserved to be able to buy it back in affordable amounts. "People have demonstrated their desire in the marketplace to have this kind of item," he said. "For the U.S. government to leave this market solely to the South Africans, to the Mexicans, and now soon, the Canadians, is foolish."[6]

## The National-Security Argument

National security was never far from the surface in these conversations about gold. The Soviet Union in particular lurked in the background and came to the forefront from time to time. During the Senate hearing, in midsummer 1978, the United States and its allies were solidly entrenched in the Cold War against the USSR and had been for more than 30 years. The relatively new-to-the-scene Carter administration was keen to avoid any appearance of weakness in relation to the Communists.

Democratic senator Adlai Stevenson of Illinois noted that the Soviet Union and South Africa were the world's major suppliers of gold. He grilled Senator Helms on the possibility of the Soviet Union benefiting from the U.S. gold program.

"If, as you indicated, the medallions enlarged the market and the demand for American gold," Stevenson said, "the effect would be presumably to increase the price of gold. And wouldn't the principal beneficiary of the increase in price be the Soviet Union?"

Helms refused to accept the premise, and turned the conversation back to one of his main bullet points. "What you're talking about," he replied, "is letting the American people buy in small quantities some of the gold held by their government rather than selling it overseas to the Soviet Union or whatever other country. I don't see how it would make any difference."

Stevenson pressed the point: "I don't have figures for the Soviet Union, but for every $10 increase in the price of gold, South African export prices are increased by roughly $230 million. An average price of $190 an ounce this year will boost gold earnings to $3.2 billion. Last year it was something over $4 billion."

Helms held his ground: "This would have no effect on either the demand or the price of gold. It would displace what the American people are now spending to buy foreign medallions, the Krugerrand, and so forth. So I am unable to respond to the senator's question because I can't accept the premise which you have given."

Would promoting the widespread sale of gold ultimately benefit the Soviet Union, a major supplier of the precious metal? This was a concern voiced by the Carter administration.

# QUESTIONS ABOUT PUBLICIZING AND SELLING THE MEDALLIONS

During the statement of Senator Garn, Senator Helms announced that "Late information has come to me. One bank has offered to buy the whole production [the first year's 1.5 million ounces] at $10 million above the bullion price." This was the Republic National Bank of New York City, whose vice president in charge of gold trading, Frederic S. Bogart, introduced himself as "a little guy from New York" and addressed the committee with Big Apple moxie. "How well are we faring with inflation? I say not too well at all. . . . As for S. 2843, the bill to make gold medallions, my question is: Why not? If we really are going to sell the metal, at least give us here in the United States a better chance to own some. It will be a good gauge of American sentiment for the value of our own currency. By the way, our bank could muster enough interest among our own dealers to guarantee the sale of a million and a half ounces of gold by the Treasury to ensure that the Treasury does not sustain a loss in the manufacturing or production." Bogart didn't back down from this optimism when questioned further by the committee.

The federal government's General Services Administration had successfully marketed millions of the Treasury's hoarded Morgan silver dollars in the early 1970s. The agency stood ready to assist in distributing new gold medallions, if called upon to do so.

As far as marketing and getting word out to the American public, Senator Helms noted, "I come from a rather erudite community. The capital city of my state has 57 colleges and there is a research triangle nearby, and I was just wondering what percentage of the people of Raleigh, North Carolina, and the immediate environs even know how to buy a Krugerrand? But they would know how to buy a medallion produced by their government." He asked the same question of Senator Garn: "How many people [in Utah] know how to buy a foreign gold coin?" Garn replied, "All I can speak for is the senior senator from Utah and I don't know how to buy one today. I would have to ask somebody, where do you go? Where do you get one?"

Joel W. Solomon, administrator of the General Services Administration, assured the assembled senators that the GSA deferred to whatever position the Treasury took in relation to the Gold Medallion bill. If the Treasury proceeded with medallion sales and chose the GSA for marketing them, he promised the agency's best efforts. "GSA is the general sales agency for the federal government," he explained, "and has had experience in recent years in the sale of precious metals, including both gold bullion and silver, as well as marketing of the Carson City silver dollars. The knowledge and expertise we have gained through these disposal actions make us confident that we could conduct a gold medallion sale." Solomon noted that in the GSA's distribution of the Treasury's millions of hoarded silver dollars (in five sales from 1972 to 1974), the cost of marketing and selling each coin had been approximately $4 plus postage.

Notwithstanding the GSA's successes in selling silver dollars, Chairman Proxmire couldn't resist needling Solomon over the agency's reputation for poor purchasing and accounting. He pointed out a Minolta camera that consumers could buy at a W. Bell & Co. discount store for $219.50; the GSA paid more than $246 apiece for the same camera. Proxmire called such examples "appalling," and told Solomon, "If you're going to market these medallions I hope you can have a better record on that than you have had in paying for calculators and so forth."

# THE U.S. MINT'S OPINION

Chairman Proxmire questioned two officers of the Treasury Department to get an understanding of the U.S. Mint's position. C. Fred Bergsten, assistant Treasury secretary for international affairs, was accompanied by Dr. Alan J. Goldman, assistant director of the Mint for technology.[7]

Goldman observed that the bill called for a ratio of two half-ounce medals for every one-ounce medal, so the 1.5 million ounces of first-year gold medals would be struck in 2.25 million pieces. "We should point out," said Goldman, "that the Mint has never undertaken a program involving the production of 2.25 million gold medals a year. The recent Bicentennial gold medal program certainly represents no precedent. In contrast to the 2.25 million medallions, the entire Bicentennial program involved the production of less than 40,000 gold medals." He believed, however, that the Mint would be able to meet the Gold Medallion Act's requirements, given "additional equipment, adequate lead time, an increase in Mint personnel ceiling, and the necessary funding by the Congress." He spelled out what would be needed: blank-inspection tables, coin-conveyor belts, and other new equipment, procured and installed for $100,000; modification and rearrangement of the manufacturing areas at the Philadelphia Mint and the West Point Bullion Depository ($250,000); and hiring of 50 additional employees, including security personnel. Adding $1.30 per planchet (for fabrication of the medal blanks by private industry, using gold supplied by the Mint), Goldman estimated an expense of $2.00 per medallion. That assumed the Mint would supply high-purity gold for the blanks, rather than .900 fine coin gold; the latter would require more refining that would add $0.50 per blank.[8]

Goldman estimated total startup costs for the program would be $1 million, to cover necessary capital and personnel expenditures plus fabrication costs for an initial 500,000 blanks. To pay for these and other expenses as the program unfolded, the Mint had general statutory authority to reimburse itself from sales. However, Goldman warned, ideally Congress should earmark $5 million for the production of the 2.25 million medals, because if sales failed to materialize the Mint would be stuck with the manufacturing costs.

Dr. Alan J. Goldman was the U.S. Mint's assistant director for technology. He spoke to the assembled senators about the Mint's production capacity. (Seen here with Mint director Donna Pope, circa 1981.)

The Mint had recent experience producing medals, for the nation's Bicentennial—but only in the tens of thousands, not in the millions, as Helms's proposed Gold Medallion Act would require.

# THE COMPETITION

Dr. Goldman's note of concern regarding sales foreshadowed the disappointing reality the American Arts Commemorative Series would face two years later. But in the midst of so much optimism and patriotic philosophizing, his tone recalls Cassandra, the Trojan princess of Greek mythology—bestowed with both the gift of prophecy and the curse of never being believed.

Americans were already buying hundreds of thousands of ounces of foreign gold coins and medallions every year. To the supporters of the Gold Medallion Act of 1978, the United States simply had to step in with its resources and expertise, and it would compete with the international bullies who were eating America's lunch.

## What Exactly Was the Krugerrand?

Senator Lugar, having already stated his support of the Gold Medallion bill, brought up the gold market's 800-pound gorilla—the Krugerrand. The coin was produced by South Africa, a republic that had voted its complete independence from Great Britain in 1961 and then officially institutionalized its long-standing system of racial segregation. This system, called *apartheid*, put the

South Africa's Krugerrand featured a portrait of national hero "Uncle Paul" Kruger (also pictured here in a 1900 *Vanity Fair* caricature) and a gamboling springbok antelope.

small South African white minority in control of the nation's vastly larger black majority, who were kept impoverished, uneducated, and disenfranchised. While the United States and other countries had their own shares of racial inequality, South Africa's abusive and state-mandated apartheid made it an international bugbear. Since the Krugerrand's debut in 1967, however, and especially since the launching of its international sales in 1970, the coin helped South Africa grow into the superpower of the gold market.[9] Lugar noted that the coin was "heavily marketed and . . . sold barely above cost." Furthermore, there was "even a suggestion that the South Africans are using the Krugerrand as a promotional device to sell gold almost in a way that [the United States] might send trade missions out to sell grain." (Edward M. Bernstein, a noted international economist and monetary theorist, opined that "The government of South Africa has a good reason for minting Krugerrands and exporting them all over the world—it wants to increase the demand for gold, its principal export."[10]) Senator Lugar noted that there was pressure on American television stations, radio stations, and newspapers to not give media coverage to the Krugerrand, because of opposition to apartheid. But still Americans were investing in the coin at the rate of some 1.6 million ounces per year.

According to C. Fred Bergsten, the Treasury Department's assistant secretary for international affairs, South Africa added only 3% to the bullion price of the Krugerrand, to cover its minting costs plus the marketing costs of the South African Chamber of Mines. Dealers would then mark up the coin for profit, but healthy competition limited that to only an additional 2% to 3% over bullion. "For this reason," Bergsten told the Committee on Banking, Housing, and Urban Affairs, "private minters of gold medallions have been unable to compete effectively with the Krugerrand." The U.S. refiner Engelhard Industries was unable to sell its American Prospector gold round to dealers without going over South Africa's 3% markup. That 3% wasn't enough for Engelhard to make a reasonable profit, given the great expense of advertising necessary to sell large quantities.

What kinds of messaging did Americans absorb in the South African promotional blitz? Newspaper and magazine advertisements for the Krugerrand promoted the coin as "the hardest cash in the world" . . . a "practically crisis-proof" hedge against paper-money devaluation and inflation . . . "the most convenient form of gold to own." Ads from Monex International encouraged investors to "Get 20 for the money and one for the show"—in other words, to "hide away" twenty Krugerrands and "show one off" (worn as jewelry, or displayed in a coin case, or given as a gift).

Paul E. Goulding, deputy administrator of the GSA, painted the following picture of the Krugerrand.[11]

> The Republic of South Africa's Krugerrand is an example of a foreign coin sold in this country. This coin, which contains one troy ounce of .91666 fine gold, is struck by the Republic of South Africa under an agreement with the Chamber of Mines, which is a consortium of private gold-mining companies in South Africa. Institutional buyers purchase Krugerrands at the point of manufacture. There is no maximum or minimum purchase limitation. Price is pegged at day-of-purchase market value of gold, plus a 3 percent surcharge imposed by the Chamber of Mines in South Africa. The purchaser is responsible for packaging and shipment of the coins back to the United States. Persons who wish to purchase Krugerrands contact their banks or dealers in local areas and order them at that day's (day-of-order) market price. These orders constitute a verbal contract at the point of order. If the banks or dealers at which the coins were ordered do not have any Krugerrands, they are ordered from banks or dealers which do possess the gold coins. The coins are always purchased at the daily gold market price, with a range in surcharge of 3 to 5 percent, in addition to the 3 percent surcharge already imposed in South Africa.

State and local sales taxes would be added to these surcharges. Goulding gave an example of a Krugerrand sold in the Washington, DC, metropolitan area on September 8, 1978, when gold was selling at $208 per ounce. The coin's final price to the consumer, after all surcharges plus district sales tax, was $231.50.

The U.S. government could have discouraged Krugerrand sales by classifying the coin as a *medallion* for customs purposes, which would have added duty costs. But the United States respected South Africa's official definition of the Krugerrand as a coin for tariff classification. "We have . . . seen what other countries do and they follow that same practice," said Assistant Treasury Secretary Bergsten. "It's a simple matter of accepting at face value what the producer says his product is."

"The cause of the Krugerrand's success is hard to measure," American Numismatic Association president Grover C. Criswell Jr. told the assembled senators, "except to say that it is a precise and exact weight, which makes price

A typically enthusiastic advertisement (1981) for South Africa's gold Krugerrand—"the world's best way to own gold," "easy to buy and easy to sell," "now offered in three new sizes."

An anti-apartheid pamphlet protesting the Krugerrand, from 1985. President Ronald Reagan would ban the coin's importation that year.

changes easy to calculate. It is not widely counterfeited or reproduced, and makes no pretense about having a numismatic worth. The backing of the South African government, together with a massive advertising campaign, have obviously not hurt sales, either. Certainly it is easier to deal with one troy ounce than a [British] sovereign weighing 0.2354 troy ounce. It's also easier to market and sell a governmental issue than it is a private issue of one ounce or more. . . . Given the widespread publicity attendant to the Krugerrand, given the 'fear' on the part of a noncollector in acquiring a coin whose gold content is expressed in four and five decimal fractions of an ounce [like the sovereign and other older foreign coins], and perhaps because there is no good alternative American bullion piece available, Krugerrand sales have soared."

Years later, in October 1985, President Ronald Reagan would ban the importation of Krugerrands to the United States, as an anti-apartheid sanction. His executive-order ban stayed in effect until South Africa abandoned apartheid in 1994. But in the late 1970s and early 1980s, the Krugerrand was the world's king of gold coins.

## Other Competing Gold Coins and Medals

Since ownership of gold was legalized for U.S. citizens in 1974, Americans had shown an interest in buying gold *coins* in particular.

Coins have advantages over gold ingots: they're smaller, making them more affordable to buy, and more convenient to store and transport; they have an implicit guarantee of quality (fineness and weight) and legal-tender status backed by their issuing countries; they're immediately recognizable (whereas a buyer might not be familiar with a wafer or round from a private mint); they often have artistic and historically significant designs.

Other forms of gold include jewelry, watches, flakes and nuggets, antiquities, and other physical objects. With wrought items like rings and necklaces, expense is added for the artistry and craftsmanship, making the gold more costly than a similar weight in coin or bullion. The secondary market for such objects can be quite unkind to an inexperienced buyer. Gold flakes or dust lack a coin's convenience of storage and easily determined weight and fineness, making them less liquid. For small investors in the 1970s, other ways of owning gold, such as exchange-traded funds, mutual funds, options, and futures, were either nonexistent or simply not competitive with good old-fashioned coinage.

In addition to the Krugerrand, older coins like the U.S. $20 double eagle (minted between 1850 and 1933, each containing 0.96750 ounce of gold), the English sovereign (minted from 1901 onward, 0.2355 ounce), Mexican 20 pesos (1917 to 1959, 0.4822 ounce) and 50 pesos (1921 to 1947, 1.2056 ounce), and the Austrian 100 corona (1908 to 1915, 0.9802 ounce) were popular types.

Trying to capture sales in the burgeoning gold market, various private firms minted rounds and wafers in sizes convenient for small investors. Chairman Proxmire questioned ANA president Criswell on the market weakness of these privately minted gold medals. "If there's a demand for gold bullion medallions, why wasn't the American Prospector more successful? Why doesn't the private market, through a private mint like the Franklin Mint, do it?"[12] His implication was clear: if the American private sector couldn't compete with the Krugerrand, what did that say about the viability of Senator Helms's proposed gold medallions?

U.S. double eagles ($20 gold coins) of the Liberty Head and Saint-Gaudens types. Circulated common dates sell for close to their bullion value.

**In addition to South Africa's Krugerrand, Americans could invest in older foreign gold coins, such as those of Great Britain, Austria, and Mexico.**

Criswell's reply was resolute. "Anything that's issued by any private firms is not popular," he said. "Gold coins have been made for years by Engelhard and private firms in both Canada and England, and they were not popular. Only when the governmental issue of the Krugerrand was promoted was it popularly sold. Anything that's issued by a private manufacturer is not going to be as popular as anything issued by a government. . . . There are a lot of people who don't trust private issues as opposed to the government. They just wouldn't buy it."

# THE POSITION OF THE AMERICAN NUMISMATIC ASSOCIATION

Criswell's comments to the Senate committee were made in his official capacity as president of the American Numismatic Association. The ANA is an organization that was founded in 1891 to promote knowledge of numismatics (the study of money) along educational, historical, and scientific lines, as well as to encourage interest in the hobby of coin collecting. It was congressionally chartered in 1912.[13] Criswell was accompanied at the Senate hearing by David L. Ganz, the ANA's legislative counsel. In his printed remarks submitted for the record, Criswell firmly supported the Gold Medallion Act of 1978.

The ANA president educated the senators on the source of much of the Treasury's 266 million troy ounces of stockpiled gold. The precious metal was not from "central banks or international transactions, but in large measure comes from American citizens who patriotically turned in the gold coins that they had on hand during the great gold recall of 1933 and 1934." Criswell evoked the image of $784 million face value of $20 gold pieces being melted into 400-ounce bars in 1935, and another $472 million in 1936 . . . plus more than $150 million in $10 gold pieces in the same years, "turned in by

**Grover C. Criswell Jr. was president of the American Numismatic Association, a congressionally chartered organization dedicated to the study of coins and the promotion of coin collecting.**

obedient citizens." All told, he stated, between 1934 and 1950 the U.S. Mint had melted more than $1.6 billion worth of previously circulating gold coins that, if not for the Gold Reserve Act of 1934, would have remained largely in private hands.

It was the position of the ANA that the American people should have the opportunity to reacquire some of that gold. Criswell further noted that U.S. gold sales would take hundreds of millions of dollars away from support of South Africa's government and its policies of apartheid. Summarizing the ANA's support of the Helms bill, he made these points:

**President Franklin Roosevelt signing the Gold Reserve Act of 1934. His decisive actions on gold ownership and convertibility helped turn around the nation's banking emergency in the Great Depression. Some Americans, however, saw them as little more than a government seizure of private property. In the 1970s, when gold became legal to own again, many wanted a chance to buy it from the Treasury's reserves.**

First, it helps the balance of payments of this country.

Second, the multiplier effect from spending money domestically has clear economic benefits.

Third, it has the effect of denying $600 million per year in assistance to South Africa.

Fourth, it returns gold to the people who gave it to the government in the first place—the American citizens. Even though present gold, as I understand from the earlier statement, is not the same gold as that which American citizens were required to turn in in 1934, billions of dollars were then taken from individuals, and should now be returned.

Finally, it raises more money for the government than its own plan does.

# SEGUE TO THE AMERICAN ARTS COMMEMORATIVE SERIES

Submitted into the record of the Senate hearing on the Gold Medallion Act of 1978 were remarks by Jim Leach, U.S. representative from Iowa and the ranking Republican member of the House Subcommittee on Historic Preservation and Coinage. Leach supported the idea of half-ounce and one-ounce gold medallions, and he used this opportunity to pitch his own similar concept: H.R. 13567, the American Arts Gold Medallion Act, which he had introduced in the House of Representatives a month earlier.[14]

Leach blasted the Treasury for hauling "the old endorsement skeleton out of the closet again as a reason for opposing gold medals." He insisted that congressional authorization would *not* imply official endorsement of gold as an investment; rather, that it would simply give average Americans an investment vehicle they could afford and be comfortable with. Diamonds and artwork are expensive and require certain expertise and costs for appraisal, he noted. Real estate is outside the average person's reach, not unlike the Treasury's ongoing sale of 400-ounce gold ingots. Small gold medallions would give Americans an easy, relatively safe way to invest in a universally recognized hard asset.

Leach brought up the subject of design. Since the 1977 proposal of a new dollar coin (the Susan B. Anthony small-sized dollar would replace the Eisenhower dollar in 1979), Leach's House subcommittee had been "besieged with suggestions for great

**Representative Jim Leach of Iowa. His bill, the American Arts Gold Medallion Act, worked its way through the House as Jesse Helms's bill was under consideration by the Senate. Leach drew from his experience with the House Subcommittee on Historic Preservation and Coinage. He was instrumental in bringing the American Arts gold medallions to life. Leach's career in elected office started in January 1977; he would serve through January 2007 and later chair the National Endowment for the Humanities.**[15]

In the 1970s the United States had plenty of coins honoring Americans for governmental and military accomplishment—but none for the arts.

Americans who deserve recognition for their contributions to our heritage." A circulating dollar coin would be limited to a single portrait, but "the striking of gold medallions offers us the possibility of recognizing a larger group than is possible on our coinage." He expanded on the opportunity the medallions presented:

> Because our coins . . . honor individuals whose contributions have been in government and politics, I am suggesting that we honor . . . 10 individuals who have been distinguished contributors to the arts—music, painting, writing, architecture, and the theatre. . . . While I have recommended the field of arts for the first five-year series, I would envision honoring other fields of achievement in the years ahead.

Leach recommended these Americans be honored: artist Grant Wood, singer Marian Anderson, writer Mark Twain, writer Willa Cather, musician Louis Armstrong, architect Frank Lloyd Wright, poet Robert Frost, sculptor Alexander Calder, actress Helen Hayes, and writer John Steinbeck.

The congressman had introduced his American Arts Gold Medallion Act on July 21, 1978. Jesse Helms's Gold Medallion Act of 1978 died, but Leach's bill went through weeks of legislative hoops, gained cosponsors, and finally was rolled into omnibus bill H.R. 14279, the Financial Institutions Regulatory and Interest Rate Control Act. President Jimmy Carter signed the act as Public Law 95-630 on November 10, 1978.

Thus were born the American Arts gold medallions—in the face of official Treasury objection at home, and well-established competitors abroad—tucked inconspicuously into title IV of a much larger bill covering much larger programs. The modest little gold medals would be the United States' first step toward a modern bullion market.

## LACKLUSTER GOLD

To get the American Arts program off the ground, Congress earmarked startup funds for production of the new gold medallions. Time was of the essence: the spot value of gold was climbing. It had started 1978 at $170 per ounce, and by the time President Carter signed the American Arts Gold Medallion Act into law that November it was at $206. Over the course of 1979 the metal rose steadily until it went over $510 in late December, averaging that month at $455. When the first medallions went on sale in July 1980, gold was selling at $644 per ounce.

The federal government's General Services Administration was put in charge of marketing and distribution. The medallions were to be "sold to the general public at a competitive price equal to the free market value of the gold contained therein" plus manufacturing and overhead costs.[16] The GSA was tasked with selling them in a way that would "encourage broad public participation" and "not preclude purchases of single pieces."

One GSA proposal was to distribute the medallions through the Federal Reserve to local banks, who would sell them directly to the public.[17] The Treasury rejected this idea and instead put into place a plan that, for the individual purchaser, was more complicated and protracted. First the prospective buyer would make a telephone call to learn the cost for a medallion on that day. This cost would vary, based on the previous day's settlement price of gold bullion traded on the Commodity Exchange of New York, plus a per-ounce surcharge to cover production and marketing expenses.[18] After learning the cost, the buyer would go to a Post Office on the same day to make payment by certified check, postal money order, or cashier's check. The gold would then be delivered from the Mint to the buyer, by mail, taking up to six weeks (as officially estimated; the actual delivery time once the program got under way was sometimes even longer).

The creators of the American Arts gold medallion program had great expectations, but from the start sales were disappointing. In the first year of issue, 1980, the Mint struck 500,000 once-ounce medals; of these, consumers bought just over 310,000. Also minted were 1,000,000 half-ounce medals, which sold to the tune of 281,000. Sales dropped dramatically in 1981, rose to the program's peak in 1982, fell again dramatically in 1983, and plummeted to dismal lows in 1984, the series' concluding year. The Treasury and GSA experimented with their

**A wood-and-velvet Treasury Department case intended to store a collector's American Arts gold medallions.**

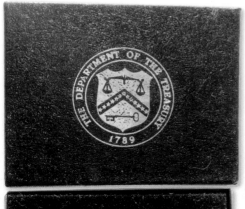

**The individual-medallion box for the 1981 Mark Twain one-ounce piece.**

**A disadvantage to this Styrofoam packaging: to remove the medallions, a collector had to tear or remove the plastic seal.**

SCULPTOR'S ORIGINAL SKETCH

SCULPTOR'S ORIGINAL SKETCH

# MARK TWAIN

The artist honored on the 1981 American Arts one ounce gold medallion triggers nostalgic sentiments. His portrait, type of humor, and literary accomplishments are familiar memories to Americans. The pen name, Mark Twain, was a registered trade mark by 1883. During his era, *The Gilded Age*, his portrait and name were printed in books, on cigar boxes, hand bills and post cards. In person, the all white suit topped by a cloud of white hair dramatized a pictorial and literary image.

Born Samuel Langhorne Clemens in Florida, Missouri on November 30, 1835, he grew up in the river town of Hannibal, Missouri, and it was this locale which later

provided the settings for *The Adventures of Tom Sawyer* and *The Adventures of Huckleberry Finn*. The reverse of the medallion depicts the central theme of Mark Twain's life and works: *Life on the Mississippi*. Of the four years, 1857–1861, spent learning the river and the work of a pilot, he wrote, "In that brief, sharp schooling, I got personally and familiarly acquainted with about all the different types of human nature that are to be found in fiction, biography, or history . . ."

Samuel Clemens' talent for observing the tone of the tale as well as details of character began developing long before his riverboat days. After his father's death in the

late 1840's, he left school to earn a living as a printer's apprentice. Publishing numerous accounts while still in his teens, he worked in Hannibal and St. Louis, Missouri and Keokuk, Iowa. In Cincinnati during this period, he decided that his purpose was "to go a travelin, so as to see the world, and then write a book about it . . ." This he did for the rest of his life.

Journalism and adventure took Mark Twain to the far west, *Roughing It* in Nevada with prospectors and with reporters in street brawls and political squabbles. Working in San Francisco in the mid 1860's, Mark Twain began to write as effectively as he talked,

humorously relating tall tales such as the "Celebrated Jumping Frog of Calaveras County" which he had heard from characters who yet live in many of his writings. Skills of talking in printers' ink further matured on his trip to the Sandwich Islands where new found admirers brought him literary contacts which lasted his entire career. Upon his return to California, public curiosity about Hawaii resulted in a lecture engagement that set his path toward becoming one of the greatest humorists of his time.

Traveling as *The Innocents Abroad*, he visited Europe and the Holy Land. His accounts of strange

places, people, and ideas, told in the language of an unsophisticated and humorous egalitarian, brought him instant admiration at home.

Mark Twain married in 1870 and lived in Connecticut. To his marriage were born four children, three of whom predeceased their father. Apparently his life, as his humor, was mixed with satire and brought opposites as strange as *A Connecticut Yankee in King Arthur's Court*. Duality of bliss and tragedy became evident in his later writings about *The Mysterious Stranger* and seemed embedded in his continual questioning of *What is Man?*

When sixty years old, Mark Twain again went to the lectern, undertaking the rigors of a world tour in order to repay debts and avoid bankruptcy. "Travelin, so as to see the world, and then write a book about it . . ." again brought solvency though not happiness. Mark Twain, who gave so much to children and to the memory of childhood, died in April 1910. He left as he had said he would—"going as he had come, with Halley's Comet." In birth, life, and death, Mark Twain dramatized a legend.

## MATTHEW PELOSO

MATTHEW PELOSO, Sculptor Engraver

Born: Salerno, Italy 1918

Education: Cooper Union; Ecole de Beaux-Arts; Rinehart School of Sculpture, Maryland Institute College of Art

Member: National Sculpture Society

Work: Free-lance sculptural commissions; Teacher of Sculpture; U.S. Mint since 1973, designer of many Mint medals

**The pamphlet for the 1981 Mark Twain one-ounce piece.**

marketing and distribution, and even the medallions' designs (see the year-by-year section later in this chapter for details), but there was no cure-all for the program's lingering illness.

| Year | Weight | Design | Mintage | Sales | Year's Sales by Weight (Ounces) |
|------|--------|--------|---------|-------|---------------------------------|
| 1980 | 1 ounce | Grant Wood | 500,000 | 312,709 | 453,521.0 |
| | 1/2 ounce | Marian Anderson | 1,000,000 | 281,624 | |
| 1981 | 1 ounce | Mark Twain | 141,000 | 116,371 | 165,036.5 |
| | 1/2 ounce | Willa Cather | 200,000 | 97,331 | |
| 1982 | 1 ounce | Louis Armstrong | 420,000 | 409,098 | 583,250.5 |
| | 1/2 ounce | Frank Lloyd Wright | 360,000 | 348,305 | |
| 1983 | 1 ounce | Robert Frost | 500,000 | 390,669 | 428,454.5 |
| | 1/2 ounce | Alexander Calder | 410,000 | 75,571 | |
| 1984 | 1 ounce | Helen Hayes | 35,000 | 33,546 | 49,832.0 |
| | 1/2 ounce | John Steinbeck | 35,000 | 32,572 | |

Critics of the American Arts program continued to push various other gold-related agendas. Some sought a full-fledged return to the monetary gold standard; others wanted at least a real legal-tender bullion *coin* (not medallions) to compete with those of South Africa. The media were reporting on such developments even before the American Arts program was two years old. Typical of the coverage was the following Associated Press report, published in the financial pages of various newspapers on February 13, 1982.[19] It announced the official recommendation of the U.S. Gold Commission that the United States develop a gold *coinage* (not medallic) program.[20]

**Panel Urges U.S. to Mint Gold Coin** — The U.S. Gold Commission recommended on Friday that the government begin minting gold coins to compete with those of South Africa and other nations in meeting Americans' desire to own gold.

The commission's recommendation—which amounts to a request for congressional action—is far short of the direct link between U.S. currency and gold sought primarily by conservative economists and politicians.

Members of the commission could still vote for such a "gold standard," in which every dollar of currency would be backed by a specified amount of gold and the government would have to redeem gold for dollars. But commission members in recent meetings have indicated such a recommendation is unlikely.

Some non-government supporters of President Reagan have urged him to take whatever steps he can toward a gold-monetary link, noting that he spoke favorably of the idea during various political campaigns.

But Reagan has made no similar remarks recently. And administration members of the commission—Treasury Secretary Donald T. Regan and economic advisers Murray Weidenbaum and Jerry Jordan—have shown no inclination to lead a charge toward gold.

The commission voted 12–3 Friday to ask Congress to pass a law telling the Treasury Department "to issue a gold-backed coin of specified weights and without dollar denomination or legal-tender status, to be manufactured from its existing stock of gold and to be sold at a small markup over the market value of the gold content."

The panel said the coin should be exempt from capital-gains and sales tax.

Rep. Chalmers P. Wylie, R–Ohio, a commission member, said the word "coin" was misleading since the gold pieces would not be legal tender and no one could be forced to accept them as payment for ordinary debts.

But other members, noting the disappointing sales of gold medallions by the Treasury Department, said the coins would not sell well if they were marketed only as "pieces."

Part of the problem, they said, is that the medallions were called "medallions" rather than "coins" as are the South African krugerrands, Canadian maple leafs and others.

Regan, who is chairman of the commission, told reporters later that the proposed new gold coin might well be more saleable than a medallion because the new piece "is a coin put out by the U.S."

The only distinction he cited, other than name, was that the coins "could be redeemable in dollars."

Ronald Reagan's administration inherited the American Arts gold medallion program from Jimmy Carter. By the time Reagan took office in January 1981, gold was dropping in value and the program was already faltering.

The terminology used in the article (with its illogical references to "coins" without denominations or legal-tender status), and the uncertainty over whether the recommended gold pieces would be coins or medals, illustrate the lingering popular (and even governmental) confusion and questions over gold sales.

The precious metal, meanwhile, was seeing its luster dim in the marketplace. From a yearly average spot price of $612 per ounce in 1980 (with highs passing $700), gold's average fell to $460 in 1981, then to $376 in 1982 . . . rallied a bit to $424 in 1983 . . . and then fell to $360 in 1984.

The writing was on the wall by the latter year, as the American Arts program struggled through the final months of its authorized five-year term. Another Associated Press notice, this one from late June 1984, painted the gloomy picture:

> **Mint Cancels Plans to Sell Medallions** — It sounded like a great idea in 1978 when gold fever was infecting speculators and people were worrying about inflation: dip into the U.S. government vault, mint medallions and make a killing for the taxpayers.
>
> An eager market, the thinking went, would not only be buying the world's prime metal but would prize the American Arts series coins [sic] with portraits of author Mark Twain, artist Grant Wood, jazzman Louis Armstrong, poet Robert Frost and actress Helen Hayes.
>
> But today, four years after the price of gold peaked and began diving, the U.S. Mint has shelved its heavily promoted campaign to turn its gold pieces into the American version of South Africa's Krugerrand and Canada's Maple Leaf.
>
> "It just hasn't worked," says Francis Frere, the mint's assistant director of marketing. "They're not selling. We've made a strong effort, but it's not working."
>
> The mint, unable to sell the coins itself, contracted with the New York firm of J. Aron and Co.
>
> The company had until September 1985 to unload 3 million ounces, but early this month the contract was canceled after J. Aron bought 1 million ounces but managed to sell only about 150,000 ounces, according to a spokesman for the firm.[21]

The depressing Associated Press report ran under headlines like "A Gold Idea That Didn't Pan Out" and "U.S. Mint Left Holding Nearly 3 Million Ounces of Fizzled Gold Frenzy." In New Hartford, Connecticut, the page-49 article was outranked in *The Day* by a front-page story on the opening of a new Filene's department store. In Utah's *Deseret News*, the story earned as many column inches as a report on wildlife smuggling. Readers of the Fort Scott, Kansas, *Tribune* found it buried on page 10 in the "National" section, just above a clarification from the Bourbon County board of commissioners noting that, in regard to a recent local resolution, "'cutting of roads' means actually cutting the surface of the road—not mowing the grass."

The American Arts gold medallions, after so much lofty congressional rhetoric, and despite high hopes and busy efforts to boost their popularity, left the national scene with a whimper.

# Today's Market for American Arts Gold Medallions

Today the American Arts gold medallions are eclipsed by their bullion-coin descendants (in particular the American Gold Eagle program, which often sells nearly a million ounces annually). Even many active coin collectors are unfamiliar with the series. The medallions haven't yet found a secondary market beyond occasional trading at or even slightly below their bullion value. An appendix in the 62nd edition (published 2008, with a cover date of 2009) of the *Guide Book of United States Coins*—the hobby's popular and best-selling "Red Book" reference guide—and similar coverage in the 70th and 71st editions (published 2012 and 2013) of the *Handbook of United States Coins* (the wholesale-pricing "Blue Book") brought them a measure of mainstream publicity, and the medallions are sometimes discussed in magazine articles and online.[22] But for 30 years they have been a largely neglected series in American numismatics.

In terms of popularity, the American Arts medallions were dead and buried, unmourned, before the decade of their birth closed—almost before the series ended. A reader of the *Los Angeles Times* wrote to staff writer Don Alpert, who manned the paper's "Your Coins" column, in March 1985. "I have been buying the U.S. gold art medals as issued. This has not been a successful series, and I find it increasingly difficult to find the new ones. I have had coin dealers refuse to get them for me, and all the ones I have talked with are uninformed and indifferent, a remarkable state of affairs." Five years later, in February 1990, another reader wrote to Alpert: "I have a number of Grant Wood and Marian Anderson medallions. How do I determine their value? These medallions are not mentioned in any of the coin magazines." Alpert described the subject as "very interesting—and in some ways mysterious," calling the American Arts program well-intentioned but ill-fated. "Your medals . . . basically trade as bullion pieces," he told the undoubtedly disappointed reader, following up with less-than-enthusiastic guidance: "You can find price quotes occasionally in the classified advertising section of *Coin World*. You might also be able to locate some interested dealers at some of the larger coin shows."

"The pricing for the American Arts medallions was very complex and was based on ever-changing bullion value," recalls numismatic historian Q. David Bowers. "After the series was complete I endeavored to find one of each variety for my reference collection—this being in pre-Internet days. It took a lot of telephone calls to finally accomplish this. I imagine that, as they were never particularly popular with numismatists and, even more important, were not face-value coins, the vast majority have been melted by now. The surviving population is probably some very small percentage of the total mintage."[23]

Professional numismatist Tom DeLorey: "I remember part of the ordering process included having the postal clerk date-stamp the order form before it was sealed in the envelope along with the payment. This was to keep people from getting a price one day and sending it in the next day only if the price of gold had gone up. Another drawback was having to call a telephone number to get the day's price. Nobody had a cell phone in 1980, except perhaps Maxwell Smart. You had to go find a pay phone."

Coverage in the 2009 edition of the Red Book brought publicity to the American Arts medallions.

Columnist Richard Giedroyc, writing in an October 2013 *Numismatic News* "Coin Clinic," noted: "From my own experience as a coin dealer, I purchased a significant number of [American Arts gold medallions] through about 2007, but have seldom encountered them since."

Rare-coin dealer and longtime *Guide Book of United States Coins* contributor Fred Weinberg remembers buying four complete sets of the medallions, with their original Mint packaging, in 2009. "With gold going over $1,100 per ounce in early 2010 [after a cumulative average of about $970 the year before], I tried very hard to find a buyer over melt, with no luck," he says. "Like many items, when the gold content is so valuable, the premium shrinks to nothing, or in some cases a negative few percentages—their gold content exceeds the collector interest."

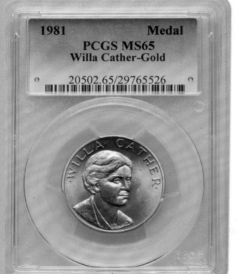

Other coin and precious-metal dealers have described buy prices of 96% of the medallions' bullion value, with corresponding sales at 99%.

All of this, of course, makes the American Arts medallions a good series for contrarian speculation, and for bargain-minded collectors. As long as the medallions trade near their gold-bullion value, any future *numismatic* premium (if they gain in popularity) or rise in gold's spot price will benefit their sellers. Some of the medallions are scarcer today than their original mintages might suggest, because of melting and other attrition; see their individual entries, following, for more details.

The three major third-party grading services (ANACS, Numismatic Guaranty Corporation of America [NGC], and PCGS) all grade and slab American Arts gold medallions. NGC and PCGS include them in their registry sets. BJ Searles, Set Registry and Special Projects Director for PCGS, says this about the firm's Modern U.S. Gold Registry Set: "Yes, these coins are modern, but building a complete set will prove challenging. . . . [It] is suspected that many of the American Arts gold medallions had been melted, making some of the issues somewhat scarce."[24]

"I have noticed a slight increase in interest, particularly for certified pieces," says John Pack, executive director of consignments for Stack's Bowers Galleries. "I think there is future potential for these." In terms of quality, numismatist and medallic sculptor Daniel Carr observes, "True MS-69 and 70 pieces are probably quite rare, since every single one I've ever looked at has at least a few small bag marks on it." Modern-coin expert Scott Schechter, vice president at NGC, says that the average certified grade for the series is MS-66, with the occasional MS-68 or 69 commanding more than a 50% premium over bullion value.[25] A prudent collector will cherrypick for eye appeal and quality, if the opportunity arises.

American Arts gold medallions certified, graded, and encapsulated by professional third-party grading firms PCGS and NGC.

# 1980 AMERICAN ARTS GOLD MEDALLIONS

**Designers:** *Frank Gasparro (Wood obverse and reverse, Anderson obverse);*
*Matthew Peloso (Anderson reverse).* **Sculptor:** *Frank Gasparro*
*(Wood obverse and reverse, Anderson obverse and reverse).*
**Composition:** *.900 gold, .100 copper.* **Diameter:** *32 mm (Wood);*
*27.4 mm (Anderson).* **Edge:** *Plain.* **Mint:** *West Point Bullion Depository.*

| Year | Weight | Design | Mintage | Sales | Estimated Surviving* | Year's Sales by Weight (Ounces) |
|------|--------|--------|---------|-------|----------------------|----------------------------------|
| 1980 | 1 ounce | Grant Wood | 500,000 | 312,709 | 250,168 | 453,521.0 |
|      | 1/2 ounce | Marian Anderson | 1,000,000 | 281,624 | 225,300 | |

*Note:* Sales figures include individual medallions as well as those sold within sets.
* After melting and other attrition.

The 1980 Grant Wood one-ounce gold medallion. Its portrait of the artist is accompanied by a rendition of his well-known 1930 oil painting *American Gothic.* Chief Engraver Frank Gasparro's initials appear under Wood's left shoulder and beneath the painting.

The inaugural year of the American Arts Commemorative Series (as the gold medallion program was called in Mint literature) honored painter Grant Wood on the one-ounce piece and singer Marian Anderson on the half-ounce.

Grant DeVolson Wood (February 13, 1891–February 12, 1942) was born near Anamosa, Iowa. His father died in 1901 and the family then moved to Cedar Rapids. Young Grant was apprenticed in a metal shop and after high school he enrolled for a year in an art school in Minneapolis. He then taught for a time in a one-room schoolhouse back in Cedar Rapids. From 1913 through the 1920s he developed his craft as an artist, enrolling in the School of the Art Institute of Chicago and studying several times in Europe (paying special attention to Impressionism and Post-Impressionism, and, in Europe, to the style of 15th-century Flemish artist Jan van Eyck). Wood was a champion of artistic regionalism (his paintings focused on the rural American Midwest) and he lectured nationwide on its importance. His 1932 cofounding of the Stone City Art Colony near Cedar Rapids was a boon to artists during the Great Depression. He taught painting from 1934 to 1941 at the University of Iowa's School of Art, where he was influential in the cultural community. Suffering

Reverse detail.

**Grant Wood in a circa-1925 self-portrait.**

The 2004 State quarter for Iowa, featuring a motif from Wood's early career as a one-room–schoolhouse teacher, with his name prominently displayed. The general design is derived from Wood's 1932 painting *Arbor Day*.

from pancreatic cancer, the artist died in 1942, one day shy of his 51st birthday. Wood had been married for several years and divorced in the 1930s, and when he died his estate went to his sister, Nan Wood Graham—the woman famously portrayed in his most widely known painting, *American Gothic*. Upon her passing in 1990, his personal effects and various artworks went to the Figge Art Museum in Davenport, Iowa.

In 2004 Wood's one-room schoolhouse would be featured on the U.S. Mint's State quarter for Iowa, in a design by sculptor-engraver John Mercanti. The motif was loosely based on the artist's 1932 painting *Arbor Day*. Wood's name was incorporated prominently in the coin's design—the largest inscription of an artist's name found on any circulating U.S. coin from 1793 to date.[26]

On the obverse of the Grant Wood American Arts gold medallion, U.S. Mint chief engraver Frank Gasparro featured a bespectacled portrait of the artist in an open-throated button-down shirt. The depiction is at once masculine and sensitive, physical and intellectual. The reverse design, a depiction of Wood's *American Gothic*, is also by Gasparro. The viewer is cast more in the role of a visitor to Wood's personal studio than as a museum observer, thanks to Gasparro's artful placement of the painting on an easel, rather than framed on a wall. In *American Gothic*—one of the most famous and instantly recognizable works of American art—Wood posed a serious-looking farmer and his spinster daughter (modeled on his dentist and his own sister) standing side by side. The farmer grips a pitchfork and stares impassively at the viewer; his daughter looks pensively into the distance. When the painting was first publicized, many sophisticated viewers had interpreted it as being critical, or at least satirical, of Midwestern culture. Wood, however, saw it as "a positive statement about rural American values, an image of reassurance at a time of great dislocation and disillusionment. The man and woman, in their solid and well-crafted world, with all their strengths and weaknesses, represent survivors."[27]

*American Gothic*, one of the artist's most famous works.

U.S. Mint plaster models of
Frank Gasparro's Grant Wood designs.

The subject of the 1980 half-ounce medallion, Philadelphia-born Marian Anderson (February 27, 1897–April 8, 1993) was one of the most renowned American singers of the 20th century, with a rich career spanning from the 1920s into the 1960s. She performed in concert and recital in the nation's major music venues, and with orchestras in the United States and Europe. The Old World's famous opera companies courted Anderson but she turned them down, preferring to sing rather than act on stage. She exhibited her rich, vibrant contralto across many traditional American and classical European forms.

Anderson was a breaker of barriers in a time when black artists struggled for recognition in the United States. By the late 1930s she already was famous, having toured the capitals of Europe to great acclaim and given more than 50 concerts in the United States, including at Carnegie Hall. Despite her renown, in 1939 the Daughters of the American Revolution refused to grant her permission to sing in a performance in Constitution Hall in Washington, DC. Their discrimination placed Anderson in a new kind of spotlight as the injustice of the situation attracted national attention. First Lady Eleanor Roosevelt resigned her membership in the DAR in protest, writing, "I am in complete disagreement with the attitude taken in refusing Constitution Hall to a great artist. . . . You had an opportunity to lead in an enlightened way and it seems to me that your organization has failed." Leaders of the NAACP, supported by President Franklin Delano Roosevelt, arranged an open-air concert on Easter Sunday, April 9, 1939, on the steps of the Lincoln Memorial, where Anderson sang before an integrated audience of more than 75,000 Americans. Her performance, opening with a matchless rendition of "My Country, 'Tis of Thee," was broadcast to millions more on the radio. In 1943 the DAR would finally invite her to Constitution Hall, to perform for an American Red Cross benefit, and she accepted graciously. Marian Anderson continued to sing until her retirement in 1965.

The 1980 Marian Anderson half-ounce gold medallion. The reverse motif was personally selected by Anderson. Frank Gasparro is credited by name, F. GASPARRO, at the truncation of Anderson's left shoulder. On the reverse, initials MP and FG identify Matthew Peloso as the medal's designer and Gasparro as its engraver.

The obverse of the Marian Anderson medallion features a youthful three-quarters–profile portrait sculpted by Frank Gasparro, chief engraver of the U.S. Mint. The singer, smiling gently with a relaxed, confident gaze, is draped in clothing evocative of an Ionic chiton on a classical Greek coin. On the reverse of the medal is a pair of hands cupping the Earth atop a background of heavenly rays—a motif modeled by Gasparro from a design by Mint sculptor-engraver Matthew Peloso, who had joined the Mint staff in 1973 and had more than a dozen coin and medal motifs to his credit. Peloso's design had its basis in a congressionally authorized national gold medal bestowed upon Anderson by President Jimmy Carter at a White House ceremony on October 16, 1978. A three-inch bronze version of this award was made for sale by the Mint to the public, and later Gasparro translated Peloso's design to the American Arts gold medallion. The Congressional Gold Medal was authorized March 8, 1977, in recognition of Marian Anderson's "highly distinguished and impressive career of more than half a century; for untiring and unselfish devotion to the promotion of the arts throughout the world, including establishment of scholarships for young people; for her strong and imaginative support to humanitarian causes; for contributions to the cause of world peace through her work as United States delegate to the United Nations; for her performances and recordings which have reached people throughout the world; for her unstinting efforts on behalf of the brotherhood of man and for the many treasured moments she has brought to the world with enormous demand on her time, talent, and energy."[28] President Carter praised Anderson for exemplifying "the finest aspects of American citizenship." In keeping with her talents, the reverse motif has musical symbolism—a depiction of the traditional American spiritual "He's Got the Whole World in His Hands." This theme was personally selected by Anderson.

Marian Anderson in a January 1940 portrait by Carl Van Vechten.

Anderson singing at Potomac Park, on the steps of the Lincoln Memorial, Easter 1939.

**U.S. Mint plasters of the
Marian Anderson medallion designs.**

## Production, Marketing, and Distribution of 1980 American Arts Gold Medallions

The entire mintage of 1980 American Arts gold medallions was produced at the U.S. Mint's West Point facility—at that time designated as a bullion depository (it would attain full status as a branch mint in 1988). The Treasury's report for fiscal-year 1980 noted that "the protection provided at the gold production and storage facilities was improved. At the West Point Bullion Depository a special security system, as well as complementary accountability procedures, was developed to protect the gold medallion program. Central to the system is an entry/exit procedure, consisting of an X-ray unit and a memory walkthrough metal detector, which appreciably increases the probability of detecting thefts."

The 1980 medals were designed without mintmarks; this was standard throughout the production of the series. They also bore no indication of the country of origin, or even of their gold content or fineness. The fact that these elements were missing would later be criticized as having discouraged investors from taking the medals seriously.

Frank Gasparro later shared his unique insight into the process of translating the Mint's three-inch bronze Marian Anderson national medal into a smaller gold format.[29]

> We were to use a press similar to that used for coining the Saint-Gaudens ten-dollar and twenty-dollar gold pieces and to strike this new gold medal under repeated pressure. This was a new challenge to us. The last time the U.S. Mint struck ten- and twenty-dollar gold coins was in 1933. I knew of no one still at the Mint who could have witnessed gold coins struck on the coining press.
>
> First, I went about preparing reduction dimensions from the three-inch Marian Anderson medal down to 1-5/16–inch diameter size, for gold

**Frank Gasparro, chief engraver of the U.S. Mint, was important in the development and artistic direction of the American Arts medallions.**

striking. I also had our transfer engraver make plans to reduce the height of relief to a low .014 inch, similar to the relief height of the U.S. silver dollar and suitable for both obverse and reverse dies. The working dies were finally prepared and ready for trial striking. Then a revelation took place. The coining press came down on the gold blank between the obverse and reverse dies with average pressure. What relief I had on the dies came up. That was all.

The gold would not spread under pressure like silver or copper coins. The gold just sunk. In striking coins, silver or copper flows or spreads. That is the reason that in the press collars are used to contain the metal in spreading and in the meanwhile to fill up the relief cavities. With gold, which is dense in content, if you have the correct relief to take all the impression, well and good. Gold will not move or spread in order to fill the remaining relief under terrific pressure.

We then had to take out the gold specimen from the coining press and to heat-anneal (soften) it in order to strike it again, under a high pressure used for medals. Still the relief of gold would not move or flow. The same thing occurred with certain areas of the reverse side. I had to go back and revise the relief to a very low height for both sides. I also lowered the relief of the nose and forehead. I did the same with the reverse areas. I came up with lowered relief dies, and these were successful.

Then the whole truth dawned on me. I saw the clear picture before me. I envisioned the great trouble that ensued with Augustus Saint-Gaudens's High Relief twenty-dollar gold pieces. They would not strike up under terrific pressure [and had to be struck three times on a medal press]. I saw the displeasure and anxiety of President Theodore Roosevelt. I envisioned all of the problems between the outside artist and the Engraving Department of the Mint. This all took place 1906–1907. I concluded that Saint-Gaudens did not take time out to study coinage production technicalities.

We must conclude with this observation that gold will sink, due to its density, and will not flow or spread satisfactorily under extreme pressure. Had a roundtable discussion taken place in 1907 among all those involved, results would have been acceptable and satisfactory, thereby resulting in the creation of well-struck coins with less wasted time and discontent. I am glad I was given the opportunity in my tenure as chief engraver at the U.S. Mint to understand the problems with striking gold coins.

In 1980 the American Arts medallions were made of 90% gold and 10% copper. This alloy would change slightly for the 1981 pieces and beyond (with silver added and the copper content reduced), which explains why those of the first year of issue can appear different in color. The first-year medals were issued in a small Styrofoam bed sealed by a plastic sheet, upon which the gold fineness and content was printed.[30] To remove a medal from its foam tray a collector had to remove the plastic, essentially damaging the original packaging.

For later issues the Mint would include an insert with a brief biography of the artist being honored on the gold medallions. This wasn't done for the first year of issue, but retroactively the Mint provided "a copy of the biographical accounts used in the 1980 informational kit" to customers who wrote to the bureau's Consumer Affairs department in Washington.[31]

The nation's 35,000 post offices were put to use as ordering facilities for the American Arts gold medallions.[32] Sales began on July 15, 1980, and the Treasury announced that the ordering period was expected to continue until September 30 (the end of the department's fiscal year). Customers were originally limited to three one-ounce and three half-ounce medals apiece. That limit was lifted later in the first year of issue.

The U.S. Postal Service reported that more than 72,000 order forms were received in San Francisco by the end of the first week of sales. Alan Goldman, the Mint's assistant director for technology, who had sounded gentle warnings during the 1978 Senate hearings on the sale of Treasury gold, was interviewed by Scripps-Howard News Service during the medallions' second week on the market. "Sales are brisk," he noted, "but things usually get wilder when the price of gold is going up." Unfortunately, gold *wasn't* going up; at the beginning of July 1980 it was around $650 per ounce, and by mid-month it had dropped closer to $615. Treasury officials no doubt were unhappy to read early newspaper reports like the following, which started out with an enticing headline ("U.S. Mint Offers Buyers 'Golden' Coin Opportunity") but by the third paragraph was damning the program with faint praise: "The response so far has been lively but not overwhelming."

> Buyers normally like to buy coins when gold prices are on the way up rather than on the way down, fearing they may get stuck with an overpriced investment. . . . There is some financial risk in buying the medallions because they are not negotiable as money and the Treasury Department won't buy them back. "You're on your own, Buster" is the way one Treasury official put it.[33]

From July 15 to September 30, 1980, the public ordered 183,000 of the one-ounce Grant Wood medallions and 164,000 of the half-ounce Marian Anderson pieces. Orders were logged through the San Francisco Old Mint, so the earliest customer checks received and processed were likely from California. Before long orders were coming in from all regions of the United States. "Preliminary analysis of the sales indicate that the intent of Congress and the Department [of the Treasury] to achieve broad geographical distribution has been achieved," the Treasury secretary would report.[34] In other words, sales of the medallions were spread far and wide across the country, as opposed to being concentrated in certain areas. Be that as it may, the sales for 1980 might best be described as a country wide and an inch deep. Americans simply weren't interested to the extent Congress had anticipated.

Stella Hackel was director of the Mint from November 1977 to April 1981, as the American Arts program was getting under way.

On September 25 the Treasury announced that it would be extending the sale of the medallions through December 31 or until the initial mintages (of 500,000 one-ounce and 1,000,000 half-ounce pieces) sold out, whichever came first. The ordering period was further extended until sales of the 1980 medallions closed on February 28, 1981.

In the October 20, 1980, issue of *New York* magazine, "Bottom Line" columnist Jack Egan heaped praise on South Africa's innovative new series of fractional-ounce gold Krugerrand coins (which had recently debuted in half-ounce, quarter-ounce, and tenth-ounce pieces). He attributed the Krugerrand's continued success to "the familiarity of the coins, thanks to vigorous promotion [South Africa had launched a $7 million advertising blitz to promote the coins in television and print media], and the excellent resale market for them around the world." Egan quoted Luis Vigdor, an executive with Manfra, Tordella & Brookes, a large wholesale-and-retail coin-and-bullion dealer, who said, "When you purchase an item, you must ask yourself how salable it is—that is really the most important question to ask when you buy gold." Vigdor went on to say, "If the United States government came out today and promoted a United States coin, pumped in the advertising dollars the South Africans have, they would get the same results the Krugerrands have gotten. They probably could have wiped out the Krugerrand and other coins like the Mexican gold peso and the Austrian krone. But in my book, they have pulled off one of the biggest mistakes ever with these two medallions." He claimed to have shipped 200 of the medallions to Europe, but dealers there were unable to sell them, and shipped them back. The reasons: they were medals and not official coins; and they featured no statement of their origin, no indication of the gold content, and no hallmark of their fineness—all necessary for a robust secondary market. Columnist Evans offered little mercy to the Treasury Department: "The success of the Krugerrand represents a vivid contrast to the United States Treasury's tepid attempts to sell gold to the American public . . . in the form of one-ounce and half-ounce commemorative medallions. The marketing, through post-office branches, has been so inept it has raised questions about whether the government actually intended to fail in its attempts to enter this expanding market. . . . Individuals

The U.S. Mint's engraving staff gathered on Friday, August 24, 1979, to celebrate Chief Engraver Frank Gasparro's 70th birthday (which fell on Sunday the 26th). Many of the engravers would design and sculpt the upcoming 1980–1984 American Arts gold medallions. Gasparro is at far left. Standing behind him is Matthew Peloso, followed (left to right) by Philip Fowler, Sherl Joseph Winter, John Mercanti, Edgar Z. Steever, and Michael Iacocca. Mercanti would serve as the Mint's 12th chief engraver from 2006 to 2011.

are not likely to buy gold where they buy postage stamps. Moreover, it is necessary to wait 45 days for delivery." On the other hand, he did note that the price "is quite favorable, comparable to the wholesale price for Krugerrands. In addition, the purchases are not subject to sales tax. But these facts have not been publicized."[35]

The lowest daily price for the 1980 gold medallions was $494 for the one-ounce and $247 for the half-ounce. This level was reached twice, on February 3 and February 28, 1981. The highest price (on September 23, 1980) was $728 and $364 respectively. The premium for the 1980 medallions was set at $12 each for the one-ounce and $6 for the half-ounce, to cover production and marketing expenses.

Some 1980 American Arts gold medallions were later sold in bulk by the U.S. Mint to J. Aron and Company and by the Mint to collectors individually and in special sets in 1984 and 1985; for more information, see the "Production, Marketing, and Distribution" entry for 1984.

## Today's Market for 1980 American Arts Gold Medallions

Gold specialist Patrick Heller estimates that at least 20% of the total 1980 mintage was melted, many of the year's medals having been purchased in bulk by bullion-trading firms that subsequently dumped them when the spot value of gold rose.[36] This would account for the attrition of about 90,000 ounces of the year's production (some 62,000 of the one-ounce Grant medallions and 56,000 of the half-ounce Anderson medallions). The Marian Anderson half-ounce has emerged as one of the scarcer and more valuable medallions of the entire American Arts series, and will likely continue to enjoy premiums above their bullion value. The Grant Wood one-ounce is still one of the more frequently seen pieces and can be found for prices closer to melt.

| 1980 Grant Wood, 1-ounce · Certified Populations and Retail Market Values | | | | | | | | |
|---|---|---|---|---|---|---|---|---|
| | Raw | <MS-65 | MS-65 | MS-66 | MS-67 | MS-68 | MS-69 | MS-70 |
| Certified | — | 13 | 30 | 29 | 25 | 12 | 4 | — |
| Value* | $1,220 | | $1,245 | $1,295 | $1,325 | $1,360 | $1,425 | |

*Recent auctions:* $1,233.75, PCGS MS-67, November 2014 (avg. gold spot value that month, $1,176). $1,703.75, NGC MS-65, October 2012 (avg. gold spot value that month, $1,747).

* "Raw" value is based on a gold spot price of $1,200 per ounce, and is for an uncertified Mint State medallion of average quality. This value may vary with the prevailing bullion value.

| 1980 Marian Anderson, 1/2-ounce · Certified Populations and Retail Market Values | | | | | | | | |
|---|---|---|---|---|---|---|---|---|
| | Raw | <MS-65 | MS-65 | MS-66 | MS-67 | MS-68 | MS-69 | MS-70 |
| Certified | — | 12 | 20 | 33 | 59 | 9 | 6 | — |
| Value* | $670 | | $695 | $720 | $750 | $800 | $900 | |

*Recent auctions:* $881.25, NGC MS-66, October 2012 (avg. gold spot value that month, $1,747). $948.75, PCGS MS-65, February 2012 (avg. gold spot value that month, $1,743).

* "Raw" value is based on a gold spot price of $1,200 per ounce, and is for an uncertified Mint State medallion of average quality. This value may vary with the prevailing bullion value.

# 1981 AMERICAN ARTS GOLD MEDALLIONS

**Designers:** *Matthew Peloso (Twain); Sherl Joseph Winter (Cather).*
**Sculptors:** *Matthew Peloso (Twain); Sherl Joseph Winter (Cather).*
**Composition:** *.900 gold, .070 copper, .030 silver.* **Diameter:** *32 mm (Twain);*
*27.4 mm (Cather).* **Edge:** *Plain.* **Mint:** *West Point Bullion Depository.*

| Year | Weight | Design | Mintage | Sales | Estimated Surviving* | Year's Sales by Weight (Ounces) |
|------|--------|--------|---------|-------|---------------------|--------------------------------|
| 1981 | 1 ounce | Mark Twain | 141,000 | 116,371 | 98,915 | 165,036.5 |
| | 1/2 ounce | Willa Cather | 200,000 | 97,331 | 82,731 | |

*Note:* Sales figures include individual medallions as well as those sold within sets.
* After melting and other attrition.

**The 1981 Mark Twain one-ounce gold medallion. The reverse evokes the Southern setting of some of his most famous novels. The initials of designer and engraver Matthew Peloso appear at the truncation of Twain's left shoulder.**

**Reverse detail.**

The gold medallions of 1981 commemorate writers Mark Twain (on the one-ounce piece) and Willa Cather (on the half-ounce).

"Mark Twain" was the pen name of American humorist and author Samuel Langhorne Clemens (November 30, 1835–April 21, 1910). He grew up in Hannibal, Missouri. The Midwest and South would be important settings in Twain's works, including *The Adventures of Tom Sawyer* (1876) and *Adventures of Huckleberry Finn* (1885). Early in his life he was a printer's apprentice, a typesetter, and a newspaper writer. Later he was a riverboat pilot on the mighty Mississippi River (from whence he derived his pen name; according to the humorist himself, "mark twain" was a cry heard from a boatman, meaning the water was two fathoms deep and safe to traverse). He was lured to Nevada during the silver- and gold-mining craze of the early 1860s; he failed as a miner but earned his living as a journalist. From there he moved to California, where he met famous artists and writers. All of these early experiences enriched Twain's craft. His humorous tall tale "The Celebrated Jumping Frog of Calaveras County" (1865), published in New York City's *The Saturday Press*, brought him national reviews. Entertaining travelogues for the *Sacramento Union* would form the foundation for his early lectures, and he racked up more and more attention and the praise of Americans from manual laborers to high society. Through his writings he championed

**Mark Twain as most Americans think of him: the celebrated man of letters in his later years, dressed and crowned in white.**

racial equality, civil rights for women and minorities, the American labor movement, and anti-imperialism. Twain was (and is) widely regarded as one of the greatest writers and humorists of the United States; William Faulkner called him "the father of American literature."[37] Today the John F. Kennedy Center for the Performing Arts honors individuals who make significant contributions to American humor with its annually presented Mark Twain Prize.

The obverse of the 1981 one-ounce medallion shows Twain in later life in a three-quarter-profile portrait by U.S. Mint sculptor-engraver Matthew Peloso. This is the great American author as most people today know him: bushy-haired, with a thick moustache and a twinkle in his eye, wearing the white flannel suit that became his signature garb after a December 1906 congressional meeting on copyrights. (Twain's dressing in white for a formal event, in Washington, DC, and in the winter, no less, caused a nationally publicized sensation. America's elder states-man of letters reveled in the attention. "When a man gets to be seventy-one years old, as I am," he told the newspaper reporters who hung on his every word, "he can wear the clothes he likes best without suffering that criticism which may come to him in his youth. . . . There is no reason why men should not wear brighter colored clothing, especially in these dark winter months."[38]) Peloso's reverse design for the Twain medallion shows a Mississippi River scene redolent of the author's adventurous tales. A majestic steamboat plows through the water, its tall crowned smokestacks sending clouds into the sky. The reason the stacks were built so tall was to keep burning cinders from falling onto the boats' decks or their cargo (often bales of Southern cotton). The fluted crowns were meant to break up the floating fiery embers so they would burn out more quickly. According to Southern lore, the term *high falutin* comes from these high, fluted smokestacks, which became more fancy and ornamental as steamboats attracted wealthy travelers. Adding even more personality to the design, a humble raft floats close to shore, its two boatmen—possibly Twain's Huck Finn and his companion, Jim—watching the passing steamer.

1910 postcards inspired by Twain's 1897 book *Following the Equator*, a travelogue of the British Empire.

Be good and you will be lonesome.

*From "Following the Equator."*
*Copyright, 1897, by Olivia L. Clemens.*

The only way to keep your health is to eat what you don't want, drink what you don't like, and do what you'd druther not.

*From "Following the Equator."*
*Copyright, 1897, by Olivia L. Clemens.*

**U.S. Mint plaster models**
**of the Mark Twain medallion designs.**

**The 1981 Willa Cather**
**half-ounce medallion.**
**A doughty plainswoman**
**has stepped from the writer's**
**stories and onto a tondo of**
**gold. SJW, the initials of**
**designer and engraver**
**Sherl Joseph Winter, is**
**at the truncation of**
**Cather's right shoulder.**

★ ★ ★ ★ ★ ★ ★ ★ ★ ★

Willa Cather (December 7, 1873–April 24, 1947) was born on a farm near Winchester, Virginia, and in her young adulthood and later life she would live in Pittsburgh and New York City—but it was America's Great Plains that set the tone for her most famous creative works. The Cather family had moved to the Nebraska prairie when Willa was nine years old, and the isolation and struggles of frontier life would figure prominently in her writing. Her short stories, a monumental biography of Christian Science founder Mary Baker Eddy, and, later, plainspoken and powerful novels established her as a major American writer. Cather was popular with critics and the public alike. The books of her "Prairie Trilogy" (*O Pioneers!*, *The Song of the Lark*, and *My Ántonia*, published from 1913 to 1918) were praised almost universally. In 1922 she won a Pulitzer Prize for *One of Ours*, a tale about an unhappy young Nebraska man who finds purpose fighting in France in the Great War. She continued to write through the Great Depression and into the 1940s, bringing to life the rugged and haunting American prairie of an earlier time.

The obverse of the Willa Cather gold medallion, by U.S. Mint sculptor-engraver Sherl Joseph

**A reflective portrait of Cather by**
**photographer Carl Van Vechten.**

A U.S. Mint galvano (electrolytic cast) of the Willa Cather medallion's obverse design, and a plaster model of the reverse.[39]

Willa Cather as a young girl, in a *carte-de-visite* portrait. Her family moved to the Great Plains when she was nine years old.

Winter, features a right-facing three-quarter–profile portrait of the writer in a lightly patterned jacket and blouse. Her hair is swept back and secured, revealing a strong expression—determined, not frowning yet not quite smiling. The reverse shows a woman in an agricultural field, her hands firmly gripping the handles of a plow, its plowshare dug into the rich Midwestern soil. Engraver Winter illustrated the field's crops with deeply carved grooves and cuts, and the sky with high-relief clouds floating in the distance. The overall effect is a rough, folk-art feel. The woman's dress is plain, workaday: a protective cap to shield her from the sun, a kerchief, a simple blouse with sleeves rolled up, an undecorated skirt, and heavy farm-working boots. She looks off to her right, away from the direction of her plowing, pausing from the day's labor. Her face is smooth, with a hint of apple-cheeked plumpness, and she wears a Mona Lisa smile. She is the very image of Cather's hardworking Great Plains characters.

## Production, Marketing, and Distribution of 1981 American Arts Gold Medallions

A Treasury fact sheet for 1981 noted that "Presentation cases appropriate for gift giving as well as an insert which includes a brief biography of the artist

**Reverse detail.**

being honored were included with the 1981 medallions. Because this was not done in the first year of the program, we did not develop a biographical insert for the 1980 Grant Wood or for the Marian Anderson medallion. A copy of the biographical accounts used in the 1980 informational kit, however, are available from Consumer Affairs, Bureau of the Mint, 501 13th Street, NW, Washington, D.C. 20220."

Like the first-year issues of 1980, those of 1981 bear no legend of UNITED STATES OF AMERICA, their edges are smooth instead of reeded, and they have no mark of their gold fineness or weight. The date is on the reverse, instead of on the obverse as it would be on a coin.

The Mint changed the composition of the American Arts medallions in 1981. The gold content was maintained at 90%, but the alloy was changed from 10% copper to 7% copper, with silver making up the remaining 3%. This modification was to improve the appearance of the medals, according to the Treasury.

There was a $14 premium for the one-ounce medallion, and a $7 premium for the half-ounce, to cover production and distribution costs, reflecting an increase over the 1980 premiums.

Sales of the 1981 medals were announced that July. "The Mint said it expects to take orders for the medallions [from July 15, 1981] until Jan. 31, 1982, unless all medallions produced are sold before then. There is a limit of 25 medallions per transaction, and customers are limited to five transactions a day for each size medallion. Thus, a customer can order up to 125 of each medallion each day. Official order forms and envelopes must be used. They can be obtained at local post offices. Because of the daily price change, the order date must be validated and signed by a postal clerk when the order is mailed. Payment must be by U.S. Postal Service money order or a certified or cashier's check. Customers in the continental United States can obtain each day's medallion price by calling a toll-free number, 800-368-5510."[40]

The Treasury launched a newspaper advertising campaign to boost sales, but public interest was even lower than for 1980. The ordering deadline for the 1981 medallions, originally set at January 31, 1982, was extended to July 5, 1982. Even with the extension, sales were only about one-third those of the program's inaugural year, for both sizes of medal.

The lowest daily price for the 1981 gold medallions was $312 for the one-ounce and $156 for the half-ounce. This level was reached on June 23, 1982. The highest price (on September 22, 1981) was $482 and $241 respectively.

Some 1981 American Arts gold medallions were later sold in bulk to bullion dealer J. Aron and Company, and by the U.S. Mint to collectors individually and in special sets in 1984 and 1985; for more information, see the "Production, Marketing, and Distribution" entry for 1984.

The third book in Cather's popular "Prairie Trilogy."

# Today's Market for 1981 American Arts Gold Medallions

The 1981 Mark Twain and Willa Cather medallions are among those more readily available in the American Arts series. For these more common pieces it's not unusual to see wholesale "buy" prices ranging from one to several percentage points *under* gold's spot value, with corresponding retail prices at or slightly above spot. The American Arts gold medallions have a lot of competition today, not just in the rich variety of alternative gold investments, but also the ease of acquiring those alternatives, many of which are popular and heavily promoted. Gold investors can choose from a smorgasbord of modern legal-tender gold bullion coins, including many U.S. Mint products. In this climate, gold bars, medals, and other non-coins sometimes have to trade at a discounted level in order to appeal to bottom-line–oriented consumers. Of course, as more and more coin collectors learn about these medallions, and come to appreciate their special status in America's numismatic history, demand should increase. With mintages that are mere fractions of modern bullion-coin production, not to mention the loss of unknown thousands of the medallions to melting over the years, the table is set for rising secondary-market prices.

Gold specialist Patrick Heller estimates "conservatively" that 15% of the 1981 mintage was melted by bulk purchasers who treated their unsold inventory as gold bullion rather than as numismatic collectibles. This would account for some 17,000 or more one-ounce Twain medallions and 14,000 or more Cather half-ounce medallions being removed from the market.

| 1981 Mark Twain, 1-ounce · Certified Populations and Retail Market Values | | | | | | | | |
|---|---|---|---|---|---|---|---|---|
| | Raw | <MS-65 | MS-65 | MS-66 | MS-67 | MS-68 | MS-69 | MS-70 |
| Certified | — | 11 | 16 | 30 | 24 | 8 | 4 | — |
| Value* | $1,220 | | $1,290 | $1,325 | $1,350 | $1,385 | $1,450 | |
| *Recent auctions:* $1,762.50, NGC MS-67, October 2012 (avg. gold spot value that month, $1,747). $1,897.50, PCGS MS-65, February 2012 (avg. gold spot value that month, $1,743). | | | | | | | | |

\* "Raw" value is based on a gold spot price of $1,200 per ounce, and is for an uncertified Mint State medallion of average quality. This value may vary with the prevailing bullion value.

| 1981 Willa Cather, 1/2-ounce · Certified Populations and Retail Market Values | | | | | | | | |
|---|---|---|---|---|---|---|---|---|
| | Raw | <MS-65 | MS-65 | MS-66 | MS-67 | MS-68 | MS-69 | MS-70 |
| Certified | — | 24 | 25 | 30 | 12 | 3 | 1 | — |
| Value* | $610 | | $640 | $660 | $690 | $715 | $750 | |
| *Recent auctions:* $851.88, NGC MS-66, October 2012 (avg. gold spot value that month, $1,747). $948.75, PCGS MS-66, February 2012 (avg. gold spot value that month, $1,743). | | | | | | | | |

\* "Raw" value is based on a gold spot price of $1,200 per ounce, and is for an uncertified Mint State medallion of average quality. This value may vary with the prevailing bullion value.

# 1982 AMERICAN ARTS GOLD MEDALLIONS

**Designers:** *John Mercanti (Armstrong); Edgar Z. Steever (Wright).*
**Sculptors:** *John Mercanti (Armstrong); Edgar Z. Steever (Wright).*
**Composition:** *.900 gold, .070 copper, .030 silver.*
**Diameter:** *32 mm (Armstrong); 27.4 mm (Wright).*
**Edge:** *Reeded.* **Mint:** *West Point Bullion Depository.*

| Year | Weight | Design | Mintage | Sales | Estimated Surviving* | Year's Sales by Weight (Ounces) |
|------|--------|--------|---------|-------|----------------------|---------------------------------|
| 1982 | 1 ounce | Louis Armstrong | 420,000 | 409,098 | 59,319 | 583,250.5 |
|      | 1/2 ounce | Frank Lloyd Wright | 360,000 | 348,305 | 50,504 | |

*Note: Sales figures include individual medallions as well as those sold within sets.*
* After melting and other attrition.

The 1982 Louis Armstrong one-ounce gold medallion. This was the first year the medallions featured the legend UNITED STATES OF AMERICA, coin-like denticles around the rim, a reeded edge, the date moved to the obverse, and an indication of weight in gold. Sculptor-engraver John Mercanti's initials appear above Armstrong's right shoulder and atop the musical staff lines.

**Reverse detail.**

In 1982 the American Arts medallions honored musician Louis Armstrong on the one-ounce gold piece and architect Frank Lloyd Wright on the half-ounce.

Louis Armstrong (August 4, 1901–July 6, 1971) was born in New Orleans, the grandson of slaves. The vibrant and tumultuous atmosphere of the Crescent City was a major force in his development as a musician growing up; he would later remark, "Every time I close my eyes blowing that trumpet of mine—I look right in the heart of good old New Orleans. . . . It has given me something to live for."[41] In the 1920s he gained fame as a cornet and trumpet player and an innovator in the uniquely American genre of jazz music. With a showman's natural charisma backed up by creativity and skill, Armstrong (nicknamed "Pops" and "Satchmo") helped transform jazz performance from group improvisation to the emphasis of extended solo expressions. He played with the top talents of the day, including Joe "King" Oliver and Hoagy Carmichael in Chicago and New York. His musical talent extended to singing, as well, with his trademark gravelly voice running a range from soft crooning to dexterous "scat" vocalization. Like Marian Anderson, Armstrong was an artist with "cross-over" appeal, his popularity transcending racial and social boundaries in a time when African-American entertainers faced long-established cultural roadblocks. Although he largely avoided politicizing his race, he famously stood up for integration during the Little Rock school-desegregation conflict of 1957. Armstrong performed to great acclaim in Europe and across the United States into the 1960s. His 1964 recording of "Hello Dolly" displaced the Beatles at number 1 on the pop charts. By the time his age kept him from active public performance in the late 1960s, the influence of "Ambassador Satch" on American popular music was firmly and permanently established.

The obverse of the Louis Armstrong gold medallion, by Mint sculptor-engraver John Mercanti, shows the performer in a youthful, informal pose. He is relaxed, smiling, and confident, dressed in a jacket and bowtie, as if pausing between sets in a Chicago jazz club and enjoying the applause of his audience. This is Louis Armstrong the artist at the top of his game—energizing American music, transforming it, making it his own, and having a ball. On the reverse we see Satchmo's famous instrument, the trumpet, set over a staff of music along with his popular title of "Ambassador of Jazz." Armstrong earned this nickname from his untiring intercontinental travels and performances under sponsorship of the U.S. State Department. Starting in the 1950s, the federal government sent jazz musicians abroad on goodwill tours, much as the Soviet Union did with its ballet troupes. At one point a *New Yorker* cartoon summed up their influence by imagining a State Department meeting for "a diplomatic mission of the utmost delicacy." The caption read, "The question is, who's the best man for it—[Secretary of State] John Foster Dulles or Satchmo?"

**A 1934 Selmer trumpet given to Armstrong by King George V of Great Britain.**

Mercanti incorporated several design changes into the Armstrong one-ounce medallion that would continue through the end of the American Arts program. Obverse and reverse both have denticles—small, regularly spaced, tooth-like projections that encircle the medallion's perimeter. On the obverse, the legend UNITED STATES OF AMERICA identifies the medallion's country of origin, punctuated by two six-pointed stars. The date, previously situated on the reverse of the medallions, is now on the obverse, as is customary in U.S. coinage. On the reverse, ONE OUNCE GOLD indicates the weight and content. These were not just whims of the designer, but were Treasury-mandated changes—intended to boost sales by making the medallions more coin-like in appearance.

**Louis Armstrong in action.**

**U.S. Mint plaster models of the one-ounce Louis Armstrong medallion.**

**The 1982 Frank Lloyd Wright half-ounce gold medallion showcases Fallingwater and its combination of manmade and natural design. The initials of Edgar Z. Steever, who designed and sculpted the medal, appear at the base of Wright's bust.**

Frank Lloyd Wright (June 8, 1867–April 9, 1959), born in Richland Center, Wisconsin, was renowned during a long and influential career in architecture and design. (He would be recognized posthumously by the American Institute of Architects as the greatest American architect of all time.) Wright's creative works included homes, churches, offices, schools, museums, hotels, and other buildings designed in a style he called *organic architecture*—a harmonious interaction of man and nature. His early work in Chicago confronted the young artist with a city of what he considered unattractive and uninspired architecture. He proved his skill working as a draftsman and designer, and made his mark on commercial and residential projects in the Windy City. Wright's brilliant and remarkably productive career would span from the 1880s into the late 1950s. He designed many building interiors, incorporating furniture, stained glass, and other elements, and developed innovative urban plans for the American landscape. He lectured throughout the United States and internationally, and wrote 20 books

**Frank Lloyd Wright in 1954: the master architect toward the end of his long and celebrated life.**

and many articles. Among his hundreds of famous works are the Darwin D. Martin house in Buffalo, New York (1903–1905); the Johnson Wax headquarters in Racine, Wisconsin (1936); Fallingwater, built as a residence suitable for the president of the Kaufmann department stores (Bear Run, Pennsylvania, 1936–1939); the Guggenheim Museum in New York City (1943–1959); and Beth Sholom Synagogue, Elkins Park, Pennsylvania (1954).

On the obverse of his American Arts gold medallion, Wright is captured in a strong profile portrait by Mint sculptor-engraver Edgar Z. Steever. His demeanor is intense, his gaze focused, his expression set in an attitude of concentration and study. The reverse of the medallion captures in gold one of the artist's most famous marriages of architecture and nature: Fallingwater. "It's a house that doesn't even appear to stand on solid ground," says the Western Pennsylvania Conservancy, which today manages the national historic landmark, "but instead stretches out over a 30' waterfall. It captured everyone's imagination when it was on the cover of *Time* magazine in 1938." Steever treats the observer to a view of Fallingwater's famous outdoor patios and the cascading streams and woods that embrace the house.

Fallingwater, one of Wright's most famous works.

**U.S. Mint plaster models of the
half-ounce Frank Lloyd Wright medallion.**

**Reverse detail.**

The 1982 half-ounce medallion, like the one-ounce, features several significant design changes that make it more coin-like than those of 1980 and 1981. The date is now on the obverse, its traditional position on U.S. coinage. Obverse and reverse both have denticles—tooth-like projections encircling the perimeter—instead of a plain rim. On the obverse, the legend UNITED STATES OF AMERICA identifies the medallion's country of origin. This is flanked by two six-pointed stars. On the reverse, ONE HALF OUNCE GOLD identifies the medallion's weight and content.

## Production, Marketing, and Distribution of 1982 American Arts Gold Medallions

In its March 1982 report to Congress, the U.S. Gold Commission supported the Treasury's planned improvement of the American Arts program's sales and distribution. The new concept under development was to sell the gold medallions directly to a network of dealers, based on the day's New York bullion price plus a 3% markup, with the dealers creating a secondary market selling directly to consumers (their profit being gained by a further markup).[42] The Bureau of the Mint would eventually report: "Alternative sales methods for the gold medallions are being implemented. The United States Mint has awarded [on December 14, 1982] a contract to J. Aron & Company to market the American Arts Gold Medallions. A new, convenient program has been developed to make the buying and selling of medallions fast and easy. J. Aron is marketing them through a network of dealers including banks, brokerage houses, and coin shops. The prices being quoted for the medallions vary slightly from dealer to dealer but are competitive with those charged for Krugerrands and other foreign gold coins."[43] The Mint advised consumers that "You may wish to call several dealers for prices before making a purchase. A list is available by calling 800-USA-GOLD."

J. Aron, a division of Goldman Sachs Group, hired the New York–based ad agency of Benton & Bowles (famous for inventing the concept of the soap opera) to handle advertising, direct marketing, and public relations. They marketed the American Arts program with the words U.S. GOLD, the letter O in the word GOLD being represented by a gold medallion.[44] A $4 million advertising blitz included television commercials featuring Bob Hope, Johnny Cash, and various Treasury bigwigs.

An April 13, 1983, article in the *New York Times* (excerpted here) described the J. Aron sales strategy.[45]

> The Treasury Department has decided to use a private dealer to sell its gold medallions in the hope that the dealer will do a better job than the Postal Service.
>
> Treasury Secretary Donald T. Regan announced today that a contract had been signed with J. Aron & Company, a precious metals company, to sell one million ounces of gold medallions annually for three years. The Postal Service has been trying to reach that goal since 1980, but has only sold about 600,000 ounces since then.
>
> "This is an excellent example of the Reagan Administration's philosophy of turning over to the private sector the things it can do best, such as marketing," Mr. Regan said, without disclosing exactly what Aron will earn for its sales

efforts. If Aron does in fact sell three million ounces through 1985, that would bring the Treasury $1.3 billion at gold's current price of about $431 an ounce.

Some analysts who follow the gold market took a slightly different view than Mr. Regan's. They said that the failure of the Postal Service to sell more medallions may have been caused less by feeble marketing efforts than by the sharp decline in gold prices. Those prices were approaching $900 an ounce in 1980, when the medallions were first introduced, only to fall as low as $300 in 1982. Sales of other gold pieces, such as the popular South African Krugerrand, also suffered, although not as much as the American medallion.

The poor sales to date have been blamed by some on the Postal Service's cumbersome and time-consuming marketing system. Purchasers have had to fill out a form, present a certified check, money order or cashier's check, and then wait up to two months before actually receiving the coins in the mail.

The price, which was adjusted by the Government every 24 hours, was based on the New York Commodity Exchange closing spot price plus a markup for mailing and handling charges of $14 per one-ounce medallion. The waiting period for delivery meant that the medallion could be more or less valuable by the time it was received.

The Postal Service has sold 438,000 ounces of the 1980 medallion and 165,000 ounces of the 1981 medallion to about 200,000 people. The 1982 medallion is just now going on sale.

John C. Whitehead, a senior partner at Goldman, Sachs & Company, the parent of Aron, said at a news conference with Mr. Regan that Aron's sales operation would be simpler than the Postal Service's. He said a nationwide network of banks, brokerage houses and coin dealers had been set up by Aron and that the selling campaign would be heavily advertised. Most private dealers take orders by phone and then arrange to either quickly deliver the coins or keep them in a vault until the customer decides to sell.

Unlike the Postal Service, Aron will maintain a two-way market and arrange for the resale of the medallions. A ready two-way market is considered to be one reason for the success in selling both Krugerrands and Canadian Maple Leafs, which promise to be the biggest competition for the United States Golds, as the American medallions are now to be known.

Mr. Regan bought the first Aron-marketed one-ounce coin from Mr. Whitehead today at a price of $450, which was a $19 markup from the London gold fixing price of $431 today. When Mr. Regan said he was not sure whether the law—which prohibits his purchase of Treasury securities—permits him to make such a purchase, Mr. Whitehead offered immediately to buy the coin back for $445.

**Files and other tools used by Mint sculptor-engraver Edgar Steever.**

"Now I learn the secrets of Goldman Sachs," joked Mr. Regan, former chief executive of Merrill Lynch & Company.

The United States Treasurer, Angela M. Buchanan, who is in overall charge of the Mint and the 264 million ounces of gold stowed at Fort Knox and other repositories, awarded the contract to Aron after a competitive bidding process last year.

The U.S. Gold Commission, in addition to giving its blessing to the new marketing strategy in its 1982 congressional report, also encouraged Congress to develop a robust program of gold *coins*—either to run alongside the medallions program or to supplant it completely—to better compete with the South African Krugerrand as an investment vehicle. J. Charles Partee, a governor of the Federal Reserve, remarked that "The procedures by which gold medallions are marketed can be substantially improved as an interim measure, but the program should be discontinued when and if the Commission's gold coin recommendation is implemented." Congressman Chalmers P. Wylie of Ohio was pessimistic about the American Arts gold medallions. He noted that "Inadequate demand for the gold medallions produced by the Treasury . . . has left the Treasury with many millions of dollars of unsold medallions." The lesson he drew from this was one of caution: Would a gold coinage program succeed if demand for the gold medallions was so low? "At least the gold medallion program should be discontinued," he wrote in a note within the commission's 1982 report, "if we are to start producing gold bullion coins in accordance with the Commission's recommendation." Eventually, in fact, the U.S. government *would* begin a gold bullion program of coins rather than medallions: the American Eagle series would launch in 1986. In the meantime, the Treasury tried to fix what was broken in the American Arts program.

Sales peaked with the 1982 issues. John Mercanti's Louis Armstrong one-ounce medallion was the series' record-setter to the tune of 409,098 pieces. Edgar Steever's Frank Lloyd Wright was the highest seller among the program's half-ounce pieces, with 348,305 sold. J. Aron and Company might not have reached its goal of selling a million ounces of gold for the year, but it certainly injected new energy into the program. Unfortunately, many of the 1982 medallions—perhaps as much as 85% of the issue—would ultimately end up in the melting pot.

The private firm's contract with the Treasury Department would be terminated earlier than planned, on June 6, 1984 (see below). Some 1982 American Arts gold medallions were later sold by the U.S. Mint individually and in special sets in 1984 and 1985; for more information, see the "Production, Marketing, and Distribution" entry for 1984.

## Today's Market for 1982 American Arts Gold Medallions

After its Treasury agreement was signed in December 1982, J. Aron and Company "had until September 1985 to unload the 3 million ounces," reported Associated Press writer David Goeller in June 1984, "but early this month the contract was canceled after J. Aron bought 1 million ounces but managed to sell only about 150,000 ounces, according to a spokesman for the firm." Goeller quoted the J. Aron spokesman: "We expected to see a response to the 3 million ounces and hoped to go back [to the Mint] for more. We felt this piece would reach many new gold buyers. But there was no incentive to buy at this time. The market was either flat or decreasing."[46]

The 1982 American Arts gold medallions present an interesting scenario in the series. Bullion specialist Patrick Heller, who analyzes investor and collector gold, tells of an exhaustive study done by Liberty Coin Service founder

R.W. Bradford in the summer of 1986. Bradford sought to determine rates of survivorship—how many of each type of American Arts gold medallion had been melted after purchase, compared to their official mintages (which the Mint released in 1986). "He amassed information from public sources on mintages, sales, and official meltage," Heller reports.[47] "He then contacted wholesalers and refiners to get estimates of how many medallions had been melted in the secondary market. Last, he surveyed dealers and investors on the relative rarity and ease of locating each medallion."

Heller summarizes Bradford's conclusions and appends his own:

> Aron did honor its purchase guarantee. However, Aron reported that they were only able to sell 15 percent of the medallions, with no breakdown of how many of each issue. Bradford made multiple attempts to have Aron confirm rumors that it had melted down the other 85 percent of the 1982 and 1983 medallions. Aron officials refused to confirm or deny these stories.
>
> Bradford concluded that Aron had melted down the remaining 85 percent of the 1982 and 1983 medallions. This information was unanimously confirmed by a number of sources close to J. Aron & Co., who were in a position to know what happened to the medallions.
>
> Another reason that Bradford believed that these medallions were melted is that no large quantities of any of these issues ever surfaced, a fact still true today. We have never even seen 200-piece groups of a single issue, despite being an active market maker in medallions.
>
> Originally Bradford assumed that none of the 1982 medallions were melted except those by J. Aron. He estimated that about 83.5 percent of 1982 issues were melted, because of a greater marketing effort in 1982, and that 87.5 percent of 1983 issues were melted.
>
> Since 1986, we estimate that another 2 percent of the original mintages of the 1982 and 1983 medallions were melted.

J. Aron and Company's contract allowed the firm to purchase the gold from the Treasury at 2% above spot value.[48] In 1983 the cumulative annual average of gold's market value was $424 per ounce; in 1984 it dropped to $361; in 1985 it dropped further to $317. It didn't climb back to its 1983 value until 1987, when it averaged $448 per ounce. For the rest of the 1980s and 1990s gold's average price generally stayed in the $350 to $400 range. Only after 2001 did its average annual value begin to steadily climb, from $312 in 2002 to $1,669 in 2012. A reasonable observer could opine, as R.W. Bradford did, that J. Aron and Company would have sought to minimize its storage and security costs, depreciation, and other expenses by liquidating all or part of its million ounces of American Arts gold, either over a period of time or as soon as the spot value allowed it to make a small profit. With no large hoards of any single medallion being known, the melting pot looks like a reasonable fate for the 1982 and 1983 pieces.

If the conclusions and estimates of large-scale melting are accurate, the 1982 and 1983 American Arts medallions are considerably scarcer today than their official mintages would imply. The market in mid-2015 does not suggest demand dramatically stronger than supply, but increased publicity of the series could change the equation.

**Smooth raised edge (1980–1981).**

**Raised edge with denticles (1982–1984).**

| 1982 Louis Armstrong, 1-ounce · Certified Populations and Retail Market Values | | | | | | | |
|---|---|---|---|---|---|---|---|
| | Raw | <MS-65 | MS-65 | MS-66 | MS-67 | MS-68 | MS-69 | MS-70 |
| Certified | — | 37 | 21 | 25 | 9 | 5 | 2 | — |
| Value* | $1,230 | | $1,300 | $1,340 | $1,375 | $1,400 | $1,450 | |

*Recent auctions:* $1,703.75, NGC MS-66, October 2012 (avg. gold spot value that month, $1,747). $1,897.50, PCGS MS-64, February 2012 (avg. gold spot value that month, $1,743).

* "Raw" value is based on a gold spot price of $1,200 per ounce, and is for an uncertified Mint State medallion of average quality. This value may vary with the prevailing bullion value.

| 1982 Frank Lloyd Wright, 1/2-ounce · Certified Populations and Retail Market Values | | | | | | | |
|---|---|---|---|---|---|---|---|
| | Raw | <MS-65 | MS-65 | MS-66 | MS-67 | MS-68 | MS-69 | MS-70 |
| Certified | — | 3 | 8 | 20 | 40 | 30 | 7 | — |
| Value* | $610 | | $645 | $670 | $690 | $700 | $720 | |

*Recent auctions:* $881.25, NGC MS-67, October 2012 (avg. gold spot value that month, $1,747). $948.75, PCGS MS-67, February 2012 (avg. gold spot value that month, $1,743).

* "Raw" value is based on a gold spot price of $1,200 per ounce, and is for an uncertified Mint State medallion of average quality. This value may vary with the prevailing bullion value.

# 1983 AMERICAN ARTS GOLD MEDALLIONS

**Designers:** *Philip E. Fowler (Frost); Michael Iacocca (Calder).*
**Sculptors:** *Philip E. Fowler (Frost); Michael Iacocca (Calder).*
**Composition:** *.900 gold, .070 copper, .030 silver.* **Diameter:** *32 mm (Frost); 27.4 mm (Calder).* **Edge:** *Reeded.* **Mint:** *West Point Bullion Depository.*

| Year | Weight | Design | Mintage | Sales | Estimated Surviving* | Year's Sales by Weight (Ounces) |
|---|---|---|---|---|---|---|
| 1983 | 1 ounce | Robert Frost | 500,000 | 390,669 | 41,020 | 428,454.5 |
| | 1/2 ounce | Alexander Calder | 410,000 | 75,571 | 7,935 | |

*Note:* Sales figures include individual medallions as well as those sold within sets.
* After melting and other attrition.

The 1983 Robert Frost one-ounce gold medallion, showcasing several lines of one of his most famous poems. Philip Fowler, the medal's designer and sculptor, is identified as P. FOWLER on the lower edge of Frost's bust.

The American Arts gold medallions of 1983 honor poet Robert Frost on the one-ounce piece and artist Alexander Calder on the half-ounce.

Robert Lee Frost (March 26, 1874–January 29, 1963) was born in San Francisco and knew from an early age that poetry was his calling. He sold his first poem at the age of 20—"My Butterfly. An Elegy" was published in the November 8, 1894, edition of the *New York Independent*. He married, attended Harvard University in the late 1890s (dropping out voluntarily because of illness), then worked his family farm in New Hampshire for nine years while crafting poems in the mornings. Frost taught English from 1906 to 1912 in schools in New Hampshire. In the latter year he moved his family overseas, to a small town outside London. It was in England that his first book of poetry, *A Boy's Will*, was published (in 1913, followed by *North of Boston* in 1914), and he met and befriended many influential contemporary poets. He returned to

New Hampshire in 1915, bought a farm, and continued his career of writing, teaching (notably at Amherst College in Massachusetts), and lecturing. Frost's creative work was distinguished by its realistic focus on New England rural life, his masterful use of American colloquial speech, and his exploration of social, cultural, and philosophical themes. His poetry earned both popular and critical acclaim, garnering four Pulitzer Prizes, and he was awarded the Congressional Gold Medal in 1960. The following year, at the age of 86, he read his poem "The Gift Outright" at the inauguration of President John F. Kennedy.

Mint sculptor-engraver Philip Fowler's portrait of Robert Frost was modeled from a photograph taken in 1959, on the poet's 85th birthday gala in New York City. The *New York World-Telegram and Sun* had sent photographer Walter Albertin to capture the occasion. Fowler's three-quarter profile rendering is reflective, gentle; he has softened a bit the poet's outward signs of age and presented him as the folksy American institution he had long since become. This is the contemplative wordsmith that many people think of when Robert Frost comes to mind. Speaking at Frost's 85th birthday dinner, however, literary critic Lionel Trilling presented another view: that instead of being "an articulate bald eagle," spoon-feeding comfortable observations in New England dialect, Robert Frost was instead "a terrifying poet . . . who made plain . . . the terrible things of human life." Later writers would explore this more complicated aspect of Frost's work.

The reverse of the Robert Frost gold medallion is the only design in the series that uses text alone to represent its artist. Engraver Fowler set several lines from Frost's 1916 poem "The Road Not Taken."

> Two roads diverged in a wood, and I —
>     I took the one less traveled by,
>     And that has made all the difference.

This is perhaps Frost's most often misunderstood popular work. In 1961 the poet himself observed that "The Road Not Taken" is "a tricky poem, very tricky." Casual readers interpret it as an affirmation of independent thinking, of marching to the beat of one's own drummer. Frost was in fact commenting on indecision, and the human tendency to look for meaning in inconsequential choices. The speaker in the poem is saying that, confronted with two wooded paths, he chose one that was "really about the same" as the other—but he admits that, somewhere "ages and ages" later, he would undoubtedly give great weight to his decision.

The artist in a moment of repose. Frost-related memorabilia is collectible; this print, signed by photographer Yousuf Karsh, sold for $1,562.50 in a 2014 Heritage auction.

Poet Robert Frost in 1959, as photographed on his 85th birthday. Mint sculptor-engraver Philip Fowler's portrait of Frost for the American Arts gold medallion was clearly inspired by this likeness.

U.S. Mint plaster models of the one-ounce Robert Frost medallion. The 1983 designs continued the coin-like features of 1982: date on the obverse, denticles, stars, and legends denoting the country of issue and the precious-metal content.

★ ★ ★ ★ ★ ★ ★ ★ ★ ★

The 1983 Alexander Calder half-ounce gold medallion. The artist is vibrant and full of life. The last name of the medal's designer and engraver, Michael Iacocca, appears lightly impressed at Calder's left shoulder.

Alexander Calder (July 22, 1898–November 11, 1976) was born in Lawnton, Pennsylvania, into a family of well-known artists. His grandfather and father had both sculpted public works in and around Philadelphia, and his mother was a professional portraitist. Young "Sandy" showed his own creative spark early on—he made his first sculpture, a clay elephant, at the age of four. The family moved several times during his childhood and Sandy was encouraged to develop as an artist. In California he became fascinated with the circus, a theme he would return to in his mature works. As a sculptor, Calder developed the *mobile*, a kinetic art form of carefully suspended or balanced sculptures that can move either through motor power or in the air's natural currents. Another of his favorite media was wire sculpture. Calder's college education was as a mechanical engineer, and his art incorporated elements of balance, motion (unusual in sculpture), and change. He created a miniature traveling circus packed in five suitcases (with which he

Alexander Calder installing a kinetic sculpture, or mobile.

narrated improvisational "Cirque Calder" shows), as well as moving push-and-pull toys; abstract sculpture that moved by pulleys and cranks; and monumental sculptures for public works (his massive steel "Mountains and Clouds," situated in the Hart Senate Office Building in Washington, DC, weighs 35 tons). Lithographs and prints, painted aircraft, hand-crafted jewelry, oil paintings, tapestries—in all, this quintessentially American artist created some 20,000 works during his long career.

Mint sculptor-engraver Michael Iacocca crafted the half-ounce Alexander Calder gold medallion. His portrait of the artist is energetic and bursting with life: Calder is captured in three-quarter profile as if turning to greet the viewer, a broad smile on his face and a merry spark in his eyes. The tousle of his hair, the laugh lines around his eyes, and the informal looseness of his shirt collar illustrate the artist's casual exuberance. On the reverse, Iacocca has depicted one of Calder's famous kinetic-sculpture creations: a mobile of delicately balanced, rounded shapes, suspended in mid-air underneath a ceiling hinted at by lines vanishing into the distance. The composition elegantly captures the gentle motion and interconnectedness of Calder's work. A recreation of the artist's bold signature is at center right, appearing almost as if scrawled in wet sand or exuberantly splashed in paint.

The cover of Calder's 1966 autobiography captures his intensity.

## Production, Marketing, and Distribution of 1983 American Arts Gold Medallions

J. Aron and Company launched its sales campaign for the American Arts gold medallions in 1983, using the trade name of U.S. GOLD and distributing the medals through a network of more than 3,200 brokerage firms, banks, and other dealers. Their agreement to purchase one million ounces of gold per

U.S. Mint plaster models of the half-ounce Alexander Calder medallion. Coin-like design elements include the date on the obverse instead of the reverse; rim-encircling denticles; heraldic stars; the legend **UNITED STATES OF AMERICA**; and a notation of gold content.

year for three years, in exchange for exclusive marketing rights, was the largest contract the U.S. Mint had ever entered into. The firm purchased the medallions at 2% over bullion value and they were sold at a 4% to 8% premium, competitive with foreign gold bullion coins.

U.S. Representative Frank Annunzio of Illinois, chairman of the House Subcommittee on Consumer Affairs and Coinage, questioned the J. Aron contract in the April 1983 issue of his numismatic newsletter. "One of my biggest fears," he said, "is that the contract gives J. Aron and Company virtually total control of all gold sales in the United States. J. Aron and Company by its own admission is the largest distributor in the world of South Africa's Krugerrands, and a primary distributor of Canada's Maple Leaf and Mexico's gold coins. Now that the company has the U.S. gold contract it could manipulate the market so as to ensure that the gold coin with the most profit potential would be pushed, while the other coins are kept in the background." He also was troubled by a provision in the contract that would have the U.S. Mint pay half the advertising costs of J. Aron's campaign, which would be millions of dollars.

J. Aron had a strong motive for promoting the medallions: its obligation to purchase three million ounces of them over three years. But despite its efforts, sales were weak. Gold's market value dropped nearly 20% in 1983, from a cumulative monthly average of $482 per ounce in January down to $389 in December. Investors were reluctant to sink money into the declining bullion market, and the American Arts medallions' weaknesses—in particular, not having legal-tender status as official U.S. coins—lowered their appeal in an already competitive environment. Of the 410,000 Calder half-ounce medallions minted, only 74,571 were sold. The Frost one-ounce medallion fared better with 390,669 sold, but this was a decline from 1982.

Based on a 1986 analysis by R.W. Bradford of Liberty Coin Service, bullion specialist Patrick Heller estimates that nearly 90% of the 1983 issues were melted starting in the 1980s. The bulk of this attrition would have been from J. Aron and Company liquidating much of the stock it was obliged to purchase under its Treasury contract.

Some 1983 American Arts gold medallions were later sold by the U.S. Mint individually and in special sets in 1984 and 1985; for more information, see the "Production, Marketing, and Distribution" entry for 1984.

## Today's Market for 1983 American Arts Gold Medallions

Dealers anecdotally cite the Calder half-ounce medallion as the scarcest issue of the American Arts series. This fits with the estimates of the bulk of its 74,571 pieces having been melted by J. Aron and Company. It is likely the series' sleeper, with the smallest number of surviving pieces available for collectors. With demand currently being low, however, its premium over more common pieces is not

A 1983 advertisement featuring
J. Aron and Company's branding of U.S. GOLD.

strong, and prices hover near bullion value for raw (not professionally graded) examples. The fact that collectors have submitted more than 150 of the Calder medallions for third-party certification to NGC alone, with additional pieces submitted to PCGS, suggests a nascent appreciation of their relative scarcity.

The one-ounce Frost medallion, too, trades near its bullion value, with stronger premiums being reserved for certified higher-grade pieces.

| 1983 Robert Frost, 1-ounce · Certified Populations and Retail Market Values | | | | | | | | |
|---|---|---|---|---|---|---|---|---|
| | Raw | <MS-65 | MS-65 | MS-66 | MS-67 | MS-68 | MS-69 | MS-70 |
| Certified | — | 12 | 9 | 10 | 12 | 9 | 18 | — |
| Value* | $1,220 | | $1,280 | $1,400 | $1,425 | $1,475 | $1,500 | |

Recent auctions: $1,703.75, NGC MS-66, October 2012 (avg. gold spot value that month, $1,747). $1,897.50, PCGS MS-66, February 2012 (avg. gold spot value that month, $1,743).

\* "Raw" value is based on a gold spot price of $1,200 per ounce, and is for an uncertified Mint State medallion of average quality. This value may vary with the prevailing bullion value.

| 1983 Alexander Calder, 1/2-ounce · Certified Populations and Retail Market Values | | | | | | | | |
|---|---|---|---|---|---|---|---|---|
| | Raw | <MS-65 | MS-65 | MS-66 | MS-67 | MS-68 | MS-69 | MS-70 |
| Certified | — | 3 | 7 | 23 | 42 | 12 | 70 | — |
| Value* | $630 | | $655 | $675 | $695 | $710 | $725 | |

Recent auctions: $881.25, NGC MS-67, October 2012 (avg. gold spot value that month, $1,747). $948.75, PCGS MS-68, February 2012 (avg. gold spot value that month, $1,743).

\* "Raw" value is based on a gold spot price of $1,200 per ounce, and is for an uncertified Mint State medallion of average quality. This value may vary with the prevailing bullion value.

# 1984 AMERICAN ARTS GOLD MEDALLIONS

**Designers:** *John Mercanti (Hayes); John Mercanti and Philip E. Fowler (Steinbeck).* **Sculptors:** *John Mercanti (Hayes); Philip E. Fowler (Steinbeck).* **Composition:** *.900 gold, .070 copper, .030 silver.* **Diameter:** *32 mm (Hayes); 27.4 mm (Steinbeck).* **Edge:** *Reeded.* **Mint:** *West Point Bullion Depository.*

| Year | Weight | Design | Mintage | Sales | Estimated Surviving* | Year's Sales by Weight (Ounces) |
|---|---|---|---|---|---|---|
| 1984 | 1 ounce | Helen Hayes | 35,000 | 33,546 | 32,875 | 49,832.0 |
| | 1/2 ounce | John Steinbeck | 35,000 | 32,572 | 31,920 | |

*Note:* Sales figures include individual medallions as well as those sold within sets.
\* After melting and other attrition.

The 1984 Helen Hayes one-ounce gold medallion. Sculptor-engraver John Mercanti's initials, JM, are on the truncation of Hayes's bust and above the O in GOLD.

The American Arts gold medallions of 1984 honor actress Helen Hayes on the one-ounce piece and writer John Steinbeck on the half-ounce. Helen Hayes (October 10, 1900–March 17, 1993)—the "First Lady of American Theater"—is one of twelve artists to have earned the coveted "EGOT" (winning all four of the coveted Emmy, Grammy, Oscar, and Tony awards). Along with Marian Anderson, she was one of only two American Arts honorees still living while the gold-medallion program was under way.

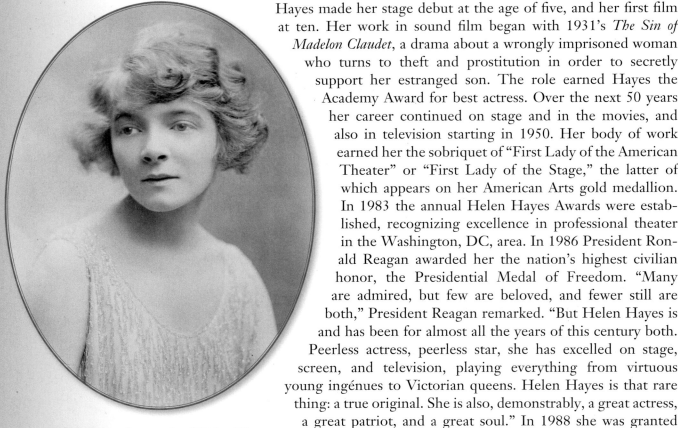

Hayes made her stage debut at the age of five, and her first film at ten. Her work in sound film began with 1931's *The Sin of Madelon Claudet*, a drama about a wrongly imprisoned woman who turns to theft and prostitution in order to secretly support her estranged son. The role earned Hayes the Academy Award for best actress. Over the next 50 years her career continued on stage and in the movies, and also in television starting in 1950. Her body of work earned her the sobriquet of "First Lady of the American Theater" or "First Lady of the Stage," the latter of which appears on her American Arts gold medallion. In 1983 the annual Helen Hayes Awards were established, recognizing excellence in professional theater in the Washington, DC, area. In 1986 President Ronald Reagan awarded her the nation's highest civilian honor, the Presidential Medal of Freedom. "Many are admired, but few are beloved, and fewer still are both," President Reagan remarked. "But Helen Hayes is and has been for almost all the years of this century both. Peerless actress, peerless star, she has excelled on stage, screen, and television, playing everything from virtuous young ingénues to Victorian queens. Helen Hayes is that rare thing: a true original. She is also, demonstrably, a great actress, a great patriot, and a great soul." In 1988 she was granted the National Medal of Arts.

A promotional portrait of Helen Hayes by the Bain News Service, one of America's earliest news-picture services. Hayes's stage debut came at the age of five years.

U.S. Mint galvanos showing the Hayes medallion designs. As with the 1982 and 1983 issues, those of 1984 included design elements associated with American coinage (stars, the name of the issuing nation, denticles around the rims, and the obverse placement of the date), as well as a statement of their weight and precious-metal alloy.

U.S. Mint sculptor-engraver John Mercanti's medallic portrait of Hayes is a virtuosic display of talent that does credit to the First Lady of the Stage. Hayes is depicted in older age in a strong and beautiful profile, her hair artfully sculpted and her jewelry elegant and simple. When the medallion is tilted the light plays off its skillfully carved details; at one angle Miss Hayes smiles gently, at another angle she almost frowns. The medal's reverse design emphasizes the performer's duality with the classic Greek theatrical masks of Comedy and Tragedy, symbols of the muses Thalia and Melpomene. An elaborately scrolled ribbon surrounds the title FIRST LADY OF THE STAGE.

America's "First Lady of Theater" was honored on a U.S. postage stamp in 2011.

John Steinbeck (February 26, 1902–December 20, 1968) is one of the best-known American authors of the 20th century. Born in small-town Salinas in rural California, he grew up working with poor migrant laborers on nearby farms. This experience would influence his later writing about some of the harsher aspects of American life. He studied English at Stanford University, though he didn't earn his degree, and lived a peripatetic life doing odd jobs in the 1920s and 1930s, married in 1930, and published his first critical success, *Tortilla Flat*, in 1935. (This would be adapted into a 1942 film of the same title, featuring Spencer Tracy and Hedy Lamarr.) The book was followed by a series of "California novels" and Dust Bowl fiction during the Great Depression, drawing on Steinbeck's knowledge of working men and their impoverished families. *The Grapes of Wrath* (1939) won a Pulitzer Prize. Equally well known are his classics *Of Mice and Men* (1937) and *East of Eden* (1952). When Steinbeck won the Nobel Prize for Literature in 1962, he was praised for "his realistic and imaginative writings, combining as they do sympathetic humour and keen social perception." His work was not without its share of controversy: *Grapes of Wrath* was critical of American capitalism, which brought a backlash against him; the book was banned by the Kern County board of supervisors for obscenity and unfair representation of the county's social conditions. Still, it was recognized as a great work and was developed into a film version, as was *Of Mice and Men*. During World War II Steinbeck was a field correspondent for the *New York Herald Tribune* and worked for the federal Office of Strategic Services. Writing was his solace from wounds, physical and psychological, brought by the war. He considered the post-war *East of Eden* his greatest work. It, too, became a film, this one starring James Dean in his movie debut. The story explored themes of depravity, charity, love, and the human struggles of guilt and freedom.

The 1984 John Steinbeck half-ounce gold medallion. U.S. Mint sculptor-engraver John Mercanti's initials appear at Steinbeck's shoulder; on the reverse, Philip Fowler's name is lightly impressed in the grass above the O in OUNCE.

**Reverse detail.**

Steinbeck's writing career continued into the 1960s, and in all he crafted 27 books, including 16 novels, 6 works of nonfiction, and 5 collections of short stories.

John Mercanti's design on the obverse is a finely sculpted portrait of Steinbeck, nearly photographic in its execution. The writer faces the viewer directly with a piercing gaze, his brow furrowed but a smile on his lips. It is a serious portrait with a hint of amusement. Steinbeck might be listening intently; he might be about to speak. "A sad soul can kill quicker than a germ," perhaps, or maybe "Writers are a little below clowns and a little above trained seals."

The reverse, by sculptor-engraver Philip Fowler, shows a dilapidated farm scene hearkening to the agricultural settings of Steinbeck's most popular works. With layers of depth, rich detail, and a masterful use of white space in the prairie sky against the weathered wood of broken fences and barns, Fowler drops the viewer directly into one of Steinbeck's poor rural environments.

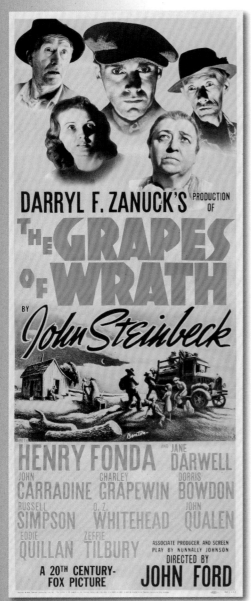

Steinbeck's novels were turned into some of the most popular American films of all time.

John Steinbeck and his 19-year-old son John visited the writer's friend, President Lyndon B. Johnson, in the Oval Office on May 16, 1966, shortly before the younger Steinbeck left for active duty in Vietnam.

## Production, Marketing, and Distribution of 1984 American Arts Gold Medallions

The Treasury mercifully allowed J. Aron and Company out of its purchasing and exclusive-marketing contract on June 6, 1984. Several months later, on October 22, the Mint resumed sales with a telephone campaign aimed at consumers who had purchased earlier issues of the American Arts gold medallions. Premiums were set at $12 over spot for the half-ounce medallions and $16 over spot for the one-ounce pieces, with all of the Mint's remaining inventory offered—medallions dating from 1980 through 1984. The telephone marketing program was originally scheduled to run through January 31, 1985, but was reopened on February 19 and ran again through March 1.

On September 10, 1985, Mint Director Donna Pope announced the sale of the gold medallions "in sets only" through a new telephone ordering system. "Customers can now purchase these medallions commemorating ten celebrated American artists, architects, writers and performers in attractive presentation sets of five one ounce or five half ounce medallions." The ordering period started on September 10 and was scheduled to end December 1, "unless supplies are sold out before that date." The Mint announced it had approximately 4,400 one-ounce sets and 5,300 half-ounce sets available. Buyers could call the old J. Aron and Company phone number, 1-800-USA-GOLD, and the price would be based on gold's value at the time the order was placed, plus a premium. When the "sets only" sales ended as scheduled on December 1, the Mint had sold 3,088 one-ounce sets and 2,951 half-ounce sets.

Final audits show the 1984 issues had the smallest sales of the series: 33,546 one-ounce Hayes medallions, and 32,572 half-ounce Steinbecks.

Unsold Mint inventory of all dates was later melted.

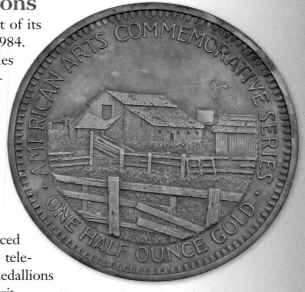

A U.S. Mint galvano showing the reverse of the Steinbeck medallion design. Both American Arts issues of 1984 included features commonly used on coins—the obverse position of the date, heraldic stars, the name of the issuing nation, and denticles around the rims—in addition to a statement of their weight and precious-metal alloy.

## Today's Market for 1984 American Arts Gold Medallions

Collectors bought 49,832 ounces total of the 1984 American Arts gold medallions. In contrast, they bought more than 497,000 examples of the Mint's 1984 commemorative gold $10 coin struck for the Los Angeles Olympiad, amounting to 240,000-plus ounces of gold. Not long after, they would buy 1,362,650 of the Mint's 1986 one-ounce American Gold Eagle $50 coins, plus another 972,000 ounces total of 1986 fractional-ounce gold coins. All of these *coins* today enjoy higher premiums (for unslabbed examples) than the 1984 American Arts medallions.

The 1984 Hayes one-ounce and Steinbeck half-ounce medallions had the lowest sales of the series. They were mostly sold directly by the Mint, by phone, to previous purchasers, rather than to national distributors or bullion dealers. For this reason it's likely most went into private collections to complete the set, or were bought by fans of Hayes and Steinbeck, and few would have been melted. Numismatist Patrick Heller conservatively estimates attrition of 2% since 1986. After the 1983 Calder half-ounce, the two issues of 1984 are likely the scarcest, and their market premiums support this scenario. "Interest in the series has started to increase in recent years," says professional numismatist Max Spiegel, vice president of sales and marketing for NGC. "High-grade examples are often difficult to locate and are eagerly sought by specialists, including participants in the NGC Registry."

| 1984 Helen Hayes, 1-ounce · Certified Populations and Retail Market Values | | | | | | | |
|---|---|---|---|---|---|---|---|
| | Raw | <MS-65 | MS-65 | MS-66 | MS-67 | MS-68 | MS-69 | MS-70 |
| Certified | — | 22 | 7 | 9 | 31 | 25 | 61 | — |
| Value* | $1,300 | | $1,340 | $1,430 | $1,475 | $1,500 | $1,600 | |

*Recent auctions:* $1,938.75, NGC MS-69, January 2013 (avg. gold spot value that month, $1,671). $1,762.50, NGC MS-67, October 2012 (avg. gold spot value that month, $1,747). $1,897.50, PCGS MS-66, February 2012 (avg. gold spot value that month, $1,743).

* "Raw" value is based on a gold spot price of $1,200 per ounce, and is for an uncertified Mint State medallion of average quality. This value may vary with the prevailing bullion value.

| 1984 John Steinbeck, 1/2-ounce · Certified Populations and Retail Market Values | | | | | | | |
|---|---|---|---|---|---|---|---|
| | Raw | <MS-65 | MS-65 | MS-66 | MS-67 | MS-68 | MS-69 | MS-70 |
| Certified | — | 0 | 7 | 17 | 36 | 15 | 73 | — |
| Value* | $650 | | $675 | $690 | $725 | $750 | $775 | |

*Recent auctions:* $851.88, NGC MS-67, October 2012 (avg. gold spot value that month, $1,747). $948.75, PCGS MS-68, February 2012 (avg. gold spot value that month, $1,743).

* "Raw" value is based on a gold spot price of $1,200 per ounce, and is for an uncertified Mint State medallion of average quality. This value may vary with the prevailing bullion value.

# 1985 AND BEYOND: WHAT MIGHT HAVE BEEN, AND WHAT WAS TO COME

By the end of 1985 the American Arts Commemorative Series had wrapped up and the nation had moved on. When the program started in 1980, the U.S. Mint was slowly getting back into the minting of gold after the long hiatus from 1934 to the early 1970s. When the medallion program ended in 1984, legal-tender *coins* were back on the table in the form of Olympic commemoratives, which would soon be joined by a $5 commemorative for the Statue of Liberty centennial (1986), then another for the bicentennial of the U.S. Constitution (1987), and many others in the 1980s and 1990s to date. More significantly, the Mint's new bullion-coin program, the American Eagles, came out in 1986 and quickly grew into what supporters of the American Arts medallions had envisioned in the late 1970s.

"The American Arts gold medallions are the predecessor to the American Gold Eagle, the world's most popular gold bullion coin," says Max Spiegel of NGC. "Despite this distinguished status the medallions have long been under-appreciated by collectors."[49]

An interesting side note to the American Arts story: On February 7, 1985, Representative Jim Leach of Iowa, who had introduced the 1978 legislation that created the American Arts program, proposed an expansion. H.R. 1055 was an amendment to the American Arts Gold Medallion Act that would have extended the series for another 10 years, honoring 20 more American artists (see the gallery on the following spread).

Leach's bill didn't get beyond the House Subcommittee on Consumer Affairs and Coinage, and the curtain officially dropped on the American Arts program. The medallions' five years on the national stage gave Congress and the Treasury a thorough education in producing, advertising, and mass-market distribution of gold. Next up would be the first of several vastly improved legal-tender bullion coinage series—not just gold coins, but also silver and platinum, destined to capture the public's attention and sell by the tens of millions.

**Gold *coins* from the U.S. Mint would soon prove more popular than its gold medallions.**

# Proposed 1985–1994 One-Ounce Medallions

Playwright and essayist
Arthur Miller.

The "Queen
of Jazz," Ella
Fitzgerald.

Writer
William
Faulkner.

Poet
Emily Dickinson.

Composer and pianist
George Gershwin.

Composer and conductor
Aaron Copland.

Old West artist
Charles
Marion Russell.

Painter and muralist
Thomas Hart Benton.

Composer and bandleader
Duke Ellington.

Social commentator and
humorist Will Rogers.

# Proposed 1985–1994 Half-Ounce Medallions

Artist Georgia O'Keeffe.

Architect
I.M Pei.

Photographer
Ansel Adams.

Singer-songwriter
Buddy Holly.

Painter John
James Audubon.

Author
Ernest Hemingway.

Actor
Henry Fonda.

Author Henry
David Thoreau.

Singer and actor
Paul Robeson.

Jazz musician
and composer
Bix Beiderbecke.

The national bird of the United States—the American bald eagle, *Haliaeetus Leucocephalus*— was selected as the emblem for the new gold and silver bullion programs that debuted in 1986.

# 4

# The American Eagle Bullion Programs (1986 to Date)

After 1984 Congress allowed the American Arts gold medallions to pass into history, and in 1986 the United States launched a new, more muscular bullion program—one that would include silver as well as gold, and, later, platinum. The American Eagles would take flight and quickly soar to new heights in global precious-metal distribution.

The right to legally own gold bullion had been taken away from Americans by Executive Order 6102 in 1933. From the passage of the Gold Reserve Act of 1934 into the 1960s, the federal government set the official value of gold at $35 per ounce. That changed on August 15, 1971, when President Richard Nixon affirmed that the United States would no longer convert dollars to gold at a fixed rate. This took the country off any semblance of a gold standard and allowed the precious metal to fluctuate with the free market. After 1974 the gold-ownership restrictions of the 1930s were nulled by new executive orders, and Americans could once again legally own gold in any form.

As discussed in chapter 3, Congress, the Treasury, and the White House wrestled with how (and whether) to sell the federal government's massive gold reserves to private buyers. The American Arts medallion program attempted but ultimately failed to provide a robust platform for making the gold available to everyday Americans. At the same time, the crippling recession of the early 1980s made gold very appealing as a financial safe-haven from rampant inflation. Even before the American Arts program had ended, U.S. congressmen such as Representative Ron Paul of Texas worked on various plans to build a domestic bullion-coin program. One constant goal was to compete with the Kru-gerrand and other foreign gold-coin investments. Canada

**The American Silver Eagle.
(shown 1.5x actual size)**

had debuted its Maple Leaf gold coins in 1979; Mexico rolled out the Libertad in 1981; and China started its Panda series in 1982. Congressman Paul's American Gold Eagle Act of 1983, which ultimately died in committee, would have had the Treasury mint two weights of gold coins called *American Eagles*. Finally Senator J. James Exon of Nebraska introduced the Gold Bullion Act of 1985, Senate Bill 1639, which was signed into law by President Ronald Reagan on December 17, 1985, as Public Law 99-185. Only a few months earlier, in September, Reagan had issued an executive order forbidding the importation of South Africa's Krugerrand coins, as a sanction against apartheid. This knocked a major competitor out of the ring.

In summary, the Gold Bullion Act of 1985:

directed the secretary of the Treasury to mint and issue gold coins in $50, $25, $10, and $5 denominations,

required the secretary to acquire the gold for such coins by purchase of gold mined from natural deposits in the United States or a U.S. territory or possession within one year after the month the ore was mined,

prohibited the secretary from paying more than the average world price for such gold,

allowed the secretary to use gold from U.S. reserves in the absence of available supplies of such mined gold at the average world price,

repealed a provision prohibiting the government from delivering any gold coin,

required any profit from the sale of such coins to be deposited in the Treasury and applied toward reducing the national debt, and

directed the secretary to ensure that the issuance of such coins resulted in no net cost to the government.

The first American Gold Eagles were stuck in a special ceremony at the West Point Bullion Depository in New York on September 8, 1986.

Silver's spot price, meanwhile, from the Great Depression into the 1960s, rose and fell in the market, typically staying between $0.30 and $0.90 per ounce. In the early 1960s it started a brisk climb in value. This rise was so dramatic that soon it was no longer profitable for countries to mint silver coins—their metal value exceeded their face value. In the 1970s and 1980s the U.S. Executive branch investigated selling off some or all of the nation's silver stockpile, which ostensibly was held for strategic purposes. Richard Nixon, Gerald Ford, Jimmy Carter, and Ronald Reagan all were convinced that ongoing domestic production of silver was greater than the amount needed by the Defense National Stockpile Center. For years Western mining interests and their friends in Congress stonewalled every executive effort to sell off the silver, fearing that a mountain of government metal (tens of millions of troy ounces) would collapse their otherwise profitable market. Finally, on June 21, 1985, Senator James McClure of Idaho introduced the Liberty Coin Act in an effort to control the way the government's

**The one-ounce
$50 denomination
of the American
Gold Eagle. (shown
1.5x actual size)**

A Proof American Platinum
Eagle. The third precious
metal was added to the U.S.
bullion programs in 1997.
(shown 1.5x actual size)

silver would be sold. It was clear by then that President Reagan and his successors would continue to push for the metal's sale, so the mining interests' protectors sought at least to avoid a massive dump on the market. Instead of the government wholesaling the silver by the millions of ounces to a few large distributors, the Liberty Coin Act authorized a new legal-tender bullion coin that could be sold one ounce at a time to the public. This widespread dissemination would help stave off a market glut.

In brief, the Liberty Coin Act:

authorized the secretary of the Treasury to mint and issue silver bullion coins,

specified the diameter, weight, fineness, general design, inscriptions, and edge format of the coins,

established the formula for pricing the coins,

defined the coins as having both numismatic and legal-tender status,

specified that the silver would come from the national stockpiles,

set the act in effect as of October 1, 1985, and

stipulated that no coins would be issued or sold before September 1, 1986.

President Reagan signed the Liberty Coin Act into law on July 9, 1985. The first American Silver Eagle was struck at a special ceremony at the U.S. Mint's San Francisco Assay Office on October 29, 1986.

Since their launch in 1986, the U.S. Mint's silver and gold American Eagle programs have sold more than 350 million ounces of silver and more than 43 million gold coins of various sizes. These coins are very popular with bullion investors nationwide. In addition, they are eagerly sought by numismatic hobbyists. On top of normal mass-produced bullion-strike coins, the Mint offers a wide range of special formats, packages, and finishes for many coins in the American Eagle series. These include anniversary sets, Proofs, Reverse Proofs, Burnished specimens, and Enhanced Uncirculated pieces. Platinum coins were added to the American Eagle lineup in 1997, also in bullion-strike and special collectible formats.

Two recently published books give collectors in-depth coin-by-coin information and history on the American Eagles. The silver series is covered in detail in *American Silver Eagles: A Guide to the U.S. Bullion Coin Program*, which features the behind-the-scenes insight of U.S. Mint chief engraver John M. Mercanti, who designed the coin's reverse. The gold and platinum series are studied in Edmund C. Moy's *American Gold and Platinum Eagles: A Guide to the U.S. Bullion Coin Programs*, which benefits from the unique perspective of the retired 38th director of the U.S. Mint.

Starting in 2006, the U.S. Mint would recreate one of America's most famous coinage designs on its first-ever series of 24K gold pieces.

# 5

# The American Buffalo .9999 Fine Gold Bullion Coins (2006 to Date)

**A**s the popular and best-selling American Eagle bullion program neared its 20th year, the Presidential $1 Coin Act of 2005 (Public Law 109-145) authorized a new suite of gold bullion coins. These would be struck in 24-karat (.9999 fine) gold, a first for the U.S. Mint, and they would feature two of America's most beloved and instantly recognizable coinage designs—the obverse and reverse of the Buffalo nickel made from 1913 to 1938.

The new act, signed into law on December 22, 2005, was intended "to require the Secretary of the Treasury to mint coins in commemoration of each of the Nation's past Presidents and their spouses, respectively, to improve circulation of the $1 coin, to create a new bullion coin, and for other purposes." The "new bullion coin" was the .9999 fine gold American Buffalo. Title II of the act described the coins:

> The initial designs of "the obverse and reverse of the gold bullion coins struck under this subsection during the first year of issuance shall bear the original designs by James Earle Fraser, which appear on the 5-cent coin commonly referred to as the 'Buffalo nickel' or the '1913 Type 1.'"

> "The coins . . . shall have inscriptions of the weight of the coin and the nominal denomination of the coin incused in that portion of the design on the reverse of the coin commonly known as the 'grassy mound.'"

"The Secretary shall acquire gold for the coins issued under this subsection by purchase of gold mined from natural deposits in the United States, or in a territory or possession of the United States, within 1 year after the month in which the ore from which it is derived was mined."

To avoid the act being used as a boondoggle for private gold-mining interests, it required that "The secretary shall not pay more than the average world price for the gold mined." The sale price of each coin would be at least the market value of the bullion at the time of its sale, plus the cost of designing and issuing the coin ("including labor, materials, dies, use of machinery, overhead expenses, marketing, and shipping").

The American Buffalos were intended to compete nationally and internationally with other mints' 24-karat gold coins, which U.S. Mint Deputy Director David A. Lebryk estimated to account for 60 percent of gold bullion-coin sales worldwide (the other 40 percent being less fine but more durable 22-karat coins). The 22-karat market was already dominated by the American Gold Eagle, and with the American Buffalo the U.S. Mint sought a share of the 24-karat market, then led by the Canadian Maple Leaf.

The authorizing legislation required that the secretary of the Treasury mint "such number of $50 gold bullion and Proof coins as the secretary

In addition to the American Buffalos, the Presidential $1 Coin Act of 2005 gave birth to several other new series of U.S. coins including Presidential dollars, circulating commemorative cents for the bicentennial of Abraham Lincoln's birth, and a new cent honoring Lincoln's preservation of the Union. (shown 1.5x actual size)

The American Buffalo gold bullion designs are familiar to every U.S. coin collector. They celebrate the Buffalo (or "Indian Head") nickel that was minted from 1913 to 1938.

may determine to be appropriate." Interestingly, in addition to allowing the Treasury secretary to change the maximum mintage quantities after one year, it also gave him authority to alter the coins' designs. "The secretary may, after consulting with the Commission of Fine Arts, and subject to review of the Citizens Coinage Advisory Committee, change the design on the obverse or reverse. . . ." So far this authority has not been invoked.

# THE FIRST BUFFALOS

The first American Buffalo gold coins were struck on June 20, 2006. Their launch ceremony was held at the West Point Mint in New York's beautiful Hudson River Valley, near the northern facilities of the United States Military Academy. U.S. Mint officials pressed two large buttons to set the presses to work, officially launching the new bullion series. "This American Buffalo gold coin will appeal to both investors who choose to hold gold and to others who simply love gold," said Deputy Director Lebryk. "These classic and beautiful American Indian and buffalo designs by James Earle Fraser, which have been American favorites since they were first used in 1913, recall a golden age of coin artistry." Two days after the ceremony the Mint transferred two of the historic gold coins to the Smithsonian Institution's National Numismatic Collection.

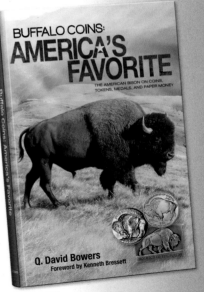

The bison, "King of the Plains," has fascinated Americans for generations. When Q. David Bowers wrote his book *Buffalo Coins: America's Favorite—The American Bison on Coins, Tokens, Medals, and Paper Money*, he chose an American Buffalo gold coin to grace the cover.

The impressive reinforced-concrete edifice of the West Point Mint. The original structure was built in 1937 and expanded in 2005. (Left to right: author Dennis Tucker, numismatist Q. David Bowers, and U.S. Mint Director of Corporate Communications Tom Jurkowsky, May 2014.)

**Working hubs used to make dies for the 2013 bullion-strike American Buffalo coinage at the West Point Mint.**

## Production and Distribution of American Buffalos

All American Buffalo gold coins, whether regular bullion strikes or special-format collector pieces, are made at the West Point Mint. The Mint has used coinage blanks fabricated by Stern-Leach, of Attleboro, Massachusetts, from gold purchased on the open market from suppliers including Johnson Matthey, Metalor, and Ohio Precious Metals, among others. The bullion-strike coins (including the 2008 Celebration coin) have a thickness of 2.62 mm. The Proof, Burnished (called *Uncirculated* in Mint literature), and Reverse Proof formats have a thickness of 2.95 mm.

The American Buffalo gold coins are legal tender, with their weight, content, and purity guaranteed by the federal government. Investors can include them in some individual retirement accounts because they meet the federal government's required fineness. Numismatic strikes—those made specifically for collectors—undergo special production processes similar to those of the American Gold Eagle bullion coins. Proofs are struck from polished coin blanks that are manually fed into a press fitted with special dies; the blank is struck multiple times to impart fine detail and high-quality fields; a white-gloved inspector examines the coin for quality; and it is then sealed in protective packaging. The Mint has also made Burnished and Reverse Proof formats, described in the 2008 and 2013 year-by-year sections below. Numismatic issues can be purchased by collectors directly from the U.S. Mint.[1] Regular bullion-strike pieces are not sold directly by the Mint to collectors and investors, but are wholesaled to a network of official distributors called *Authorized Purchasers*, who in turn sell them to secondary retailers. Authorized Purchasers include banks, investment firms, and other non-numismatic channels, as well as large precious-metal and coin marketers. To qualify as an Authorized

**Mintmark location on numismatic issues.**

**2014-dated American Buffalo gold bullion coins fresh off the press at West Point, May 14, 2014.**

Purchaser, a firm must be an experienced and established market-maker in bullion coins; provide a liquid two-way market for the coins; be audited annually; have an established and broad retail-customer base for distribution; and have a tangible net worth of $5 million to $50 million (depending on the bullion product). Authorized Purchasers of gold must have sold more than 100,000 ounces of gold bullion coins over any 12-month period since 1990. Their initial order must be for at least 1,000 ounces, with reorders in increments of 500 ounces.

The fact that the U.S. Mint follows this distribution model shows that valuable lessons were learned from the unsuccessful American Arts gold medallion program (and from the very successful American Eagle bullion coin programs). "The United States Mint is interested in ensuring that the coins minted and issued under its gold and platinum bullion coin programs are distributed effectively and efficiently and in a manner that ensures that the bullion coins are competitive with bullion products produced by other international mints," the Mint states.[2]

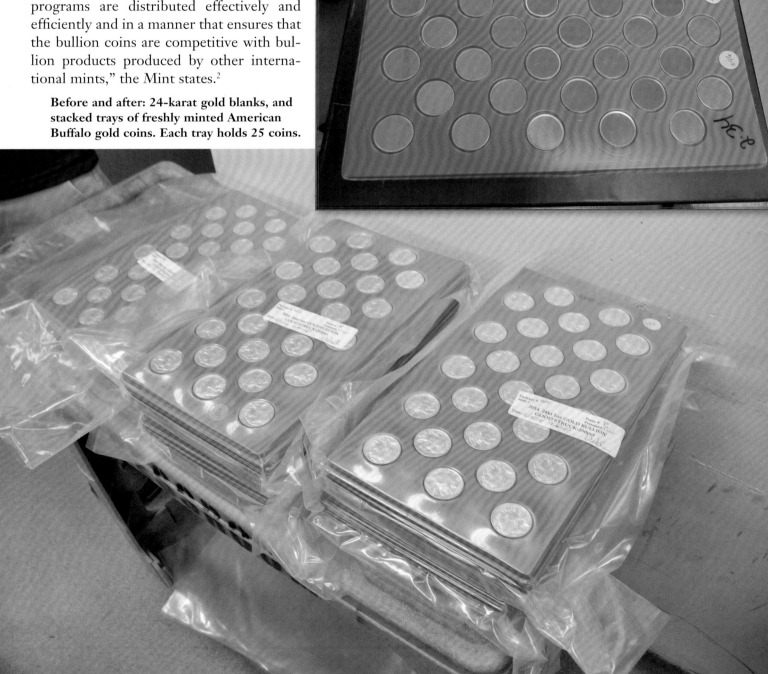

**Before and after: 24-karat gold blanks, and stacked trays of freshly minted American Buffalo gold coins. Each tray holds 25 coins.**

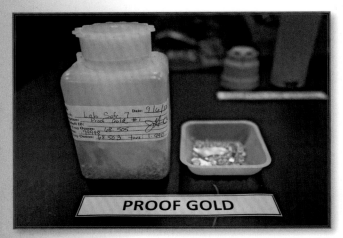

PROOF GOLD

Gold used for assaying at the West Point Mint.
24-karat gold is .9999 fine, compared to 22-karat
gold, which is .9167 fine. American Buffalos are
24-karat, and American Gold Eagles are 22-karat.

A white-gloved Mint technician observing
freshly struck Reverse Proof coins dated 2013—
the centennial year of the Buffalo nickel.

To accomplish this goal, the United States Mint seeks to use private sector distribution channels that ensure that the coins are:

A. as widely available to the public as possible;

B. bought and sold at prices/premiums that are in line with other similar bullion coin products in the marketplace; and

C. bought and sold in a manner that ensures relatively low transaction costs.

Due in part to the commodity-like, investment nature of these coins characterized by constantly fluctuating coin prices, the United States Mint has determined that the most effective and efficient means for bullion coin distribution is through the use of the well-established gold/platinum bullion coin distribution network in the private sector. This network typically consists of hundreds of coin and precious metal dealers, participating banks, brokerage companies, and other financial intermediaries.

From 2006 to 2008, the Mint assigned each numismatic version of the American Buffalo an issue price that didn't fluctuate even if the market value of gold rose or fell. Since 2009, all numismatic versions have been priced according to a flexible published-in-advance table. Under this plan, introduced in January 2009, the Mint's prices can change weekly, based on a range of the average market price for gold. "Pricing for precious-metal numismatic products varies by the average cost of the underlying metal," the Mint announced. "We use our pricing-range table the week prior to sale in order to determine the product's price. If the average weekly price of the precious metal moves up or down into another cost range, the price of the product will also go up or down, respectively, by a fixed amount." The Mint further noted that "The price of each gold product consists of the following components: cost of metal, cost to manufacture (including overhead), and margin." It gave an example of gold spot-priced at $1,100 per ounce. "At this spot price, the respective approximate average ranges for each component as a percentage of total price are as follows: cost of metal, 66 to 75%; cost to manufacture (including overhead), 11 to 19%, and margin, 13%."

The following is a sample of the sliding-scale pricing of the American Buffalo Proof gold coins.

| Preceding week's average price of gold | Proof American Buffalo price |
|---|---|
| $1,100.00 to $1,149.99 | $1,410.00 |
| $1,150.00 to $1,199.99 | $1,460.00 |
| $1,200.00 to $1,249.99 | $1,510.00 |

Unlike the American Gold Eagle and First Spouse gold-coin series, Proofs in the American Buffalo bullion program after 2008 have had no maximum mintage or household ordering limits.

## Packaging for the American Buffalos

The bullion-strike versions of the American Buffalo are individually packaged in plastic capsules that are then sheet-wrapped in a polyvinyl-chloride (PVC) covering. A "mint box" of 500 American Buffalo gold coins measures 17.5 x 12.5 x 4 inches and has a shipping weight of about 40 pounds. The higher-premium collector formats are presented in elegant boxes with distinctive finishing touches, accompanied by a certificate of authenticity.

Over time, the occasional American Buffalo gold coin has toned, to one degree or another and in various patterns, with an orange-red color. Some collectors find this effect attractive and others prefer untoned pieces. Similar toning has been observed on some First Spouse gold coins. Such toning is rare and does not indicate a deleterious flaw in the coin.

## "First Strike," "First Releases," and "Early Releases" Designations

The U.S. Mint does not have a program or designation for the first or earliest coins struck by a set of dies, or for the coins produced first or earliest in a particular year or series. Still, terms such as First Strike, Early Strike, and Early Release have sometimes been used in retailers' advertising, often centered

**U.S. Mint packaging for numismatic versions of the American Buffalo gold coin, sold directly by the Mint to collectors.**

around the Mint's bullion programs. In 2006 the Mint released the following clarification regarding coins popularly described in marketing literature as being "First Strike":

The United States Mint has received inquiries from consumers regarding use of the term "first strike." The term has appeared in connection with the advertising and grading of 2005 and 2006 silver, gold, and platinum Proof and bullion American Eagle coins, and the new 2006 24-karat Proof and bullion American Buffalo gold coins. Currently, there is no widely accepted and standardized numismatic industry definition of "first strike." Coin dealers and grading services may use this term in varying ways. Some base its use on dates appearing on United States Mint product packaging or packing slips, or on the dates of product releases or ceremonial coin strike events. Consumers should carefully review the following information along with each dealer's or grading service's definition of "first strike" when considering a purchase of coins with this designation.

The United States Mint has not designated any 2005 or 2006 American Eagle coins or 2006 American Buffalo coins as "first strikes," nor do we track the order in which we mint such coins during their production. The United States Mint held a launch ceremony for the 2006 American Buffalo Gold Coin on June 20, 2006, two days before its release on June 22, at which two Proof coins and two Burnished coins were ceremonially struck. However, those coins were not individually identified and were put in regular inventory after the ceremony. The United States Mint did not hold any striking ceremonies for the 2005 or 2006 American Eagle coins.

The United States Mint strives to produce coins of consistently high quality throughout the course of production. Our strict quality controls assure that coins of this caliber are produced from each die set throughout its useful life. Our manufacturing facilities use a die set as long as the quality of resulting coins meets United States Mint standards, and then replace the dies, continually changing sets throughout the production process. For bullion American Eagle and American Buffalo coins, the United States Mint makes an average of about 6,000 coins from one die set. For Proof versions of the 2006 American Buffalo coins, the yield is an average of about 1,500 coins per die set. For Proof versions of the American Eagle coins, the yield is an average of about 300–500 coins per die set. This means that coins may be minted from new die sets at any point and at multiple times while production of a coin is ongoing, not just the first day or at the beginning of production. To put this in context, in 2005 the United States Mint produced approximately 356,500 one-ounce gold, 8,891,000 silver, and 6,300 one-ounce platinum American Eagle bullion coins.

American Eagle and American Buffalo coins are not individually numbered and the United States Mint does not keep track of the order or date of minting of individual bullion or Proof coins. The United States Mint begins production several weeks before these coins are scheduled to be released. By the release dates for 2005 and 2006 bullion coins, the United States Mint had already minted approximately 50% of the projected sales numbers for these coins. Any dates on shipping boxes containing Uncirculated bullion coins sent to Authorized Purchasers are strictly for quality control and accounting purposes at the United States Mint at West Point.

The date on the box represents the date that the box was packed, verified as 500 ounces, and sealed, and the date of packaging does not necessarily correlate with the date of manufacture. The date on shipping labels and packing slips for Proof coins, which are sent directly to United States Mint customers from our fulfillment center, is the date the item was packed and shipped by the fulfillment center. The other numbers on the shipping label and packing slip are used to track the order and for quality control.

PCGS and NGC state their positions on their Web sites.

PCGS says, "The PCGS First Strike program designates coins issued in the first 30 days of the Mint's release. This designation not only adds value to modern coins, but takes modern coin collecting to another level with multiple Mint releases each year. There are two ways to obtain the First Strike designation: 1. The package mailed to PCGS has a postmark date prior to the PCGS cutoff date for that particular coin/issue. Only the coins need to be mailed to PCGS and received within the first 30 days of issue. 2. Submit the coins in the original unopened shipping box from the U.S. Mint with a postmark date prior to the specified PCGS cutoff date." The firm charges an additional $18 fee per coin for the First Strike designation, and offers a bulk submission program.

NGC says, "NGC offers the Early Releases designation for selected coins received by NGC or an NGC-approved depository during the first 30 days of release. The term EARLY RELEASES will be noted as part of the description on the special blue Early Releases label. Other special and series-specific labels available from NGC may also be used in combination with the Early Releases designation. To qualify for Early Releases, all coins must generally be received by NGC or an NGC-approved depository within 30 days of their release. Coins being sent directly to NGC do not need to be accompanied by original packaging or shipped in sealed Mint boxes, but must arrive within the time period described above. The Early Releases request must be noted on the submission invoice, and additional service fees apply for the special label and designation verification. This is the default label for coins received within their first 30 days of issue. Alternatively, NGC offers the First Releases designation, which has the same definition as Early Releases."

**Proof packaging.**

**2006 bullion strike.**

**2006-W Proof.**

# 2006 American Buffalo

*Composition: .9999 gold. Actual Gold Weight: 1 ounce. Diameter: 32.7 mm. Thickness: 2.62 mm (bullion); 2.95 mm (Proof). Edge: Reeded. Mint: West Point. Mintmark: None (for bullion strikes); W (for Proofs). Issue Price: spot price plus markup (bullion); $800 (Proof). Release Date: June 22, 2006.*

The first batch of American Buffalo gold coins was struck ceremonially at the West Point Mint on June 20, 2006. Two specimens from this initial mintage are priceless—literally invaluable, as no amount of money can purchase them. These two coins (one Proof and one Uncirculated) reside permanently in the National Numismatic Collection at the Smithsonian Institution in Washington, DC, and they belong to every American as part of our heritage.[3]

The main production of 2006 coins was made available for sale to collectors and investors on June 22, 2006. Excitement was high for the first 24-karat (.9999 fine) gold coin produced by the U.S. Mint. The artful recreation of James Earle Fraser's classic Indian Head and Buffalo designs, derived from the Buffalo nickel of 1913 to 1938, added more fuel to the fire.

Regular bullion strikes were available through the Mint's distribution network of Authorized Purchasers and their secondary level of retailers. This network was already well established and active in the ongoing sale of silver, gold, and platinum American Eagles. The bullion coins were sold at the current spot price of gold plus a markup.

Also available were coins struck in Proof format and packaged individually in attractive display boxes. Collectors and investors could purchase these special coins directly from the Mint. "The American Buffalo gold Proof coin will be encapsulated in plastic to protect its pristine, Proof finish," the Mint announced. "It is packaged in a blue United States Mint gift box and accompanied by a custom-designed Certificate of Authenticity." The Proof coins bear a W mintmark, for West Point, on the obverse. Sales were limited to 10 Proof coins per order and household, and the maximum Proof mintage was capped at 300,000. Customers could order the coins from the Mint's secure Web site at www.USMint.gov, by phone at 1-800-USA-MINT, and by a toll-free TTY line (1-888-321-MINT) for hearing- and speech-impaired customers.

The new coins were the talk of the hobby community through 2006. Collectors discussed every facet of their production, designs, packaging, distribution, and certified grading. Online forums entertained ongoing conversations about whether or not to remove the bullion strikes from their original capsules and plastic wraps; how the coins were faring on eBay and other venues in the secondary market; and whether the Mint would eventually issue fractional-ounce sizes. At the 2006 American Numismatic Association World's Fair of Money, held in Denver that summer, Red Book senior editor Kenneth Bressett and die-variety specialist Bill Fivaz remarked favorably on the coins' faithful recreation of Fraser's original textured-field designs.

Sales of the 2006 Proof coins nearly reached their maximum mintage, with a final audit of 246,267 sold. This astounding number is even more remarkable when compared to the number of Proof one-ounce American Gold Eagles sold that year: a mere 47,092.

Bullion-strike sales exceeded 330,000, the high-level mark for the series. This demand for the American Buffalo gold coins siphoned some sales from the Mint's ongoing American Gold Eagle bullion program, which sold 120,000 fewer one-ounce coins in 2006 than in 2005. The Buffalo outsold the Eagle by more than 100,000 units.

Thanks to these high mintages, coins from the first year of production are readily available on the secondary market. Their value has appreciated with the spot price of gold, with high-grade certified examples commanding a premium from specialists and registry-set collectors.

**Mintage: 337,012 bullion; 246,267 Proof**

| Certified Populations and Retail Market Values | | | | | | | | |
|---|---|---|---|---|---|---|---|---|
| **2006** | **Raw MS** | **<MS-69** | **MS-69** | **MS-70** | **Raw PF** | **<PF-69** | **PF-69** | **PF-70** |
| **Certified** | — | 57 | 37,203 | 43,576 | — | 36 | 13,311 | 16,053 |
| **Value*** | $1,350 | | $1,410 | $1,560 | $1,450 | | $1,525 | $1,725 |

*Recent auctions:* $1,416, MS-69, August 2014 (avg. gold spot value that month, $1,296). $1,675, PF-70DC, March 2015 (avg. gold spot value that month, $1,179).

\* "Raw" value is based on a gold spot price of $1,200 per ounce, and is for an uncertified bullion strike or Proof coin of average quality. This value may vary with the prevailing bullion value.

2007 bullion strike.

# 2007 AMERICAN BUFFALO

*Composition: .9999 gold. **Actual Gold Weight:** 1 ounce. **Diameter:** 32.7 mm. **Thickness:** 2.62 mm (bullion); 2.95 mm (Proof). **Edge:** Reeded. **Mint:** West Point. **Mintmark:** None (for bullion strikes); W (for Proofs). **Issue Price:** spot price plus markup (bullion); $825.95 (Proof). **Release Date:** January (bullion); May 23, 2007 (Proof).*

The novelty of the Mint's new 24-karat gold American Buffalo program wore off during the second year of issue, resulting in lower but still significant sales. The series continued to dominate the online discussion forums such as the Collectors Universe Message Board (forums.collectors.com) and the Collectors Society Message Board (boards.collectors-society.com). Across both product options, hobbyists and investors purchased nearly 200,000 of the coins.

The Proof coins of 2007 had a lower mintage cap than those of 2006, with a maximum issue of 200,000 pieces. "To ensure the broadest and fairest access to United States Mint products, a limit of 100 units per order and per household is in effect," the Mint announced on May 21. "Accordingly, all orders for American Buffalo gold Proof coins will go immediately into backorder status to ensure compliance with this policy. The United States Mint may re-evaluate this limit and adjust or remove it at any time." The limit of 100 coins was later lifted. With gold's spot value rising through the year, climbing nearly $100 per ounce, the Mint later increased the Proof coin price from $825.95 to $899.95. Proof sales for the year were just under 59,000 coins.

The year 2007 marked the beginning of the Mint's second 24-karat gold-coin program. For information on the First Spouse gold coins that debuted this year, see chapter 6.

2007-W Proof.

2008 bullion strike.

2008-W Proof
$5 tenth-ounce.

Mintage: 136,503 bullion; 58,998 Proof

| Certified Populations and Retail Market Values | | | | | | | | |
|---|---|---|---|---|---|---|---|---|
| 2007 | Raw MS | <MS-69 | MS-69 | MS-70 | Raw PF | <PF-69 | PF-69 | PF-70 |
| Certified | — | 8 | 10,942 | 15,103 | — | 18 | 4,406 | 4,863 |
| Value* | $1,360 | | $1,425 | $1,575 | $1,460 | | $1,525 | $1,725 |

*Recent auctions:* $1,410, MS-69, July 2013 (avg. gold spot value that month, $1,287). $1,469, PF-69DC, September 2013 (avg. gold spot value that month, $1,349).

\* "Raw" value is based on a gold spot price of $1,200 per ounce, and is for an uncertified bullion strike or Proof coin of average quality. This value may vary with the prevailing bullion value.

# 2008 AMERICAN BUFFALO

*Composition:* .9999 gold. *Actual Gold Weight:* 1/10 ounce; 1/4 ounce; 1/2 ounce; 1 ounce. *Diameter:* 16.5 mm (1/10 oz.); 22 mm (1/4 oz.); 27 mm (1/2 oz.); 32.7 mm (1 oz.). *Thickness:* 2.62 mm (1-oz. bullion); 2.95 mm (1-oz. Burnished and Proof). *Edge:* Reeded. *Mint:* West Point. *Mintmark:* None (for bullion strikes); W (for collector versions). *Issue Price:* spot price plus markup (bullion); $1,018.88 (Celebration coin); $1,228.88 (Double Prosperity set); various prices (Proof); various prices (Burnished). *Release Dates:* February 5, 2008 (bullion and Celebration coin); July 22, 2008 (Proof and Burnished coins and sets); August 1, 2008 (Double Prosperity set).

For the American Buffalo gold bullion program, the third year was a charm. Collectors had a field day as the U.S. Mint offered more Buffalo varieties and product options in 2008 than in any year before or since. In addition to regular bullion strikes, the Mint produced Proofs; a new numismatic format called *Uncirculated* (cataloged here and in the Red Book as *Burnished*); a Celebration coin; a Double Prosperity set; fractional-ounce Burnished and Proof coins; a four-coin Proof set; and a four-coin Burnished set.

**2008 bullion strikes.** 2008 was the first year of the modern Great Recession—a financially turbulent period that saw Americans abandoning the sorely weakened U.S. dollar, banks, and the stock market, and throwing their cash into silver, gold, and platinum bullion. The U.S. Mint went into overtime to keep up with demand. The American Buffalo's older sister program, the American Gold Eagle, saw sales soar from 140,000 one-ounce coins in 2007 to 710,000 in 2008. Sales of the 24-karat gold Buffalo, while less dramatic, jumped nearly 30 percent, with investors buying 53,000 more bullion-strike coins than in 2007.

Demand spiked in September and in that month actually exceeded the Mint's supply on hand. Authorized Purchasers received a memorandum saying that the Mint was working diligently to meet demand but that its supplies of blanks were "very limited." The Mint temporarily rationed the quantities of coins that Authorized Purchasers could buy. Then the agency was forced to suspend sales for several weeks while it produced an additional 25,000 American Buffalo coins. This final mintage of 2008-dated bullion strikes was put on the market in November and sold until depleted.

The American Buffalo bullion strikes were available only in the one-ounce size that had been offered since 2006.

**2008 Proofs.** The Mint opened sales for its 2008-W American Buffalo Proof coins on July 22. No mintage limits or household ordering limits were set; customer demand would ultimately determine the coins' production.

Market research had led the secretary of the Treasury to authorize the Mint to strike and issue the Proof coins in fractional-ounce sizes in addition to the traditional one-ounce. Mint Director Edmund Moy, who was confirmed in that post by the U.S. Senate in July 2006, recalls, "Planning the fractional American Buffalo coins was one of my early key tasks as director of the Mint."[4]

With gold's market price averaging about $940 per ounce in July 2008, the four Proof sizes, their denominations, and their July 22 issue prices were:

| tenth ounce | $5 | $159.95 |
| quarter ounce | $10 | $329.95 |
| half ounce | $25 | $619.95 |
| one ounce | $50 | $1,199.95 |
| four-coin set | | $2,219.95 |

Each individually sold coin was encapsulated in protective plastic and mounted in an elegant, custom-designed hardwood presentation case with a certificate of authenticity. The four-coin sets included a custom hardwood box with a matte finish and a leatherette embellishment. The interior tray that holds the coins can be positioned at an angle for displaying. In total, 7,803 four-coin Proof sets were bought.

**2008-W Proof $10 quarter-ounce.**

Gold's month-average spot value saw a $100-per-ounce drop from July to August 2008, and then a slower decline through November, in which month it averaged $760 per ounce. Reacting to this decline, and to lower the resulting high premium for its Proof gold coins, the Mint adjusted its pricing for the Proof American Buffalos on November 13, 2008. The following January the Mint would introduce a new sliding-scale pricing structure for its gold and platinum numismatic/collectible offerings (e.g., Proof and Burnished coins). The new structure would allow the Mint to adjust its pricing more nimbly, on a weekly basis, based on the metals' market activity. In the meantime, stuck at their original issue price through the summer and fall of 2008, the Proof American Buffalos were too expensive (compared to their actual bullion value) to be attractive to collectors. Additionally, some collector interest was siphoned off by the year's new Burnished coins. By the time the Proofs' pricing was adjusted downward in mid-November there was little time left for collectors to buy the coins before the Mint moved on, resulting in a very low final mintage for the one-ounce. Because of this low mintage, the 2008-W one-ounce American Buffalo Proof gold coin is ranked among the 100 Greatest U.S. Modern Coins, in the book of the same title by Scott Schechter and Jeff Garrett. "Sales for the Proof gold Buffalo were strong in 2007, with about 60,000 units sold," they note, "but dropped off [to less than one-third that] in 2008. This mintage was surprisingly small and is, by far, the lowest for any Proof one-ounce U.S. gold bullion coin. It is little more than half the lowest figure for any Proof gold Eagle. Among Proof bullion coins, the 2008 Buffalo's low mintage makes this coin an obvious standout."

**2008-W Proof $25 half-ounce.**

**2008-W Proof
$50 one-ounce.**

**2008-W Burnished
$5 tenth-ounce.**

The Mint deemed the fractional-ounce experiment not worthy of repeating, and late in 2008 it announced that it would return to minting only one-ounce American Buffalo coins in 2009. This announcement, coupled with the lowered issue price, led to a quick sellout of its remaining 2008-W Proof coin inventory, after which no more were struck.

Today the 2008-W Proofs command hefty premiums in the secondary market.

**2008 Burnished coins.** 2008 brought another innovation to the American Buffalo program. The Mint introduced to the series a new finish format that had been used on some American Gold Eagles in 2006, 2007, and 2008. Called

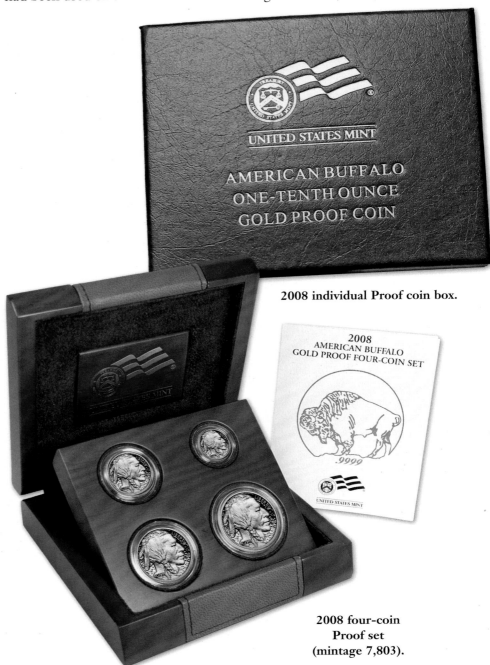

**2008 individual Proof coin box.**

**2008 four-coin
Proof set
(mintage 7,803).**

*Uncirculated* by the Mint to distinguish them from Proofs and regular bullion strikes, coins of this format were struck on specially burnished planchets. The surface finish of a Burnished American Buffalo is difficult to distinguish visually from that of a regular bullion strike, but the presence of a W mintmark (for the West Point Mint) makes it readily identifiable. The mintmark is located on the obverse, to the left of the Indian's neck.

The Burnished coins went on sale July 22, alongside the program's Proof coinage. As with the Proofs, they were made in one-ounce and fractional sizes, sold individually and in four-coin sets. These coins and sets came with special hardwood packaging and certificates of authenticity. Collectors bought a total of 6,049 of the Burnished four-coin sets.

Gold was near a monthly average high for the year when the Burnished coins were released, and they were issue-priced at a premium to reflect their collectible status.

| tenth ounce | $5 | $129.95 |
| quarter ounce | $10 | $289.95 |
| half ounce | $25 | $539.95 |
| one ounce | $50 | $1,059.95 |
| four-coin set | | $1,959.95 |

2008-W Burnished
$10 quarter-ounce.

As gold's market value dropped in August and started a slow decline through the summer and fall, the Burnished coins appeared more and more overpriced relative to their bullion value. Sales were slow until the Mint finally adjusted its prices on November 13. By then the Mint's inventory of tenth-ounce Burnished coins was sold out, and the decision was made not to produce more of that size. In fact, all of the fractional-ounce coins of 2008 would prove to be one-year issues. The Mint in late 2008 announced that it would discontinue the smaller-denomination coins in 2009 and would go back to minting only one-ounce American Buffalo coins.

2008 four-coin Burnished set (mintage 6,049).

2008-W Burnished
$25 half-ounce.

**2008-W Burnished $50 one-ounce.**

The Burnished 2008-W American Buffalo $10 quarter-ounce is ranked no. 94 among the 100 Greatest U.S. Modern Coins, in the book of the same title. Authors Scott Schechter and Jeff Garrett note, "To date, the 2008-W is the only quarter-ounce Uncirculated version of the gold Buffalo coin and, with fewer than 10,000 examples, it's an attractive scarcity." The $5 tenth-ounce is featured in *Top 50 Most Popular Modern Coins*, by Eric Jordan and John Maben, who opine, "If the Mint ever chooses to strike fractional [Burnished] gold Buffalos regularly to complement the fractional Gold Eagles in the bullion program, the 2008-W $5 issue would likely become an immediate and strong key." They write that "its classic good looks, long-term potential, and affordable price make it a collector favorite."

The 2008-W Burnished $50 one-ounce American Buffalo currently leads the herd as the lowest-mintage issue of the entire program. Only 9,074 pieces were sold, making it even scarcer than the $5 tenth-ounce. Like all of the Burnished American Buffalos, it is available on the secondary market only for a very strong premium, particularly when certified at MS-70.

**2008 Celebration Coin.** The year's special numismatic festivities started on February 1 when the Mint announced that in four days a new "Celebration Coin" would be released in time for the Lunar New Year, which would begin February 7. "The American Buffalo 2008 Celebration coin is a special numismatic product, featuring a 24-karat American Buffalo gold coin, being introduced in the year 2008 because the number '8' is traditionally associated with wealth and prosperity in Asian-American cultures," the Mint announced. It was the inaugural product in a line the Mint called its "Celebration Series."

**2008 American Buffalo Celebration coin (mintage: 24,558).**

Edmund Moy, director of the U.S. Mint and himself of Chinese descent, remarked, "In many Asian cultures, there is a tradition of buying gold for loved ones to show how much you care for them. The introduction of the American Buffalo 2008 Celebration coin will be an exceptional opportunity for both first-time Asian-American buyers, as well as our long-term gold-coin collectors."

The product itself consisted of a regular bullion-strike American Buffalo dated 2008, packaged in a plastic capsule and nestled in a bright-red plush gift box with a specially decorated red sleeve. It also included a custom-designed certificate of authenticity that featured the signature of Director Moy and his personal chop mark, a stamp in Chinese characters. Jaime Hernandez, PCGS Price Guide editor, has noted, "There is no difference between a regular non–Celebration coin and a Celebration coin except for the packaging. Therefore PCGS did not recognize these coins any differently and did not implement any special programs or insert labels for the Celebration coins." Max Spiegel, vice president of sales and marketing for NGC, says, "NGC does not offer a special pedigree for these coins. We didn't offer one at the time of issue, and at this point it is not possible to verify that the coin is original to the Mint's packaging."

The idea behind the Mint's new Celebration Series was to offer coins in an outreach initiative to appeal to Americans who were not already collecting them. "The United States Mint will explore introducing various numismatic coin products that are packaged and positioned to celebrate special gift-giving occasions and events," a spokeswoman said. "The American Buffalo 2008 Celebration coin is part of a pilot program to test the viability of this initiative."

While the Celebration coins obviously were geared toward Asian and Asian-American customers, especially as gifts for the Lunar New Year, anyone interested could buy them. The Mint brought the coins to Phoenix, Arizona, as part of its suite of products at the American Numismatic Association's National Money Show in early March 2008. Mint officials described the show as "the perfect opportunity to get newly released United States Mint coin products or obtain 2007-dated options before they are discontinued." That April the coins were featured in the Mint's Spring gift catalog. "Spring is the time of rebirth and renewal," said Director Moy. "And like spring, the products offered in this catalog herald the rebirth of great coin design and a renewed sense of the American spirit." The Celebration coins were also promoted in the Mint's 2008 holiday-season gift catalog, published in October. "Our gift catalog showcases the exceptional artistry of genuine United States Mint coinage," Moy said. "We encourage customers to place their orders early."

Over the course of the 2008 Celebration coin's offering, collectors and investors purchased a total of 24,558 of the specially packaged good-luck coins. This mintage is in addition to the year's main mintage of 189,500 bullion strikes.[5]

**2008 Double Prosperity Set.** On July 22, 2008, the Mint announced that the second product in its Celebration Series would go on sale August 1. Called the Double Prosperity set, it included one American Buffalo half-ounce coin and one American Eagle half-ounce coin, both in the Burnished format. The coins were packaged in an attractive hardwood box with the date 8-08-08 and a certificate of authenticity bearing the facsimile signature of Mint Director Ed Moy and his personal chop mark in red. Many hobbyists remarked on the beauty of the sets' presentation.

"The number '8' is traditionally associated with prosperity in Asian cultures," the Mint noted. "The triple '8' date is highly significant as it occurs only once every 100 years."

The set was issue-priced at $1,228.88, about $120 higher than the combined prices of the two Burnished coins and $400 higher than their bullion value. Many collectors found the premiums disagreeable, and sales were slow. The Mint brought the sets to the nation's largest coin show, the American Numismatic Association World's Fair of Money, held in August 2008 in Baltimore, telling collectors that "It's a great time to purchase a special gift or add a new item to your collection." A week later Mint Director Moy was at the San Francisco Mint, giving invited journalists a tour along with Plant Manager Larry Eckerman and showcasing the appeal of the Double Prosperity set as the

**2008 American Buffalo Double Prosperity set (mintage: 7,751).**

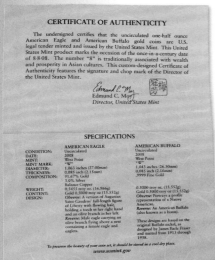

**CERTIFICATE OF AUTHENTICITY**

The undersigned certifies that the uncirculated one-half ounce American Eagle and American Buffalo gold coins are U.S. legal tender minted and issued by the United States Mint. This United States Mint product marks the occasion of the once-in-a-century date of 8-8-08. The number "8" is traditionally associated with wealth and prosperity in Asian cultures. This custom-designed Certificate of Authenticity features the signature and chop mark of the Director of the United States Mint.

*Edmund C. Moy*
Edmund C. Moy
*Director, United States Mint*

**SPECIFICATIONS**

| | AMERICAN EAGLE | AMERICAN BUFFALO |
|---|---|---|
| CONDITION: | Uncirculated | Uncirculated |
| DATE: | 2008 | 2008 |
| MINT: | West Point | West Point |
| MINT MARK: | "W" | "W" |
| DIAMETER: | 1.063 inches (27.00mm) | 1.043 inches (26.50mm) |
| THICKNESS: | 0.085 inch (2.15mm) | 0.083 inch (2.16mm) |
| COMPOSITION: | 91.67% Gold | .9999 Fine Gold |
| | 3.0% Silver | |
| | Balance Copper | |
| WEIGHT: | 0.5455 troy oz. (16.966g) | 0.5000 troy oz. (15.552g) |
| CONTENT: | Gold 0.5000 troy oz (15.552g) | Gold 0.5000 troy oz (15.552g) |
| DESIGN: | *Obverse:* A version of Augustus Saint-Gaudens' full-length figure of Liberty with flowing hair, holding a torch in her right hand and an olive branch in her left. *Reverse:* Male eagle carrying an olive branch flying above a nest containing a female eagle and eaglets. | *Obverse:* Portrays a profile representation of a Native American. *Reverse:* An American Buffalo (also known as a bison). These designs are based on the original Buffalo nickel, as designed by James Earle Fraser and minted from 1913 through 1938. |

To preserve the beauty of your coin set, it should be stored in a cool dry place.
www.usmint.gov

**Double Prosperity set certificate of authenticity.**

world prepared for the upcoming Games of the XXIX Olympiad in Beijing, China. "The 8-8-08 Double Prosperity set presents a once-in-a-lifetime opportunity for coin collectors and the general public," Moy said. "The date 8-8-08 occurs only once every 100 years. To mark this occasion, this is also the first time the United States Mint has paired two gold coins in custom-designed packaging, making this set a unique product for the Asian-American community." The set was highlighted as "well crafted" and "an exceptional gift" in the Mint's 2008 *Gift Catalog*, issued in October. In November the Mint lowered the set's issue price by $150, which removed some of the lingering collector hesitation. Then it sold out its inventory of individual half-ounce Burnished American Buffalos, which made the Double Prosperity set the only primary-market source of the coins. This, too, encouraged more sales late in the year. The final audit of sets sold was 7,751.

Before long the 2008 Double Prosperity set was living up to its name, earning strong prices on the secondary market and bringing financial prosperity to its lucky buyers. Today the set commands a hefty premium of more than double its bullion value.

**Mintage: 17,429 (tenth-ounce Burnished); 18,884 (tenth-ounce Proof)**

| Certified Populations and Retail Market Values, Tenth-Ounce (Burnished and Proof) | | | | | | | | |
|---|---|---|---|---|---|---|---|---|
| **2008** | **Raw MS** | **<MS-69** | **MS-69** | **MS-70** | **Raw PF** | **<PF-69** | **PF-69** | **PF-70** |
| **Certified** | — | 3 | 1,436 | 4,966 | — | 7 | 2,016 | 4,298 |
| **Value*** | $500 | | $530 | $625 | $610 | | $635 | $725 |

*Recent auctions:* $540, MS-70, March 2015 (avg. gold spot value that month, $1,179). $823, PF-70DC, June 2015 (avg. gold spot value that month, $1,182).

\* "Raw" value is based on a gold spot price of $1,200 per ounce, and is for an uncertified Burnished or Proof coin of average quality.

**Mintage: 9,949 (quarter-ounce Burnished); 13,125 (quarter-ounce Proof)**

| Certified Populations and Retail Market Values, Quarter-Ounce (Burnished and Proof) | | | | | | | | |
|---|---|---|---|---|---|---|---|---|
| **2008** | **Raw MS** | **<MS-69** | **MS-69** | **MS-70** | **Raw PF** | **<PF-69** | **PF-69** | **PF-70** |
| **Certified** | — | 8 | 571 | 2,974 | — | 10 | 847 | 3,131 |
| **Value*** | $1,280 | | $1,360 | $1,475 | $1,525 | | $1,575 | $1,750 |

*Recent auctions:* $1,116, MS-70, March 2015 (avg. gold spot value that month, $1,179). $1,300, PF-70DC, July 2015 (avg. gold spot value that month, $1,130).

\* "Raw" value is based on a gold spot price of $1,200 per ounce, and is for an uncertified Burnished or Proof coin of average quality.

**Mintage: 16,908 (half-ounce Burnished); 12,169 (half-ounce Proof)**

| Certified Populations and Retail Market Values, Half-Ounce (Burnished and Proof) | | | | | | | | |
|---|---|---|---|---|---|---|---|---|
| **2008** | **Raw MS** | **<MS-69** | **MS-69** | **MS-70** | **Raw PF** | **<PF-69** | **PF-69** | **PF-70** |
| **Certified** | — | 18 | 1,486 | 3,564 | — | 5 | 1,176 | 3,134 |
| **Value*** | $1,310 | | $1,360 | $1,675 | $1,660 | | $1,725 | $1,850 |

*Recent auctions:* $1,600, MS-70, March 2015 (avg. gold spot value that month, $1,179). $1,234, PF-69DC, September 2013 (avg. gold spot value that month, $1,349).

\* "Raw" value is based on a gold spot price of $1,200 per ounce, and is for an uncertified Burnished or Proof coin of average quality.

**Mintage: 189,500 (one-ounce bullion strike, excluding Celebration coins); 24,558 (Celebration coin); 18,863 (one-ounce Proof)**

| Certified Populations and Retail Market Values, One-Ounce (Bullion and Proof) | | | | | | | | |
|---|---|---|---|---|---|---|---|---|
| **2008** | **Raw MS** | **<MS-69** | **MS-69** | **MS-70** | **Raw PF** | **<PF-69** | **PF-69** | **PF-70** |
| **Certified** | — | 9 | 11,447 | 11,365 | — | 11 | 1,184 | 3,114 |
| **Value*** | $1,350 | | $1,400 | $1,550 | $3,000 | | $3,170 | $3,525 |
| | *Recent auctions:* $1,645, MS-69, March 2014 (avg. gold spot value that month, $1,336). $2,585, PF-69DC, November 2013 (avg. gold spot value that month, $1,276). | | | | | | | |

* "Raw" value is based on a gold spot price of $1,200 per ounce, and is for an uncertified bullion strike or Proof coin of average quality. This value may vary with the prevailing bullion value. 2008 Celebration coins are regular bullion strikes in special U.S. Mint packaging; their mintage is separate from (not included as part of) that of the main mintage of regular bullion strikes. When in their original packaging they command a small premium over the value of the regular bullion strike.

**Mintage: 9,074 (one-ounce Burnished)**

| Certified Populations and Retail Market Values, One-Ounce (Burnished) | | | |
|---|---|---|---|
| **2008** | **Raw MS** | **<MS-69** | **MS-69** | **MS-70** |
| **Certified** | — | 4 | 714 | 2,507 |
| **Value*** | $3,000 | | $3,060 | $3,530 |
| | *Recent auction:* $2,056, MS-69, September 2013 (avg. gold spot value that month, $1,349). | | |

* "Raw" value is based on a gold spot price of $1,200 per ounce, and is for an uncertified Burnished coin of average quality.

**Mintage: 7,803 (four-coin Proof set)**

| Retail Market Values, Four-Coin Proof Set | | | |
|---|---|---|---|
| **2008** | **Raw PF** | **PF-69** | **PF-70** |
| **Value*** | $7,100 | $7,500 | $8,200 |
| | *Recent auction:* $7,475, PF-70UC, May 2011 (avg. gold spot value that month, $1,510). | | |

* "Raw" value is based on a gold spot price of $1,200 per ounce, and is for an uncertified set of Proof coins of average quality in its original U.S. Mint packaging.

**Mintage: 6,049 (four-coin Burnished set)**

| Retail Market Values, Four-Coin Burnished Set | | | |
|---|---|---|---|
| **2008** | **Raw MS** | **MS-69** | **MS-70** |
| **Value*** | $6,550 | $6,675 | $7,150 |
| | *Recent auction:* $6,613, uncertified, August 2010 (avg. gold spot value that month, $1,216). | | |

* "Raw" value is based on a gold spot price of $1,200 per ounce, and is for an uncertified set of Burnished coins of average quality in its original U.S. Mint packaging.

**Mintage: 7,751 (Double Prosperity set)**

| Retail Market Values, Double Prosperity Set | | | |
|---|---|---|---|
| **2008** | **Raw MS** | **MS-69** | **MS-70** |
| **Value*** | $2,900 | $3,000 | $3,100 |
| | *Recent auction:* $2,185, uncertified, September 2010 (avg. gold spot value that month, $1,271). | | |

* "Raw" value is based on a gold spot price of $1,200 per ounce, and is for an uncertified set of Burnished coins (one half-ounce American Buffalo and one half-ounce American Gold Eagle) of average quality in its original U.S. Mint packaging.

# 2009 American Buffalo

**Composition:** *.9999 gold.* **Actual Gold Weight:** *1 ounce.* **Diameter:** *32.7 mm.*
**Thickness:** *2.62 mm (bullion); 2.95 mm (Proof).* **Edge:** *Reeded.*
**Mint:** *West Point.* **Mintmark:** *None (for bullion strikes); W (for Proofs).*
**Issue Price:** *spot price plus markup (bullion); $1,360 (Proof).*
**Release Date:** *October 15, 2009 (bullion); October 29, 2009 (Proof).*

2009 bullion strike.

2009-W Proof.

2009 was a remarkable year for collectors of U.S. gold bullion coins, including the American Buffalos. A combination of factors would lead to the program's second-highest bullion-strike sales and second-*lowest* Proof sales up to that point.

The economic turmoil of 2008 had brought a huge increase in popular demand for precious metals as hedges against inflation. The U.S. Mint was so focused on keeping up with demand for its main gold-bullion program, the American Gold Eagle, that it diverted efforts from other programs through much of 2009. In fact, it even canceled certain collector coins in order to mint as many bullion coins as possible. "Because of unprecedented demand for American Eagle gold and silver bullion coins, the United States Mint suspended production of 2009 Proof and Uncirculated versions of these coins," the Mint announced October 6. "All available 22-karat gold and silver bullion blanks are being allocated to the American Eagle gold and American Eagle silver bullion coin programs, as mandated by Public Law 99-185 and Public Law 99-61, respectively. Both laws direct the agency to produce these coins in quantities sufficient to meet public demand. The Proof and Uncirculated versions of the American Eagle gold and silver coins are not mandated by law."

Until mid-June 2009, the Mint continued its 2008 rationing of the number of coins its Authorized Purchasers could buy. In addition to reserving all of its 22-karat blanks for the American Eagle bullion strikes, the Mint also held off production of its 24-karat American Buffalo coins through the spring, summer, and fall. The hobby community was getting anxious by the summer of 2009, and rumors circulated that the Mint would cancel the regular bullion-strike coins and only make Proofs that year, or possibly cancel the entire program. Although these rumors were unfounded, it would be early winter 2009 before the year's coinage got under way.

In its October 6, 2009, press release, the Mint announced release dates for the stalled American Buffalo bullion-strike and Proof coins. Having been dogged by delays as it worked to meet exploding demand, the Mint stressed that these dates were considered *tentative.* October 15 was the planned release date for the bullion coin, and October 29 for the one-ounce Proof. The fractional-ounce coins in Proof and Burnished formats had already been officially canceled after their 2008 debut (and would never make another appearance in the Mint's product lineup).

As planned, the American Buffalo bullion strikes were released to Authorized Purchasers in mid-October and were galloping into the marketplace on the 15th. Collectors and investors were hungry for the long-delayed coins and by December 4 the Mint's entire production run of 200,000 coins was sold out. No more 2009-dated bullion strikes would be produced. At that point, all gold bullion offerings from the U.S. Mint were either sold out, suspended, or limited. (Sales of the 22-karat one-ounce American Gold Eagle bullion coins were suspended on November 25, 2009. The Mint announced the suspension to Authorized Purchasers in a memo citing a depleted inventory due to "continued strong demand." Additional coins were expected to be available by mid-December.)

No Burnished American Buffalo gold coins were minted in 2009; the 2008-W issues would end up being the program's first and last in that format. "As a result of the numismatic product portfolio analysis conducted late last year," the Mint announced in October, "fractional denominations of the American Buffalo Gold Proof and Uncirculated coins, as well as the American Buffalo four-coin set, are no longer offered for sale."

The Mint's Proof American Buffalos were released on October 29, as tentatively anticipated earlier that month. It was back to business as usual, but with the coins' price based on the Mint's new sliding-scale pricing structure (introduced in January 2009) that followed gold's weekly market value. "Each 2009 American Buffalo gold Proof coin is presented in an elegant hardwood box with a matte finish and a faux leather inset," stated the Mint's promotional literature. "The coins are exhibited on a platform which can stand at an angle for display when the box is open. A custom-designed certificate of authenticity signed by the director of the United States Mint is also included."

As with the year's regular bullion strikes, sales of the 2009-W Proofs were strong, thanks to built-up collector demand. Hobbyists and investors bought more than 19,000 coins in their first three days (exceeding the entire demand of the previous year). The Mint had produced enough inventory to last through March 2010 before the Proofs sold out on the 29th. By that time their price had increased $50, to $1,410. The agency's final audit revealed the 2009-W Proofs to have the second-lowest one-ounce Proof mintage up to that time, totaling just over 49,300 pieces.

**Mintage: 200,000 bullion; 49,306 Proof**

| Certified Populations and Retail Market Values | | | | | | | | |
|---|---|---|---|---|---|---|---|---|
| 2009 | Raw MS | <MS-69 | MS-69 | MS-70 | Raw PF | <PF-69 | PF-69 | PF-70 |
| Certified | — | 18 | 11,580 | 18,517 | — | 4 | 1,429 | 5,517 |
| Value* | $1,360 | | $1,425 | $1,575 | $1,460 | | $1,525 | $1,750 |

*Recent auctions:* $1,469, MS-69, July 2014 (avg. gold spot value that month, $1,311). $1,586, PF-70DC, January 2014 (avg. gold spot value that month, $1,245).

* "Raw" value is based on a gold spot price of $1,200 per ounce, and is for an uncertified bullion strike or Proof coin of average quality. This value may vary with the prevailing bullion value.

# 2010 American Buffalo

*Composition: .9999 gold. **Actual Gold Weight:** 1 ounce. **Diameter:** 32.7 mm.*
***Thickness:** 2.62 mm (bullion); 2.95 mm (Proof). **Edge:** Reeded.*
***Mint:** West Point. **Mintmark:** None (for bullion strikes); W (for Proofs).*
***Issue Price:** spot price plus markup (bullion); $1,510 (Proof).*
***Release Date:** April 29, 2010 (bullion); June 3, 2010 (Proof).*

2010 bullion strike.

2010-W Proof.

Production and distribution of American Buffalo bullion-strike coins was off to a smoother start in 2010 than it had been in 2009. The Mint's controlled rationing of bullion coins available to its Authorized Purchasers was lifted in March 2010. The year's new American Buffalo coins were available in late April through the distribution network of Authorized Purchasers and their secondary retailers. The market value of gold had been on a slow but steady climb since February, and, excepting a dip in July, the metal's spot price continued its gentle climb all year. Customer demand for the 24-karat gold coins was steady. It took five months for collectors and investors to buy the entire 209,000-coin press run, and on September 27 the Mint announced the close of sales for the 2010 bullion strikes. The agency's memo to Authorized Purchasers was short and to the point: "The United States Mint has depleted its inventory of 2010 American Buffalo One Ounce Gold Bullion Coins. No additional inventory will be made available."

The year's Proofs went on sale June 3, 2010, with collectors able to buy the coins directly from the Mint. Gold's spot value in May had averaged $1,205 per ounce, and the Proof American Buffalo coins went on sale at $1,510. The hobby community absorbed 12,778 Proofs as of June 8, and then an average of about 110 coins per day for the next 11 months. CoinUpdate.com reported on the first month of sales on July 7:

> By June 13, 2010, sales of 17,465 coins had been recorded. In the following two weekly periods, sales of 2,054 and 1,540 were recorded. This week sales have slowed down even more to just 798 coins. After roughly one month of availability total sales have now reached 21,857. Last year's 2009 Proof gold Buffalo had managed to sell 37,885 coins after one month's time.

As gold's spot price increased the Mint adjusted the Proofs' price based on its published sliding-scale structure. Its inventory of Proof coins lasted into May of 2011, with the sellout of the 2010-W Proofs being announced on May 10. After final auditing, the mintage of 2010-W Proof American Buffalo coins was 49,263—just under the 49,306 2009-W coins (which had sold in half the time).

**Mintage: 209,000 bullion; 49,263 Proof**

| 2010 | Raw MS | <MS-69 | MS-69 | MS-70 | Raw PF | <PF-69 | PF-69 | PF-70 |
|---|---|---|---|---|---|---|---|---|
| Certified | — | 15 | 5,264 | 9,405 | — | 7 | 869 | 3,585 |
| Value* | $1,360 | | $1,425 | $1,575 | $1,460 | | $1,525 | $1,725 |

*Recent auctions:* $1,410, MS-70, November 2013 (avg. gold spot value that month, $1,276). $1,528, PF-70DC, March 2015 (avg. gold spot value that month, $1,179).

\* "Raw" value is based on a gold spot price of $1,200 per ounce, and is for an uncertified bullion strike or Proof coin of average quality. This value may vary with the prevailing bullion value.

# 2011 AMERICAN BUFFALO

**Composition:** *.9999 gold.* **Actual Gold Weight:** *1 ounce.* **Diameter:** *32.7 mm.*
**Thickness:** *2.62 mm (bullion); 2.95 mm (Proof).* **Edge:** *Reeded.*
**Mint:** *West Point.* **Mintmark:** *None (for bullion strikes); W (for Proofs).*
**Issue Price:** *spot price plus markup (bullion); $1,760 (Proof).*
**Release Date:** *March 14, 2011 (bullion); May 19, 2011 (Proof).*

The bullion-strike American Buffalo gold coins of 2011 were offered earlier in the year than the 2010 issue had been. The U.S. Mint's network of Authorized Purchasers and their secondary retailers was selling the coins to the public by March 14. There were no ordering limits placed by the Mint on its Authorized Purchasers, unlike in the earlier years of the Great Recession, when demand often exceeded the immediate supply of coinage blanks.

Gold was strong through much of 2011, with its spot price surging nearly $250 that summer and its annual average going up $450 compared to 2010. Customer demand for the 2011 bullion coins started slower than for 2010. On March 30, editor Dave Harper of *Numismatic News* wrote:

> The gold Buffalo bullion coin seems to be a one-week wonder. Only 4,000 coins were sold this week as compared to last week's debut number of 31,000. Naturally the rhythm of the marketplace dictates weekly sales totals, but is buyer interest in this coin already limited?[6]

**2011 bullion strike.**

A total of 38,000 coins were sold in March. By the time the bullion-strike inventory sold out, the final mintage stood at 174,500.

On May 10, 2011, the Mint's associate director for sales and marketing announced that the agency was increasing the price of the American Buffalo bullion-coin presentation boxes it sold to retailers. "A lot of 100 presentation cases will be offered for sale at a price of $299.95."

The 2011-W Proof American Buffalo gold coins went on sale May 19, 2011, about a week after the 2010 Proof sold out. Gold had been on the rise since January, and the issue price was set at $1,760, the highest in the program's history. Collector interest was slow to build given the higher cost. Another factor may have been at work: competition for collectors' hobby budgets. The Mint's congressionally mandated requirement to focus first on *bullion-coin* production, at the expense of limited-edition collector-format coins, had been lifted in late 2010. This allowed the Mint to create more collector coins in 2011, including resuming the Burnished format of the popular American Gold Eagle. For whatever combination of reasons, sales of the 2011-W American Buffalo were down about 40 percent compared to 2010.

**Mintage: 174,500 bullion; 28,683 Proof**

| Certified Populations and Retail Market Values | | | | | | | | |
|---|---|---|---|---|---|---|---|---|
| **2011** | **Raw MS** | **<MS-69** | **MS-69** | **MS-70** | **Raw PF** | **<PF-69** | **PF-69** | **PF-70** |
| **Certified** | — | 1 | 4,690 | 5,672 | — | 2 | 564 | 2,943 |
| **Value*** | $1,360 | | $1,425 | $1,575 | $1,460 | | $1,580 | $1,780 |
| | *Recent auctions:* $1,410, MS-70, November 2014 (avg. gold spot value that month, $1,176). $1,586, PF-70DC, August 2014 (avg. gold spot value that month, $1,296). | | | | | | | |

**2011-W Proof.**

* "Raw" value is based on a gold spot price of $1,200 per ounce, and is for an uncertified bullion strike or Proof coin of average quality. This value may vary with the prevailing bullion value.

# 2012 American Buffalo

**Composition:** .9999 gold. **Actual Gold Weight:** 1 ounce. **Diameter:** 32.7 mm.
**Thickness:** 2.62 mm (bullion); 2.95 mm (Proof). **Edge:** Reeded.
**Mint:** West Point. **Mintmark:** None (for bullion strikes); W (for Proofs).
**Issue Price:** spot price plus markup (bullion); $1,960 (Proof).
**Release Date:** March 5, 2012 (bullion); March 15, 2010 (Proof).

*2012 bullion strike.*

The Mint's network of Authorized Purchasers began distributing 2012 American Buffalo bullion coins on March 5, 2012. Gold had started the year strong, averaging $1,656 and $1,743 per ounce in January and February, but by early March it was sliding downward. Initial sales for the 2012 American Buffalo were slow, with 5,500 coins sold on the first day. Overall investors bought about 25 percent fewer coins than in 2011. (Sales were similarly weaker in the Mint's American Gold Eagle program for 2012.)

The 2012-W Proof American Buffalo debuted for sale on March 15, priced at $1,960 according to the Mint's sliding-scale structure that followed the weekly spot value of gold. Despite the Mint's best efforts to get the hobby community excited about the coins (including bringing them to the American Numismatic Association's two annual coin shows, the National Money Show held in Denver in May, and the World's Fair of Money held in Philadelphia in August), collector interest was low. The Mint's production inventory lasted into mid-January 2013. The final mintage of just under 20,000 coins was a continuation of the Proofs' downward trend of recent years.

**Mintage: 132,000 bullion; 19,715 Proof**

| Certified Populations and Retail Market Values | | | | | | | | |
|---|---|---|---|---|---|---|---|---|
| 2012 | Raw MS | <MS-69 | MS-69 | MS-70 | Raw PF | <PF-69 | PF-69 | PF-70 |
| Certified | — | 1 | 1,348 | 2,800 | — | 6 | 455 | 2,352 |
| Value* | $1,360 | | $1,430 | $1,585 | $1,465 | | $1,625 | $2,225 |
| | *Recent auctions:* $1,586, MS-70, April 2014 (avg. gold spot value that month, $1,299). $1,998, PF-70DC, October 2014 (avg. gold spot value that month, $1,222). | | | | | | | |

\* "Raw" value is based on a gold spot price of $1,200 per ounce, and is for an uncertified bullion strike or Proof coin of average quality. This value may vary with the prevailing bullion value.

# 2013 American Buffalo

**Composition:** .9999 gold. **Actual Gold Weight:** 1 ounce. **Diameter:** 32.7 mm.
**Thickness:** 2.62 mm (bullion); 2.95 mm (Proof and Reverse Proof).
**Edge:** Reeded. **Mint:** West Point. **Mintmark:** None (for bullion strikes);
W (for collector versions). **Issue Price:** spot price plus markup (bullion);
$1,790 (Proof); $1,640 (Reverse Proof). **Release Date:** January 2, 2013
(bullion); May 23, 2013 (Proof); August 8, 2013 (Reverse Proof).

*2012-W Proof.*

The numismatic new year kicked off with American Gold Eagles and American Buffalos debuting for sale on the same day, January 2, 2013. Once again, Authorized Purchasers' access to the bullion strikes was unrestricted by rationing, and investors herded together an impressive 72,500 of the Buffalo coins in January. After the initial excitement (a typical spike seen in most first-month sales), demand backed off to 11,500 coins in February and 11,000 in March—but even with the slowdown, 2013's first-quarter sales were more than double those of 2012.

On the world markets, gold's month-average spot price dropped more than $100 per ounce between March and April, nearly $200 lower than its January average. The cheaper metal fueled an increase in American Buffalo sales in April, up to 37,000 coins. By the end of that month, the 2013 coins had reached sales equal to the entire mintage of 2012. Gold's value continued to decline through June, rallied a bit in the summer, and then resumed its downward trend. This activity helped maintain investor interest in the Mint's 24-karat American Buffalo bullion coins. By the time the inventory sold out, 239,000 coins were accounted for. This was nearly double the program's sales for 2012.

In April 2013 the U.S. Mint announced that it would release a special Reverse Proof version of the American Buffalo later in the year, to commemorate the 100th anniversary of the debut of James Earle Fraser's Buffalo nickel.

Before the Reverse Proof was launched, the Mint released the usual Proof version for sale on May 23. Collector anticipation of the exotic Reverse Proof stole some thunder from the herd of Buffalo Proofs, and 2013 sales ended up being the lowest in the one-ounce Proof's history. By the time the Mint's inventory sold out on December 10, the 2013-W logged in at 18,594 sold. The previous low had been the 2008-W Proof at 18,863.

The Reverse Proof, meanwhile, was the talk of the hobby community through the spring and summer. On June 10, 2013, Paul Gilkes of *Coin World* described the production process of the special Reverse Proof coins:

2013 bullion strike.

> At 8:45 a.m. Eastern Daylight Time June 4, the first Reverse Proof 2013-W American Buffalo $50 gold coin was struck at the West Point Mint, inaugurating full-scale production for an issue to be offered by the U.S. Mint later this year.
>
> After the 1-ounce .9999 fine gold coin was struck, it was placed inside a special envelope on which was recorded the date, time and shift of production, serial numbers of the obverse and reverse dies used, and identification of the specific Gräbener coinage press on which the coin was struck.
>
> The enveloped coin was then secured inside a vault to preserve the historical record for the issue.
>
> The obverse and reverse dies on the Gräbener GMP 360 coinage press used to produce the Reverse Proof coins are oriented to strike with a vertical motion. The upper or hammer die bears the American Buffalo coin's obverse image, while the lower or anvil die carries the reverse design.
>
> A press operator feeds the planchets between the coinage dies one at a time by hand, using dedicated tongs.
>
> Each coin is struck three times between the dies, with each strike of the dies exerting 120 tons of pressure, to ensure the planchet's metal completely fills the design elements in the obverse and reverse dies. The outward expansion of the coin is restrained by a reeded edge collar die, which imparts the reeded edge.
>
> After the three designated strikes, the collar retracts and the struck coin rests on top of the anvil die until it can be safely removed with tongs.[7]

2013-W Proof.

On July 11 the Mint released more news about the upcoming coin:

> Collectors, mark your calendars! The United States Mint will begin accepting orders for the 2013 American Buffalo Gold Reverse Proof coin (product code BV1) at noon Eastern Time (ET) on August 8, 2013. The

**2013-W Reverse Proof.**

coin will be available for a four-week period ending September 5 at 5 p.m. (ET). There is no mintage limit for this prod uct. Customer demand will determine the number of coins produced. The coin is being minted and sold to mark the 100th anniversary of the designs appearing on the original Type I Buffalo nickel.

The American Buffalo Gold Reverse Proof coin is struck in .9999 fine, 24-karat gold at the United States Mint at West Point. The coin is produced in the same manner as a traditional Proof coin. However, unlike the traditional Proof coin, which has a mirror-like background and frosted design elements, the Reverse Proof coin has a frosted background and mirror-like design elements.

The coin's obverse (heads) and reverse (tails) designs are based on James Earle Fraser's original designs, first appearing in 1913. The obverse depicts the profile of a Native American, while the reverse depicts an American buffalo (also known as a bison). Each coin is presented in an elegant matte-finish hardwood box with a faux leather inset. A certificate of authenticity is included.

Collectors were understandably excited about the potential of the new Reverse Proof American Buffalos. A Reverse Proof finish had been used on the 2006-W American Gold Eagle one-ounce coin, and that issue was already a strong winner in the secondary marketplace. Reverse Proofs in the American Silver Eagle series also were popular and valuable. The American Buffalo program hadn't seen a new variety since 2008, when fractional-ounce sizes and Burnished coins had been available for a single year. As Scott Schechter and Jeff Garrett write in *100 Greatest U.S. Modern Coins*, "There was never a time that collectors weren't asking for a Reverse Proof gold Buffalo. The coin debuted in 2006, the same year as the 20th-anniversary Reverse Proof gold and silver American eagles. As new Reverse Proof silver eagles came out in 2011 and 2012, collectors were asking, 'Where is the Reverse Proof Buffalo?!'" From the spring of 2013 until early August, hobbyists lit up the online discussion boards and wrote letters to the editors of the trade papers about the soon-to-be-released coins.

The hobby's pent-up demand exploded on Thursday, August 8, when the Reverse Proof coins finally went on sale. Within 30 minutes 12,630 of the coins were ordered. The next day that number was pushed to 21,009 coins—more than what would be the year's entire mintage of the Proof format. That weekend sales reached 24,883.

The Mint had been offering free standard shipping and reduced expedited shipping on Web orders since July 26 (an offer that would run through September 30), which sweetened the deal for collectors ordering the Reverse Proof online.

Adding further to the excitement around the Reverse Proof coin, the Mint teamed up with the Bureau of Engraving and Printing at a shared booth at the American Numismatic Association World's Fair of Money in Chicago, the week after sales started. "The BEP and Mint are very pleased to announce that Treasurer of the United States Rosie Rios will attend the ANA World's Fair of Money convention on Thursday, August 15. Treasurer Rios will hold a public forum to take questions from the audience and to discuss issues pertaining to the BEP, the Mint, and Department of the Treasury."

At the ANA show, Mint Deputy Director Richard A. Peterson took part in the ribbon-cutting ceremony on August 13, signed autographs, and held a public forum. He also brought 1,000 of the new Reverse Proof American Buffalo coins to the U.S. Mint booth, giving the collecting public its first chance to see the coins before purchasing them. This was fuel added to the Reverse Proof fire, and all 1,000 coins sold out that afternoon. Soon dealers at the show were offering premiums to anyone who had bought one of the coins and was willing to part with it. NGC and PCGS began grading the coins and slabbing them with special "Chicago ANA" labels. The Mint quickly ordered another 1,000 coins shipped up from West Point to the show to meet collector demand. These "went on sale Friday," reported editor Dave Harper of *Numismatic News*. "The purchase limitation was reduced from Tuesday's five coins to three coins. The result was the lines became lengthier and lasted longer than on Tuesday."[8]

Michael Zielinski reported on the Reverse Proof sales in a September 10, 2013, column at CoinUpdate.com:

> For the remainder of the sales period, the odometer [at the Mint's Web site] was updated each weekday with a new total. The sales changes between updates ranged from a low of 263 units to a high of 2,548 units. During the course of the offering, the U.S. Mint also sold 1,000 units from their booth at the ANA convention on both August 13 and August 16.
>
> For the final days of availability, sales moved up by 1,683 units, 1,434 units, and 1,924 units to conclude at 47,836. This sales total is preliminary and indicated as an approximation of orders accepted through all sales channels. It will be subject to adjustments due to order cancellations and returns. As it stands, the final indicated sales figure is far below the high for a numismatic issue of the series established by the 2006 Proof at 246,267 units, but well above the low of 9,074 units for the one ounce 2008-W Uncirculated [Burnished] coin.

The new Reverse Proof format, and the excitement ignited around its debut and sale, was a shot in the arm for the American Buffalo program. Even though the quantity placed the Reverse Proof among the higher-mintage issues of the series, it continues to command a premium above most others in the secondary market. It was ranked no. 74 in the third edition of *100 Greatest U.S. Modern Coins*, with authors Schechter and Garrett remarking, "As the only Reverse Proof in the series and without another on the horizon, the long-term outlook for this issue to remain one of the 100 Greatest U.S. Modern Coins is very good."

**Mintage: 239,000 bullion; 18,599 Proof**

| Certified Populations and Retail Market Values, Bullion and Proof | | | | | | | | |
|---|---|---|---|---|---|---|---|---|
| **2013** | **Raw MS** | **<MS-69** | **MS-69** | **MS-70** | **Raw PF** | **<PF-69** | **PF-69** | **PF-70** |
| **Certified** | — | 6 | 1,175 | 7,003 | — | 3 | 541 | 2,745 |
| **Value\*** | $1,360 | | $1,420 | $1,525 | $1,460 | | $1,625 | $2,230 |
| *Recent auctions:* $1,293, MS-70, April 2015 (avg. gold spot value that month, $1,198). $2,233, PF-70DC, June 2015 (avg. gold spot value that month, $1,182). | | | | | | | | |

\* "Raw" value is based on a gold spot price of $1,200 per ounce, and is for an uncertified bullion strike or Proof coin of average quality. This value may vary with the prevailing bullion value.

**2014 bullion strike.**

**2014-W Proof.**

**Mintage: 47,836 Reverse Proof**

| Certified Populations and Retail Market Values, Reverse Proof | | | | |
|---|---|---|---|---|
| 2013 | Raw MS | <MS-69 | MS-69 | MS-70 |
| Certified | — | 79 | 4,091 | 8,875 |
| Value* | $1,710 | | $1,765 | $2,075 |

*Recent auction:* $1,934, PF-70, June 2015 (avg. gold spot value that month, $1,182).

\* "Raw" value is based on a gold spot price of $1,200 per ounce, and is for an uncertified Reverse Proof coin of average quality. This value may vary with the prevailing bullion value.

# 2014 American Buffalo

*Composition: .9999 gold. **Actual Gold Weight:** 1 ounce. **Diameter:** 32.7 mm. **Thickness:** 2.62 mm (bullion); 2.95 mm (Proof). **Edge:** Reeded. **Mint:** West Point. **Mintmark:** None (for bullion strikes); W (for collector versions). **Issue Price:** spot price plus markup (bullion); $1,640 (Proof). **Release Date:** January 2, 2014 (bullion); May 8, 2014 (Proof).*

Distribution of the 2014-dated American Buffalo bullion strike began on January 2, 2014, with investors buying 41,500 of the coins that month. Sales flattened to 12,000 coins per month in February and March. Gold's spot price was rising in the marketplace, but a downturn in April brought an increase in American Buffalo purchases—up to 17,500 that month. The year's sales closed at 177,500 coins total, a respectable quantity but about 25 percent short of 2013.

The 2014-W Proof went on sale May 8, with no mintage cap and no household ordering limits, as was usual for the American Buffalo program. The coin enjoyed an early surge of collector interest, perhaps riding the tailcoats of the 2013-W Reverse Proof and the low-mintage 2013-W Proof. Hobbyists and investors bought almost 8,000 of the 2014-W in its first week of sales. "This is much stronger than the opening sales figures for the product over the past two years," noted Michael Zielinski in a May 13, 2014, report at CoinUpdate. com. "The 2013-dated offering had opened with sales of 4,863 pieces and the 2012-dated offering had opened at 4,110 units."

As was the case in 2013, the year's Proof coins were featured in the Mint's lineup at the American Numismatic Association World's Fair of Money, again held in Chicago in August 2014. In December the Mint's inventory was declared sold out, with the mintage standing at 20,557.

**Mintage: 180,500 bullion; 20,557 Proof**

| Certified Populations and Retail Market Values | | | | | | | | |
|---|---|---|---|---|---|---|---|---|
| 2014 | Raw MS | <MS-69 | MS-69 | MS-70 | Raw PF | <PF-69 | PF-69 | PF-70 |
| Certified | — | 0 | 1,534 | 5,094 | — | 0 | 383 | 2,479 |
| Value* | $1,360 | | $1,425 | $1,530 | $1,600 | | $1,680 | $1,900 |

*Recent auctions:* $1,410, MS-70, August 2015 (avg. gold spot value that month, $1,117). $1,645, PF-70UC, April 2015 (avg. gold spot value that month, $1,198).

\* "Raw" value is based on a gold spot price of $1,200 per ounce, and is for an uncertified bullion strike or Proof coin of average quality. This value may vary with the prevailing bullion value.

# 2015 AMERICAN BUFFALO

**Composition:** *.9999 gold.* **Actual Gold Weight:** *1 ounce.* **Diameter:** *32.7 mm.*
**Thickness:** *2.62 mm (bullion); 2.95 mm (Proof).* **Edge:** *Reeded.* **Mint:*
*West Point.* **Mintmark:** *None (for bullion strikes); W (for collector versions).*
**Issue Price:** *spot price plus markup (bullion); $1,590 (Proof).*
**Release Date:** *January 2015 (bullion); April 9, 2015 (Proof).*

Sale of the 2015 bullion version of the American Buffalo gold coins started that January, with investors buying 34,500 of the coins in the first month—a 16 percent decrease from the previous year's opening month. For several months sales were weaker than in 2014, perhaps a cautious reaction to gold's long downward trend on the international markets, but by August had reached 146,000 coins, nearly a third of that quantity thanks to a dramatic surge in June and July. This was an increase compared to the 125,000 coins sold in the same eight-month period in 2014.

The U.S. Mint brought samples of the 2015-W American Buffalo Proof coins to the Whitman Coin and Collectibles Expo in Baltimore in March 2015, giving the public an advance look at the year's coins. Sales of the coins started on April 9, with the initial pricing set at $1,590—the lowest Proof release price since the 2010 issue. In June, Paul Gilkes of *Coin World* reported: "Current sales recorded by the U.S. Mint for the Proof 2015-W American Buffalo $50 gold coin are half of the coin's 2014 sales totals. The U.S. Mint's latest sales report indicates 10,821 of the 2015-W American Buffalo gold Proof coins were sold through June 14."[9]

**2015 bullion strike.**

Later in the year, the Mint brought the Proof coins as part of its suite of products at the American Numismatic Association World's Fair of Money, held in August in Chicago. Customers who bought the coin at the show received a complimentary reusable bag with images of former President and First Lady John and Jackie Kennedy (a tie-in to the Jackie Kennedy First Spouse gold coin launched that year).

Although all mintages of recent years are considered unsettled until the Mint's official final audit (which accounts for returns), based on sales figures into the fourth quarter it appears 2015's mintages will be higher than those of 2014. The American Buffalos remain a popular way for investors and collectors to add 24-karat gold to their portfolios and coin collections.

**Mintage: ~181,500 bullion (as of November 2015);
~15,411 Proof (as of November 2015)**

| Certified Populations and Retail Market Values | | | | | | | | |
|---|---|---|---|---|---|---|---|---|
| 2015 | Raw MS | <MS-69 | MS-69 | MS-70 | Raw PF | <PF-69 | PF-69 | PF-70 |
| Certified | — | 0 | 1,664 | 3,529 | — | 2 | 262 | 1,772 |
| Value* | $1,350 | | $1,400 | $1,500 | $1,590 | | $1,640 | $1,825 |
| | *Recent auction:* $1,410, MS-70, August 2015 (avg. gold spot value that month, $1,117). | | | | | | | |

\* "Raw" value is based on a gold spot price of $1,200 per ounce, and is for an uncertified bullion strike or Proof coin of average quality. This value may vary with the prevailing bullion value.

**2015-W Proof.**

Dolley Madison re-enactor Lucinda Frailly of Canton, Ohio, in period costume, describing Madison's accomplishments to First Lady Laura Bush and Mint Director Edmund Moy during the unveiling of the final First Spouse gold bullion coin of 2007.

# 6

# The First Spouse Gold Bullion Coins (2007–2016)

**B**y 2007 the United States was more than 20 years into its successful modern gold-bullion programs. Collectors and investors were buying hundreds of thousands of ounces of American Gold Eagles annually. The American Buffalo 24-karat coins had been introduced the year before and were off to a galloping start. Next in the lineup was a gold-coinage series designed as a companion to the Mint's soon-to-roll-out Presidential dollars. The new bullion program's 24-karat coins would honor and commemorate the nation's First Ladies.

## DETAILS OF THE PRESIDENTIAL $1 COIN ACT

The Presidential $1 Coin Act of 2005 (Public Law 109-145) was the legislation that authorized the U.S. Mint's First Spouse gold bullion coins. It was enacted "to require the secretary of the Treasury to mint coins in commemoration of each of the nation's past presidents and their spouses, respectively, to improve circulation of the $1 coin, to create a new bullion coin, and for other purposes."[1] The act was considered and passed in the Senate on November 18, 2005; considered and passed in the House on December 13; and signed into law by President George W. Bush on December 22.

Relevant to the First Spouse coins, the text of the act noted the following:

**The First Spouse gold bullion coins are the same diameter as the Presidential dollar each corresponds to. (shown 1.5x actual size)**

"First Spouses have not generally been recognized on American coinage."

"Although the Congress has authorized the Secretary of the Treasury to issue gold coins with a purity of 99.99 percent, the Secretary has not done so." [This was in 2005, when the American Buffalo 24-karat gold coins had yet to be released.]

"Bullion coins are a valuable tool for the investor and, in some cases, an important aspect of coin collecting."

The 2005 act ordered that, starting in 2007 to coincide with the debut of the Presidential dollar coins, "the Secretary shall issue bullion coins . . . that are emblematic of the spouse of [each] President." It spelled out the coins' specifications: they would have the same diameter as the Presidential dollars [26.5 mm]; they would weigh 1/2 ounce; and they would contain 99.99% pure gold. In terms of designs, the obverse of each coin would feature:

the name and likeness of the spouse of each president during the president's period of service,

the years during which she was the spouse of the president during the president's period of service, and

a number indicating the order of the period of service in which such president served.

On each coin's reverse:

images emblematic of the life and work of the First Spouse whose image is borne on the obverse,

the inscription "United States of America," and

an inscription of the nominal denomination of the coin, $10.

The legislation's focus on *First Spouses* rather than *First Ladies* avoided any confusion over cases where a president was widowed or unmarried and the usual ceremonial functions of First Lady were carried out by a daughter or other relative; or if he was married but someone other than his wife performed some or all of the duties typically assigned to the First Lady (as was the case when various presidential wives were too sick or frail).

In cases where a president served without a spouse, the act ordered that "the image on the obverse of the bullion coin corresponding to the $1 coin relating to such President shall be an image emblematic of the concept of 'Liberty'—

"as represented on a United States coin issued during the period of service of such President; or

as represented, in the case of President Chester Alan Arthur, by a design incorporating the name and likeness of Alice Paul, a leading strategist in the suffrage movement, who was instrumental in gaining women the right to vote upon the adoption of the 19th amendment and thus the ability to participate in the election of future Presidents, and who was born on January 11, 1885, during the term of President Arthur; and

The Mint struck special bronze medals as companions to the gold First Spouse bullion coins. (shown enlarged)

the reverse of such bullion coin shall be of a design representative of themes of such President, except that in the case of [the Alice Paul coin] the reverse of such coin shall be representative of the suffrage movement."

The act further specified that if two presidential spouses served during an executive term (in the case of death of one and remarriage to another), a separate coin would be designed and issued for each.

# DESIGNERS OF THE
# FIRST SPOUSE GOLD COINS

Some U.S. Mint coinage designers are full-time Treasury employees who work in the sculpting-engraving department at the Philadelphia Mint. Others are talented outside designers brought into the mix through the Mint's Artistic Infusion Program, launched in 2003.

The Mint's team of sculptor-engravers and medallic sculptors in Philadelphia, all of whom have designed and engraved First Spouse coins, includes the following artists (in the order they started working at the Mint):

**Jim Licaretz.** A graduate of the Pennsylvania Academy of the Fine Arts, Jim Licaretz earned a J. Henry Schiedt Memorial Travel Scholarship as well as a Philadelphia Board of Education four-year scholarship. From 1986 to 1989 he held a position as a medallic sculptor with the U.S. Mint. He worked for Franklin Porcelain and the Franklin Mint, was a master sculptor at Mattel, and managed the sculpting department at Artistic Solutions and Production in California, in addition to holding faculty positions at the Fleisher Art Memorial in Philadelphia, Otis School of Art and Design in Los Angeles, and Academy of Art College in San Francisco. After studying abroad he returned to the U.S. Mint as a medallic sculptor in 2006. Licaretz's work can be seen at the British Museum, the Royal Coin Cabinet, the National Museum of Economy in Stockholm, the American Numismatic Society, and the Smithsonian Institution.

**Mint Medallic Sculptor Jim Licaretz at work. Today all of the Mint's engraving staff use computer-aided design in addition to traditional sketching.**

**Sculptor-Engraver
Charles Vickers at
the Philadelphia Mint.**

**Tools and clay used by
Mint Sculptor-Engraver
Don Everhart to design
First Spouse gold coins and
other numismatic works.**

**Charles L. Vickers.** Born and raised in northeast Texas, Charles Vickers served in the U.S. Army's 101st Airborne Division, then studied at New York's Art Students League and Frank Reilly School of Art, as well as the Pratt Institute and the School of Visual Arts. In 1976 he moved to Pennsylvania and started a successful career at the Franklin Mint. He left as a senior sculptor in 1985 and launched his own business, an art studio that gained worldwide recognition. His private sculpting credits include the official medal of the Ronald Reagan Library, the official christening medal of the USS *Ronald Reagan*, the Pope John Paul II 25th-Anniversary Medal, and the official presidential inaugural medal of George W. Bush. Vickers joined the U.S. Mint's sculpting-engraving staff in December 2003. He crafts many of his coinage and medallic designs "the old-fashioned way," in bas-relief, while also working with the department's modern computer programs.

**Don Everhart.** Born in York, Pennsylvania, Don Everhart earned his Bachelor of Fine Arts in painting from Kutztown State University in 1972. He joined the Franklin Mint as a designer in 1973 and rose to the position of staff sculptor. In 1980 he left to develop his freelance career, working in figurines, plates, coins, medals, and other media for such prominent firms as Walt Disney and Tiffany, as well as international mints including the Royal Norwegian Mint and British Royal Mint. Everhart's numerous sculptural commissions include a 24-piece bronze installation for Georgetown University's Sports Hall of Fame. His work has been exhibited internationally and resides in several permanent collections, including those of the Smithsonian Institution, the British Museum, the American Numismatic Society, and the National Sculpture Society. Everhart joined the U.S. Mint's team of sculptor-engravers in January 2004.

**Sketches and plaster
models of the 2013 Ida
McKinley First Spouse
coin, in Medallic Sculptor
Phebe Hemphill's office,
Philadelphia Mint
engraving department.**

**Joseph F. Menna.** College for Joseph Menna was the University of the Arts in Philadelphia and graduate school at the New York Academy of Art in Manhattan, supplemented by studies at the Pennsylvania Academy of the Fine Arts, the Art Students League, and the Sculpture Center. He finished his studies in Russia, then worked as a figure sculptor at an American fine-art foundry, creating monumental and life-sized statues and portraits. His work in the world of collectible sculpture includes clients such as DC Entertainment, Mattel, Fisher-Price, and Hasbro. Menna had 18 years of professional experience in traditional and digital art before he joined the staff of the U.S. Mint as its first full-time digitally skilled artist in 2005. "He became a teacher and a mentor to the Mint's staff in everything related to digital sculpting," recalls retired chief engraver John Mercanti. "I nicknamed him the 'Yoda' of the new technology."[2] In addition to his work for the Mint, Menna maintains an active freelance career and is recognized internationally as a leader in digital sculpture.

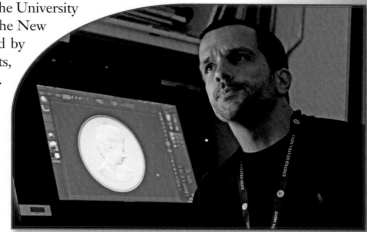

**Mint Medallic Sculptor Joseph Menna with a computer model and sketches of the 2013 Edith Roosevelt First Spouse coin.**

**Phebe Hemphill.** A graduate of the Pennsylvania Academy of the Fine Arts and a student of sculptor EvAngelos Frudakis in Philadelphia, Phebe Hemphill joined the sculpture department of the Franklin Mint in 1987. For 15 years she worked there on many porcelain and medallic projects. She was a staff sculptor for three years with McFarlane Toys in Bloomingdale, New Jersey, before joining the U.S. Mint as a medallic sculptor in 2006. Her freelance work has included sculpture in figurines, medallions, dolls, toys, and garden ornaments, and her artistry has been exhibited by the National Sculpture Society, the American Medallic Sculpture Association, West Chester University, and the F.A.N. Gallery in Philadelphia.

**Michael Gaudioso.** A graduate of the University of the Fine Arts in Philadelphia, Michael Gaudioso earned a Master of Fine Arts from the New York Academy Graduate School of Figurative Art. In the 1990s he studied sculpture at the Repin Institute in St. Petersburg, Russia. Gaudioso is a classically trained draftsman and sculptor and has taught figure drawing at Villanova University. He worked as a master painter and designer for America's oldest and largest stained-glass studio, Willet Hauser, before joining the U.S. Mint in 2009. His work for the Mint includes a combination of traditional clay-based sculpture and modern digital production, all grounded in his training and experience as a classical artist.

**Mint Medallic Sculptor Michael Gaudioso working in plaster.**

**Mint Medallic Sculptor
Renata Gordon with a computer
sketch for the Helen Taft coin.**

**Renata Gordon.** A gifted painter as well as a sculptor, Renata Gordon earned her Bachelor of Fine Arts in sculpture in 2010 from the University of the Fine Arts in Philadelphia. She studied coin and medal design, as well as traditional and digital sculpture, as an intern at the U.S. Mint for three years, and then joined the Mint's sculptor-engraver department in March 2011. Her freelance commissions include public and private murals and portraiture.

First Spouse coin designers who are members of the Mint's Artistic Infusion Program include:

**William C. Burgard.** Art-festival director, portraitist, and illustrator William Burgard is a faculty lecturer at the Penny W. Stamps School of Art & Design, University of Michigan.

**Thomas Cleveland.** Born in Hugo, Oklahoma, Thomas Cleveland attended Texas A&M Commerce and launched his art career in Houston in 1984. His clients have included Coca-Cola, General Motors, Nickelodeon, McDonald's, and other household-name companies. Cleveland began teaching art in 1997 and founded the Artist Within Studio School in 2004.

**Chris Costello.** The Art Institute of Fort Lauderdale and Northeastern University in Boston are where Chris Costello studied advertising design, graphic design, and visual communication. He is a professional designer, illustrator, typographer, Web designer, and fine artist. His clients include Random House, Simon and Schuster, Oxford University Press, and HarperCollins.

**Barbara Fox.** A graduate of the University of California, Davis, Fox is a fine artist and illustrator whose paintings are exhibited and collected internationally. She teaches watercolor-painting in classes nationwide. Her design and illustration clients include Timex, Disney, American Greetings, and the Franklin Mint.

**Linda L. Fox.** Fine artist, digital illustrator, layout designer, and teacher Linda Fox earned her Bachelor's degree in studio art from Arizona State University, supplemented by master artists' workshops at Scottsdale Artists' School. Her fine-art portraits have appeared in local and national exhibits.

**Susan Gamble.** One of the original AIP coin designers (having joined in 2004), Gamble is a graduate of the Virginia Commonwealth University School of the Arts. She has more than 30 years' experience as a graphic designer and illustrator. Much of her work revolves around foundations that preserve America's history and its natural beauty. Private commissions include illustrations of historic Spanish missions across America, presidential portraiture, and the Air Force Combat Action Medal. She has designed numerous U.S. coins and medals.

**Joel Iskowitz.** Known in both the numismatic and the philatelic worlds, Joel Iskowitz is one of the few living artists whose artwork has been displayed in the Pentagon, the U.S. Capitol, and the White House. For more than 30 years he has created a body of work including paintings, book covers, public art, coins, medals, and postage stamps. His artistry is in the collections of many government institutions and museums including the Smithsonian, the Abraham Lincoln Presidential Museum, the New-York Historical Society Museum, and the Museum of American Illustration. He lectures on art at universities and other venues nationwide.

**Justin Kunz.** A painter, concept artist, illustrator, and teacher, Justin Kunz has a Bachelor of Fine Arts in illustration from Brigham Young University and a Master of Fine Arts in painting from Laguna College of Art and Design. He has worked in game-development studios including Disney Interactive and Blizzard Entertainment, and his paintings are exhibited throughout the United States. He is an assistant professor in the Department of Visual Arts at Brigham Young.

**Richard Masters.** A professor of art at the University of Wisconsin, Oshkosh, Richard Masters studied design and drawing at the University of Iowa, graduating with a Master of Fine Arts in 1990. He has exhibited in five solo shows and more than fifty national and international juried exhibitions since 1997. Masters was one of the earliest members of the U.S. Mint's Artistic Infusion Program, having joined in 2004.

**Mary Beth Zeitz Medley.** One of the first members of the U.S. Mint's Artistic Infusion Program, Mary Beth Medley (née Zeitz) studied art at the Université de Montpellier France. Her paintings and other artwork are internationally licensed and appear in stores such as Target; Kohl's; Bed, Bath and Beyond; and Linens 'n Things.

**Frank Morris.** Art school for Frank Morris included the University of Memphis, Art Center College of Design, New York Art Students League, and New York Academy of Art. After 20 years as a professional artist in New York City, Morris continues to work as a book and advertising illustrator, graphic designer, portrait artist, and public artist.

November 20, 2006, National Portrait Gallery, Washington: Joel Iskowitz, an Artistic Infusion Program designer who would work on several of the Presidential dollars and First Spouse gold coins, talks with Representative Carolyn Maloney of New York at the unveiling ceremony for the new Presidential dollars. Maloney and Representative Mike Castle of Delaware were sponsors of the 2005 Presidential $1 Coin Act.

**Benjamin Sowards.** Official portraiture, gallery painting, children's-book illustration, and young-adult fantasy are among the artistic genres of Ben Sowards. He completed undergraduate and graduate studies at Laguna College of Art and Design and Brigham Young University, and now teaches traditional painting and digital art at Southern Utah University, where he directs the illustration program.

**Donna Weaver.** After studying sculpting, painting, and printmaking at the Art Academy of Cincinnati, Donna Weaver graduated with a Bachelor of Fine Arts in 1966. She worked for several Kentucky toy companies, including Kenner Toys and Hasbro, sculpting action figures and other toys. She served as a sculptor-engraver at the Philadelphia Mint from 2000 until her retirement in 2006, during which time she designed or sculpted more than 40 coins and medals. She is renowned as the reviver of the art of miniature bas-relief wax portraiture, popular in the United States between 1750 and 1840. Today she sculpts wax portraits, exhibits her art in galleries, and does commissioned works in addition to having returned to the U.S. Mint as an AIP designer.

**David Westwood.** A creative director, graphic designer, cartoonist, and custom illustrator, David Westwood has worked for advertising agencies in London and Los Angeles, illustrated and designed for television and movie promotions, designed album covers for 20 performers, and written and illustrated 8 published books.

**Gary Whitley.** A self-employed artist living in Washington State, Gary Whitley specializes in historical and natural-history art for museums, aquariums, and zoos, using a variety of media. His work is contracted by the National Park Service's Southeast Region.

**A Philadelphia Mint technician reviewing a design sketch for the 2012 Frances Cleveland coin (Variety 2).**

# PRODUCTION AND DISTRIBUTION OF THE FIRST SPOUSE GOLD COINS

The coinage act gave the secretary of the Treasury the authority to determine the maximum number issued of each First Spouse coin. These quantities were to be announced before their issuance.

The coins were sold directly by the Mint to collectors and investors, rather than through the network of Authorized Purchasers and secondary retailers that distributed the American Eagle and American Buffalo coins. By law, each coin would be sold at a price equal to or greater than the sum of its face value plus the cost of designing and issuing the coin (including labor, materials, dies, use of machinery, overhead expenses, marketing, and shipping).

Other sections of the act defined the formats of the coins, the source of their raw materials, and other factors:

> Quality of coins.—The bullion coins minted under this Act shall be issued in both Proof and Uncirculated [cataloged in this book as *Burnished*] qualities.
>
> Source of gold bullion.—
>
> In general.—The Secretary shall acquire gold for the coins issued under this subsection by purchase of gold mined from natural deposits in the United States, or in a territory or possession of the United States, within 1 year after the month in which the ore from which it is derived was mined.
>
> Price of gold.—The Secretary shall pay not more than the average world price for the gold mined. . . .
>
> Legal tender.—The coins minted under this title shall be legal tender. . . .
>
> Treatment as numismatic items.—[All] coins minted under this subsection shall be considered to be numismatic items.

The Mint announced the First Spouse gold coin release schedule as follows:

| Maximum Work Hub Tonnages Safety Limits | |
|---|---|
| **Denomination** | **Maximum Tonnage (Standard Tons)** |
| Penny | 223 |
| Nickel | 223 |
| Dime | 223 |
| Quarter | 342 |
| Half Dollar | 342 |
| Golden Dollar | 342 |
| 1/10 Ounce Gold/Platinum | 223 |
| 1/4 Ounce Gold/Platinum | 342 |
| 1/2 Ounce Gold/Platinum | 342 |
| 1 Ounce Gold/Platinum | 342 |
| 1 1/2" Silver Commemorative | 433 |
| Silver Bullion | 433 |
| $5 Gold | 342 |
| $10 First Spouse | 342 |
| 1 5/16" Medal | 433 |
| 1 1/2" Medal | 433 |

*Maximum tonnages must not be exceeded under any circumstances due to potential personal injury and/or press or tooling damage

Posters directing Mint technicians on the creation of First Spouse coinage dies.

| Year | | Featured Spouse or Design | Years of Service or Presidency |
|---|---|---|---|
| 2007 | 1 | Martha Washington | 1789–1797 |
| 2007 | 2 | Abigail Adams | 1797–1801 |
| 2007 | 3 | Thomas Jefferson's Liberty | 1801–1809 |
| 2007 | 4 | Dolley Madison | 1809–1817 |
| 2008 | 5 | Elizabeth Monroe | 1817–1825 |
| 2008 | 6 | Louisa Adams | 1825–1829 |
| 2008 | 7 | Andrew Jackson's Liberty | 1829–1837 |
| 2008 | 8 | Martin Van Buren's Liberty | 1837–1841 |
| 2009 | 9 | Anna Harrison | 1841 |
| 2009 | 10* | Letitia Tyler | 1841–1842 |
| 2009 | 10* | Julia Tyler | 1844–1845 |
| 2009 | 11 | Sarah Polk | 1845–1849 |
| 2009 | 12 | Margaret Taylor | 1849–1850 |
| 2010 | 13 | Abigail Fillmore | 1850–1853 |
| 2010 | 14 | Jane Pierce | 1853–1857 |
| 2010 | 15 | James Buchanan's Liberty | 1857–1861 |
| 2010 | 16 | Mary Todd Lincoln | 1861–1865 |
| 2011 | 17 | Eliza Johnson | 1865–1869 |
| 2011 | 18 | Julia Grant | 1869–1877 |
| 2011 | 19 | Lucy Hayes | 1877–1881 |
| 2012 | 20 | Lucretia Garfield | 1881 |
| 2012 | 21 | Alice Paul | 1881–1885 |
| 2012 | 22** | Frances Cleveland (first term) | 1885–1889 |
| 2012 | 23 | Caroline Harrison | 1889–1893 |
| 2012 | 24** | Frances Cleveland (second term) | 1893–1897 |
| 2013 | 25 | Ida McKinley | 1897–1901 |
| 2013 | 26 | Edith Roosevelt | 1901–1909 |
| 2013 | 27 | Helen Taft | 1909–1913 |
| 2013 | 28*** | Ellen Wilson | 1913–1914 |
| 2013 | 28*** | Edith Wilson | 1915–1921 |
| 2014 | 29 | Florence Harding | 1921–1923 |
| 2014 | 30 | Grace Coolidge | 1923–1929 |
| 2014 | 31 | Lou Hoover | 1929–1933 |
| 2014 | 32 | Eleanor Roosevelt | 1933–1945 |
| 2015 | 33 | Elizabeth Truman | 1945–1953 |
| 2015 | 34 | Mamie Eisenhower | 1953–1961 |
| 2015 | 35 | Jacqueline Kennedy | 1961–1963 |
| 2015 | 36 | Claudia Taylor "Lady Bird" Johnson | 1963–1969 |
| 2016 | 37 | Patricia Ryan "Pat" Nixon | 1969–1974 |
| 2016 | 38 | Elizabeth Bloomer "Betty" Ford | 1974–1977 |
| 2016 | 40 | Nancy Reagan | 1981–1989 |

* The coins for Letitia Tyler and Julia Tyler are both numbered 10 in the First Spouse series, because Letitia and Julia were both married to John Tyler while he served as the nation's 10th president. ** Frances Cleveland served as First Lady in two non-consecutive periods (her husband's presidential terms were separated by the four-year presidency of Benjamin Harrison). For this reason she is honored on two coins. *** The coins for Ellen Wilson and Edith Wilson are both numbered 28 in the First Spouse series, because Ellen and Edith were both married to Woodrow Wilson while he served as the nation's 28th president.

The coins were all struck at the West Point Mint and issued four per year (or five per year, if a president had two wives while in office) in a fairly regular schedule. Fluctuations in demand and production caused an occasional delayed release or period of unavailability. Often the Mint kept each issue on sale in its product catalog for 12 months after its release. "Flexibility" was the key, however, as the Mint constantly gauged customer demand, and some coins and formats were discontinued before or after 12 months elapsed. If inventory for a particular coin reached zero and collector demand was dwindling, the Mint was apt to announce a sellout and remove the coin from its product catalog, rather than striking another press run.

In the program's first two years, 2007 and 2008, each First Spouse coin was released at an issue price set by the U.S. Mint, and that price stayed the same throughout its ordering period whether the market value of gold rose or fell. The ninth First Spouse coin, that of Anna Harrison (2009), was the first to be priced according to a new Mint-established plan for platinum and gold numismatic products, implemented on January 12, 2009. Under the new plan the Mint's prices changed based on a range of the average market price for gold. This allowed the sales team to monitor gold's activity and respond to changes, up and down, in the bullion markets. "Pricing for precious-metal (e.g., platinum, 24-k gold, 22-k gold) numismatic products varies by the average cost of the underlying metal," the Mint announced. "We use our pricing-range table the week prior to sale in order to determine the product's price. If the average weekly price of the precious metal moves up or down into another cost range, the price of the product will also go up or down, respectively, by a fixed amount." The Mint further noted that "The price of each gold product consists of the following components: cost of metal, cost to manufacture (including overhead), and margin." It gave an example of gold spot-priced at $1,100 per ounce. "At this spot price, the respective approximate average ranges for each component as a percentage of total price are as follows: cost of metal, 66 to 75%; cost to manufacture (including overhead), 11 to 19%, and margin, 13%."

Below is a sample of the sliding-scale pricing of the First Spouse gold coins.

The W mintmark, for West Point, is on the obverse underneath the coin's year date.

Varieties of attractive U.S. Mint packaging for numismatic collector versions of the First Spouse gold coins.

| Preceding week's average price of gold | Burnished First Spouse price | Proof First Spouse price |
| --- | --- | --- |
| $1,100.00 to $1,149.99 | $716.00 | $729.00 |
| $1,150.00 to $1,199.99 | $741.00 | $754.00 |
| $1,200.00 to $1,249.99 | $766.00 | $779.00 |

# BULLION OR COMMEMORATIVES?

The First Spouses are an interesting hybrid with characteristics of both investor-oriented bullion pieces and collector-oriented commemorative coins.

**Bullion:** Their authorizing legislation clearly refers to them as *bullion*; Section 103 identifies them as such, using the phrase *First Spouse Bullion Coin Program* and stating that "the Secretary shall issue bullion coins."

**Commemoratives:** Section 103.5. refers to them as "coins commemorating first spouses." It orders that "The bullion coins minted under this Act shall be issued in both Proof and Uncirculated qualities"; these formats are generally classified by the U.S. Mint as being "numismatic" rather than bullion. In fact,

Section 103.10. states that "all coins minted under this subsection shall be considered to be numismatic items."

Not doing much to clarify the distinction, the opening definition of the act states its objectives as being:

1. *to require the secretary of the Treasury to mint coins in commemoration of each of the nation's past presidents and their spouses, respectively*—Obviously this requirement resulted in the Presidential dollars and the First Spouse coins.
2. *to improve circulation of the $1 coin*—Not related to the gold coins, the act included plans for the Federal Reserve and the Treasury to work together to increase dollar-coin circulation.[3]
3. *to create a new bullion coin*—This refers to the American Buffalo, defined under Title II of the act.
4. *for other purposes*—Unspecified, but Title III lays out new plans for the Lincoln cents dated 2009 and beyond.

Under these objectives, the American Buffalo is the bullion coin, and the First Spouses are the "coins minted in commemoration" of the presidents' wives.

Perhaps this hybrid nature is summed up best in Section 101.13, which states that "bullion coins are a valuable tool for the investor and, in some cases, an important aspect of coin collecting." Many of the catalog entries that follow dramatically illustrate that duality. The First Spouses are bullion coins and commemoratives at the same time.

# THE FUTURE OF THE FIRST SPOUSES

"When I became Mint director in 2006," recalls Ed Moy, "one of the key issues on my plate was making sure of the successful launch of the Presidential dollar coins and their companion First Spouse gold bullion coins."[4]

Today, whether they're collected for sentimental reasons or hoarded as hedges against inflation, the First Spouse coins have found their niche among gold buyers. The audience for the coins is diverse. It includes hobbyists who add one or two of each issue to keep their collections complete and up to date; precious-metal investors seeking 24-karat gold in coin form; and people who don't consider themselves numismatists but are attracted to the occasional design that interests them. The first issues in 2007 established a "field population" of tens of thousands of coins, while low-mintage issues of later years added a limited-supply challenge to assembling a complete collection. After slow activity in the early 2010s, popular mainstream sales skyrocketed in 2015 with the Jackie Kennedy coin. This introduced (or re-introduced) many Americans to the First Spouse coins. The expanded audience might bring additional mainstream interest to earlier issues. Many collectors enjoy the so-called Liberty subset. From the start of the series, many specialists have sought the finest grades (MS-70 and PF-70) not only for their personal aesthetic satisfaction but also to compete with other collectors in the NGC and PCGS set registries.[5] Some invest in "First Strike" or "Early Release" coins—those pieces acknowledged by the grading firms as coming from the earliest Mint production (usually the first 30 days) for each type. Several of the First Spouse gold coins have been ranked in the *100 Greatest U.S. Modern Coins* (by Scott Schechter and Jeff Garrett) and among the *100 Greatest Women on Coins* (by Ron Guth). As more collectors work to assemble collections based on those popular books, demand for the included coins will increase.

# MARTHA WASHINGTON (2007)

*Designer: Joseph F. Menna (obverse); Susan Gamble (reverse). Sculptor: Joseph F. Menna (obverse); Don Everhart (reverse). Composition: .9999 gold. Actual Gold Weight: 1/2 ounce. Diameter: 26.49 mm. Edge: Reeded. Mint: West Point. Issue Price: $410.95 (Burnished); $429.95 (Proof). Release Date: June 19, 2007.*

On May 10, 2007, the U.S. Mint announced that it would start taking orders for the Martha Washington First Spouse gold coin (as well as the Abigail Adams coin) at 12:00 noon Eastern Time on June 19. Prices were set at $410.95 for the Burnished version and $429.95 for the Proof. Ordering limits were set at five coins per household for each format. Maximum mintage for the type would be 40,000, capped at 20,000 Burnished and 20,000 Proof. The coins sold out within hours.

Burnished.

Susan Gamble, a Master Designer in the Mint's Artistic Infusion Program (AIP), designed the coin's reverse, showing Martha Washington during the Revolutionary War, sewing a button onto her husband's uniform jacket.[6] While the former British colonies were struggling for independence, Martha's obvious concern for the fighting forces—officers and their families, as well as regular soldiers—earned her the respect and admiration of the troops and the nickname "First Lady of the Continental Army." Gamble's design is well balanced, with detail, texture, and white space contributing to the whole. On the obverse, Mint Medallic Sculptor Joseph Menna's portrait of Washington bespeaks the First Lady's dignity and modesty.

"Martha Washington is known to have organized sick wards and persuaded the society ladies of Morristown to roll bandages from their fine napkins and tablecloths, as well as to repair uniforms and knit shirts for the poorly equipped Continental soldiers," the Mint noted in its promotional literature. "Her presence in the encampments of the Continental Army was an example to other officer's wives and a significant factor in lifting the morale of her husband's tired, cold, and hungry troops."

After the issue sold out, in the early summer of 2007 collectors eagerly tuned in to eBay to watch as the Martha Washington gold coins hit the secondary market. The popular online-auction venue attracted interested bidders from beyond the numismatic community, adding to the demand and driving prices up. There was an active amount of "flipping," where a speculator would purchase a quantity of the coins from the Mint (ordering the household maximum of 10 coins and enlisting friends to do the same), study and compare them under magnification, send the finest examples to PCGS or NGC for grading, and quickly put the 69s and especially the 70s up for bid, seeking to profit from the hobby community's excitement over a new coinage issue in high certified grades. By mid-summer the coins were seeing premiums of $100 over their issue price (nearly a 25% increase). Some buyers held back their finest coins, hoping for the market to mature and grow after the super-fast Mint sellout, and expecting holiday gift-giving demand to bring a further rise in prices. First Strike and 70-graded coins were quick to earn strong premiums, especially in eBay auctions with low starting bids, which caused bidding frenzies. The slightest delivery delay from the Mint added to the anticipation and excitement. Soon registry-set collectors and aficionados of ultra-modern coins added to the demand for the highest-graded coins.

Proof.

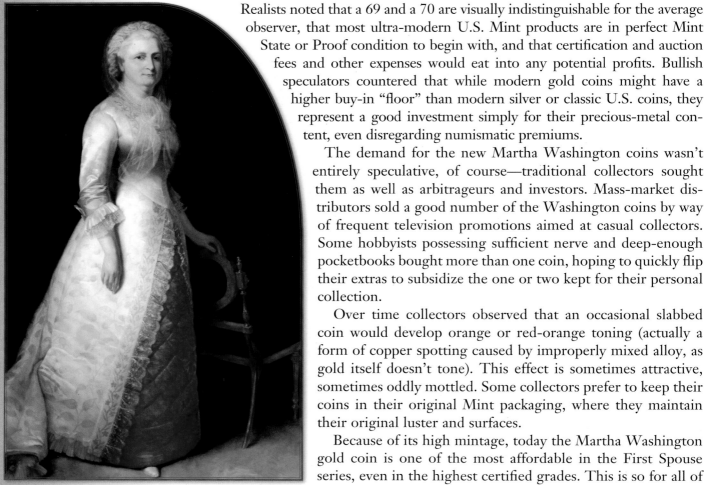

Martha Washington (1731–1802); First Lady from April 30, 1789, to March 4, 1797.

Realists noted that a 69 and a 70 are visually indistinguishable for the average observer, that most ultra-modern U.S. Mint products are in perfect Mint State or Proof condition to begin with, and that certification and auction fees and other expenses would eat into any potential profits. Bullish speculators countered that while modern gold coins might have a higher buy-in "floor" than modern silver or classic U.S. coins, they represent a good investment simply for their precious-metal content, even disregarding numismatic premiums.

The demand for the new Martha Washington coins wasn't entirely speculative, of course—traditional collectors sought them as well as arbitrageurs and investors. Mass-market distributors sold a good number of the Washington coins by way of frequent television promotions aimed at casual collectors. Some hobbyists possessing sufficient nerve and deep-enough pocketbooks bought more than one coin, hoping to quickly flip their extras to subsidize the one or two kept for their personal collection.

Over time collectors observed that an occasional slabbed coin would develop orange or red-orange toning (actually a form of copper spotting caused by improperly mixed alloy, as gold itself doesn't tone). This effect is sometimes attractive, sometimes oddly mottled. Some collectors prefer to keep their coins in their original Mint packaging, where they maintain their original luster and surfaces.

Because of its high mintage, today the Martha Washington gold coin is one of the most affordable in the First Spouse series, even in the highest certified grades. This is so for all of the 2007 issues.

Reverse detail.

**Mintage: 17,661 Burnished; 19,167 Proof**

| | Raw MS | <MS-69 | MS-69 | MS-70 | Raw PF | <PF-69 | PF-69 | PF-70 |
|---|---|---|---|---|---|---|---|---|
| **Certified** | — | 8 | 1,902 | 3,753 | — | 33 | 2,302 | 3,360 |
| **Value\*** | $750 | | $770 | $805 | $760 | | $770 | $820 |

*Recent auctions:* $664, MS-70, August 2014 (avg. gold spot value that month, $1,296). $646, PF-69DC, October 2014 (avg. gold spot value that month, $1,222).

\* "Raw" value is based on a gold spot price of $1,200 per ounce, and is for an uncertified Burnished or Proof coin of average quality. This value may vary with the prevailing bullion value.

# ABIGAIL ADAMS (2007)

*Designer: Joseph F. Menna (obverse); Thomas Cleveland (reverse). **Sculptor:** Joseph F. Menna (obverse); Phebe Hemphill (reverse). **Composition:** .9999 gold. **Actual Gold Weight:** 1/2 ounce. **Diameter:** 26.49 mm. **Edge:** Reeded. **Mint:** West Point. **Issue Price:** $410.95 (Burnished); $429.95 (Proof). **Release Date:** June 19, 2007.*

The U.S. Mint's announcement of May 10, 2007, set the start of sales for the Abigail Adams gold coin at 12:00 noon Eastern Time on June 19. The issue prices would be the same as for the Martha Washington coin, the first in the series (released on the same day). Orders were limited to five coins per household for each format, Burnished and Proof. Maximum mintage for the type would be 40,000 coins, divided equally between the two formats.

Artistic Infusion Program Master Designer Thomas Cleveland designed the reverse, showing a youthful Abigail Adams writing a letter to her husband while he served in the Second Continental Congress. John Adams valued his wife's advice above the counsel of any other contemporary, holding that her political wisdom equaled that of his professional colleagues. In one letter, Abigail urged her husband to "remember the ladies" as the new nation was being formed. This advice is featured as an inscription in Cleveland's design, which was sculpted by U.S. Mint Medallic Sculptor Phebe Hemphill. On the obverse Joseph Menna brought a superb level of intricate detail to the clothing and features of the First Lady, rendering the older Mrs. Adams in a portrait of quiet strength.

Burnished.

Like the Martha Washington coins that went on sale at the same time, the Abigail Adams coins sold out in a matter of hours. In the secondary market, high-grade and First Strike examples of the Adams gold coins followed the trajectory enjoyed by the Washingtons, with 70-graded coins in particular earning strong premiums by the winter months of 2007. Once again, eBay auctions, with their broad mainstream audience, saw higher prices than traditional numismatic sales to savvy collectors and dealers.

For months the First Spouse coins were a hot topic within the hobby community. Collectors scrutinized their purchases, eager to discuss pieces struck with insignificantly misaligned dies or unusual toning or frosting, and comparing their certification results to others' experiences. Of course MS-70 and PF-70 slabs—with their high demand and auction records—continued to be the coveted goal.

Today the Abigail Adams gold coin remains one of the most affordable in the First Spouse series, thanks to its high mintage.

Proof.

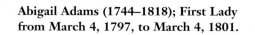

**Abigail Adams (1744–1818); First Lady from March 4, 1797, to March 4, 1801.**

**Reverse detail.**

**Draped Bust
half cent (1800–1808).**

**Burnished.**

**Mintage: 17,142 Burnished; 17,149 Proof**

| | Certified Populations and Retail Market Values | | | | | | | |
|---|---|---|---|---|---|---|---|---|
| | **Raw MS** | **<MS-69** | **MS-69** | **MS-70** | **Raw PF** | **<PF-69** | **PF-69** | **PF-70** |
| **Certified** | — | 7 | 2,225 | 3,432 | — | 36 | 2,459 | 2,871 |
| **Value\*** | $750 | | $770 | $805 | $755 | | $770 | $810 |

*Recent auctions:* $764, MS-70, September 2014 (avg. gold spot value that month, $1,239). $611, PF-69DC, October 2014 (avg. gold spot value that month, $1,222).

\* "Raw" value is based on a gold spot price of $1,200 per ounce, and is for an uncertified Burnished or Proof coin of average quality. This value may vary with the prevailing bullion value.

# THOMAS JEFFERSON'S LIBERTY (2007)

*Designer: Robert Scot (obverse); Charles L. Vickers (reverse). **Sculptor:** Phebe Hemphill (obverse); Charles L. Vickers (reverse). **Composition:** .9999 gold. **Actual Gold Weight:** 1/2 ounce. **Diameter:** 26.49 mm. **Edge:** Reeded. **Mint:** West Point. **Issue Price:** $410.95 (Burnished); $429.95 (Proof). **Release Date:** August 30, 2007.*

Hobby observers anticipated a hot market for the third coin of the First Spouse series. This issue was the first of four that would feature an allegorical Miss Liberty rather than an actual First Lady. Thomas Jefferson's wife, Martha, had died some 19 years before he won the presidency, and he never remarried, so the nation had no First Lady during his two terms in office. To keep the coinage series complete (with one coin for each presidency), the Presidential $1 Coin Act of 2005 provided that, in the event a president had served without a spouse, his First Spouse coin would feature "a design emblematic of Liberty as it appeared on a United States coin issued during his time in office."

The image for Jefferson's coin is Mint Medallic Sculptor Phebe Hemphill's resculpted version of Miss Liberty from Chief Engraver Robert Scot's Draped Bust half cent of 1800 to 1808. "This beautiful coin captures a classic image of Liberty from Jefferson's time," said Mint director Ed Moy, "connecting us to the history of our coinage."

There are special elements of appeal for the four Liberty designs. Viewed by collectors as a self-contained "short set," they make a more attainable (less expensive) goal than acquiring one of every type in the First Spouse gold series. On top of that the Liberty coins recreate the classic designs of popular older coins. For these reasons, enthusiasts in 2007 expected strong demand for the Jefferson's Liberty coins. By mid-September, market-makers in modern coins were advertising buy prices up to $550 per raw coin (which would yield a quick $100-plus profit for the seller), and retailing 70-graded coins for up to $900. Sellers on eBay advertised the coins at prices above their official Mint issue price, even before they were delivered.

As predicted, Jefferson's Liberty did garner the series' highest mintages up to that point, in both Proof and Burnished formats—a distinction they still maintain, as mintages never again got close to their first-year highs.

Not long after their August 30 release, it became evident that the Jefferson's Liberty coins would not enjoy a repeat of the sustained strong secondary markets of their Washington and Adams predecessors. The Mint placed an order limit of one coin of each format per household, which allowed for broader, more equitable distribution—speculators had a harder time grabbing up large quantities. "The Mint got out its bulldozer and leveled the playing field," is how one collector put it. Once the coins were in collectors' and dealers' hands, they started to flow in to the professional third-party grading firms for certification. The Jefferson coin had the largest certified population of First Strike 70s. This combination of factors—broad distribution throughout the collector base, and a large quantity of perfect First Strike coins—dampened the secondary market. Everyone who wanted a nice example of the coin had one.

Rare-coin dealer Wayne Herndon made this observation in November 2007: "The real question is not what happened to the Jefferson, but what happened to the Washington and Adams. The Jefferson did exactly what it should have done based on the mintage, interest, etc. Somehow, some way, a lot of people got it into their heads that is would be a great series and the first two sold out quickly. Slow delivery contributed to the apparent lack of supply vs. demand. As a result, the first two ended up being the exceptions, not Jefferson." Presciently, Herndon went on: "I predict this series will see some pieces with mintages in the low four figures. Those are the ones that will have some potential."[7]

Scott Schechter and Jeff Garrett, too, have noted the potential of the Liberty gold coins. "Collectors like them because of the way they honor numismatic history, recasting old designs in a new way," they write in *100 Greatest U.S. Modern Coins*. As a set, the First Spouse Liberty gold coins are ranked in the third edition of the *100 Greatest* book at no. 58. Their ranking will undoubtedly climb closer to no. 1 if the program grows in popularity, as the Mint anticipates it will with recent popular First Ladies taking center stage. (The maximum mintage of the Jacqueline Kennedy gold coin was tripled to meet expected demand.) Eric Jordan and John Maben write in *Top 50 Most Popular Modern Coins*: "One of the best things that can happen to a series is to have a large population of good-looking common dates in the hands of the public to get them started without the intimidating hurdle of a high collector premium. Jefferson's Liberty is this coin in the four-coin Liberty gold subset."

**Proof.**

**Reverse detail.**

Regarding the aesthetics of the Jefferson's Liberty coin, collectors were charmed by the Mint's use of the early-1800s half-cent portrait of Miss Liberty. America's copper half cents and large cents have been popular collectibles since they went obsolete in the late 1850s. Today a solid and growing collector base benefits from the educational and fraternal missions of hobby groups such as Early American Coppers, whose members keep the series alive with ongoing research (they publish new findings regularly, and were instrumental in sharing their scholarship in Q. David Bowers's *Guide Book of Half Cents and Large Cents*, 2015). EAC nationwide has more than 1,200 members who congregate at coin shows and online at www.eacs.org. Undoubtedly many of these enthusiasts bought this First Spouse "Liberty" coin to complement their half cent and large cent collections.

The *reverse* of the coin, on the other hand, won few kudos with its text-heavy design. U.S. Mint Sculptor-Engraver Charles Vickers depicted Thomas Jefferson's grave monument, located on the grounds of his Monticello estate, in minutely textured detail. He overset the obelisk with the president's self-penned epitaph: "Here was buried Thomas Jefferson, author of the declaration of American independence, of the statute of Virginia for religious freedom and father of the University of Virginia. Born April 2, 1743, O.S. Died July 4, 1826." Surrounding this well-balanced but lengthy inscription are the standard legends UNITED STATES OF AMERICA and E PLURIBUS UNUM, plus the denomination of $10, the weight of 1/2 OZ., and the purity of .9999 FINE GOLD. "Enjoy the obverse," remarked some hobby wags, "but don't flip the coin over"—no offense to the very talented Mr. Vickers, who was tasked with fitting nearly 50 words into a one-inch–diameter circle of gold.

**Mintage: 19,823 Burnished; 19,815 Proof**

| | | | | Certified Populations and Retail Market Values | | | | |
|---|---|---|---|---|---|---|---|---|
| | **Raw MS** | **<MS-69** | **MS-69** | **MS-70** | **Raw PF** | **<PF-69** | **PF-69** | **PF-70** |
| **Certified** | — | 4 | 856 | 2,318 | — | 11 | 1,240 | 2,017 |
| **Value\*** | $750 | | $770 | $805 | $755 | | $770 | $810 |
| *Recent auction:* $705, PF-69DC, October 2014 (avg. gold spot value that month, $1,222). | | | | | | | | |

\* "Raw" value is based on a gold spot price of $1,200 per ounce, and is for an uncertified Burnished or Proof coin of average quality. This value may vary with the prevailing bullion value.

# DOLLEY MADISON (2007)

**Designer:** *Don Everhart (obverse and reverse).* **Sculptor:** *Joel Iskowitz (obverse); Don Everhart (reverse).* **Composition:** *.9999 gold.* **Actual Gold Weight:** *1/2 ounce.* **Diameter:** *26.49 mm.* **Edge:** *Reeded.* **Mint:** *West Point.* **Issue Price:** *$509.95 (Burnished); $529.95 (Proof).* **Release Date:** *November 19, 2007.*

On November 15, 2007, the U.S. Mint announced it would begin selling the Dolley Madison First Spouse coin on November 19 at 12:00 noon. "Orders will be limited to one per option per household for the first week of sales," Mint spokesman Michael White said. "The Mint will reevaluate this limit following the initial sales period and either extend, adjust, or eliminate it." The maximum mintage for the type would be 20,000 coins of each format, Burnished and Proof.

The fourth and final First Spouse coin of 2007 returned to real-life portraiture with a gently smiling visage of Dolley Madison on the obverse, and an artful full-body standing portrait on the reverse.

Burnished.

The latter captures the First Lady in the midst of saving the executive mansion's Cabinet papers and the famous Gilbert Stuart painting of George Washington from seizure by advancing British troops in August 1814. Collectors remarked on the attractiveness of the reverse tableau. Both sides of the coin were designed by Mint Sculptor-Engraver Don Everhart.

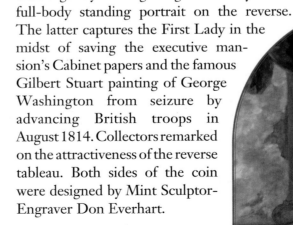

Reverse detail.

**Dolley Madison (1768–1849); First Lady from March 4, 1809, to March 4, 1817.**

By the time the Dolley Madison First Spouse coin was released, some of the bloom was off the rose of the new gold bullion series. The tulip-mania aftermarket of the Washington and Adams coins had given way to calmer activity with Jefferson's Liberty. The latter attracted a great number of orders, and the official limit of two coins per household helped spread them evenly among interested buyers, which stabilized the supply-and-demand equation and kept aftermarket prices under control. Then demand for the Madison coin softened a bit compared to the high sales of the Jefferson coins. The rising price of gold undoubtedly discouraged some earlier buyers from continuing with the series.

The Mint initially limited one Dolley Madison coin of each format per household, to allow collectors to acquire the coins without speculators cornering the entire issue. Collectors had their fill, and the ordering limit was raised to 10 per household in December 2007. The Madison coins sold several thousand pieces fewer than the Jefferson in both formats, failing to reach sellout levels before they were pulled from the Mint's catalog a year after the first day of sales. Coins in Mint inventory at that point were melted. After all sales and returns were accounted for, the Madison coins had the lowest Burnished mintage for 2007, and the second-lowest Proof mintage. Even so, compared to later years' quantities these mintages would seem as grand and monumental as Montpelier, the Madison family's plantation estate.

Proof.

**Mintage: 12,340 Burnished; 17,943 Proof**

| Certified Populations and Retail Market Values | | | | | | | | |
|---|---|---|---|---|---|---|---|---|
| | Raw MS | <MS-69 | MS-69 | MS-70 | Raw PF | <PF-69 | PF-69 | PF-70 |
| **Certified** | — | 5 | 363 | 1,184 | — | 20 | 882 | 1,207 |
| **Value*** | $750 | | $770 | $810 | $760 | | $770 | $820 |
| | *Recent auctions:* $705, MS-70, July 2014 (avg. gold spot value that month, $1,311). $635, PF-69DC, October 2014 (avg. gold spot value that month, $1,222). | | | | | | | |

* "Raw" value is based on a gold spot price of $1,200 per ounce, and is for an uncertified Burnished or Proof coin of average quality. This value may vary with the prevailing bullion value.

# ELIZABETH MONROE (2008)

***Designer:*** *Joel Iskowitz (obverse); Donna Weaver (reverse).* ***Sculptor:*** *Don Everhart (obverse); Charles L. Vickers (reverse).* ***Composition:*** *.9999 gold.* ***Actual Gold Weight:*** *1/2 ounce.* ***Diameter:*** *26.49 mm.* ***Edge:*** *Reeded.* ***Mint:*** *West Point.* ***Issue Price:*** *$599.95 (Burnished); $619.95 (Proof).* ***Release Date:*** *February 28, 2008.*

The first issue of First Spouse coins for 2008—that of Elizabeth Monroe—went on sale February 28, 2008, with household limits of one coin of each format (Burnished and Proof) for the first week of sales. Starting with this issue the Mint let customer demand decide the distribution between Burnished and Proof formats, capping the entire production at 40,000 rather than setting a limit of 20,000 of each. Mint salespeople brought the coins to the American Numismatic Association's March 7–9 National Money Show in Phoenix, Arizona, as part of a suite of new product offerings.

First Lady Elizabeth Monroe was important in refurbishing the executive mansion after its main building was burned in the War of 1812. This significance is memorialized in the reverse design of her First Spouse gold coin.

Burnished.

**Proof.**

**Reverse detail.**

Artistic Infusion Program Assistant Designer Donna Weaver depicted Monroe at an 1818 reception for the reopening of the mansion, by that time unofficially known as the "White House" (because its smoke-damaged exteriors were painted white during its restoration). Weaver's design, sculpted by Charles Vickers, is a beautifully crafted mixture of ornamental details and finely wrought portraiture. The First Lady wears furs, pearls, formal gloves, and an ostrich-plumed headdress in front of a richly carved mirror frame and vase. In the Proof version, the mirror is cleverly given a polished reflective finish, with the surrounding architecture in matte. On the obverse, Joel Iskowitz's portrait of Monroe, sculpted by Don Everhart, shows the First Lady as an attractive and stylishly dressed socialite, very much the daughter of a wealthy New York City family and wife of a famous American statesman.

With this first release for 2008 it was evident that demand for the First Spouse coins was softening. The Mint removed its ordering limits per household in an effort to spur sales. The April 15 issue of *Numismatic News*, which hit newsstands in early April, listed purchases as 3,632 Burnished and 6,180 Proof. By the time the Mint closed sales for the Elizabeth Monroe issue in early 2009, the mintage stood at 4,462 Burnished and 7,800 Proof—less than half that of the immediately preceding Dolley Madison coins. Of course, in the market for ultra-modern coins, low sales today can translate into high prices tomorrow; the Elizabeth Monroe was the first of the First Spouse coins to break away from the family and, over time, enjoy markedly higher and stable premiums in "raw" form (ungraded, in original Mint packaging).

The Mint switched to a larger plastic-capsule size for the Elizabeth Monroe issue.

**Elizabeth Monroe (1768–1830); First Lady from March 4, 1817, to March 4, 1825.**

**Mintage: 4,462 Burnished; 7,800 Proof**

| | | | | Certified Populations and Retail Market Values | | | | |
|---|---|---|---|---|---|---|---|---|
| | **Raw MS** | **<MS-69** | **MS-69** | **MS-70** | **Raw PF** | **<PF-69** | **PF-69** | **PF-70** |
| **Certified** | — | 0 | 148 | 626 | — | 7 | 572 | 640 |
| **Value*** | $850 | | $865 | $1,055 | $810 | | $870 | $1,325 |

*Recent auctions:* $728.50, MS-70, November 2013 (avg. gold spot value that month, $1,276). $544, PF-69DC, November 2014 (avg. gold spot value that month, $1,176).

* "Raw" value is based on a gold spot price of $1,200 per ounce, and is for an uncertified Burnished or Proof coin of average quality. This value may vary with the prevailing bullion value.

# LOUISA ADAMS (2008)

*Designer: Susan Gamble (obverse); Joseph F. Menna (reverse).* **Sculptor:** *Phebe Hemphill (obverse); Joseph F. Menna (reverse).* **Composition:** *.9999 gold.* **Actual Gold Weight:** *1/2 ounce.* **Diameter:** *26.49 mm.* **Edge:** *Reeded.* **Mint:** *West Point.* **Issue Price:** *$599.95 (Burnished); $619.95 (Proof).* **Release Date:** *May 29, 2008.*

The U.S. Mint announced on May 27, 2008, that the Louisa Adams First Spouse gold coin would go on sale at 12:00 noon Eastern Time on May 29. As with other recent issues, orders were capped for the first week at one coin per format per household, with an issue-wide limit of 40,000 coins in both formats.

"It could not have been easy for Louisa Catherine Adams, wife of our nation's sixth president, John Quincy Adams, to follow in the footsteps of her esteemed mother-in-law and former First Lady Abigail Adams," the Mint's press release opined. "Despite her predecessor's legacy, however, Louisa—an accomplished musician, hostess, and writer on the subjects of women's rights and abolitionism—managed to make her mark in Washington society and in political circles. Louisa staunchly supported her husband's career and was invaluable in furthering his initiatives."

Before she was First Lady, Louisa made the family home in Europe while her husband worked as a diplomat. The coin's obverse portrait, designed by Susan Gamble and sculpted by Phoebe Hemphill, blends classical beauty with sartorial elegance. Joseph Menna's reverse design captures Louisa's bravery and determination as she embarked on a harrowing winter journey from Russia toward Belgium, while Europe was embroiled in the Napoleonic Wars, to join her husband, who was negotiating an end to America's naval war with Britain. At one point during her journey her Russian carriage was stopped by hostile French troops who assumed she was Russian herself and wanted her killed. Louisa cleverly had her servants "reveal" that she was Emperor Napoleon's sister traveling in disguise—then she stepped from the coach and rallied the exhausted troops in perfect French, securing their passage.

**Burnished.**

Louisa Adams (1775–1852); First Lady from March 4, 1825, to March 4, 1829.

Napoleon's overzealous soldiers had nothing on the challenge faced by the Louisa Adams First Spouse coin in 2008: deflated collector interest. By the end of the sales period barely 10,000 of the coins had been purchased, making French toast of the Mint's 40,000-coin mintage limit. The low mintage, of course, has not hurt the coin's value in the aftermarket. By this point in the First Spouse bullion program, bullish collectors were looking at the long game, knowing that low mintages today can blossom into tomorrow's sleeper hits.

**Proof.**

Reverse detail.

Capped Bust
half dollar (1807–1836).

Burnished.

**Mintage: 3,885 Burnished; 6,581 Proof**

| | | Certified Populations and Retail Market Values | | | | | | |
|---|---|---|---|---|---|---|---|---|
| | Raw MS | <MS-69 | MS-69 | MS-70 | Raw PF | <PF-69 | PF-69 | PF-70 |
| Certified | — | 3 | 210 | 571 | — | 14 | 505 | 582 |
| Value* | $850 | | $875 | $1,055 | $810 | | $870 | $1,325 |

*Recent auctions:* $1,116.25, MS-70, August 2014 (avg. gold spot value that month, $1,296). $646.25, PF-69DC, June 2015 (avg. gold spot value that month, $1,182).

\* "Raw" value is based on a gold spot price of $1,200 per ounce, and is for an uncertified Burnished or Proof coin of average quality. This value may vary with the prevailing bullion value.

# ANDREW JACKSON'S LIBERTY (2008)

*Designer: John Reich (obverse); Justin Kunz (reverse). Sculptor: Don Everhart (reverse). Composition: .9999 gold. Actual Gold Weight: 1/2 ounce. Diameter: 26.49 mm. Edge: Reeded. Mint: West Point. Issue Price: $599.95 (Burnished); $619.95 (Proof). Release Date: August 28, 2008.*

On August 21, 2008, the Mint announced that it would begin accepting orders for the next First Spouse gold coin on August 28. Mintage was set at a maximum of 40,000 coins across both product options, Burnished and Proof, with customer demand determining the quantity produced of each format. The household limit, previously capped at one coin of each format for the first week of sales, was raised to 10 coins of each format for the first week in an effort to stimulate purchasing.

Once again the provisions of the Presidential $1 Coin Act of 2005 were invoked due to a president having served without a spouse. Andrew Jackson's wife Rachel died shortly before he took office, leaving him grief-stricken and the nation without an official First Lady from 1829 to 1837. The gold coin for the seventh presidency featured "an obverse design emblematic of Liberty as represented on a United States coin issued during the president's period of service and a reverse image emblematic of that president." The figure of Miss Liberty was derived from Mint engraver John Reich's Capped Bust, Lettered Edge, silver half dollar of 1807 to 1836. The reverse design by Artistic Infusion Program Master Designer Justin Kunz shows a military equestrian portrait of Jackson as "Old Hickory"—the moniker by which he became known for leading American forces against the British Army in the War of 1812. Don Everhart's sculpting of Kunz's design has remarkable depth and nuanced detail.

The hobby community's reaction to the coin was mixed. Why did collectors *not* buy Jackson's Liberty in droves? Some in 2008 were saving their hobby money for the upcoming 2009 Ultra High Relief gold coin. Some were disgruntled with the issue price of the latest First Spouse coin—about 50% above gold's spot value. Some collectors found the prospect of completing the set of First Spouse coins too daunting to continue (or begin), especially with the uncertainty of gold's value fluctuating. Collectors of modern issues felt the pressure of many other Mint products competing for their discretionary income. And the interest of some hobbyists had cooled after the market couldn't sustain the initial firestorm of excitement over the program's first two coins the year before.

Even with this chill, Andrew Jackson's Liberty was appealing enough to gin up total sales about 20% higher than the preceding Louisa Adams issue. The attractive designs of the Jackson coin, with a classic American coinage motif of Miss Liberty and the dramatic horseback portrait of the famous war hero, strengthened its appeal. So did its status as one of only four members of the subset of Liberty coins in the First Spouse series. As a group the four coins are ranked at no. 58 in *100 Greatest U.S. Modern Coins*, with numismatic historians Scott Schechter and Jeff Garrett saying "For most collectors and dealers, the Liberty coins are truly the greatest First Spouse gold coins." Eric Jordan and John Maben included Jackson's Liberty among the Top 50 Most Popular Modern Coins, in their 2012 book of the same name.

All of the 2007 coins and half of the preceding 2008 issues had sold more Proofs than did Jackson's Liberty, but none after it (until 2015) would reach its level of 7,684 Proof coins. Its Burnished mintage level would not be exceeded by a predecessor until nine coins down the line—the next in the Liberty subset, James Buchanan's Liberty, in 2010.

**Proof.**

**Mintage: 4,609 Burnished; 7,684 Proof**

| | Raw MS | <MS-69 | MS-69 | MS-70 | Raw PF | <PF-69 | PF-69 | PF-70 |
|---|---|---|---|---|---|---|---|---|
| **Certified** | — | 0 | 170 | 633 | — | 10 | 487 | 745 |
| **Value\*** | $850 | | $875 | $1,055 | $860 | | $880 | $1,425 |

*Recent auctions:* $998.75, MS-70, July 2015 (avg. gold spot value that month, $1,130). $822.50, PF-69DC, June 2015 (avg. gold spot value that month, $1,182).

\* "Raw" value is based on a gold spot price of $1,200 per ounce, and is for an uncertified Burnished or Proof coin of average quality. This value may vary with the prevailing bullion value.

# Martin Van Buren's Liberty (2008)

*Designer: Christian Gobrecht (obverse); Thomas Cleveland (reverse). Sculptor: Jim Licaretz (reverse). Composition: .9999 gold. Actual Gold Weight: 1/2 ounce. Diameter: 26.49 mm. Edge: Reeded. Mint: West Point. Issue Price: $524.95 (Burnished); $549.95 (Proof). Release Date: November 25, 2008.*

The U.S. Mint started accepting orders for the Martin Van Buren First Spouse gold coin at 12 noon on November 25, 2008. The issue price was set about $75 lower than that of its predecessor coin, following gold's activity in the bullion markets. As with the Andrew Jackson coin that had debuted three months earlier, the Mint set an order limit of 10 coins per format (Burnished and Proof) per household for the first week, reserving the right to evaluate sales and either extend, adjust, or eliminate the limit after that. The total mintage was capped at 40,000 pieces, to be distributed between the Burnished and Proof coins according to buyers' demand.

Collector interest waned a bit for this issue, the third in the First Spouse program's four-coin Liberty subset, despite its attractive engraving of Christian Gobrecht's classic Liberty Seated design. This motif had been used on the silver dime from 1837 to 1891, and on other U.S. silver coins in various time spans of the same era. The reason the 2008 gold bullion coin for Van Buren's

**Liberty Seated silver dollar (1840–1873).**

**Burnished.**

**Proof.**

presidency featured no First Lady is that his wife, Hannah, had died of tuberculosis in 1819, early in his political career, when he was a member of the New York State Senate. Van Buren never remarried. Their son's wife, Sarah Angelica Singleton Van Buren, performed many of the hostess functions for the White House during her father-in-law's presidency.

The reverse tableau shows Martin Van Buren as a youth reading a book outside the Kinderhook, New York, tavern run by his father, with a traveler on horseback in the background. When Martin was growing up, the tavern, situated along a post road, was a meeting place for conversation, debate, and voting. Politicians traveling between New York City and the state capital of Albany stopped there. From this exposure young Van Buren developed a taste for politics and the philosophy of law. The coin's richly detailed scene, with its well-balanced blend of natural, architectural, and human elements, was designed by Artistic Infusion Program Master Designer Thomas Cleveland and sculpted by Mint Medallic Sculptor Jim Licaretz.

Numismatics offers many opportunities to cross-pollinate a sophisticated coin collection. No doubt more than just a few of Van Buren's Liberty gold coins are kept company by much older silver half dimes, dimes, quarters, half dollars, and silver dollars that date back to the generation of "The Red Fox of Kinderhook." Consider the Liberty Seated Collectors Club ("Uniting Collectors of Liberty Seated Coinage Since 1973," online at www.lsccweb.org). That particular hobby group is very active, and proved its numismatic chops in sharing information, research, and insight for Q. David Bowers's *A Guide Book of Liberty Seated Silver Coins* (2016). How many of its 600-plus members treated themselves to one or more of these artful gold pieces? New members will undoubtedly feel the same attraction.

Due to its low mintage, and ongoing collector demand for the four coins of the Liberty subset, Van Buren's Liberty has emerged as the aftermarket winner among the First Spouse issues of 2007 and 2008. In both Burnished and Proof format it typically carries a premium of 25% to 50% over the other coins of those years. "In time, some standout rarities will definitely be recognized among [the First Spouse coins]," write Scott Schechter and Jeff Garrett in the third edition of *100 Greatest U.S. Modern Coins*. The Liberty subset of First Spouse gold coins is ranked at no. 58 in that volume. Eric Jordan and John Maben give Van Buren's Liberty an overall score of 4.0 in their book *Top 50 Most Popular Modern Coins*, calling it "the undisputed king of the Liberty subset," with "classic good looks that attract both classic and modern collectors."

**Mintage: 3,826 Burnished; 6,807 Proof**

| | **Raw MS** | **<MS-69** | **MS-69** | **MS-70** | **Raw PF** | **<PF-69** | **PF-69** | **PF-70** |
|---|---|---|---|---|---|---|---|---|
| | | | **Certified Populations and Retail Market Values** | | | | | |
| **Certified** | — | 0 | 201 | 719 | — | 15 | 484 | 785 |
| **Value\*** | $925 | | $1,025 | $1,110 | $1,260 | | $1,280 | $1,625 |

*Recent auctions:* $1,057.50, MS-70, June 2014 (avg. gold spot value that month, $1,279). $1,292.50, PF-70UC, June 2014 (avg. gold spot value that month, $1,279).

\* "Raw" value is based on a gold spot price of $1,200 per ounce, and is for an uncertified Burnished or Proof coin of average quality. This value may vary with the prevailing bullion value.

# ANNA HARRISON (2009)

*Designer: Donna Weaver (obverse); Thomas Cleveland (reverse).* **Sculptor:** *Joseph F. Menna (obverse); Charles L. Vickers (reverse).* **Composition:** *.9999 gold.* **Actual Gold Weight:** *1/2 ounce.* **Diameter:** *26.49 mm.* **Edge:** *Reeded.* **Mint:** *West Point.* **Issue Price:** *$614 (Burnished); $629 (Proof).* **Release Date:** *March 5, 2009.*

**Burnished.**

The U.S. Mint unveiled the designs of the upcoming 2009 First Spouse coins on December 23, 2008.

"The First Spouse gold coin designs give us a glimpse into the fascinating lives of the women who supported, promoted, and often advised the men who led our country," said Mint Director Ed Moy.

For Anna Harrison, that glimpse involved an activity close to the First Lady's heart: education. Her mother had died when she was young, and from 12 to 15 years of age Anna boarded as a student with Isabella Marshall Graham, a widowed teacher and philanthropist who believed in equal education for women. Graham was one of the first American women to form a charitable organization, providing food, shelter, schooling, and jobs for poor widows and orphans. It is likely that young Anna helped her teach the children she cared for. At the age of 20 she married soldier William Henry Harrison, and the couple would eventually have six sons and four daughters of their own. Anna educated them in reading, writing, Bible studies, Greek philosophy, the works of Shakespeare, and other classics. Her devotion to such enlightenment is captured by Thomas Cleveland's coinage design showing her surrounded by children, reading to them from a book. Charles Vickers sculpted the reverse, skillfully imparting a multi-layered level of detail and texture to the scene.

The Anna Harrison First Spouse gold coin went on sale March 5, 2009. "Mintage . . . is limited to 40,000 across both product options," the Mint announced on February 25. "The ratio of Proof coins to Uncirculated coins produced will be determined by customer demand within the total maximum issuance of 40,000. A limit of 10 coins per product option per household will be in effect during the first week of sales. At the end of the initial sales period, the United States Mint will reevaluate this limit and either extend, adjust, or eliminate it."

The Anna Harrison gold coin was the first to be priced according to the U.S. Mint's new pricing structure for platinum and gold numismatic products, which was implemented January 12, 2009. Under this plan, product prices could change based on a range of the average market price for gold or platinum. The coin's issue price was $614 for the Burnished version and

**Anna Harrison (1775–1864); First Lady from March 4, 1841, to April 4, 1841.**

**Proof.**

**Reverse detail.**

$629 for the Proof, and its Mint price changed several times over the course of its offering, as gold's spot value fluctuated. Collector demand declined a bit from the preceding year, making Anna Harrison's gold piece the program's lowest seller—at least temporarily. Fewer than 10,000 pieces were sold all together. As is often the case with modern Mint issues, yesterday's snoozer is today's hot ticket; Anna Harrison commands some of the highest premiums in the First Spouse series.

The Harrison gold coin was offered in the Mint's product catalog for a year—far longer than Anna Harrison served as First Lady. In fact, she never even served in the executive mansion: William Henry Harrison died 30 days into his office, before his wife was able to make the journey to Washington. She was the first First Lady to be widowed while holding the title, and she was First Lady for the shortest period of time. In her old age Anna lived with her son John and his family, and she encouraged the education of her grandson, Ben—who would grow up to become President Benjamin Harrison.

**Mintage: 3,645 Burnished; 6,251 Proof**

| | Raw MS | <MS-69 | MS-69 | MS-70 | Raw PF | <PF-69 | PF-69 | PF-70 |
|---|---|---|---|---|---|---|---|---|
| **Certified** | — | 0 | 116 | 656 | — | 7 | 333 | 550 |
| **Value\*** | $1,100 | | $1,270 | $1,350 | $1,000 | | $1,025 | $1,360 |

*Certified Populations and Retail Market Values*

*Recent auctions:* $911, MS-70, January 2015 (avg. gold spot value that month, $1,252). $881, PF-70DC, August 2014 (avg. gold spot value that month, $1,296).

\* "Raw" value is based on a gold spot price of $1,200 per ounce, and is for an uncertified Burnished or Proof coin of average quality. This value may vary with the prevailing bullion value.

**Burnished.**

# LETITIA TYLER (2009)

*Designer: Phebe Hemphill (obverse); Susan Gamble (reverse). Sculptor: Phebe Hemphill (obverse); Norman E. Nemeth (reverse). Composition: .9999 gold. Actual Gold Weight: 1/2 ounce. Diameter: 26.49 mm. Edge: Reeded. Mint: West Point. Issue Price: $614 (Burnished); $629 (Proof). Release Date: July 2, 2009.*

The First Spouse gold coin for Letitia Tyler went on sale at 12 noon on July 2, 2009. Its issue price was pegged to the U.S. Mint's new gold pricing structure, established on January 12 of that year, whereby certain numismatic product prices would slide up or down according to a regularly adjusted scale, based on the changing precious-metals market.

For a variety of reasons, collectors stayed away from this coin. Some were disenchanted with the issue price—$614 for a half-ounce gold coin, when its precious-metal value was averaging about $470 for the month. Others saved their hobby budget for the Mint's flashy new Ultra High Relief MMIX (2009) Saint-Gaudens gold coin. And some had simply lost interest in the First Spouse series, as reflected in far fewer online bulletin-board discussions about the coins, compared to 2007 and 2008. The Mint kept the Letitia Tyler coin in its product lineup until June 3, 2010, and in its 11 months it mustered sales of only 3,240 Burnished pieces and 5,296 Proofs.

Proof.

**Letitia Tyler (1790–1842);
First Lady from April 4, 1841,
to September 10, 1842.**

The attractive designs and engraving of the coin were no detraction. Phebe Hemphill's portrait of Tyler shows a pretty and serene woman, looking younger than her 50 years. President John Tyler and his wife had a happy and fruitful marriage, with four daughters and three sons living to maturity. Letitia herself was not in the best of health, however. Two years before her husband became president, she suffered a paralyzing stroke. She lived upstairs in the executive mansion during his presidency, coming down only once, in January 1842, for their daughter Elizabeth's wedding. The phantom First Lady was well accustomed to managing a household, however—she had organized the family's 1,200-acre plantation in Virginia, and raised their children—so she was able to direct some of the presidential entertainments and coordinate some household affairs from behind the scenes. Sadly, her health continued to decline, and she passed away in September 1842, the first First Lady to die in office. The reverse of the Letitia Tyler gold coin shows her in happier times, playing with her eldest children at Cedar Grove Plantation, the Virginia home of her own childhood, where she would eventually be buried.

Reverse detail.

How has Letitia Tyler fared in the long run? As the old saying goes, "Pay me now, or pay me later." Collectors who didn't like a 30% premium over bullion value for the gold coin in 2009 can expect to pay a 100% premium today, thanks to the simple economic law of supply and demand.

**Mintage: 3,240 Burnished; 5,296 Proof**

| | Raw MS | <MS-69 | MS-69 | MS-70 | Raw PF | <PF-69 | PF-69 | PF-70 |
|---|---|---|---|---|---|---|---|---|
| **Certified Populations and Retail Market Values** | | | | | | | | |
| **Certified** | — | 0 | 229 | 548 | — | 8 | 234 | 513 |
| **Value\*** | $1,150 | | $1,275 | $1,360 | $1,210 | | $1,230 | $1,375 |

*Recent auctions:* $1,532, MS-70, June 2013 (avg. gold spot value that month, $1,342). $1,528, PF-70DC, August 2014 (avg. gold spot value that month, $1,296).

\* "Raw" value is based on a gold spot price of $1,200 per ounce, and is for an uncertified Burnished or Proof coin of average quality. This value may vary with the prevailing bullion value.

# Julia Tyler (2009)

**Designer:** *Joel Iskowitz (obverse and reverse).* **Sculptor:** *Don Everhart.* **Composition:** *.9999 gold.* **Actual Gold Weight:** *1/2 ounce.* **Diameter:** *26.49 mm.* **Edge:** *Reeded.* **Mint:** *West Point.* **Issue Price:** *$619 (Burnished); $629 (Proof).* **Release Date:** *August 6, 2009.*

**Burnished.**

**Proof.**

The First Spouse gold coin of Julia Tyler debuted for sale on August 6, 2009, some five weeks after its predecessor, that of Letitia Tyler. A parallel might be drawn to the speed with which President John Tyler remarried: he began courting Julia Gardiner a few months after his wife Letitia passed away in September 1842, and they were wed, in secret, in June 1844. The president was a youthful 54 years of age, and his new wife, the high-spirited daughter of a prominent New York landowner and politician, was 24. Their wedding was announced to the nation after the fact. The official reason given for the secrecy was that the Gardiner family was still in mourning for Julia's father, who had died in a freak cannon explosion that February.

"Julia Gardiner Tyler was part of a well-known New York family," the U.S. Mint noted in its promotional literature. "Though she presided as first spouse for only eight months, the second Mrs. Tyler quickly made her mark. Julia was popular in Washington society and used her considerable charm to promote her husband's political agenda, especially the annexation of Texas. She is credited with starting the custom of playing James Sanderson's 'Hail to the Chief' to announce the president's arrival on official occasions, a tradition that continues to this day."

The reverse of the coin shows Julia and John Tyler dancing in formal attire against a clean blank field—an appealing use of white space by U.S. Mint Artistic Infusion Program Master Designer Joel Iskowitz. The First Lady took her public role seriously, publicized her social activities, and became the first "celebrity" presidential wife, spending her own money to appear in public in lavish dress and a coach drawn by eight white Arabian horses. She granted permission for her name to be used in the title of the "Julia Waltzes" (popular sheet-music polkas), and was the first First Lady to publicly dance at the White House—hence the significance of Iskowitz's design.

The Julia Tyler gold coin sold in numbers even smaller than those of Letitia Tyler. Its issue was

**Julia Tyler (1820–1889); First Lady from June 26, 1844, to March 4, 1845.**

similar in details, as far as ordering limits and issue price. It was removed from the Mint's catalog after 10 months, when the Jane Pierce coin went on sale in June 2010. By that time its Mint price had risen from $619 to $766 for the Burnished version, and from $629 to $779 for the Proof, due to the rising price of gold. The two Tyler spouses share strong premiums in today's market. Collector demand and low mintage combine to bring double their bullion value for uncertified examples.

Reverse detail.

**Mintage: 3,143 Burnished; 4,844 Proof**

| Certified Populations and Retail Market Values | | | | | | | | |
|---|---|---|---|---|---|---|---|---|
| | Raw MS | <MS-69 | MS-69 | MS-70 | Raw PF | <PF-69 | PF-69 | PF-70 |
| Certified | — | 2 | 178 | 733 | — | 10 | 356 | 485 |
| Value* | $1,155 | | $1,275 | $1,360 | $1,210 | | $1,230 | $1,375 |
| | Recent auctions: $1,293, MS-70, June 2015 (avg. gold spot value that month, $1,182). $1,116, PF-70DC, September 2014 (avg. gold spot value that month, $1,239). | | | | | | | |

* "Raw" value is based on a gold spot price of $1,200 per ounce, and is for an uncertified Burnished or Proof coin of average quality. This value may vary with the prevailing bullion value.

# SARAH POLK (2009)

***Designer:*** *Phebe Hemphill (obverse and reverse).* ***Sculptor:*** *Phebe Hemphill (obverse and reverse).* ***Composition:*** *.9999 gold.* ***Actual Gold Weight:*** *1/2 ounce.* ***Diameter:*** *26.49 mm.* ***Edge:*** *Reeded.* ***Mint:*** *West Point.* ***Issue Price:*** *$641 (Burnished); $654 (Proof).* ***Release Date:*** *September 3, 2009.*

On Tuesday, September 1, 2009, the U.S. Mint announced that the Sarah Polk First Spouse gold coin would be released at 12:00 noon Eastern Time two days hence. Its mintage was limited to 40,000 pieces total for the Proof and Burnished product options, with customer demand determining the quantity produced of each format. As with recent issues, the Mint initially limited orders to 10 coins per product option per household for the first week of sales. After that the Mint would reevaluate the limit and either continue it, adjust it, or remove it. The ordering limit would eventually be dropped, and the coins were part of the Mint's product catalog for about a year. During that time its price fluctuated according to the market value of gold, following the Mint's established sliding scale.

Burnished.

Sarah Polk (1803–1891); First Lady from March 4, 1845, to March 4, 1849.

**Proof.**

**Reverse detail.**

"Sarah Childress Polk received an education traditionally available only to the most privileged young women of her time," the Mint's promotional literature noted, "which made her especially fitted to assist a husband with a political career. She devoted her married life to husband James K. Polk's political career, organizing his campaigns, writing speeches, handling his correspondence, and developing a network of valuable political friendships. Skilled in tactful conversation, Mrs. Polk enjoyed wide popularity and deep respect. She instituted many changes at the White House, including its refurbishment and the installation of gas lighting."

Not mentioned: the religiously conservative Sarah banned (at least temporarily) dancing, liquor, and card games at White House receptions. Compared to her predecessor, the vivacious First Lady Julia Tyler, Mrs. Polk earned the nickname "Sahara Sarah."

The obverse of Sarah Polk's gold coin is graced by an attractive portrait by Medallic Sculptor Phebe Hemphill, showing the First Lady's famous ringlets of hair and her pursed smile. The reverse, also by Hemphill, features one of the series' few designs showing both wife and husband. The scene at first glance appears homespun and domestic, with Sarah gesturing to a paper she's holding while James regards it. The tableau has deeper meaning, however, symbolizing the First Lady's great influence in the president's professional life. Sarah acted as her husband's personal secretary, deciding what news and information was important enough to bring to him, and acting as a liaison to the general public and even to government officials. "She is certainly master of herself," observed Vice President George Dallas, "and I suspect of someone else, also."

This was the first and only coin of the First Spouse program to be entirely designed and sculpted, obverse as well as reverse, by a single individual.

Near the end of its run, in September 2010, the Mint was selling the Sarah Polk gold coin for $766 (Burnished) and $779 (Proof). The total mintage was higher than that of Julia Tyler, but didn't even reach 9,000 coins. Today the Burnished coin, unslabbed, has appreciated in value by about 20% over the closing Mint price (40% over its original issue price). It sells at a premium over the higher-mintage Proof.

**Mintage: 3,489 Burnished; 5,151 Proof**

| Certified Populations and Retail Market Values | | | | | | | |
|---|---|---|---|---|---|---|---|
| | **Raw MS** | **<MS-69** | **MS-69** | **MS-70** | **Raw PF** | **<PF-69** | **PF-69** | **PF-70** |
| **Certified** | — | 1 | 163 | 539 | — | 3 | 173 | 594 |
| **Value*** | $930 | | $1,025 | $1,410 | $810 | | $830 | $1,025 |

*Recent auctions:* $823, MS-69, January 2015 (avg. gold spot value that month, $1,252). $998, PF-70, August 2014 (avg. gold spot value that month, $1,296).

* "Raw" value is based on a gold spot price of $1,200 per ounce, and is for an uncertified Burnished or Proof coin of average quality. This value may vary with the prevailing bullion value.

# MARGARET TAYLOR (2009)

*Designer: Phebe Hemphill (obverse); Mary Beth Zeitz (reverse).* **Sculptor:** *Charles L. Vickers (obverse); Jim Licaretz (reverse).* **Composition:** *.9999 gold.* **Actual Gold Weight:** *1/2 ounce.* **Diameter:** *26.49 mm.* **Edge:** *Reeded.* **Mint:** *West Point.* **Issue Price:** *$741 (Burnished); $754 (Proof).* **Release Date:** *December 3, 2009.*

On November 25, 2009, the U.S. Mint announced it would begin accepting orders for the Margaret Taylor First Spouse gold coin at noon Eastern Time on December 3. Maximum mintage was set at 40,000 across all product options, with the ratio of Proof to Burnished coins to be determined by customer demand. Pricing for the coin was based on the Mint's sliding-scale retail structure for numismatic products containing precious metals. A limit of 10 coins per format per household was in effect for the first few weeks of sales. Demand was modest, and the Mint lifted this limit in January 2010 in an effort to encourage interest in the coins.

Margaret Taylor (1788–1852); First Lady from March 4, 1849, to July 9, 1850.

Burnished.

Margaret "Peggy" Mackall Smith, from a wealthy Maryland family, was married to Zachary Taylor when he was a young U.S. Army lieutenant. They made their life together in remote military posts and camps from Louisiana to northern Wisconsin as he established his Army career and grew the family business. The obverse of the Margaret Taylor gold coin shows us the kind of woman who would devote herself to a life of such hardship after growing up in comfort. Taylor's portrait was designed by Phebe Hemphill and sculpted by Charles Vickers, both full-time artists on the Mint staff. It shows a strong and determined Margaret Taylor—from the artist's imagining, as no photographs or other likenesses of her have been authenticated. An account from November 1848, shortly before the Taylors entered the White House, describes her thus: "Dress plain, and in good taste; manners dignified and easy, countenance rather stern but it may be the consequence of military association. Person tall and commanding, demeanor retiring, with no palpable predilection for high station; and, judging from appearance, one would suppose the White House offers no peculiar attractions. . . ."[8] Vickers, sculpting from Hemphill's design, graced the portrait with exquisite detail, finely rendering the First Lady's lace collars and even the tiny cameo profile on her brooch.

Proof.

The reverse of the gold coin was designed by Artistic Infusion Program Associate Designer Mary Beth Zeitz and sculpted by Medallic Sculptor Jim Licaretz. It shows Margaret during the Second Seminole War, about 12 years before the White House. Her husband was assigned to Florida, where he defeated the Seminole Indians in one of the largest battles of the 1800s, was promoted to brigadier general and placed in command of all U.S. troops in

Reverse detail.

the state, and became known as "Old Rough and Ready." Margaret Taylor is shown at the bedside of a wounded and heavily bandaged American soldier, offering comfort and care. It is a scene of great empathy and tenderness.

The president's wife was in delicate health as First Lady, and she entrusted public engagements and White House hostess functions to their popular young daughter, "Miss Betty." Zachary Taylor died 18 months into his presidency, and grieving Margaret followed him two years later.

The Margaret Taylor gold coin was part of the Mint's product lineup for one year. Sales ended on December 2, 2010, at which point the catalog price was $841 (Burnished) and $854 (Proof). Gold at that time was running about $1,390 per ounce in the bullion market. Collectors and investors bought just over 8,500 coins, slightly fewer than the preceding Sarah Polk issue. Supply and demand have kept the secondary-market numismatic value about 33% ahead of their precious-metal value.

**Mintage: 3,627 Burnished; 4,936 Proof**

| | Certified Populations and Retail Market Values | | | | | | | |
|---|---|---|---|---|---|---|---|---|
| | **Raw MS** | **<MS-69** | **MS-69** | **MS-70** | **Raw PF** | **<PF-69** | **PF-69** | **PF-70** |
| **Certified** | — | 0 | 116 | 872 | — | 9 | 316 | 582 |
| **Value\*** | $825 | | $850 | $1,110 | $800 | | $825 | $1,110 |
| | *Recent auctions:* $754, MS-70, December 2014 (avg. gold spot value that month, $1,202). $823, PF-70, August 2014 (avg. gold spot value that month, $1,296). | | | | | | | |

\* "Raw" value is based on a gold spot price of $1,200 per ounce, and is for an uncertified Burnished or Proof coin of average quality. This value may vary with the prevailing bullion value.

# ABIGAIL FILLMORE (2010)

***Designer:*** *Phebe Hemphill (obverse); Susan Gamble (reverse).* ***Sculptor:*** *Phebe Hemphill (obverse); Joseph F. Menna (reverse).* ***Composition:*** *.9999 gold.* ***Actual Gold Weight:*** *1/2 ounce.* ***Diameter:*** *26.49 mm.* ***Edge:*** *Reeded.* ***Mint:*** *West Point.* ***Issue Price:*** *$716 (Burnished); $729 (Proof).* ***Release Date:*** *March 18, 2010.*

The designs of the upcoming 2010 First Spouse gold coins were unveiled by the Mint on December 21, 2009. The first of them, for Abigail Fillmore, went on sale March 18, 2010, at 12 noon Eastern Time. Two significant changes accompanied its release: the maximum mintage was lowered from 40,000 coins to 15,000 (across both formats, Burnished and Proof, with customer demand determining how many of each); and the Mint set no household ordering limit. Whether these changes were factors or not, collectors and investors did buy about 12% more than the preceding issue.

Phebe Hemphill designed and sculpted the obverse portrait of Abigail Powers Fillmore, showing the steady gaze of an educated and intellectually curious woman. Like Anna Harrison before her, First Lady Abigail Fillmore is remembered for her connection to education. "She developed a passion for learning early in life," the Mint's publicist noted. "Financial circumstances forced her to begin working at the age of 16 as a teacher while she continued her own education. While teaching at the New Hope Academy in Sempronius, New York, she met future husband, Millard Fillmore. After their marriage, she continued to teach for another two years until their first child was born, making her the first presidential spouse to hold a paying job after her marriage. Throughout

Burnished.

her life, she continued her zeal for self-improvement by reading voraciously, attending lectures and Congressional debates, and participating in political discussions. Perhaps her most lasting contribution as First Lady was her work in establishing a permanent White House library, for which President Fillmore asked Congress to appropriate funds. With $2,000 authorized for the project, Fillmore acquired several hundred volumes to start the collection in a second-floor oval parlor, where she enjoyed entertaining such guests as authors Washington Irving, Charles Dickens, and William Makepeace Thackeray. She also spent many hours selecting and arranging books for the library."

Abigail Fillmore (1798–1853); First Lady from July 9, 1850, to March 4, 1853.

Susan Gamble's reverse design, sculpted by Mint medallic sculptor Joseph Menna, depicts Abigail Fillmore in the surroundings that delighted her. The First Lady is in the White House parlor library, carrying four large, heavy books while shelving a smaller volume. No fewer than 50 books are visible in the charming composition—undoubtedly a favorite design of the Numismatic Bibliomania Society, a group of collectors of coin- and money-related books, catalogs, and similar literature.[9]

Proof.

The Fillmore gold coin was part of the Mint's product line for more than a year, with the Burnished format offered until late March 2011 and the Proof until May 5 (when the Eliza Johnson coin went on sale). At final audit, just more than 9,600 coins were sold—an increase over each of the 2009 coins except that of Anna Harrison, which, interestingly, also featured a First Lady holding a book. Perhaps the Numismatic Bibliomania Society's membership appreciated the connection of coins and literature enough to push sales upward? Today the Fillmore coin enjoys aftermarket premiums of 50% or more over its precious-metal value. This illustrates the First Spouse program's hybrid status as a *bullion* series (like the American Gold Eagles, which trade as commodities) with strong *collector-coin* elements (more like the U.S. Mint's commemorative coinage).

Reverse detail.

**Mintage: 3,482 Burnished; 6,130 Proof**

| | Raw MS | <MS-69 | MS-69 | MS-70 | Raw PF | <PF-69 | PF-69 | PF-70 |
|---|---|---|---|---|---|---|---|---|
| **Certified Populations and Retail Market Values** | | | | | | | | |
| **Certified** | — | 0 | 97 | 698 | — | 3 | 181 | 664 |
| **Value*** | $950 | | $1,025 | $1,110 | $900 | | $930 | $1,030 |
| | *Recent auctions:* $852, MS-70, July 2015 (avg. gold spot value that month, $1,130). $793, PF-70DC, August 2014 (avg. gold spot value that month, $1,296). | | | | | | | |

\* "Raw" value is based on a gold spot price of $1,200 per ounce, and is for an uncertified Burnished or Proof coin of average quality. This value may vary with the prevailing bullion value.

**Burnished.**

**Proof.**

# JANE PIERCE (2010)

*Designer: Donna Weaver (obverse and reverse). Sculptor: Don Everhart (obverse); Charles L. Vickers (reverse). Composition: .9999 gold. Actual Gold Weight: 1/2 ounce. Diameter: 26.49 mm. Edge: Reeded. Mint: West Point. Issue Price: $766 (Burnished); $779 (Proof). Release Date: June 3, 2010.*

The U.S. Mint announced on May 28, 2010, that it would begin accepting orders for the Jane Pierce First Spouse gold coin on June 3, at 12 noon Eastern Time. As with the year's earlier Abigail Fillmore coin, the maximum mintage was set at 15,000 total, with customer demand determining how many would be Burnished and how many Proof. The Mint set no household ordering limit. The issue price of $766 (Burnished) or $779 (Proof) was based on the Mint's sliding-scale schedule that followed the preceding week's average gold price, plus manufacturing costs and margin.

U.S. Mint Artistic Infusion Program Master Designer Donna Weaver crafted the stately portrait of Pierce on the obverse. She repeated the dignified three-quarter-profile pose in a wider scene on the reverse, showing the First Lady seated in the visitors' gallery of the Old Senate Chamber in the U.S. Capitol Building.

If there is a hint of melancholy to this coin and its portraiture, it's with good reason: by the time Franklin Pierce was sworn in as the nation's 14th president, he and his wife had lost all three of their children. One boy died in infancy, another at the age of four from epidemic typhus. Then, just two months before Pierce's inauguration, their only surviving child, 11-year-old Benny, was killed when their railroad passenger car broke loose and rolled down an embankment. For two years Jane Pierce mourned her last son, praying and writing apologetic letters to him (she felt God was punishing the Pierces for her husband's political ambitions). Finally she emerged from mourning and took on some of the usual social duties of First Lady.

Seated in the Senate visitors' gallery, Mrs. Pierce would likely have been listening to the chamber's debates over slavery, an increasingly contentious issue in American politics in the mid-1850s.

The Mint's sales period for the Jane Pierce coins was shorter than many others in the series. The Proof version was removed from the Mint catalog after nine months, on March 4, 2011, and the Burnished followed it on

**Jane Pierce (1806–1863); First Lady from March 4, 1853, to March 4, 1857.**

March 22. Final mintages were the lowest among the 2010 issues—significantly so for the Proof format, which was only two-thirds that of the next coin in the series.

Today the Jane Pierce gold coin enjoys a premium in Proof, typically selling for 10% more than other recent issues.

**Reverse detail.**

**Mintage: 3,338 Burnished; 4,775 Proof**

| Certified Populations and Retail Market Values | | | | | | | | |
|---|---|---|---|---|---|---|---|---|
| | **Raw MS** | **<MS-69** | **MS-69** | **MS-70** | **Raw PF** | **<PF-69** | **PF-69** | **PF-70** |
| **Certified** | — | 0 | 74 | 547 | — | 6 | 290 | 514 |
| **Value\*** | $850 | | $875 | $960 | $1,000 | | $1,030 | $1,225 |

*Recent auctions:* $940, MS-70, August 2014 (avg. gold spot value that month, $1,296). $1,116, PF-70DC, August 2014 (avg. gold spot value that month, $1,296).

\* "Raw" value is based on a gold spot price of $1,200 per ounce, and is for an uncertified Burnished or Proof coin of average quality. This value may vary with the prevailing bullion value.

**Liberty Head
quarter eagle (1840–1907).**

# JAMES BUCHANAN'S LIBERTY (2010)

*Designer: Christian Gobrecht (obverse); David Westwood (reverse). Sculptor: Joseph F. Menna (reverse). Composition: .9999 gold. Actual Gold Weight: 1/2 ounce. Diameter: 26.49 mm. Edge: Reeded. Mint: West Point. Issue Price: $766 (Burnished); $779 (Proof). Release Date: September 2, 2010.*

The design of the 2010 James Buchanan's Liberty gold bullion coin was unveiled in Washington, DC, on December 21, 2009. On June 29, 2010, the U.S. Mint announced that the coin would be released for sale on September 2. As with other recent issues, the combined mintage for Burnished and Proof pieces was capped at 15,000, with customer demand determining the quantities of each format. No household ordering limits were set.

This was the fourth and final First Spouse gold coin in the so-called Liberty subset. "Because President James Buchanan did not have a spouse," the Mint announced, "the obverse of his corresponding First Spouse Gold Coin features a design emblematic of Liberty as it appeared on a U.S. coin issued during his time in office." It features a reproduction of the Liberty Head design by Christian Gobrecht, minted on the quarter eagle ($2.50 gold piece) from 1840 through 1907. (In an interesting case of "what might have been," the Citizens Coinage Advisory Committee, which advises the Treasury on coin designs, had leaned toward using the Flying Eagle cent of 1856 to 1858.)

The Liberty Head motif was the dominant obverse element of U.S. gold coins minted from the late 1830s to the early 1900s. Undoubtedly Gobrecht's elegant and popular design attracted a share of collector interest above and beyond that of First Spouse specialists and bullion investors. Writing about the Proof format in particular, Eric Jordan and John Maben have noted, "This attractive $10 Proof gold coin is the last issue of an affordable four-coin set

**Burnished.**

**Proof.**

**Reverse detail.**

that is in some ways a tour of the great designs of the 1800s that can't be acquired in a cameo Proof format any other way. . . . It's the *only* option if you like the look of high-grade antique Proof gold but have to live within a reasonable budget."[10]

As to why there was no First Spouse in James Buchanan's life, modern historians and biographers support the idea that the Pennsylvania politician was gay. For whatever reason, he is the only U.S. president to have remained a lifelong bachelor. Unrelated to his personal life, many presidential historians rank Buchanan as one of the nation's worst chief executives. Despite grand ideas he proved unable to map out a plan for peace as the country became more and more split by the slavery question. The Southern states seceded in the waning months of his presidency, and the Civil War erupted shortly after. Avoiding these political failings, the reverse design of the Buchanan's Liberty coin focuses not on his presidential tenure but on his early life. Artistic Infusion Program Associate Designer David Westwood envisioned Buchanan as a young man keeping a ledger in his father's country store in Pennsylvania. It is a scene of quiet work and dedication—the boy who would grow up to be an "incorruptible statesman" (as honored on his congressionally approved memorial in Washington, DC), rather than the beleaguered president overwhelmed by national events.

Buchanan's Liberty was the most popular of the First Spouse gold coins of 2010 in each format, and one of the last of the program's issues to exceed a mintage of 10,000. In the first three days of sales, the Mint sold more than 6,000 pieces total, nearing the halfway point of the issue's maximum coinage. Collector interest continued to be strong, and the Mint announced a second round of minting just weeks into the sales period. Ultimately more than 12,000 coins were purchased before the Mint closed its sales of the Proof version on February 8, 2011, and of the Burnished version on April 11.

Demand for the Liberty subset keeps the secondary-market prices of this issue relatively high, despite its larger-than-average mintage.

**Mintage: 5,162 Burnished; 7,110 Proof**

| Certified Populations and Retail Market Values | | | | | | | | |
|---|---|---|---|---|---|---|---|---|
| | Raw MS | <MS-69 | MS-69 | MS-70 | Raw PF | <PF-69 | PF-69 | PF-70 |
| **Certified** | — | 0 | 88 | 803 | — | 1 | 433 | 931 |
| **Value\*** | $850 | | $875 | $1,110 | $900 | | $960 | $1,220 |
| *Recent auctions:* $999, MS-70, August 2014 (avg. gold spot value that month, $1,296). $999, PF-70DC, August 2014 (avg. gold spot value that month, $1,296). | | | | | | | | |

\* "Raw" value is based on a gold spot price of $1,200 per ounce, and is for an uncertified Burnished or Proof coin of average quality. This value may vary with the prevailing bullion value.

# Mary Todd Lincoln (2010)

*Designer: Phebe Hemphill (obverse); Joel Iskowitz (reverse). Sculptor: Phebe Hemphill (obverse and reverse). Composition: .9999 gold. Actual Gold Weight: 1/2 ounce. Diameter: 26.49 mm. Edge: Reeded. Mint: West Point. Issue Price: $841 (Burnished); $854 (Proof). Release Date: December 2, 2010.*

On June 29, 2010, the U.S. Mint announced that it anticipated releasing the Mary Todd Lincoln First Spouse gold coin on December 2. This tentative launch date was confirmed in another press announcement of November 24. The maximum mintage was raised from 15,000 coins—which was the cap for the three other issues of 2010—to 20,000, with the ratio of Burnished to Proof being determined by customer demand. Mary Lincoln's connection to one of the most popular and famous of American presidents was the reason for the increased maximum mintage. There was no household limit to the number of coins ordered. As with other recent gold issues, the Lincoln First Spouse coin was priced by the Mint's sliding scale that followed the average market price of the precious metal.

Mary Todd Lincoln cuts an intriguing and controversial figure among the First Ladies of the United States. In her time (and even today), detractors painted her as out of touch with reality, jealous, high-strung, and extravagant in frivolous spending during the Civil War. Supporters note that she was a savvy advisor to her husband and an active partner in his political career despite their sometimes turbulent marriage, and that her wartime spending was to increase

Burnished.

the prestige of the presidency and the Union. She was not, as some Northern critics theorized, a Confederate spy, despite having grown up in Kentucky, the daughter of an influential slave-owning businessman. Socializing at a young age with the likes of neighbor and family friend Senator Henry Clay, Mary Todd cultivated an interest in politics. In her early twenties she was living with her sister's family in Springfield, Illinois, when she met attorney and state legislator Abe Lincoln. They wed in 1842, and several years later he was elected to the U.S. House of Representatives. Mary focused on advancing her husband's

Mary Todd Lincoln (1818–1882); First Lady from March 4, 1861, to April 15, 1865.

Proof.

**Reverse detail.**

political interests, which culminated in his bid for the presidency. In the White House she continued her role as advisor and confidant.

Phebe Hemphill's portrait of Mary Todd Lincoln shows a relaxed and confident woman, beautifully attired in a floral headpiece, earrings, and necklace. Inspired by a Mathew Brady photograph, Hemphill's vision is of the educated and stylish Lexington socialite who steered her husband to the executive mansion—not the nervous, increasingly unhinged victim of family tragedies, who would later be committed by her son to a private asylum. Joel Iskowitz's reverse design is a tour de force, one of the most dramatic of the series. The scene is of injured Union soldiers in a hospital during the war. Some are sprawled on the ground. One is lying on a bench; another hobbles on crutches. All of the men, in fact, have crutches—symbolic of the huge number of amputations and grievous limb injuries suffered during the Civil War. This is not a clean, sterile environment of peaceful rest and recuperation. Uniforms are in disarray. The hobbling soldier has no beard—a mere youth, cut by war. The barrel of a rifle intrudes into the scene at the left, over the head of a wounded soldier: more symbolism, of the constant wartime threat of injury and death. Into this grim scene comes a figure of hope and charity: Mary Todd Lincoln, the First Lady herself, bearing gifts of books and flowers to entertain and refresh the weary troops. She often made such visits during the war, distributing fresh fruit, comforting the wounded, writing letters for them to their families. "I am sitting by the side of our soldier boy," she wrote to the mother of a soldier at Campbell General Hospital, not far from the White House, in the summer of 1864. "He has been quite sick, but is getting well. He tells me to say to you that he is all right."[11]

The U.S. Mint declared the Mary Todd Lincoln gold coin sold out in Burnished format in June 2011, after slightly more than six months of production and sales. The Proof version stayed in the Mint's product lineup several more months, until November 9. With a total mintage of 10,556 pieces, the Lincoln issue was the last of the First Spouse coins to break the 10,000 mark—until Jackie Kennedy came along four years later and sold more than that quantity in a single day.

**Mintage: 3,695 Burnished; 6,861 Proof**

| | | | | | | | | |
|---|---|---|---|---|---|---|---|---|
| **Certified Populations and Retail Market Values** | | | | | | | | |
| | **Raw MS** | **<MS-69** | **MS-69** | **MS-70** | **Raw PF** | **<PF-69** | **PF-69** | **PF-70** |
| **Certified** | — | 0 | 115 | 515 | — | 3 | 333 | 736 |
| **Value*** | $850 | | $875 | $1,075 | $900 | | $930 | $1,300 |

*Recent auctions:* $823, MS-70, October 2014 (avg. gold spot value that month, $1,222). $881, PF-70DC, August 2014 (avg. gold spot value that month, $1,296).

* "Raw" value is based on a gold spot price of $1,200 per ounce, and is for an uncertified Burnished or Proof coin of average quality. This value may vary with the prevailing bullion value.

# ELIZA JOHNSON (2011)

*Designer: Joel Iskowitz (obverse); Gary Whitley (reverse). Sculptor: Don Everhart (obverse); Phebe Hemphill (reverse). Composition: .9999 gold. Actual Gold Weight: 1/2 ounce. Diameter: 26.49 mm. Edge: Reeded. Mint: West Point. Issue Price: $916 (Burnished); $929 (Proof). Release Date: May 5, 2011.*

The U.S. Mint announced the issue date of the Eliza Johnson First Spouse gold coin on December 29, 2010, publicizing that it would be released on March 3, 2011. A month prior to release, the Mint announced the designs of all four First Spouse coins slated for 2011.

The Eliza Johnson rollout was delayed two months, and the coin actually debuted for sale on May 5, 2011, the same day as the bullion-grade American Gold Eagle. Gold's spot price had been on the rise since the start of the year, so the Johnson coin's issue price was higher than that of its predecessor. (The Mint's selling price was based on its sliding scale that followed the market value of gold, and it would change over the course of the offering.) By April it was clear the Mary Todd Lincoln coin would barely reach half of its maximum mintage of 20,000 coins, so the mintage cap of the Eliza Johnson coin returned to the "Buchanan's Liberty" level of 15,000 across both formats, Burnished and Proof. There was no household ordering limit.

Burnished.

Eliza Johnson (née McCardle), born and raised in Tennessee, is credited as a strong influence in the life of her husband Andrew, a tailor at the time they were introduced. They met in their teens and married when she was only 16 years old. The better-educated Eliza tutored her young husband in his reading, writing, and arithmetic. Andrew Johnson would become both a voracious reader and a successful businessman, and Eliza encouraged him in his political career while staying out of the limelight herself. Andrew was elected to positions in local, state, and federal government up to the office of vice president under Abraham Lincoln. After the Great Emancipator was assassinated in 1865, Andrew Johnson became the nation's 17th president and Eliza joined him in the White House, moving from her wartime home in Nashville. As First Lady, poor health and a retiring disposition led Eliza to largely confine her role to that of hostess for formal dinners and the visits of foreign heads of state. She directed her daughters in the

Proof.

Eliza Johnson (1810–1876);
First Lady from April 15,
1865, to March 4, 1869.

**Reverse detail.**

office's more public appearances and responsibilities. While she was never the most vibrant or accessible presidential spouse, nor was she quite the shut-in invalid that some biographers have described.

Two notable public appearances by Eliza Johnson were a reception held for Queen Emma of Hawaii and a celebration of her husband's birthday. The reverse of her First Spouse gold coin shows three youths dancing at the children's ball held for the president's 60th birthday, a fête attended by 300 of their grandchildren's friends and schoolmates and the sons and daughters of various Washington officials, diplomats, and White House staff. The children were given red-carpet treatment, the executive mansion's rooms were filled with flowers, and entertainment was provided by Marine Band musicians and students from a local dance academy. The only parents present were the president and First Lady themselves and their adult children, the official hosts of the party. Eliza, seated in an armchair, greeted each young guest. The event was a testimony to her love of children, and is engagingly illustrated in Artistic Infusion Program Associate Designer Gary Whitley's reverse motif, sculpted by Phebe Hemphill. In it, a boy and two girls dance merrily to a tune sawed out by a Marine Corps fiddler in the background.

The Mint sold the Eliza Johnson coins for more than 12 months—a longer selling period than usual. With sales declining and its inventory depleted, the Mint declared the Burnished format sold out on June 5, 2012, rather than minting more. The Proof version was declared sold out on June 20. The combined mintage of just under 6,800 coins was a new series low (one that would be broken later in the year). Today the Eliza Johnson coins enjoy a robust premium over their bullion value in all grades and formats.

**Mintage: 2,905 Burnished; 3,887 Proof**

| | Certified Populations and Retail Market Values | | | | | | | |
|---|---|---|---|---|---|---|---|---|
| | **Raw MS** | **<MS-69** | **MS-69** | **MS-70** | **Raw PF** | **<PF-69** | **PF-69** | **PF-70** |
| **Certified** | — | 1 | 63 | 422 | — | 1 | 200 | 425 |
| **Value*** | $875 | | $900 | $1,575 | $870 | | $910 | $1,130 |
| | *Recent auctions:* $1,294, MS-70, August 2014 (avg. gold spot value that month, $1,296). $763, PF-70DC, June 2015 (avg. gold spot value that month, $1,182). | | | | | | | |

* "Raw" value is based on a gold spot price of $1,200 per ounce, and is for an uncertified Burnished or Proof coin of average quality. This value may vary with the prevailing bullion value.

# JULIA GRANT (2011)

**Designer:** *Donna Weaver (obverse); Richard Masters (reverse).* **Sculptor:** *Michael Gaudioso (obverse); Charles L. Vickers (reverse).* **Composition:** *.9999 gold.* **Actual Gold Weight:** *1/2 ounce.* **Diameter:** *26.49 mm.* **Edge:** *Reeded.* **Mint:** *West Point.* **Issue Price:** *$916 (Burnished); $929 (Proof).* **Release Date:** *June 23, 2011.*

On June 16, 2011, the U.S. Mint announced that it would begin accepting orders for the Julia Grant First Spouse gold coin on June 23, starting at noon Eastern Time. The issue's mintage limit was set at 15,000 coins, proportioned between the Burnished and Proof formats as customer demand dictated. No household ordering limit was set. Pricing was based on the Mint's sliding-scale structure that followed the market value of gold.

The day before the Julia Grant gold coin went on sale, Ian Russell, president of GreatCollections, addressed hobbyists who were skeptical of the First Spouse program. "I know people say they aren't popular," he wrote, "but they have probably been one of the best investments in numismatics over the past two to three years. I like them."[12] Sales for the Grant issue would increase slightly over the preceding Johnson issue, with customer demand having settled near the 7,000-coin mark, about half of the Mint's established maximum mintage. The Proof format continued to be more popular than Burnished by about a 30% margin. Today both formats command numismatic premiums well over their intrinsic gold value.

The subject of the coin, born Julia Boggs Dent, was the daughter of a wealthy slaveholding businessman in Missouri. She grew up at White Haven, a plantation west of St. Louis, which is where she met Ulysses S. Grant, a West Point classmate of her brother's. They married in their 20s despite Ulysses's father disapproving of Julia's family (for owning slaves) and her father disapproving of Ulysses for his unpromising military career. Like many military wives, Julia joined her husband in most of his garrison and camp positions, and during the Civil War this often put her close to battle. Ulysses rose to the rank of general before the conflict's first year was over. "Unconditional Surrender Grant" would ride out the war as a national hero and the Commanding General of the United States Army. His popularity led to an electoral-landslide victory in the presidential election of 1868, making him the youngest chief executive (at age 46) up to that point.

**Burnished.**

In the White House Julia Grant brought refreshing energy to the position of First Lady. The nation had been wracked by a long and devastating war, the assassination of Abraham Lincoln, and the impeachment of Andrew Johnson. Julia returned the White House to a level of happiness not enjoyed since the days of Julia Tyler, 25 years before. She entertained lavishly and often, with guests partaking of expensive wines and liquors; she dressed in finery and jewels befitting the nation's triumphant commander-in-chief; she hosted a glittering East Room wedding for their daughter Nellie in 1874. The obverse portrait of Julia Grant, designed by Donna Weaver and sculpted by Michael Gaudioso, shows the First Lady in a ruffled outfit and earrings, her hair immaculately coiffed. The reverse design features a younger Julia during her courtship—she and Ulysses are on horseback, riding at her family's estate of White Haven. Charles Vickers's engraving of a design by Artistic Infusion Program Master Designer Richard Masters is an engaging and lively portrayal with attractive detail.

**Julia Grant (1810–1876); First Lady from March 4, 1869, to March 4, 1877.**

**Proof.**

Reverse detail.

By March of 2012 the U.S. Mint, after gauging sales, decided not to order another press run for the Proof version of the Julia Grant coins. The issue was declared sold out in Proof format at the end of the month. As was typically the case with the First Spouse program, "sold out" meant only that the Mint's existing inventory had been purchased and that no more would be minted. It did not mean that the mintage limit of 15,000 coins had been met. The Burnished pieces would continue to sell until August 28, 2012. In total, counting both formats, collectors and investors bought 6,835 of the coins.

Mintage: 2,892 Burnished; 3,943 Proof

| Certified Populations and Retail Market Values | | | | | | | | |
|---|---|---|---|---|---|---|---|---|
| | Raw MS | <MS-69 | MS-69 | MS-70 | Raw PF | <PF-69 | PF-69 | PF-70 |
| Certified | — | 0 | 56 | 385 | — | 5 | 277 | 337 |
| Value* | $860 | | $900 | $1,120 | $875 | | $900 | $1,075 |

*Recent auctions:* $940, MS-70, August 2014 (avg. gold spot value that month, $1,296). $881, PF-70DC, August 2014 (avg. gold spot value that month, $1,296).

* "Raw" value is based on a gold spot price of $1,200 per ounce, and is for an uncertified Burnished or Proof coin of average quality. This value may vary with the prevailing bullion value.

# Lucy Hayes (2011)

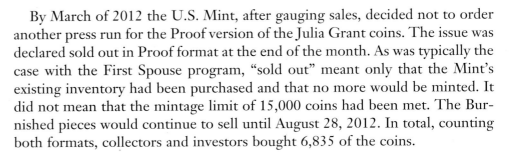

**Designer:** *Susan Gamble (obverse); Barbara Fox (reverse).* **Sculptor:** *Don Everhart (obverse); Joseph F. Menna (reverse).* **Composition:** *.9999 gold.* **Actual Gold Weight:** *1/2 ounce.* **Diameter:** *26.49 mm.* **Edge:** *Reeded.* **Mint:** *West Point.* **Issue Price:** *$1,041 (Burnished); $1,054 (Proof).* **Release Date:** *September 1, 2011.*

Burnished.

On August 30, 2011, the U.S. Mint announced that it would begin accepting orders for the Lucy Hayes First Spouse gold coin two days hence, at noon Eastern Time on September 1. The ratio of Proof coins to Burnished coins would be determined by customer demand, with the total maximum mintage being capped at 15,000. Pricing was based on the market value of gold, following the Mint's sliding scale. Gold bullion was at a peak, and the Hayes issue debuted with the highest prices of the First Spouse program, at more than $1,000 per coin.

First Lady Julia Grant had brought an entertaining vitality back to the White House after years of war and political strife. The open liquor bar, however, would dry up with her successor. Lucy Hayes was serious and devoutly Christian,

Lucy Hayes (1831–1889);
First Lady from March 4,
1877, to March 4, 1881.

and she supported her husband's opinions on alcoholic beverages. Their ban on booze in the executive mansion gave Rutherford Hayes's administration the nickname of "the Cold Water Regime" and earned his wife the sobriquet of "Lemonade Lucy." In the Hayes White House, the water flowed like wine.

Mrs. Hayes ran the presidential mansion more as the household of their family life than as a center of public events. She championed the family and home life as the solid foundation of the United States. "America is the cradle of the future for all the world," she said. "Elevate woman, and you lift up the home; exalt the home and you lift up the nation." The obverse of her First Spouse gold coin (designed by Susan Gamble and sculpted by Don Everhart) gives us a serious-looking portrait of the First Lady.

While her state dinners were sober and sedate, when it came to children Lucy Hayes was an enthusiastic hostess who loved to plan parties. She is famous for having arranged the first Easter egg roll held at the White House—a scenario acted out on the reverse of her First Spouse gold coin. Artistic Infusion Program Associate Designer Barbara Fox designed the tableau, and Joseph Menna sculpted it. Lucy Hayes, smiling happily, claps her hands to cheer on a boy and girl who are pushing Easter eggs with spoons on the White House lawn. This is a delightful scene showing the other side of the stern teetotaler: a family-oriented woman, loving and supportive of the nation's youth.

The market value of gold stayed high during the months the Lucy Hayes coins were on sale, although it did drop a bit so the Mint's selling price decreased by about $100. After about 11 months the inventory of Burnished coins dried up, and rather than order another press run the Mint reported the Burnished version sold out on August 6, 2012. The final mintage—a mere 2,196 coins—was the lowest of the First Spouse program, and indeed the smallest mintage of any modern U.S. gold coin. The Proof format stayed on sale for the rest of the year, with the Mint's "Last Chance" sale ending on December 31, 2012. Today the Lucy Hayes coins command some of the highest premiums in the series.

Proof.

Reverse detail.

**Mintage: 2,196 Burnished; 3,868 Proof**

| Certified Populations and Retail Market Values | | | | | | | | |
|---|---|---|---|---|---|---|---|---|
| | **Raw MS** | **<MS-69** | **MS-69** | **MS-70** | **Raw PF** | **<PF-69** | **PF-69** | **PF-70** |
| **Certified** | — | 0 | 67 | 266 | — | 1 | 271 | 275 |
| **Value\*** | $1,225 | | $1,450 | $1,850 | $900 | | $920 | $1,200 |
| | *Recent auctions:* $1,763, MS-70, February 2015 (avg. gold spot value that month, $1,227). $999, PF-70DC, August 2014 (avg. gold spot value that month, $1,296). | | | | | | | |

\* "Raw" value is based on a gold spot price of $1,200 per ounce, and is for an uncertified Burnished or Proof coin of average quality. This value may vary with the prevailing bullion value.

**Burnished.**

**Proof.**

# LUCRETIA GARFIELD (2011)

*Designer:* Barbara Fox (obverse); Michael Gaudioso (reverse). *Sculptor:* Phebe Hemphill (obverse); Michael Gaudioso (reverse). *Composition:* .9999 gold. *Actual Gold Weight:* 1/2 ounce. *Diameter:* 26.49 mm. *Edge:* Reeded. *Mint:* West Point. *Issue Price:* $1,016 (Burnished); $1,029 (Proof). *Release Date:* December 1, 2011.

On November 22, 2011, the U.S. Mint announced that the Lucretia Garfield First Spouse gold coin would go on sale at noon Eastern Time, December 1. As with the other issues of 2011, its potential mintage was capped at 15,000 pieces across all product options, with customer demand determining the ratio of Proof to Burnished coins. Pricing was set by the Mint's fluctuating scale that followed the bullion value of gold.

This final First Spouse issue of 2011 honored the woman born Lucretia ("Crete") Rudolph in Hiram, Ohio, in 1832. She met her future husband, James Garfield, when they both were students at Geauga Seminary in Chester, Ohio. He was attracted to her wit and intelligence. Both were 26 years old when they married and set up their household in 1858. When the Civil War erupted in 1861 James, by then a state senator, enthusiastically recruited soldiers in Ohio, was granted a regimental colonelcy, and entered active-duty command by the end of the year. His military service separated the couple until 1863, when James entered the U.S. House of Representatives. The Garfields built a network of intellectual friends in the nation's capital, attending literary society meetings together, making social calls, dining, traveling, and otherwise enjoying each other's company inseparably. Lucretia was a valued advisor to her husband; she enjoyed listening to political debates and would report her findings and opinions to him. Congressman Garfield was elected to the presidency in 1880, and he, Lucretia, and their five teenaged and younger children entered the White House. The more frivolous social duties of First Lady didn't interest the intellectual Lucretia, but she was welcoming and hospitable, hosting enjoyable dinners and twice-weekly receptions. (Ignoring pressure from pro-temperance associates, she lifted the Hayes administration's ban on alcohol in the White House.) Lucretia investigated restoring the White House's furnishings and decorations to their historical origins, one of her personal interests, and

**Lucretia Garfield (1832–1918); First Lady from March 4, 1881, to September 19, 1881.**

she made plans to invite famous musicians, writers, and artists to White House dinners. Unfortunately these pursuits were cut short on July 2, 1881, when President Garfield was shot by a frustrated office-seeker. He died 11 weeks later.

We see some of the same melancholy of Jane Pierce's 2010 First Spouse gold coin in the portrait of Lucretia Garfield from 2011. "Oh, why am I made to suffer this cruel wrong?" she asked the president's doctor on the evening he finally succumbed from his gunshot wound and unsanitary medical care. The widowed Lucretia would live another 36 years without her husband, in the privacy of their old farm in northern Ohio. There's something in the eyes of Barbara Fox's portrait of the First Lady, sculpted by Phebe Hemphill, that speaks of the tragedy and sadness that awaited her in the summer of 1881. The coin's reverse tableau, designed and sculpted by Michael Gaudioso, looks to happier times, with a vision of the creatively inclined First Lady in a studio, seated painting at an easel. The scene is quiet, contemplative, and warmly personal, completely focused on the artist absorbed in her art.

**Reverse detail.**

When the preceding 2011 First Spouse issue, that of Lucy Hayes, sold out unexpectedly on August 6, 2012 (with a very low final sales number), speculators eagerly turned to the Lucretia Garfield coin. Collectors, investors, and dealers (most likely more of the latter) hurriedly placed orders for some 500 of the coins in early August. Many of the orders were put on "back order" and ultimately canceled by the Mint, and the Burnished Garfield issue was declared sold out on August 9. As with the Hayes Proof coins, the Garfield Proofs would stay on sale in the Mint's catalog for another several months, finally being removed on December 31, 2012. Collectors knew that the Burnished Garfield would be a low-mintage issue, judging by preliminary sales numbers (which are never final, but have to be reconciled with returns). The final audit would show the Lucretia Garfield First Spouse gold coin to have a series-low mintage of just 2,168 pieces. Today the Burnished version in particular commands strong premiums in the secondary market.

**Mintage: 2,168 Burnished; 3,653 Proof**

| Certified Populations and Retail Market Values | | | | | | | | |
|---|---|---|---|---|---|---|---|---|
| | Raw MS | <MS-69 | MS-69 | MS-70 | Raw PF | <PF-69 | PF-69 | PF-70 |
| Certified | — | 0 | 38 | 260 | — | 4 | 212 | 268 |
| Value* | $1,200 | | $1,400 | $2,000 | $900 | | $925 | $1,200 |

*Recent auctions:* $1,410, MS-70, March 2015 (avg. gold spot value that month, $1,179). $1,116, PF-70DC, August 2014 (avg. gold spot value that month, $1,296).

\* "Raw" value is based on a gold spot price of $1,200 per ounce, and is for an uncertified Burnished or Proof coin of average quality. This value may vary with the prevailing bullion value.

**Burnished.**

**Proof.**

# ALICE PAUL (2012)

*Designer:* Susan Gamble (obverse); Phebe Hemphill (reverse). *Sculptor:* Phebe Hemphill (obverse and reverse). *Composition:* .9999 gold. *Actual Gold Weight:* 1/2 ounce. *Diameter:* 26.49 mm. *Edge:* Reeded. *Mint:* West Point. *Issue Price:* $1,041 (Burnished); $1,054 (Proof). *Release Date:* October 11, 2012.

In December 2011, Secretary of the Treasury Timothy Geithner directed that the U.S. Mint suspend minting and issuing Presidential dollars for circulation. "Regular circulating demand for the coins will be met through the Federal Reserve Bank's existing inventory of circulating coins minted prior to 2012," the Mint announced, noting that it would still offer various products and packages containing the dollar coins. Although the Presidential $1 Coin Act of 2005 tied the First Spouse coins to the Presidential dollars, this change had no effect on the issuance of the gold pieces.

On April 23, 2012, the U.S. Mint announced the design of the year's first First Spouse gold coin. "Public Law 109-145, the Presidential $1 Coin Act of 2005, contains a provision for the continuity of the First Spouse Coin Program in the event that a president served without a first spouse. In the case of President Chester Arthur, who was widowed before he took office, the Act specifically requires that the obverse (heads side) design for his corresponding First Spouse gold coin incorporate the name and likeness of Alice Paul, a leading strategist in the suffrage movement who was born during his term. The Act specifies that the reverse (tails side) design be representative of the suffrage movement."

The mintage limit for the Alice Paul coin was lowered from the previous year's 15,000 to 13,000, with customer demand determining how many would be Burnished and how many Proof.

Complications in striking the coins delayed their release until late in the year. They finally went on sale October 11, 2012. Initial demand was strong, perhaps with some buyers anticipating a short sales period and therefore a low mintage. Nearly a quarter of the mintage limit was ordered in the first week.

As with the prior year's issues, the 2012 First Spouse coins were priced by the Mint's sliding scale based on the fluctuating market value of gold. They started out higher than $1,000 per coin, but a decline in the spot value led to prices as low as $840 for the Proof format and $820 for the Burnished. The Proof coins remained on sale into the summer of 2013, with the Mint declaring them sold out on July 16. The final Proof mintage, after an official audit accounting for returned and melted coins, was 3,505. The Burnished version remained in the Mint's product catalog until December 31, 2013, with a final mintage of 2,798.

Some collectors bemoaned the U.S. Mint's "political correctness" in depicting suffragist Alice Paul instead of a coinage-inspired Miss Liberty to represent the

**Alice Paul (1885–1977).**

presidency of widower Chester Alan Arthur. This complaint mischaracterizes the source of the design: the U.S. Congress, not the Mint. Alice Paul was written into the First Spouse program's authorizing legislation.

Reverse detail.

The coin's obverse design departs from others in the series with the word SUF-FRAGIST underneath Alice Paul's portrait, instead of the ordinal of Arthur's presidency (21st) and the year-date range of his term (1881–1885). The portrait, designed by Susan Gamble and sculpted by Phebe Hemphill, has Alice facing the viewer with a steady and determined gaze that embodies her strength and courage. Alice was born in New Jersey in 1885 and raised in the Quaker traditions of public service and gender equality. She studied social work but soon realized that "I was never going to be a social worker, because I could see that social workers were not doing much good in the world. . . . you couldn't change the situation by social work." The "situation" was the inequality endured by women worldwide. In England in her early 20s Alice developed a more militant advocacy for women's rights, taking part in protests and being jailed for voicing her beliefs. She returned to the United States energized and well known. She publicized the cause of equal rights—in particular the right of women to vote—on a national scale, organizing a 1913 parade march in Washington, DC, the day before Woodrow Wilson's inauguration as president. The lead banner in the march read, "We Demand an Amendment to the United States Constitution Enfranchising the Women of the Country." Alice Paul and other suffragists pushed the right-to-vote agenda for several more years, facing arrest, harassment, and even brutal confinement to psychiatric wards, which only fueled popular support for their cause. Finally in June 1919 the U.S. Senate passed the Constitution's 19th amendment, which was ratified in August 1920, guaranteeing women the right to vote. The reverse of the Alice Paul First Spouse gold coin, designed and sculpted by Phebe Hemphill, shows Alice in action, marching for equality with an American flag and a sash reading VOTES FOR WOMEN. Her stride is bold, and the energy of the motif, with the flag and the sash in motion, captures the suffragist's forward movement.

The Alice Paul gold coin is something of an anomaly in the First Spouse series, illustrating neither a First Lady nor a purely symbolic coinage-inspired representation of Liberty. However, no other suffragist embodies the ideals of American liberty—and the human urge to fight and to endure personal suffering for the liberty of others—more so than Alice Paul. Yes, there are coins from the era of Chester Arthur's presidency that depict Liberty and could have been used, making this the fifth in the series' Liberty subset. The Morgan dollar, the Indian Head cent, the Liberty Head nickel, and the Indian Princess Head $3 gold piece come to mind. But as a *living* symbol of American liberty, Alice Paul fits the First Spouse gold coin quite nicely.

## Mintage: 2,798 Burnished; 3,505 Proof

| Certified Populations and Retail Market Values | | | | | | | | |
|---|---|---|---|---|---|---|---|---|
| | Raw MS | <MS-69 | MS-69 | MS-70 | Raw PF | <PF-69 | PF-69 | PF-70 |
| Certified | — | 0 | 39 | 346 | — | 3 | 207 | 308 |
| Value* | $800 | | $820 | $875 | $880 | | $900 | $975 |
| *Recent auctions:* $881, MS-70, September 2014 (avg. gold spot value that month, $1,239). $764, PF-70DC, August 2014 (avg. gold spot value that month, $1,296). | | | | | | | | |

\* "Raw" value is based on a gold spot price of $1,200 per ounce, and is for an uncertified Burnished or Proof coin of average quality. This value may vary with the prevailing bullion value.

**Burnished.**

**Proof.**

# FRANCES CLEVELAND, VARIETY 1 (2012)

*Designer: Joel Iskowitz (obverse); Barbara Fox (reverse). **Sculptor:** Don Everhart (obverse); Michael Gaudioso (reverse). **Composition:** .9999 gold. **Actual Gold Weight:** 1/2 ounce. **Diameter:** 26.49 mm. **Edge:** Reeded. **Mint:** West Point. **Issue Price:** $1,016 (Burnished); $1,029 (Proof). **Release Date:** November 15, 2012.*

Although the designs of the 2012 First Spouse gold coins were officially announced as early as April 23, production challenges delayed their sales until early winter. The coin marking Frances Cleveland's first of two terms as First Lady was released for sale on November 15, 2012. The maximum mintage was set at 13,000 across all production options, with customer demand determining the ratio of Proof coins to Burnished coins. Pricing was set by the U.S. Mint's published schedule that fluctuated based on the market value of gold.

Frances Cleveland is a special case in the First Spouse gold coin program. She is the only First Lady to have served two non-consecutive terms (1886 to 1889, and 1893 to 1897), because her husband's two presidential terms were separated by that of Benjamin Harrison. For this reason she appears on two individual coin varieties in the series. (First Ladies who served consecutive terms were honored on a single coin each.)

Frances Clara Folsom (called "Frank" after an uncle) was born in 1864 in Buffalo, New York, to lawyer Oscar Folsom and his wife Emma. A longtime friend of Oscar's, Grover Cleveland, doted on baby Frances, and when Oscar died in a carriage accident in 1875 with no will, Grover was court-appointed as administrator of his estate. This brought him closer to young Frances, supervising her upbringing along with her mother. In the meantime his law practice and political career propelled Grover into higher and higher public offices; he was elected governor of New York in 1882 and then won the presidency in 1884. Frances's mother granted permission for Grover to correspond with her while she was in college and he was in the White House. He proposed marriage to her shortly after she graduated in 1885.

The American public surprisingly was not scandalized by the age difference between the president and his bride—she was only 21 years old, the youngest First Lady ever, and he was 49 when they married in 1886. Leading up to the nuptials Frances Cleveland became a celebrity, with newspapers clamoring for details. The White House wedding (the first and only wedding of a sitting president) was a small, private ceremony, held in the Blue Room. After the wedding Frances's beauty and charm won her widespread popularity. Private firms struck commemorative medals celebrating her, along with sundry trinket boxes, sheet music, refreshments, and other products bearing her face and even her name. Advertisers enthusiastically used her portrait, not worrying about getting permission, to hawk everything from candy to cigars. Young American women copied her clothes and her hairstyles. Newspapers put her on their covers knowing that sales would boom.

Unable to stem the tide of this commercial exploitation, Frances Cleveland decided to use her celebrity for goals more important than selling chocolates and newspapers. She became a strong advocate of women's charities and orphanages, supported educational opportunities for female factory workers,

Reverse detail.

and helped the careers of young lady musicians. She started a weekly White House reception for working-class women, held on Saturday so they could meet the First Lady on their day off. Clerks, shopgirls, and servants could go to the executive mansion and speak with the president's wife in the beautiful East Room. This revolutionary environment is captured on the reverse of the Frances Cleveland, Variety 1, gold coin, designed by Barbara Fox and sculpted by Michael Gaudioso. The popular young First Lady is seen greeting three everyday American women dressed in their finest clothes and obviously delighted with the opportunity. It is a charming populist scene that captures the energy and excitement of the First Lady's weekly receptions.

**Frances Cleveland (1864–1947); First Lady from June 2, 1886, to March 4, 1889 (first term).**

Grover Cleveland lost the 1888 presidential election, but Frances knew that their days in the White House weren't over. She is said to have told the staff to keep up the home and its furnishings because she and her husband would be back in four years. She was right.

The U.S. Mint's Frances Cleveland, Variety 1, coins were available in its product catalog through 2013, with sales closing on December 31. The market value of gold fluctuated down, up, and down over the course of the year, starting in January with a monthly average of $1,671 per ounce and closing in December with an average of $1,225. The general downward trend of gold likely explains why demand dropped about 11% for the coin, compared to its predecessor, which had a five-week head-start in sales. With current supply and demand so close for the Alice Paul and Frances Cleveland coins, they enjoy the same premiums in the secondary market.

**Mintage: 2,454 Burnished; 3,158 Proof**

| | Raw MS | <MS-69 | MS-69 | MS-70 | Raw PF | <PF-69 | PF-69 | PF-70 |
|---|---|---|---|---|---|---|---|---|
| **Certified Populations and Retail Market Values** | | | | | | | | |
| **Certified** | — | 0 | 25 | 252 | — | 2 | 116 | 231 |
| **Value*** | $800 | | $820 | $875 | $880 | | $900 | $975 |

*Recent auctions:* $911, MS-70, February 2015 (avg. gold spot value that month, $1,227). $646, PF-69DC, October 2014 (avg. gold spot value that month, $1,222).

* "Raw" value is based on a gold spot price of $1,200 per ounce, and is for an uncertified Burnished or Proof coin of average quality. This value may vary with the prevailing bullion value.

**Burnished.**

**Proof.**

# CAROLINE HARRISON (2012)

*Designer: Frank Morris (obverse); Donna Weaver (reverse). Sculptor: Michael Gaudioso (obverse); Charles L. Vickers (reverse). Composition: .9999 gold. Actual Gold Weight: 1/2 ounce. Diameter: 26.49 mm. Edge: Reeded. Mint: West Point. Issue Price: $1,016 (Burnished); $1,029 (Proof). Release Date: December 6, 2012.*

The U.S. Mint announced the designs of all four 2012 First Spouse gold coins in April of that year. However, production delays caused by striking difficulties would keep collectors and investors waiting until December to get their hands on the Caroline Harrison coin. The Mint began accepting orders at noon Eastern Time on December 6. As with the other 2012 coins, mintage was capped at 13,000 across all options, with customer demand setting the ratio of Proof to Burnished coins. The Mint's pricing was based on its sliding-scale structure, which followed the market price of gold bullion. The issue prices of $1,016 and $1,029 would fall over the coins' 12 months of sales, as gold decreased in bullion value.

The subject of the third 2012 coin was born Caroline Lavinia Scott in Ohio in 1832. Her father was a minister and a professor of science and mathematics, and she and her siblings grew up well educated, surrounded by books, music, and art. Caroline enrolled in the Oxford (Ohio) Female Institute, which her father presided over, studying painting, theater, literature, and art. She taught piano music while in school. During this time she was courting Benjamin Harrison, one of her father's students from Farmer's College. They would marry in 1853. Caroline volunteered in patriotic associations during the Civil War, while Benjamin organized troops and eventually took on a military command. After the war he entered the U.S. Senate and the Harrisons moved their family to Washington. Benjamin was elected president in 1888, defeating incumbent Grover Cleveland.

Caroline Harrison brought charm, humor, and a creative eye to her position as First Lady—diplomatic traits that bolstered the social capital of her less friendly and outgoing husband. Upset by the crowded and dilapidated condition of sections of the White House, she secured a budget from Congress to upgrade and renovate the historic mansion, and had electricity and new plumbing installed. She was famous for her love of flowers, in particular orchids, and her devotion to the arts. Her interest in china-painting—the decoration of glazed porcelain plates, vases, and similar objects—helped popularize that art form in America. These personal interests are embodied in the First Spouse gold coin's reverse, designed by Donna Weaver and sculpted by Charles Vickers. The dominant theme is a spray of orchids, which Caroline established as the official floral decoration for White House receptions and dinners. To the right is a set of paintbrushes, symbolizing the First Lady's lifelong passion for the arts in general and painting in particular.

Caroline Harrison's interest in aesthetics and the life of the mind was balanced by hands-on activity in public affairs. She helped found the Daughters of the American Revolution in order to promote the nation's history, and served as the group's first president general. She was active in church life and social-welfare clubs, promoted American business, and called for the admission of women as students in the Johns Hopkins School of Medicine.

Reverse detail.

**Caroline Harrison (1832–1892); First Lady from March 4, 1889, to October 25, 1892.**

Late in 1891 Caroline contracted tuberculosis, and as she weakened she found the official duties of First Lady to be too taxing. A summer retreat to the Adirondacks in 1892 failed to rally her strength and she returned to Washington. She passed away in the White House that October.

The Caroline Harrison First Spouse gold coin was not a barnburner in the sales department. With gold trending downward through 2013, and with the third 2012 First Spouse released so soon after the second, demand for the coin was—not surprisingly—lower than for the Frances Cleveland coin, which was lower than for the Alice Paul. Today, thanks to collector demand being higher than the limited supply, all of the 2012 issues command similar premiums in the aftermarket.

**Mintage: 2,436 Burnished; 3,046 Proof**

| Certified Populations and Retail Market Values | | | | | | | | |
|---|---|---|---|---|---|---|---|---|
| | **Raw MS** | **<MS-69** | **MS-69** | **MS-70** | **Raw PF** | **<PF-69** | **PF-69** | **PF-70** |
| **Certified** | — | 0 | 10 | 299 | — | 1 | 69 | 272 |
| **Value*** | $800 | | $820 | $875 | $880 | | $900 | $1,075 |
| | *Recent auctions:* $793, MS-70, August 2014 (avg. gold spot value that month, $1,296). $1,028, PF-70DC, August 2014 (avg. gold spot value that month, $1,296). | | | | | | | |

\* "Raw" value is based on a gold spot price of $1,200 per ounce, and is for an uncertified Burnished or Proof coin of average quality. This value may vary with the prevailing bullion value.

**Burnished.**

**Proof.**

# FRANCES CLEVELAND, VARIETY 2 (2012)

*Designer: Barbara Fox (obverse); Joseph F. Menna (reverse).* **Sculptor:** *Phebe Hemphill (obverse); Joseph F. Menna (reverse).* **Composition:** *.9999 gold.* **Actual Gold Weight:** *1/2 ounce.* **Diameter:** *26.49 mm.* **Edge:** *Reeded.* **Mint:** *West Point.* **Issue Price:** *$991 (Burnished); $1,004 (Proof).* **Release Date:** *December 20, 2012.*

The second variety of Frances Cleveland First Spouse coin went on sale December 20, 2012. It would be part of the Mint's product catalog until December 31, 2013; over the course of its offering, the market value of gold rose and fell, and the Mint's weekly issue prices fluctuated with it, dipping as much as $150 lower than its December 2012 debut prices.

As she'd predicted in 1889, First Lady Frances Cleveland did indeed return to the White House after a four-year hiatus. In the meantime she and Grover, living in New York City, had become parents. Their daughter "Baby Ruth" caused a national sensation because of the family's celebrity. Parenthood softened Grover's reputation of having been a rough-edged philanderer in his bachelor days. After the Clevelands returned to the executive mansion in 1893, Frances gave birth to another daughter—the first child born to a sitting president—and then another, in 1895. She brought a kindergarten teacher to the White House in the first formal school held there. The media were as fascinated with the Cleveland children as they were with Frances, and for privacy's sake the family maintained a personal home close to the White House. The ever-popular First Lady needed a social secretary to handle the volume of her fan mail.

She was the first First Lady to officially visit a head of state (the queen regent of Spain, who was touring Washington), and she was sympathetic to the cause of Princess Kaiulani of Hawaii, whose aunt had been dethroned by American businessmen.

After their second stay in the White House ended the Clevelands retired to Princeton, New Jersey, and were soon joined by two sons. Grover passed away in 1908, and in 1913 Frances became the first First Lady to remarry. She died in 1947 in Baltimore and was buried beside the president in Princeton.

Barbara Fox's portrait of Frances in her second term shows the First Lady as pretty and stylish as she was in the late 1880s—perhaps a bit more mature, no longer the 21-year-young lady, but a mother and the president's faithful wife of nearly a dozen years. The reverse, designed and engraved by Joseph Menna, shows the presi-

**Frances Cleveland (1864–1947); First Lady from March 4, 1893, to March 4, 1897 (second term).**

dential couple in a telling scene: President Cleveland in the middle background, and his wife, the celebrity First Lady, waving to an adoring crowd.

All of the 2012 First Spouse gold coins have similar values in the secondary market, with retail and auction prices markedly higher than their bullion value.

**Reverse detail.**

**Mintage: 2,425 Burnished; 3,104 Proof**

| Certified Populations and Retail Market Values | | | | | | | | |
|---|---|---|---|---|---|---|---|---|
| | Raw MS | <MS-69 | MS-69 | MS-70 | Raw PF | <PF-69 | PF-69 | PF-70 |
| Certified | — | 0 | 20 | 266 | — | 3 | 92 | 242 |
| Value* | $800 | | $820 | $875 | $880 | | $900 | $975 |
| | Recent auctions: $881, MS-70, September 2014 (avg. gold spot value that month, $1,239). $881, PF-70DC, June 2015 (avg. gold spot value that month, $1,182). | | | | | | | |

\* "Raw" value is based on a gold spot price of $1,200 per ounce, and is for an uncertified Burnished or Proof coin of average quality. This value may vary with the prevailing bullion value.

# IDA MCKINLEY (2013)

*Designer: Susan Gamble (obverse); Donna Weaver (reverse). **Sculptor:** Phebe Hemphill (obverse); Renata Gordon (reverse). **Composition:** .9999 gold. **Actual Gold Weight:** 1/2 ounce. **Diameter:** 26.49 mm. **Edge:** Reeded. **Mint:** West Point. **Issue Price:** $820 (Burnished); $840 (Proof). **Release Date:** November 14, 2013.*

The U.S. Mint announced the designs for the 2013 First Spouse gold coins on August 6 of that year. They had been delayed by ongoing discussion between the Citizens Coinage Advisory Committee and the Commission of Fine Arts. "The first 2013 coin, honoring Ida Saxton McKinley, will be available in early fall," said Mint press contact Carolyn Fields. "Specific release dates for all five coins will be posted to the United States Mint's product schedule at www.usmint.gov/catalog once established." Production was postponed as the Mint worked to reduce finning, a technical problem whereby a wire rim of extra metal builds up at a coin's edges as it's struck.[13] "The production team is working through this problem," the Mint announced on September 23, "and we are confident we will be able to resolve the issue." The McKinley coins finally went on sale November 14, 2013, at noon Eastern Time. Their maximum mintage was set at 10,000 across all product options, with customer demand determining the ratio of Proof to Burnished coins. This was a reduction from the maximum of 13,000 coins established the previous year.

The subject of the First Spouse program's first coin of 2013 was born Ida Saxton, eldest daughter of a

**Burnished.**

**Ida McKinley (1847–1907); First Lady from March 4, 1897, to September 14, 1901.**

**Proof.**

**Reverse detail.**

prominent Canton, Ohio, banker, and granddaughter of the founder of the city's first newspaper. She was sent to Pennsylvania to attend the Brook Hall Seminary finishing school, and in 1867 she met her future husband, William "Bill" McKinley, at a picnic. He was a successful attorney who had recently started getting into politics, and Ida worked at her father's bank as a cashier—an important managerial position normally held by a man. She and Bill began courting in 1869, after her grand tour of Europe. They wed on January 25, 1871, when she was 23 and he was 27. Their first daughter was born on Christmas Day that year. Their second daughter was born in the spring of 1873 and died in infancy that summer. This loss sent the already delicate and nervous Ida into a lasting depression and her health became more fragile, worsening further after their first daughter died of typhoid fever in 1875.

Despite developing epilepsy in 1873, Ida insisted that her husband continue his legal and political careers. She held strong beliefs, supporting women's rights to vote and to pursue higher education, and, later, protecting native Filipinos as the United States became involved in the Philippines. Declining health made her a semi-invalid, dependent on Bill's attention and protection; her epileptic seizures sometimes occurred in public, including one at the ball held for his inauguration as governor of Ohio. When they became president and First Lady, he broke diplomatic etiquette at state dinners by seating her next to him instead of at the far end of the table. Historian Blanche Wiesen Cook describes how, when Ida was about to suffer a seizure, Bill would gently cover her face with a kerchief to hide her contortions, carry on, and then quietly remove it. Although the details of her illness were kept private, the president's patience and his loving devotion to his wife were well known in the nation's capital. Ohio congressman Mark Hanna observed, "President McKinley has made it pretty hard for the rest of us husbands here in Washington."

Ida was traveling with her husband when he was shot twice at close range by an assassin in Buffalo, New York, in September 1901. She was not personally with the president when he was attacked, but his thoughts were with her: "My wife," he said to his secretary, "be careful, Cortelyou, how you tell her. Oh, be careful." He died a few days later. Ida McKinley would later write to an old friend, "I am more lonely every day I live." She visited his grave almost daily and joined him six years later.

The reverse of her First Spouse gold coin illustrates the pastime that occupied Ida McKinley's life as a semi-invalid: crotcheting slippers. These became gifts for friends and, along with personally designed floral arrangements, Ida contributed them to charities, which would auction them to benefit their programs. The scene, as designed by Donna Weaver and sculpted by Renata Gordon, is a clever combination of negative space and delicately implied motion. On the obverse the sumptuous detail of Susan Gamble's portrait of McKinley, sculpted by Phebe Hemphill, mirrors the woven intricacy of the lanyard encircling the First Lady's hands on the reverse.

"December 31, 2013, is the final day the West Point Mint can strike 2013 coins," noted Steve Roach, then editor of *Coin World*, in an October 2013 column. "Sales can continue indefinitely, and without a clear sales deadline, it seems that it is becoming increasingly tough to motivate collectors to buy these coins from the Mint." Still, he continued, "Those who are already invested in the series can look at the bright side. Today's low demand translates to low mintages, creating tomorrow's rarities."[14] A couple years after their debut, with gold's bullion value around $1,200 per ounce, the Ida McKinley First Spouse coin is worth its initial issue price or slightly more. Given its low mintage, if demand rises there's no place for its value to go but up.

**Mintage: ~1,973 Burnished; ~1,769 Proof**

| | Raw MS | <MS-69 | MS-69 | MS-70 | Raw PF | <PF-69 | PF-69 | PF-70 |
|---|---|---|---|---|---|---|---|---|
| **Certified Populations and Retail Market Values** | | | | | | | | |
| **Certified** | — | 0 | 20 | 248 | — | 2 | 131 | 229 |
| **Value\*** | $750 | | $770 | $870 | $815 | | $830 | $870 |
| Recent auctions: $823, MS-70, July 2014 (avg. gold spot value that month, $1,311). $1,093, PF-70DC, July 2015 (avg. gold spot value that month, $1,130). | | | | | | | | |

\* "Raw" value is based on a gold spot price of $1,200 per ounce, and is for an uncertified Burnished or Proof coin of average quality. This value may vary with the prevailing bullion value.

# EDITH ROOSEVELT (2013)

*Designer: Joel Iskowitz (obverse); Chris Costello (reverse).* **Sculptor:** *Joseph F. Menna (obverse); Don Everhart (reverse).* **Composition:** *.9999 gold.* ***Actual Gold Weight:*** *1/2 ounce.* **Diameter:** *26.49 mm.* **Edge:** *Reeded.* **Mint:** *West Point.* **Issue Price:** *$820 (Burnished); $840 (Proof).* **Release Date:** *November 21, 2013.*

**Burnished.**

On November 14, 2013—the day the Ida McKinley First Spouse coins went on sale—the U.S. Mint announced that it would begin accepting orders for the program year's second coin, that of Edith Roosevelt, on November 21. The maximum mintage would be 10,000 coins across all product options, with customers, not the Mint, determining the ratio of Burnished versus Proof coins.

The coin's subject, née Edith Kermit Carow, was born in Norwich, Connecticut, in 1861. Her father was an import-export merchant and her maternal grandfather was a railroad president and Union Army brigadier general. She and her sister grew up in New York City as next-door neighbors and childhood friends of the wealthy and philanthropic Roosevelt family, including Theodore ("Teedie," or T.R.), two years her senior. Edith and T.R. were close companions, but they were separated when he left for Harvard College and later married a schoolmate's cousin. His first wife died less than two days after the birth of their daughter. Nearly two years later T.R. proposed marriage to Edith; they kept their engagement secret for appearance's sake, and were wed after a year.

**Edith Roosevelt (1861–1948); First Lady from September 14, 1901, to March 4, 1909.**

Edith's personality was down-to-earth and reserved—a good balance for her larger-than-life husband's. Motherhood was the main focus of her energy, as she managed the family household and raised six children, including the daughter from T.R.'s first marriage. She

**Proof.**

**Reverse detail.**

quietly supported his career as he served as a New York State assemblyman, New York City police commissioner, assistant secretary of the Navy, colonel of the Rough Riders, governor of New York, and vice president. After William McKinley was assassinated and "the Colonel" became president, Edith devoted herself to turning the White House into a home suitable for a large, rambunctious family. She transformed the second floor of the West Wing into their private domain, and followed the lead of Frances Cleveland, whom she knew, in remodeling and upgrading the property. Under Edith and with the enthusiastic support of her husband, the White House became an executive mansion appropriate to the greatest nation in the world, and America's social center. She protected her children from the insatiable newspapers, but did allow photographer Frances Benjamin Johnston to photograph them (and their menagerie of beloved pets) and released the photos to the press, to satisfy national curiosity. "A lady's name should appear in print only three times," she said. "At her birth, marriage, and death." In spite of her private nature Edith was a vigorously active hostess of formal festivities, state receptions, smaller parties, and afternoon musicals. One famous reception was that of Prince Henry of Prussia, brother of Kaiser Wilhelm II of Germany. On the personal side, the Roosevelts' eldest daughter, nicknamed "Princess Alice" by the press, was introduced as a debutante during the family's White House years and was later married in the mansion.

In an article in the Fall 2013 issue of the *Theodore Roosevelt Association Journal*, Michael F. Moran describes his championing of the Edith Roosevelt gold coin's designs while he served on the Citizens Coinage Advisory Committee.[15] "The best image of Edith was the photograph taken in 1900 that [biographer] Sylvia Morris termed the 'Goddess Picture.' To me it showed a woman both elegant and self-confident in the prime of her life. It was all the more outstanding in that Edith Roosevelt was genuinely camera-shy. Her preferred pose seems nearly always to have included wearing a large hat with the netting pulled down, a veil, if you will, between the camera and her." The Goddess Picture was one of the inspirations for Joel Iskowitz's beautiful obverse portrait of Edith, perfectly rendered by Joseph Menna. On the reverse Chris Costello's design, sculpted by Don Everhart, symbolizes Edith's restoration of the White House with an Ionic column overlaid with an architect's compass, and a view of the executive mansion from the South Lawn.

Collectors purchased about two-thirds more of the Edith Roosevelt Proof gold coin than that of Ida McKinley. It would be the year's best seller in the Proof format, and the second-highest seller in Burnished. Today all of the 2013 coins see similar pricing in the secondary market, although this might change as demand increases or decreases for various issues.

**Mintage: ~1,913 Burnished; ~2,851 Proof**

| | Raw MS | <MS-69 | MS-69 | MS-70 | Raw PF | <PF-69 | PF-69 | PF-70 |
|---|---|---|---|---|---|---|---|---|
| **Certified Populations and Retail Market Values** | | | | | | | | |
| **Certified** | — | 0 | 14 | 244 | — | 1 | 71 | 281 |
| **Value*** | $750 | | $770 | $870 | $815 | | $830 | $870 |
| | *Recent auctions:* $856, MS-70, June 2015 (avg. gold spot value that month, $1,182). $1,180, PF-70DC, August 2015 (avg. gold spot value that month, $1,117). | | | | | | | |

* "Raw" value is based on a gold spot price of $1,200 per ounce, and is for an uncertified Burnished or Proof coin of average quality. This value may vary with the prevailing bullion value.

# HELEN TAFT (2013)

*Designer:* William C. Burgard (obverse); Richard Masters (reverse).
*Sculptor:* Phebe Hemphill (obverse); Charles L. Vickers (reverse).
*Composition:* .9999 gold. *Actual Gold Weight:* 1/2 ounce. *Diameter:*
26.49 mm. *Edge:* Reeded. *Mint:* West Point. *Issue Price:* $795
(Burnished); $815 (Proof). *Release Date:* December 2, 2013.

As was the case with the other First Spouse gold coins of 2013, the release of the Helen Taft issue was delayed by design debates and production challenges until late in the year. On November 26, five days after the Edith Roosevelt coin went on sale, the U.S. Mint announced that the Helen Taft coin would be offered starting at 12 noon on December 2: "Maximum mintage for the coins is set at 10,000 units across all product options. Customer demand will determine the ratio of Proof coins to Uncirculated [Burnished] coins produced within the total maximum mintage."

**Burnished.**

Helen Louise "Nellie" Herron was born in Cincinnati, Ohio, in 1861, the fourth child of John Williamson Herron, whose law partner, Rutherford B. Hayes, would later become governor of Ohio and president of the United States. On her mother's side, her grandfather and an uncle were members of Congress. Nellie was a creative and intellectual young woman, studying at the Cincinnati College of Music and teaching before she married a young lawyer named William Howard Taft in 1886. After a quick honeymoon and a three-month tour of Europe they settled in Cincinnati, where Nellie raised their children and encouraged William's escalating judicial and political careers. Her ambition was for him to eventually win the presidency. In 1901 federal affairs took the family to the Philippines, where "Big Bill" headed up the new civilian government after the United States won the Spanish-American War. She upset some in the American military establishment by giving respect and appreciation to the native Filipinos, inviting them to social events, learning their languages and customs, and publicly working to better their lives. She continued to advise and encourage her husband in his political career, offering guidance in personal letters and private discussions. During the presidential campaign of 1908 she was careful to shield her more "liberated" activities from the press—she enjoyed playing cards (for money, no less!), smoking cigarettes, and drinking beer. Finally Nellie's ultimate goal was met and she and Bill entered the White House

Helen Taft (1861–1943);
First Lady from
March 4, 1909, to
March 4, 1913.

**Proof.**

**Reverse detail.**

as president and First Lady in 1909. After he was sworn in, Nellie was the first First Lady to ride in the inaugural parade alongside her husband.

Nellie Taft made many changes in the culture of the White House. She took the traditional and prestigious position of the mansion's ushers—up to that point all white—and replaced them with African-American men. This was a daring move and a respectful nod to the nation's minorities. She served alcohol despite pressure from abolitionist groups, and updated the president's transportation from horse-drawn carriages to automobiles. She relaxed the strict social codes of White House etiquette, allowing divorced people (formerly forbidden) to attend official events, and inviting all members of Congress and their families, as well as military personnel stationed locally. She expanded the White House's social calendar and its accommodations in order to invite more Americans to musical concerts and other events. All of this activity was despite suffering a stroke, which required her to relearn how to speak, just two months into her term as First Lady. She never stopped studying politics and advising her husband, who praised her as "self-contained, independent, and of unusual application." The shrewd Mrs. Taft described herself as having "the satisfaction of knowing almost as much as he about the politics and intricacies of any situation . . . and my life was filled with interests of a most unusual kind."

A lasting accomplishment of Nellie's was the planting of more than 3,000 Japanese cherry trees in the Washington Tidal Basin and the creation of West Potomac Park. She was inspired by Luneta Park in Manila, where Filipinos of all races and social standing attended musical concerts together. Nellie personally planted the first two saplings with the wife of the Japanese ambassador on March 27, 1912. The reverse of her First Spouse gold coin, designed by AIP artist William Burgard and sculpted by Phebe Hemphill, shows representative branches of cherry blossoms. A December 2013 report at www.mintnewsblog.com observed that the Commission of Fine Arts "praised the abstracted cherry blossom design as a strong symbol" and that the Citizens Coinage Advisory Committee "gave the design their strongest possible recommendation and felt that it was elegant, beautiful, and would produce a very attractive coin."[16] Richard Masters's obverse portrait of Nellie, sculpted by Charles Vickers, is a robust forward-facing view of the First Lady reminiscent of an Alphonse Mucha painting.

In the sales department the Helen Taft gold coins started out stronger than the two earlier issues of 2013 (with two days more of sales in their first reporting period, and an issue price $25 lower, which likely spurred some interest). They were among the Mint's best sellers for the week in its entire product catalog, with 1,467 Proofs and 982 Burnished coins sold—nearly 25 percent of the maximum mintage.

**Mintage: ~1,940 Burnished; ~2,603 Proof**

| | Certified Populations and Retail Market Values | | | | | | | |
|---|---|---|---|---|---|---|---|---|
| | Raw MS | <MS-69 | MS-69 | MS-70 | Raw PF | <PF-69 | PF-69 | PF-70 |
| **Certified** | — | 0 | 27 | 227 | — | 1 | 98 | 212 |
| **Value*** | $750 | | $770 | $870 | $815 | | $830 | $870 |
| | *Recent auctions:* $852, MS-70, July 2015 (avg. gold spot value that month, $1,130). $999, PF-70DC, June 2015 (avg. gold spot value that month, $1,182). | | | | | | | |

\* "Raw" value is based on a gold spot price of $1,200 per ounce, and is for an uncertified Burnished or Proof coin of average quality. This value may vary with the prevailing bullion value.

# ELLEN WILSON (2013)

**Designer:** *Frank Morris (obverse); Don Everhart (reverse).* **Sculptor:** *Charles L. Vickers (obverse); Don Everhart (reverse).* **Composition:** *.9999 gold.* **Actual Gold Weight:** *1/2 ounce.* **Diameter:** *26.49 mm.* **Edge:** *Reeded.* **Mint:** *West Point.* **Issue Price:** *$795 (Burnished); $815 (Proof).* **Release Date:** *December 9, 2013.*

On December 6, 2013, the U.S. Mint announced that it would begin fulfilling orders for the Ellen Wilson First Spouse gold coin at 12 noon three days thence. The maximum mintage would be 10,000, with the number of Proof and Burnished coins determined by customer demand. As was customary by this time, the Mint accepted orders through its online catalog at www.usmint.gov/catalog, and at 1-800-USA-MINT (872-6468). Hearing- and speech-impaired customers with TTY equipment were able to order at 1-888-321-MINT (6468). A shipping and handling fee of $4.95 was added to all domestic orders.

Burnished.

Ellen Louise Axson was born in Savannah, Georgia, to a Presbyterian pastor and his wife, a teacher. Both of her grandfathers also were Presbyterian ministers. In her infancy she was moved from city to city because of the dangers of living in the Southern battle zone during the Civil War. Her mother died shortly before Ellen's 23rd birthday, and a young Atlanta lawyer named Thomas Woodrow Wilson (the son of one of her father's longtime friends) noticed her at the funeral service. They became engaged while she cared for her ailing father and Woodrow continued his postgraduate studies at Johns Hopkins University. They would marry in 1885 and then move to Pennsylvania after he was offered a teaching position at Bryn Mawr College. Ellen assisted her husband in his academic research while raising their three daughters. (For their first two children, Ellen returned to her native Georgia to give birth, lightheartedly insisting that they wouldn't be born Yankees.)

In 1890 the family entered a new stage in Princeton, New Jersey, as Woodrow began a distinguished professorship and in 1902 was promoted to president of Princeton University. Ellen was active in the academic social scene, formed a local women's organization, restored the university president's mansion, and entertained luminaries such as businessman J.P. Morgan, former U.S. president Grover Cleveland, writer Mark Twain, and educator Booker T. Washington.

Woodrow Wilson transitioned from academe into public service, ultimately winning the U.S. presidency in the election of 1912. As First Lady, Ellen's style was simple but welcoming, and she maintained a rigorous schedule of entertaining. The Wilsons did not hold an inaugural ball (an

**Ellen Wilson (1860–1914); First Lady from March 4, 1913, to August 6, 1914.**

Proof.

**Reverse detail.**

unnecessary and wasteful expense, she felt), but two of their daughters would later be married in the White House. Ellen pursued her longtime hobbies of sketching and painting. She set up a studio on the executive mansion's third floor and gave many of her creations to charitable organizations. She personally and publically supported the improvement of housing for poor Washingtonians, many of them black, in the capital city's slums. Closer to the presidential home, Ellen created the first White House Rose Garden—an accomplishment remembered on the reverse of her First Spouse gold coin. Designed and sculpted in fine detail by Don Everhart, the reverse shows a bloom of roses in the foreground with the presidential mansion in the back. The portrait of Ellen Wilson, envisioned by AIP artist Frank Morris and sculpted by Charles Vickers, is stately, dignified, and somewhat homespun. Ellen was not extravagant; as First Lady she spent less than $1,000 per year on clothing. "I am naturally the most unambitious of women and life in the White House has no attractions for me," she said. She was only 54 years old when she died of kidney disease, not halfway through her husband's first term as president—the third First Lady to die in the White House, after Letitia Tyler (1842) and Caroline Harrison (1892).

From December 9 through December 15, 2013, the Mint recorded sales of 1,327 Proofs and 932 Burnished coins of the Ellen Wilson type. This was a slightly weaker showing than for the Helen Taft issue that debuted a week earlier. Ultimately the last three issues of 2013—those of Taft and the two Wilson spouses—would sell at about the same level, averaging around 2,500 Proofs and 1,900 Burnished each. Today they enjoy the same premiums on the secondary market.

**Mintage: ~1,980 Burnished; ~2,511 Proof**

| | Raw MS | <MS-69 | MS-69 | MS-70 | Raw PF | <PF-69 | PF-69 | PF-70 |
|---|---|---|---|---|---|---|---|---|
| **Certified** | — | 0 | 22 | 309 | — | 0 | 132 | 201 |
| **Value\*** | $750 | | $770 | $870 | $815 | | $830 | $870 |

*Certified Populations and Retail Market Values*

*Recent auctions:* $898, MS-70, July 2015 (avg. gold spot value that month, $1,130). $957, PF-70DC, December 2014 (avg. gold spot value that month, $1,202).

\* "Raw" value is based on a gold spot price of $1,200 per ounce, and is for an uncertified Burnished or Proof coin of average quality. This value may vary with the prevailing bullion value.

# EDITH WILSON (2013)

**Designer:** *David Westwood (obverse); Joseph F. Menna (reverse).*
**Sculptor:** *Michael Gaudioso (obverse); Joseph F. Menna (reverse).*
**Composition:** *.9999 gold.* **Actual Gold Weight:** *1/2 ounce.* **Diameter:**
*26.49 mm.* **Edge:** *Reeded.* **Mint:** *West Point.* **Issue Price:** *$795*
*(Burnished); $815 (Proof).* **Release Date:** *December 16, 2013.*

The Edith Wilson First Spouse gold coin—the program's final issue of 2013—was released by the U.S. Mint on December 16. As with the year's other First Spouse coins, its debut had been delayed by design reviews and production challenges. Maximum mintage was set at 10,000 coins, with Burnished and Proof quantities to be determined by customer demand.

**Burnished.**

This was the second coin to honor a wife of President Woodrow Wilson; Ellen Wilson died during his first term and he married Edith Bolling Galt 16 months later. Edith had been widowed for seven years when she met the president in March 1915. The two were introduced by a cousin of his, who was fulfilling some of the social functions of First Lady since Ellen's death. Edith and Woodrow quickly fell in love; he proposed within three months and they were married that December.

Edith Bolling was born in 1872 in Wytheville, Virginia, the seventh of eleven children of a lawyer and circuit judge who was a direct descendant of Pocahontas. The pro-Confederacy Bolling family had been wealthier before the Civil War. When Edith was growing up the household included grandmothers, aunts, and cousins, plus the nine siblings. She was schooled at home; left the strictly regimented Martha Washington College after one miserable semester; and later happily attended Powell's School for Girls in Richmond for a time, before her father decided to invest the expense into educating his sons instead. At the age of 23 she married Norman Galt, whose family owned a famous jewelry store in Washington, not far from the White House. Galt's death in his early 40s, in 1908, left Edith wealthy and in charge of the family business, for which she hired a manager.

The Great War was in its second year when Edith became First Lady. She was interested mainly in protecting her husband's health and comfort, and she stayed near him at most times, including while he held meetings in the Oval Office. Woodrow often worked from his private office in the White House, which gave Edith access to him even during "presidential" hours; she screened his mail and limited visitors who tried to demand his time. This bypassed functions normally held by professional advisors and secretaries. After the United States entered the war in 1917 Edith became even more involved in Woodrow's work, and he trusted her with classified information. She led austerity programs, encouraging Americans to raise funds for the troops and conserve food resources. When she traveled with the president to Europe for the signing of the Treaty of Versailles, ending the war, her presence raised the office of the First Lady to an international status equaling that of Europe's queens.

**Proof.**

The aspect of Edith's life honored on her First Spouse gold coin is the important role she played after October 1919, when her husband suffered a stroke that practically incapacitated him for five months. Edith, feeling Woodrow's life depended on his being able to fulfill his presidential mandate, strengthened what she called her "stewardship." She told congressmen and others (including the public) that the president was simply exhausted from stress. She vigorously

**Edith Wilson (1872–1961); First Lady from December 18, 1915, to March 4, 1921.**

**Reverse detail.**

screened his communications and limited physical access to him, acting as a go-between and delivering her own notes and interpretations of his wishes to Congress. Despite the eventual grumbling of critics, who saw a "petticoat government" in the works, she insisted that she never personally made any public-policy decisions and only protected her husband's health during his recovery.

Joseph Menna's design for the reverse of the Edith Wilson coin, which he sculpted himself, symbolizes Edith's care of her stroke-crippled husband. The president's hand leans on a cane, and his wife's rests gently on top of it, her wedding ring visible. It is a gesture of protection, guidance, support, and love, in an uncluttered design of quiet strength.

The Edith Wilson coin sold at levels nearly identical to its predecessor, with collectors buying close to 2,000 Burnished pieces and almost 2,500 Proofs. Precise sales figures have yet to be tallied in the Mint's final audit. On the secondary market, none of the 2013 First Spouse gold coins have emerged as leaders for the year; they all enjoy the same modest premiums over their bullion value. Those professionally certified at the 70 level attract higher auction bids and retail sales.

**Mintage: ~1,974 Burnished; ~2,464 Proof**

| Certified Populations and Retail Market Values | | | | | | | | |
|---|---|---|---|---|---|---|---|---|
| | Raw MS | <MS-69 | MS-69 | MS-70 | Raw PF | <PF-69 | PF-69 | PF-70 |
| **Certified** | — | 0 | 33 | 249 | — | 0 | 62 | 228 |
| **Value*** | $745 | | $765 | $860 | $810 | | $825 | $870 |
| | *Recent auctions:* $876, MS-70, July 2015 (avg. gold spot value that month, $1,130). $646, PF-68DC, June 2015 (avg. gold spot value that month, $1,182). | | | | | | | |

\* "Raw" value is based on a gold spot price of $1,200 per ounce, and is for an uncertified Burnished or Proof coin of average quality. This value may vary with the prevailing bullion value.

# FLORENCE HARDING (2014)

**Designer:** *Thomas Cleveland (obverse); Thomas Cleveland (reverse).* **Sculptor:** *Joseph F. Menna (obverse); Don Everhart (reverse).* **Composition:** *.9999 gold.* **Actual Gold Weight:** *1/2 ounce.* **Diameter:** *26.49 mm.* **Edge:** *Reeded.* **Mint:** *West Point.* **Issue Price:** *$845 (Burnished); $865 (Proof).* **Release Date:** *July 10, 2014.*

In early July 2014 the U.S. Mint announced that the year's first coin in the First Spouse series would go on sale July 10. The mintage cap remained the same as for the previous year's coins: 10,000 maximum, with the ratio of Burnished to Proof coins being left up to collector demand. Prices were set according to the Mint's sliding scale based on the market value of gold.

The design of the Florence Harding coin is rich in symbolism that captures many aspects of its subject's life as First Lady. She was born Florence Mabel Kling in 1860, the eldest child of Marion, Ohio, banker and businessman Amos Kling. Young Florence worked from the age of eight in her father's businesses as a clerk and even as a rent collector. She dreamed of becoming a concert pianist and started her studies at the Cincinnati Conservatory of Music, but eloped before finishing and common-law married Henry Atherton DeWolfe when she was 19. They had one child, a son, in 1880, but DeWolfe abandoned the family in 1882 and the couple was divorced in 1886.

**Burnished.**

Florence's second marriage, in 1891, was more mature, and longer-lasting. Her new husband, Warren Gamaliel Harding, was owner of the *Marion Star* newspaper. When he fell ill in 1894 Florence took over management of the business and ran it like a pro—creating a circulation department, negotiating contracts, training newsboys (some say she invented the idea of paper routes for young boys, an idea that spread nationally), building the first local news-wire service, and increasing the newspaper's distribution. Warren recovered from his illness, but Florence continued to manage the paper for more than 10 years while also supporting her husband's growing political career. This took them to the office of lieutenant governor, the U.S. Senate, and finally the White House.

As First Lady, Florence Harding took an active role in national politics and held a strong influence over her husband, advising him on Cabinet selections and other decision-making. A popular perception was that she told her husband, "Well, Warren Harding, I got you the presidency. Now what are you going to do with it?" She saw her role as being bigger than just a social hostess and homemaker. She supported women's rights, looked after the welfare of war veterans, and strongly championed the protection of animals. Her years in newspaper management gave her a skillful understanding of media relations. At the same time, Florence didn't ignore the ceremonial and social functions of being First Lady: she coordinated elegant parties, brought after-dinner motion pictures to the White House, befriended a wide circle of high-profile personalities, and quietly served alcohol despite Prohibition. Warren Harding died of a cerebral hemorrhage while traveling in California in the third year of his presidency. Grief-stricken Florence's health was poor, as well, and she followed him into the Great Beyond a little over a year later.

In a rare instance for the First Spouse program, the obverse and reverse of the Florence Harding coin were both designed by the same artist. Thomas Cleveland's reverse design assembles elements symbolic of Florence's life in a visual mélange evocative of the Art Deco style. The ballot box and ballots represent American women's recently won right to vote. Florence was the first First Lady to vote for a U.S. president (her husband, naturally). The pen and the camera represent her work as a newspaper manager and as a media-relations expert in Warren's political campaigns, and her correspondence with military service members and their families. The stylized initials WWV memorialize her concern and support for veterans of the World War.

The U.S. Mint's mintage numbers for the Florence Harding gold coin are awaiting their final audit. As of November 2, 2015, accounting for returns, the Mint reported 2,372 Proofs and 1,723 Burnished coins sold. In any of the older U.S. coinage series, these low

Proof.

Reverse detail.

Florence Harding (1860–1924);
First Lady from March 4, 1921,
to August 2, 1923.

quantities would qualify the First Spouse coins as major rarities. With demand currently limited to a small number of enthusiastic collectors and speculators, prices are still reasonable on the secondary market.

**Mintage: ~1,723 Burnished; ~2,372 Proof**

| | Raw MS | <MS-69 | MS-69 | MS-70 | Raw PF | <PF-69 | PF-69 | PF-70 |
|---|---|---|---|---|---|---|---|---|
| **Certified Populations and Retail Market Values** | | | | | | | | |
| **Certified** | — | 0 | 33 | 249 | — | 0 | 62 | 228 |
| **Value*** | $745 | | $765 | $860 | $810 | | $825 | $870 |
| | *Recent auctions:* $876, MS-70, November 2014 (avg. gold spot value that month, $1,176). $892, PF-70DC, December 2014 (avg. gold spot value that month, $1,202). | | | | | | | |

\* "Raw" value is based on a gold spot price of $1,200 per ounce, and is for an uncertified Burnished or Proof coin of average quality. This value may vary with the prevailing bullion value.

# GRACE COOLIDGE (2014)

*Designer: Joel Iskowitz (obverse); Frank Morris (reverse). Sculptor: Phebe Hemphill (obverse); Jim Licaretz (reverse). Composition: .9999 gold. Actual Gold Weight: 1/2 ounce. Diameter: 26.49 mm. Edge: Reeded. Mint: West Point. Issue Price: $845 (Burnished); $865 (Proof). Release Date: July 17, 2014.*

**Burnished.**

On the day the Florence Harding gold coins went on sale, July 10, 2014, the U.S. Mint announced that the year's second First Spouse coins would be available the following week, starting July 17. The Grace Coolidge coins would have a mintage cap of 10,000, with customer interest determining how that quantity was split between Burnished and Proof pieces. Orders would be accepted online, as usual, at www.USMint.gov/catalog, and by phone at 1-800-USA-MINT. Hearing- and speech-impaired collectors could order with TTY equipment at 1-888-321-MINT. Grace Coolidge, who worked to raise awareness of, and opportunities for, Americans with disabilities, would have appreciated that equal-opportunity access to her coins.

Grace Anna Goodhue was an only child, born in 1879 in Burlington, Vermont. Her father was a church deacon and an inspector of steamboats for the Lake Champlain Transportation Company. Grace's mother taught her to cook meals, clean, knit clothes, tend the

**Grace Coolidge (1879–1957); First Lady from August 2, 1923, to March 4, 1929.**

garden, and take care of other household tasks. At the University of Vermont she studied education and graduated with a degree in teaching. She used this experience to teach deaf and hearing-impaired children to lip-read at the Clarke Schools for Hearing and Speech in Northampton, Massachusetts. Two years after graduating college Grace met Calvin Coolidge; they courted and were married the next year.

Calvin, a lawyer, entered politics two years into their marriage. Grace kept a low public profile as he climbed the state political ladder from the Massachusetts General Court to the legislature to the office of the lieutenant governor. After a term as governor Cal was elected vice president of the United States, and the family (by then including two young sons) moved to Washington, where he took office in 1921. Grace continued to maintain a low-key presence, avoiding controversial topics and publicly supporting the Red Cross, the Visiting Nurse Association, education for the deaf, community service, and other non-political causes and programs. In 1923 the Coolidges became president and First Lady after the death of Warren Harding. As First Lady, Grace ran a dignified and unpretentious household. Unlike her recent predecessors, she stayed out of her husband's political arena, and he similarly kept official matters to himself and his professional colleagues. In 1924 the family lost youngest son Calvin to a blood infection; Grace had the nation's sympathy, and instead of withdrawing she quietly threw herself back into her role as First Lady. After the White House she continued to support her husband and promoted charitable causes. She resumed working with the deaf, wrote for magazines, supported the military, and helped refugees during World War II.

Proof.

Frank Morris's design for the reverse of the Grace Coolidge gold coin, sculpted by Jim Licaretz, shows three hands uplifted to spell the letters USA in American Sign Language. In the background are the White House and its lawns. The design is attractively textured and layered with depth. It symbolizes the First Lady's quiet patriotism and her promotion of education for the deaf and hearing-impaired.

If more than 4,000 collectors decide they want to build a type collection of First Spouse gold coins (acquiring one of each design), recent low-mintage issues like the Grace Coolidge will emerge as aftermarket winners. Supply and demand dictate as much. In the meantime, "slow and steady wins the race" for collectors and investors who patiently acquire and hold the coins while their prices are close to bullion value.

Reverse detail.

**Mintage: ~1,734 Burnished; ~2,315 Proof**

| | Raw MS | <MS-69 | MS-69 | MS-70 | Raw PF | <PF-69 | PF-69 | PF-70 |
|---|---|---|---|---|---|---|---|---|
| **Certified** | — | 0 | 9 | 159 | — | 0 | 106 | 205 |
| **Value\*** | $750 | | $770 | $870 | $815 | | $830 | $870 |

Certified Populations and Retail Market Values

*Recent auctions:* $875, MS-70, November 2014 (avg. gold spot value that month, $1,176). $705, PF-69DC, June 2015 (avg. gold spot value that month, $1,182).

\* "Raw" value is based on a gold spot price of $1,200 per ounce, and is for an uncertified Burnished or Proof coin of average quality. This value may vary with the prevailing bullion value.

# LOU HOOVER (2014)

*Designer: Susan Gamble (obverse); Richard Masters (reverse).* **Sculptor:** *Michael Gaudioso (obverse); Jim Licaretz (reverse).* **Composition:** *.9999 gold.* **Actual Gold Weight:** *1/2 ounce.* **Diameter:** *26.49 mm.* **Edge:** *Reeded.* **Mint:** *West Point.* **Issue Price:** *$845 (Burnished); $865 (Proof).* **Release Date:** *August 14, 2014.*

**Burnished.**

**Proof.**

Lou Hoover was an active and intelligent First Lady, well known as a scholar and a linguist. (She and her husband, Herbert, had practiced their Chinese while he was stationed in Shanghai as an engineer. For private conversations in the White House, they would sometimes converse in Mandarin. She also spoke Spanish, French, and Italian.)

The eldest daughter of banker Charles Henry of Waterloo, Iowa, Lou grew up as a bit of a tomboy—an athlete and outdoorswoman in an era when such traits were unconventional for young ladies. Biographers Anne Beiser Allen and Jon Wakelyn describe how her father took young Lou camping in the hills when the family lived in California; she learned to ride a horse, collect rocks and minerals, and hunt animals, preserving her kills as an amateur taxidermist. She became the first female geology major at Stanford University, which is where she met her future husband, Herbert Hoover, who became wealthy as a mining expert and engineer.

**Lou Hoover (1874–1944); First Lady from March 4, 1929, to March 4, 1933.**

Lou was very much a woman of the world. The couple traveled to many remote and even dangerous parts of China in their early years, and were present during the anti-imperialist Boxer Rebellion (1899–1901). Together they translated medieval scientist Georgius Agricola's encyclopedia of mining and metallurgy, creating what remains the standard English version of his work. During the Great War, the Hoovers coordinated relief for Belgian refugees. This drive to help others carried forward into her time as First Lady. Lou Hoover personally helped hundreds—probably thousands—of needy Americans who appealed to her for assistance during the Great Depression. She hired secretaries to help answer all of these appeals, and spent her own money as well as encouraging wealthy friends to give to those in dire straits. After she died, Herbert was cleaning out Lou's desk and he found checks that people had sent to repay her generosity. She'd never cashed them.

Another mark of Lou's time as First Lady was her frequent and enthusiastic use of the radio to communicate with the American people. She took the medium seriously, and had a recording system set up in the White House so she could hone her delivery. Her civic speeches were broadcast and she was a guest speaker on numerous radio programs, encouraging those with the means to volunteer to help others, and promoting causes such as the Girl Scouts of the USA (she had served as the organization's national president in the early 1920s). Lou Hoover's masterful use of the radio and her "bully pulpit" as First Lady are captured in Richard Masters's design for her First Spouse gold coin. In it, rays emanate from a 1920's-style cathedral radio, with the legend FIRST PUBLIC ADDRESS / APRIL 19, 1929.

The Lou Hoover First Spouse gold coins went on sale August 14, 2014, with their prices set at $845 (Burnished) and $865 (Proof). As with the other issues of the year, their total mintage was capped at 10,000 coins, with no set limit for either format. The Mint's final audit has not been completed yet, but all indications are that fewer than 4,000 coins were purchased. Today the issues of 2014 all enjoy similar premiums in the secondary market.

**Reverse detail.**

**Mintage: ~1,722 Burnished; ~2,258 Proof**

| | Raw MS | <MS-69 | MS-69 | MS-70 | Raw PF | <PF-69 | PF-69 | PF-70 |
|---|---|---|---|---|---|---|---|---|
| **Certified** | — | 0 | 18 | 199 | — | 1 | 65 | 185 |
| **Value*** | $750 | | $780 | $890 | $815 | | $850 | $900 |

*Certified Populations and Retail Market Values*

*Recent auctions:* $905, MS-70, November 2014 (avg. gold spot value that month, $1,176). $881, PF-70DC, August 2015 (avg. gold spot value that month, $1,117).

\* "Raw" value is based on a gold spot price of $1,200 per ounce, and is for an uncertified Burnished or Proof coin of average quality. This value may vary with the prevailing bullion value.

# ELEANOR ROOSEVELT (2014)

**Designer:** *Chris Costello (obverse and reverse).* **Sculptor:** *Phebe Hemphill (obverse); Renata Gordon (reverse).* **Composition:** *.9999 gold.* **Actual Gold Weight:** *1/2 ounce.* **Diameter:** *26.49 mm.* **Edge:** *Reeded.* **Mint:** *West Point.* **Issue Price:** *$820 (Burnished); $840 (Proof).* **Release Date:** *September 4, 2014.*

Anna Eleanor Roosevelt was born into a wealthy New York City family. Through her father she was a niece of Theodore Roosevelt—a New York State assemblyman at the time of her birth in 1884, and destined to become president of the United States. Privately tutored, she was intelligent although not self-confident as a child (her confidence would grow with age). She married her father's fifth cousin, Franklin Delano Roosevelt, in 1905.

"Mrs. Roosevelt was considered the eyes, ears, and feet for her partially paralyzed husband," the Mint said in its literature promoting her First Spouse gold coin. "She reported directly and in great detail to the president regarding her many trips inside and outside the country at his request and at her own behest." The First Lady was not shy in voicing her own opinions about life and culture in the United States. As described in chapter 3, she publicly resigned her membership in the Daughters of the American Revolution when that group refused to allow Marian Anderson, an African-American singer, to perform at DAR Constitution Hall in 1939. She personally volunteered to visit the homeless and

**Burnished.**

Proof.

Reverse detail.

Eleanor Roosevelt (1884–1962);
First Lady from
March 4, 1933, to April 12, 1945.

work in soup kitchens during the Great Depression, and visited the troops (including in war zones) after the United States entered the Second World War. Like her predecessor, Lou Hoover, Eleanor used the radio to address the American people in a weekly program. She also wrote a popular syndicated newspaper column ("My Day") and lectured widely. This was *not* the quiet, domestic First Lady of yesteryear, focusing only on White House social duties and entertaining. She fought injustice, vocally and with vigor. After the White House Eleanor remained active as a delegate to the newly formed United Nations, the first chair of the UN Commission on Human Rights, and chair of John F. Kennedy's Presidential Commission on the Status of Women.

The reverse of the Eleanor Roosevelt gold coin was designed by Chris Costello and sculpted by Renata Gordon. The motif evokes the global significance of Eleanor's selfless work. Harry S. Truman called her the "First Lady of the World" for her humanitarian efforts. "What other single human being has touched and transformed the existence of so many?" asked diplomat Adlai Stevenson at a memorial address to the United Nations in 1962. "She would rather light candles than curse the darkness, and her glow has warmed the world." Costello symbolizes these sentiments with Eleanor's hand lighting a candle, the curvature of the globe enlightened in the background.

The Eleanor Roosevelt gold coin garnered the strongest opening sales of the four 2014 releases. In its first reporting cycle (September 4–7, 2014), the Mint announced sales of 1,810 coins total (1,181 Proof and 629 Burnished). This was higher than the 1,593 coins reported in the first sales cycle for Lou Hoover, 1,541 for Grace Coolidge, and 1,481 for Florence Harding. The Roosevelt Proof ended up with the highest mintage of the year, due to the First Lady's widespread popularity, which broadened its audience beyond the numismatic market. Overall sales, however, did not reach even half the Mint's maximum limit of 10,000 coins. The inventory from its 2014 press run carried over into 2015 sales, with the Proof Roosevelts selling out on January 16, 2015, and the Burnished coins selling out on March 18. At that point, because the Mint cannot strike more of the coins after their year of issue, the Eleanor Roosevelt coins were declared sold out—even while the Mint was still selling its remaining inventory of 2014 Hoover, Coolidge, and Harding coins.

Once the Mint completes its final audits, all of the 2014 issues will emerge as keys and semi-keys within the series.

**Mintage: ~1,886 Burnished; ~2,377 Proof**

| Certified Populations and Retail Market Values | | | | | | | | |
|---|---|---|---|---|---|---|---|---|
| | Raw MS | <MS-69 | MS-69 | MS-70 | Raw PF | <PF-69 | PF-69 | PF-70 |
| Certified | — | 1 | 22 | 204 | — | 2 | 55 | 184 |
| Value* | $750 | | $800 | $910 | $815 | | $850 | $910 |
| | *Recent auctions:* $916, MS-70, November 2014 (avg. gold spot value that month, $1,176). $823, PF-69DC, June 2015 (avg. gold spot value that month, $1,182). | | | | | | | |

\* "Raw" value is based on a gold spot price of $1,200 per ounce, and is for an uncertified Burnished or Proof coin of average quality. This value may vary with the prevailing bullion value.

# ELIZABETH "BESS" TRUMAN (2015)

*Designer: Joel Iskowitz (obverse and reverse). Sculptor: Phebe Hemphill (obverse); Charles L. Vickers (reverse). Composition: .9999 gold. Actual Gold Weight: 1/2 ounce. Diameter: 26.49 mm. Edge: Reeded. Mint: West Point. Issue Price: $770 (Burnished); $790 (Proof). Release Date: April 16, 2015.*

The U.S. Mint announced the upcoming 2015 First Spouse gold coins on March 16, giving collectors advance notice of who designed and sculpted each coin, and what they would look like. In this year the coinage program entered the era of post–World War II First Ladies, beginning with Elizabeth "Bess" Truman, whose coin went on sale Thursday, April 16.

Mintage was limited to no more than 10,000 units across all product options, with customer demand determining the ratio of Proof coins to Burnished coins. Reflecting gold's decline in the market, the Mint set the issue prices $50 lower than those of the Eleanor Roosevelt coins that debuted some seven months earlier.

**Burnished.**

The girl who would grow up to be First Lady Bess Truman was born Elizabeth Virginia Wallace in 1885 in Independence, Missouri. When Harry Truman was six years old his family moved to Independence from nearby Grandview, and from fifth grade through high school he and Bess were schoolmates. They married in 1919. Harry served as a U.S. senator from Missouri from 1935 until 1945, when he was selected as Franklin Roosevelt's vice president. He filled his new role for only 82 days before Roosevelt died in office, making Harry president and Bess First Lady. She was not entirely happy with her position, disliking the lack of privacy. She entertained during the White House social

**Proof.**

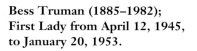
Bess Truman (1885–1982); First Lady from April 12, 1945, to January 20, 1953.

Reverse detail.

season, including hosting garden parties for servicemen, but otherwise spent most of her husband's presidency away from Washington. Bess didn't share Eleanor Roosevelt's passion for constant communication with the media and the American public. Asked what she was planning to wear to an event, she would reply, "It's none of their damned business." She once said, "I am not the one elected. I have nothing to say to the public," and observed that "A woman's place in public life is to sit beside her husband, be silent, and be sure her hat is on straight." She allowed precisely one question-and-answer press conference during her time as First Lady. One of the reporters asked Bess what she wanted to do after Harry left office. Her reply was, "Return to Independence."

The Trumans did just that after his presidency. Bess lived to the age of 97, making her the longest-lived First Lady in American history.

For her gold coin, Joel Iskowitz's portrait subtly captures some of the First Lady's feelings about the "formalities and pomp of the artificiality," as Harry Truman put it, that went along with life in the White House. She is dressed plainly, and is neither frowning nor quite smiling, but looking almost as if she'd rather be back in Missouri. "CCAC member Michael Moran said the rendition is very close in appearance to an autographed photo of the first lady that was handed out by the White House," Paul Gilkes reported in *Coin World*. "The image of Mrs. Truman in the autographed photo is one Mrs. Truman preferred, Moran said."[17] The reverse design, also by Iskowitz, features a locomotive wheel on a railroad track, symbolizing Bess's support of her husband on his 1948 whistle-stop campaign for reelection. It is a fitting symbol for her quiet, steady, lifelong work: spectators marvel at the locomotive engine, passengers comfortably enjoy the carriages, and children are thrilled as the caboose blows the train's whistle—all while the wheel steadfastly performs its duty, unsung. Bess Truman traveled 22,000 miles during her husband's successful 1948 campaign.

Low mintages continued to be the order of the day with the First Spouse gold coins. The U.S. Mint was cautious with its production, preferring to strike fewer pieces with the option of going back for another press run if demand warranted it, rather than carrying excess inventory. In the Mint's first week of reported sales, sales reached 1,913 coins in both formats. By early July 2015 the Bess Truman coins were back-ordered. Another round of production at the West Point Mint refreshed the supply, and by early October the Mint had sold just under 3,700 coins in both formats, with sales ongoing. Retailers priced 70-graded specimens at a handsome premium over their issue prices, and eBay auction results into autumn of 2015 illustrated the market value of these highest-graded coins.

**Mintage: ~1,585 Burnished; ~2,220 Proof**

| Certified Populations and Retail Market Values | | | | | | | | |
|---|---|---|---|---|---|---|---|---|
| | **Raw MS** | **<MS-69** | **MS-69** | **MS-70** | **Raw PF** | **<PF-69** | **PF-69** | **PF-70** |
| **Certified** | — | 0 | 18 | 213 | — | 2 | 77 | 204 |
| **Value*** | $790 | | $825 | $925 | $830 | | $875 | $950 |

*Recent auctions:* $1,051, MS-70, June 2015 (avg. gold spot value that month, $1,182). $1,425, PF-70DC, May 2015 (avg. gold spot value that month, $1,199).

* "Raw" value is based on a gold spot price of $1,200 per ounce, and is for an uncertified Burnished or Proof coin of average quality. This value may vary with the prevailing bullion value.

# Marie "Mamie" Eisenhower (2015)

**Designer:** *Richard Masters (obverse); Barbara Fox (reverse).* **Sculptor:** *Joseph F. Menna (obverse); Renata Gordon (reverse).* **Composition:** *.9999 gold.* **Actual Gold Weight:** *1/2 ounce.* **Diameter:** *26.49 mm.* **Edge:** *Reeded.* **Mint:** *West Point.* **Issue Price:** *$770 (Burnished); $790 (Proof).* **Release Date:** *May 7, 2015.*

The Mamie Eisenhower First Spouse gold coin went on sale May 7, 2015. There was no individual or household ordering limit, but the mintage was capped at 10,000 across all product options, with customer demand setting the ratio of Proof to Burnished coins. As with the other coins in the First Spouse program, all were minted at West Point, encapsulated in a highly polished, dome-chested, lacquered hardwood presentation case, and accompanied by a certificate of authenticity.

Marie "Mamie" Geneva Dowd was born in Boone, Iowa, in 1896, the daughter of a wealthy meat-packing company executive. She met her future husband, Dwight D. "Ike" Eisenhower, in 1915, while she was wintering in San Antonio, Texas, and he was on his first Army tour of duty at Fort Sam Houston. They fell in love and were married in 1916, after which they moved frequently as Ike's military career demanded, including overseas—27 moves over the course of 37 years. His success as Supreme Allied Commander in Europe during World War II, including command of Operation Overlord and the liberation of France, propelled General Eisenhower into national politics after the war. The slogan of his 1952 presidential campaign was "I Like Ike," a theme echoed in Barbara Fox's reverse design for the second First Spouse gold coin of 2015. "I Like Mamie" is seen on a promotional button held up by a woman's hand—a reflection of Mrs. Eisenhower's own popularity on the campaign trail. Mamie kept an old-fashioned view of feminine domesticity: "I never knew what a woman would want to be liberated from," she once said, and she summed up the family roles as, "Ike runs the country, and I turn the lamb chops." She made an energetic and outgoing First Lady, known for her love of pretty clothes and jewelry and her pride in her husband and their home. She kept the White House busy in a flurry of seasonal decorations and entertainments, and hosted a record number of foreign dignitaries in the new age of convenient air travel. Although Mamie felt that women shouldn't work outside the home, she also believed that their influence and

**Burnished.**

insight could be powerful. Ike apparently agreed. "Let me try this out on Mamie," he once said during an economic conference. "She's a pretty darn good judge of things."

In the first three days of sales, collectors and investors bought 587 Burnished examples of the Mamie Eisenhower First Spouse coin and 1,035 Proofs—a total of about 16 percent of the mintage limit. By early October the numbers would stand at 1,611 and 2,378, respectively. This represented an increase over the Bess Truman coins, although as of press date the Mint has not released its final audit of sales.

**Mamie Eisenhower (1896–1979); First Lady from January 20, 1953, to January 20, 1961.**

**Proof.**

**Reverse detail.**

Mintage: ~1,665 Burnished; ~2,472 Proof

| Certified Populations and Retail Market Values | | | | | | | | |
|---|---|---|---|---|---|---|---|---|
| | Raw MS | <MS-69 | MS-69 | MS-70 | Raw PF | <PF-69 | PF-69 | PF-70 |
| **Certified** | — | 0 | 29 | 184 | — | 1 | 176 | 197 |
| **Value\*** | $790 | | $825 | $925 | $830 | | $875 | $950 |

*Recent auctions:* $1,162, MS-70, July 2015 (avg. gold spot value that month, $1,130). $1,214, PF-70DC, July 2015 (avg. gold spot value that month, $1,130).

\* "Raw" value is based on a gold spot price of $1,200 per ounce, and is for an uncertified Burnished or Proof coin of average quality. This value may vary with the prevailing bullion value.

# JACQUELINE KENNEDY (2015)

*Designer: Susan Gamble (obverse); Benjamin Sowards (reverse). Sculptor: Phebe Hemphill (obverse); Jim Licaretz (reverse). Composition: .9999 gold. Actual Gold Weight: 1/2 ounce. Diameter: 26.49 mm. Edge: Reeded. Mint: West Point. Issue Price: $770 (Burnished); $790 (Proof). Release Date: June 25, 2015.*

**Burnished.**

The U.S. Mint, anticipating the mainstream popularity of the Jackie Kennedy First Spouse gold coin, raised its mintage limit from the 10,000 of 2015's earlier issues to 30,000. This was the first increase to the mintage cap since the 2010 Mary Todd Lincoln issue was raised from 15,000 coins to 20,000. The move proved wise—after the Kennedy coins went on sale at 12 noon Eastern Time on June 25, 2015, the Mint sold 10,894 pieces in the first day (7,102 Proofs and 3,792 Burnished).

Jacqueline Lee "Jackie" Bouvier was born in 1929, the eldest daughter of Wall Street stockbroker John Vernou Bouvier III and socialite Janet Norton Lee. She studied at George Washington University, earned a degree in French literature in 1951, and worked for the *Washington Times-Herald* as a photographer. In 1952 she met World War II veteran John F. Kennedy, at the time a U.S. representative from Massachusetts, soon to be on his way to the Senate. They were married in 1953. John's career took him to the White House as the nation's 35th president.

Jackie brought a renewed sense of style and fashion to the role of First Lady, glamorizing the Kennedy White House with an aura of celebrity that brought their household the nickname of "Camelot." She was a popular hostess of foreign dignitaries and heads of state, and in the post-war era of jet travel official state visits became more frequent. She allowed White House guests to drink cocktails, and invited artists, musicians, writers, and other creative visitors to socialize with international VIPs. Jackie organized and oversaw the

**Jacqueline Kennedy (1929–1994); First Lady from January 20, 1961, to November 22, 1963.**

restoration and redecoration of the executive mansion—a significant and complicated project after years of neglect—and the redesign was broadcast nationally, showcasing the beautiful and important home of America's president. This effort led to her cofounding of the White House Historical Association. Beloved in the United States, Jackie was equally popular abroad. During a visit to Paris, where she charmed the French public with her knowledge of their history and her fluent parlance, the press jokingly referred to the president as the man who was accompanying Jacqueline Kennedy.

Jackie was riding in the presidential motorcade with her husband when he was assassinated in Dallas in November 1963. The nation was horrified by his violent death, and media attention focused intensely on his courageous and poised widow. Jackie led President Kennedy's funeral procession on foot and lit the eternal flame at his gravesite in Arlington National Cemetery. A British correspondent reported that "Jacqueline Kennedy has given the America people . . . one thing they have always lacked: *majesty*."

Proof.

The First Lady's lovely portrait was designed by Susan Gamble and elegantly sculpted by Phebe Hemphill. The reverse design, sculpted by Jim Licaretz, is by Benjamin Sowards. It shows a blossom of the saucer magnolia that Jackie Kennedy had planted in the White House garden and near her husband's eternal flame in Arlington. "The petals stretch across the globe," the Mint noted, "its tips connecting the points of some of her most notable diplomatic visits," in the United States, South America, Europe, and Asia.

Distribution got off to a slow start for Proof versions of the Jackie Kennedy coin that were ordered through the Mint's Web site. The Proof was listed as being on back order starting on day one, June 25. The Office of Corporate Communications issued a statement: "The Mint underestimated the initial demand for the 2015 First Spouse Series one-half-ounce gold coins (Jacqueline Kennedy) and, unfortunately, the products went on back order very quickly after sales started. As of June 30, additional product arrived at our distribution center in Memphis that will clear a majority of the back orders. The Mint has resumed production and we expect to fulfill all customer demand in the coming days and weeks. We apologize to our customers for the delay." On July 1, Adam Stump, deputy director of the Mint's office of corporate communications, noted that the coins were available in both formats at the Philadelphia Mint and Denver Mint retail shops, and at the gift shop in its Washington, DC, headquarters. By early November 2015, collectors and investors had purchased 5,262 of the Burnished coins and 10,635 Proofs, totaling more than half of the production limit. As of this book's press date, sales are ongoing and the hobby community awaits a final mintage audit.

Reverse detail.

**Mintage: ~5,262 Burnished; ~10,635 Proof**

| Certified Populations and Retail Market Values | | | | | | | | |
|---|---|---|---|---|---|---|---|---|
| | Raw MS | <MS-69 | MS-69 | MS-70 | Raw PF | <PF-69 | PF-69 | PF-70 |
| **Certified** | — | 0 | 71 | 749 | — | 2 | 579 | 1,073 |
| **Value*** | $770 | | $800 | $900 | $800 | | $850 | $950 |

*Recent auctions:* $860, MS-70, August 2015 (avg. gold spot value that month, $1,117). $936, PF-70DC, August 2015 (avg. gold spot value that month, $1,117).

* "Raw" value is based on a gold spot price of $1,200 per ounce, and is for an uncertified Burnished or Proof coin of average quality. This value may vary with the prevailing bullion value.

**Burnished.**

**Proof.**

Claudia Taylor "Lady Bird" Johnson (1912–2007); First Lady from November 22, 1963, to January 20, 1969.

# CLAUDIA TAYLOR "LADY BIRD" JOHNSON (2015)

*Designer:* Linda L. Fox (obverse); Chris Costello (reverse). *Sculptor:* Michael Gaudioso (obverse); Renata Gordon (reverse). *Composition:* .9999 gold. *Actual Gold Weight:* 1/2 ounce. *Diameter:* 26.49 mm. *Edge:* Reeded. *Mint:* West Point. *Issue Price:* $745 (Burnished); $765 (Proof). *Release Date:* August 27, 2015.

For the Lady Bird Johnson First Spouse gold coin, the U.S. Mint once again capped its production limit at 10,000, in keeping with all of the 2015 coins except for its immediate predecessor, that of Jackie Kennedy. The latter had debuted to great excitement two months earlier, selling more than 10,000 coins in its first day.

Claudia Alta Taylor was born in Karnack, Texas, near the Louisiana border, in 1912. Her father was a wealthy businessman and landowner by the time she was born, but he himself had grown up as a poor sharecropper's son. Little Claudia was raised in the antebellum plantation mansion her father bought on the edge of town. Her lifelong nickname came from her childhood nurse, who said she was as "purty as a ladybird." She even used the name *Bird Taylor* on her marriage certificate.

Lady Bird was a serious student in high school and earned degrees in arts and journalism from the University of Texas. In 1934 she met a young legislative secretary and political hopeful named Lyndon Baines Johnson; he swept her off her feet and they were married in November of that year. Lady Bird was an intelligent project manager and she used part of her inheritance to finance LBJ's campaign for Congress. She ran his office while he volunteered for the Navy during World War II, and in 1955 she helped keep his staff organized after he suffered a heart attack while serving as Majority Leader of the U.S. Senate. She bought a radio station and a television station, and her business acumen made the Johnsons wealthy. She was the first presidential wife to have become a millionaire in her own right.

John F. Kennedy asked Lady Bird to take an active role in the presidential campaign of 1960, when her husband was running as vice president. She filled in for Jackie Kennedy, who had to limit her engagements because she was pregnant. Lady Bird traveled 35,000 miles through 11 states and appeared at 150 campaign events over the course of about two and a half months.

After Kennedy was assassinated in 1963, the Johnsons became president and First Lady. In her new role she embraced the causes of conservation and beautification of America's roadways and countryside. She modernized the office of the First Lady, being the first to have a press secretary and chief of staff of her own, as well as an outside liaison to Congress. She campaigned vigorously for her husband's 1964 election bid. In the first solo whistle-stop tour conducted by a First Lady, she traveled through eight Southern states giving speeches and promoting the Civil Rights Act.

**Reverse detail.**

Chris Costello's beautifully designed reverse of Lady Bird's First Spouse gold coin honors her work as a protector of the nation's natural scenery. Visible in the design are the Jefferson Memorial and the Washington Monument, with manicured lawns and growing flowers in the foreground. The legend reads BEAUTIFY OUR CITIES, PARKS & HIGHWAYS. Lady Bird worked with the American Association of Nurserymen to protect wildflowers and have them planted along the nation's roads. Thanks to her advocacy the Highway Beautification Act, passed in 1965, became known as "Lady Bird's Bill." When she was awarded the Presidential Medal of Freedom in 1977, it was in part for these conservation efforts. "One of America's great First Ladies, she claimed her own place in the hearts and history of the American people," read the medal's citation. "In councils of power or in homes of the poor, she made government human with her unique compassion and her grace, warmth and wisdom. Her leadership transformed the American landscape and preserved its natural beauty as a national treasure."

During the first week of sales (from August 27 through September 2), collectors and investors purchased more than 25 percent of the Lady Bird Johnson coin's maximum mintage. The total included 1,070 Burnished coins and 1,471 Proofs. By November 2, those numbers stood at 1,335 and 2,002, respectively. As of press date, sales are ongoing. The Mint always has the option to order another production run at West Point to replenish its inventory before year's end. None of the First Spouse coins can be minted past their year of issue, so for any given coin whatever quantity is available on December 31 is effectively the end of its mintage.

**Mintage: ~1,335 Burnished; ~2,002 Proof**

| Certified Populations and Retail Market Values | | | | | | | | |
|---|---|---|---|---|---|---|---|---|
| | Raw MS | <MS-69 | MS-69 | MS-70 | Raw PF | <PF-69 | PF-69 | PF-70 |
| Certified | — | n/a | n/a | n/a | — | n/a | n/a | n/a |
| Value* | $755 | | $800 | $875 | $775 | | $820 | $900 |
| *Recent auctions:* $785, MS-70, September 2015 (avg. gold spot value that month, $1,125). $799, PF-69DC, September 2015 (avg. gold spot value that month, $1,125). | | | | | | | | |

\* "Raw" value is based on a gold spot price of $1,200 per ounce, and is for an uncertified Burnished or Proof coin of average quality. This value may vary with the prevailing bullion value.

# 2016 AND BEYOND

**Designers:** *To be announced.* **Sculptors:** *To be announced.* **Composition:** *.9999 gold.* **Actual Gold Weight:** *1/2 ounce.* **Diameter:** *26.49 mm.* **Edge:** *Reeded.* **Mint:** *West Point.* **Issue Prices:** *To be announced.* **Release Dates:** *To be announced.*

The First Spouse gold coin program will continue into 2016 with three scheduled issues: those of First Ladies Pat Nixon, Betty Ford, and Nancy Reagan. Rosalynn Carter is not included in the program because her husband, President Jimmy Carter, was still living in 2015, and the Presidential $1 Coin Act of 2005 states that "No coin issued . . . may bear the image of a living former or current President, or of any deceased former President during the 2-year period following the date of the death of that President." This means there will be no Jimmy Carter Presidential dollar, and therefore no accompanying Rosalynn Carter First Spouse gold coin. Ronald Reagan passed away in 2004, and so is eligible for a Presidential dollar, and therefore Nancy Reagan will be featured on a First Spouse gold coin in 2016, making her the only living First Lady to be so honored.

Where will the First Spouse gold coins go, value-wise, after the entire program is "secondary market," with no more current issues available directly from the Mint? Coin dealers and researchers generally acknowledge that thousands of the 2007 and 2008 coins were melted during the dramatic run-up of gold's bullion value following the Crash of 2008. In time the true rarity of those earlier issues, notwithstanding their officially registered mintages, will become better known.

Patricia Ryan "Pat" Nixon (1912–1993); First Lady from January 20, 1969, to August 9, 1974.

They will likely remain affordable even though thousands were melted, simply because their original mintages were so high. Some collectors feel that the later issues, with total sales of less than 4,000 coins in many instances, should continue to rise in value with age, as more collectors come to appreciate the series. Others, however, point out that the First Spouse program started with a bang and quickly lost steam, is expensive to collect, appears to have a thin collector base, and is tied largely to the coins' bullion value, with a relatively small number of high-grade examples enjoying stronger demand and therefore higher prices.

One thing is certain: there will always be a demand for these coins, given their precious-metal content and their connections to some of the most interesting and influential ladies in American history.

One of the obverse sketches for the Pat Nixon First Spouse gold coin, favored by both the Citizens Coinage Advisory Committee and the Commission of Fine Arts. The reverse design preferred by the CCAC shows stylized figures standing hand-in-hand around a globe, symbolizing Nixon's emphasis of the value of every American citizen. The reverse favored by the CFA shows her welcoming a person in a wheelchair to the White House. This represents the First Lady's goal of making the White House more accessible to everyone. She is depicted in pants instead of a traditional dress because she was the first First Lady to wear pants in public.

Elizabeth Bloomer "Betty" Ford
(1918–2011); First Lady from
August 9, 1974, to January 20, 1977.

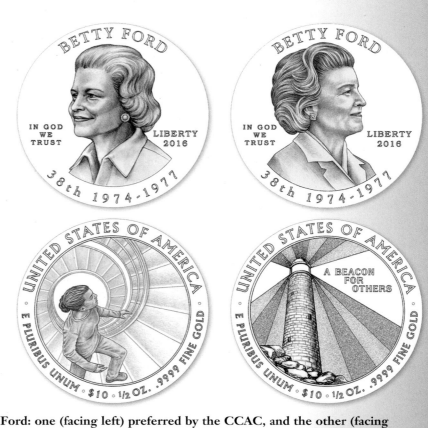

Two different portraits of First Lady Betty Ford: one (facing left) preferred by the CCAC, and the other (facing right) by the CFA. For the reverse, the CCAC favored a design showing a young woman climbing a spiral staircase, symbolic of Betty Ford's legacy of inspiring others to recover from addiction. The CFA preferred the sketch showing a lighthouse, but with the words SHEDDING LIGHT instead of A BEACON FOR OTHERS.

The obverse design
favored by both the
Citizens Coinage
Advisory Committee
and the Commission of
Fine Arts, as well as by
Nancy Reagan herself; and
the reverse design selected by
the CCAC. This depicts Reagan with
two youths, along with her anti-drug
message of "Just Say No."

Nancy Reagan (born 1921);
First Lady from January 20,
1981, to January 20, 1989.

A ram's-eye view of the Grand Canyon, and the five-ounce silver 2010 America the Beautiful bullion coin celebrating the national park.

# 7

# The America the Beautiful Silver Bullion Coins (2010 to Date)

In 1999 the U.S. Mint rolled out one of its most successful and popular modern coinage series—a series that would, in a meandering way, lead to the largest and heaviest silver coins ever created by the United States.

Officially called the United States Mint 50 State Quarters® Program, it involved a creative redesign of the Washington quarter dollar, which had been in circulation since 1932. From 1999 through 2008 the reverse of the quarter was used as a canvas to celebrate each of the states in the order they joined the Union, starting with Delaware and ending with Hawaii. Each coin was designed to highlight a distinctive symbol, landmark, or other feature of its state. The Georgia quarter showed one of that state's famous peaches; New Hampshire featured the famous "Old Man of the Mountain" landmark; and of course New York had the Statue of Liberty. Five times each year a new coin design was rolled out with publicity and promotional events. The program was a boon for education and state tourism—and a shot in the arm for the hobby of coin collecting, with millions of casual new collectors joining the ranks. Books were written about the State quarters; hobby companies sold thousands upon thousands of folders, albums, and maps to store and display the coins; and Americans young and old were checking their pocket change to see if they could find the ones they needed for their collections.

The State quarters program was so successful that the Mint expanded it in 2009 to include coins for the District of Columbia and the five U.S. territories (Puerto Rico, Guam, American Samoa, the U.S. Virgin Islands, and the Northern Mariana Islands).

The Statue of Liberty, situated in New York Harbor, was featured on a 2001 State quarter—one of 50 coins in the 1999–2008 series.

In December 2008, as the State quarters were winding down, Congress approved two new coinage programs through the America's Beautiful National Parks Quarter Dollar Coin Act. This legislation created another round of 56 circulating quarter dollars, honoring national parks and other historic sites in each of the states, the District of Columbia, and the territories. Additionally, it authorized a related new silver bullion coin program. Since 2010, when the "America the Beautiful" (or "National Park") quarters debuted, the Mint has struck five-ounce silver coins, three inches in diameter, each one reproducing the design of its smaller circulation-strike quarter dollar.

Title II of the coinage act discussed these "Bullion Investment Products."

(1) In General.—The Secretary [of the Treasury] shall strike and make available for sale such number of bullion coins as the Secretary determines to be appropriate that are exact duplicates [changed in December 2010 to "likenesses"] of the quarter dollars issued under subsection (t), each of which shall—

(A) have a diameter of 3.0 inches and weigh 5.0 ounces; [this subparagraph was changed in December 2010 to "have a diameter determined by the Secretary that is no less than 2.5 inches and no greater than 3.0 inches and weighs 5.0 ounces"]

(B) contain .999 fine silver;

(C) have incused into the edge the fineness and weight of the bullion coin; [this subparagraph was deleted in December 2010]

(D) bear an inscription of the denomination of such coin, which shall be 'quarter dollar'; and

(E) not be minted or issued by the United States Mint as so-called 'fractional' bullion coins or in any size other than the size described in paragraph (A).

(2) Availability for Sale.—Bullion coins minted under paragraph (1)—

(A) shall become available for sale no sooner than the first day of the calendar year in which the circulating quarter dollar of which such bullion coin is a duplicate is issued; and

(B) may only be available for sale during the year in which such circulating quarter dollar is issued.

The changes noted in brackets above were enacted later in order to try to solve some of the production challenges the Mint encountered in striking the coins. (See below, under "Production and Distribution of the Silver Bullion Coins," for more information.)

# SELECTION OF THE NATIONAL PARKS AND HISTORIC SITES

A five-step process was set up for the selection of sites to be honored on the National Park quarters and their related silver bullion coins.

**Step 1.** The U.S. Mint initiated the site selection process by contacting the chief executive of each host jurisdiction (state, District of Columbia, or territory) through a formal letter of request to identify one preferred and three ranked alternative national sites in that jurisdiction. The Mint provided resources and access to lists of applicable national sites to each chief executive. National sites for consideration included any site under the supervision, management, or conservancy of the National Park Service, the United States Forest Service, the United States Fish and Wildlife Service, or any similar department or agency of the federal government.

**Step 2.** With due consideration to the requirement that the national site chosen for each host jurisdiction was to be the most appropriate in terms of natural and historic significance, and after giving full and thoughtful consideration to national sites not under the jurisdiction of the secretary of the Interior, the chief executive provided the Mint his or her recommendation for the national site to be honored on the respective quarter, as well as three recommended alternative national sites in order of preference.

Public launch ceremonies are held for the National Park quarters. They often feature special guests, local students, high-school bands and Junior ROTC groups, artists and performers, and cultural presentations. U.S. Mint officials, state elected officials, and representatives from the honored site give speeches and hand out coins. Here, a member of the Pollen Trail Dancers performs the Eagle Dance at the launch ceremony for the Grand Canyon National Park quarter.

**Step 3.** The Mint reviewed all the recommendations and established a candidate list of the 56 national sites.

**Step 4.** The Mint consulted with the secretary of the Interior to ensure appropriateness of each of the 56 national site recommendations based on their natural or historic significance, and to validate the date on which each recommended site was established as a national site.

**Step 5.** Having consulted with each chief executive and the secretary of the Interior, and having giving full and thoughtful consideration to national sites that are not under the jurisdiction of the secretary of the Interior, the Mint reconciled all comments and recommended a final candidate list determined to be the most appropriate in terms of natural and historic significance to the secretary of the Treasury, who approved the final national site list. The approved list also established the order in which each quarter dollar would be released, at a rate of five per year, beginning in 2010.

**U.S. Mint Director Ed Moy and Grand Canyon National Park Superintendent Steve Martin ceremoniously launch the park's new quarter.**

The national sites were registered as follows:

| Year | Jurisdiction | Site | Legal Authority | Date Established |
|------|--------------|------|-----------------|------------------|
| 2010 | Arkansas | Hot Springs National Park | 4 Stat. 505 | 4/20/1832 |
|      | Wyoming | Yellowstone National Park | 17 Stat. 32 | 3/1/1872 |
|      | California | Yosemite National Park | 26 Stat. 650 | 10/1/1890 |
|      | Arizona | Grand Canyon National Park | 27 Stat. 469 | 2/20/1893 |
|      | Oregon | Mt. Hood National Forest | 28 Stat. 1240 | 9/28/1893 |
| 2011 | Pennsylvania | Gettysburg National Military Park | 28 Stat. 651 | 2/11/1895 |
|      | Montana | Glacier National Park | 29 Stat. 907 | 2/22/1897 |
|      | Washington | Olympic National Park | 29 Stat. 901 | 2/22/1897 |
|      | Mississippi | Vicksburg National Military Park | 30 Stat. 841 | 2/21/1899 |
|      | Oklahoma | Chickasaw National Recreation Area | 32 Stat. 641 | 7/1/1902 |
| 2012 | Puerto Rico | El Yunque National Forest | 32 Stat. 2029 | 1/17/1903 |
|      | New Mexico | Chaco Culture National Historical Park | 35 Stat. 2119 | 3/11/1907 |
|      | Maine | Acadia National Park | 39 Stat. 1785 | 7/8/1916 |
|      | Hawaii | Hawai'i Volcanoes National Park | 39 Stat. 432 | 8/1/1916 |
|      | Alaska | Denali National Park and Preserve | 39 Stat. 938 | 2/26/1917 |
| 2013 | New Hampshire | White Mountain National Forest | 40 Stat. 1779 | 5/16/1918 |
|      | Ohio | Perry's Victory and International Peace Memorial | 40 Stat. 1322 | 3/3/1919 |
|      | Nevada | Great Basin National Park | 42 Stat. 2260 | 1/24/1922 |
|      | Maryland | Fort McHenry National Monument and Historic Shrine | 43 Stat. 1109 | 3/3/1925 |
|      | South Dakota | Mount Rushmore National Memorial | 43 Stat. 1214 | 3/3/1925 |

**In Columbia Falls, Montana, Glacier National Park Superintendent Chas Cartwright hands out new quarters to students of Canyon Elementary School.**

| Year | Jurisdiction | Site | Legal Authority | Date Established |
|------|-------------|------|-----------------|------------------|
| 2014 | Tennessee | Great Smoky Mountains National Park | 44 Stat. 616 | 5/22/1926 |
| | Virginia | Shenandoah National Park | 44 Stat. 616 | 5/22/1926 |
| | Utah | Arches National Park | 46 Stat. 2988 | 4/12/1929 |
| | Colorado | Great Sand Dunes National Park | 47 Stat. 2506 | 3/17/1932 |
| | Florida | Everglades National Park | 48 Stat. 816 | 5/30/1934 |
| 2015 | Nebraska | Homestead National Monument of America | 49 Stat. 1184 | 3/19/1936 |
| | Louisiana | Kisatchie National Forest | 49 Stat. 3520 | 6/3/1936 |
| | North Carolina | Blue Ridge Parkway | 49 Stat. 2041 | 6/30/1936 |
| | Delaware | Bombay Hook National Wildlife Refuge | 45 Stat. 1222 | 6/22/1937 |
| | New York | Saratoga National Historical Park | 52 Stat. 608 | 6/1/1938 |
| 2016 | Illinois | Shawnee National Forest | 54 Stat. 2649 | 9/6/1939 |
| | Kentucky | Cumberland Gap National Historical Park | 54 Stat. 262 | 6/11/1940 |
| | West Virginia | Harpers Ferry National Historical Park | 58 Stat. 645 | 6/30/1944 |
| | North Dakota | Theodore Roosevelt National Park | 56 Stat. 326 | 2/25/1946 |
| | South Carolina | Fort Moultrie (Fort Sumter National Monument) | 62 Stat. 204 | 4/28/1948 |
| 2017 | Iowa | Effigy Mounds National Monument | 64 Stat. A371 | 10/25/1949 |
| | District of Columbia | Frederick Douglass National Historic Site | 76 Stat. 435 | 9/5/1962 |
| | Missouri | Ozark National Scenic Riverways | 78 Stat. 608 | 8/27/1964 |
| | New Jersey | Ellis Island National Monument (Statue of Liberty) | 79 Stat. 1490 | 5/11/1965 |
| | Indiana | George Rogers Clark National Historical Park | 80 Stat. 325 | 7/23/1966 |

Treasurer of the United States
Rosie Rios hands out Fort
McHenry National Monument
and Historic Shrine quarters
to visitors 18 and under
at the quarter launch.

Hawai'i Volcanoes National Park quarters
awaiting distribution to local students.

The Fort McHenry Guard Fife and Drum Corps.

| Year | Jurisdiction | Site | Legal Authority | Date Established |
|---|---|---|---|---|
| 2018 | Michigan | Pictured Rocks National Lakeshore | 80 Stat. 922 | 10/15/1966 |
| | Wisconsin | Apostle Islands National Lakeshore | 84 Stat. 880 | 9/26/1970 |
| | Minnesota | Voyageurs National Park | 84 Stat. 1970 | 1/8/1971 |
| | Georgia | Cumberland Island National Seashore | 86 Stat. 1066 | 10/23/1972 |
| | Rhode Island | Block Island National Wildlife Refuge | 62 Stat. 240 | 4/12/1973 |
| 2019 | Massachusetts | Lowell National Historical Park | 92 Stat. 291 | 6/5/1978 |
| | Northern Mariana Islands | American Memorial Park | 92 Stat. 487 | 8/18/1978 |
| | Guam | War in the Pacific National Historical Park | 92 Stat. 487 | 8/18/1978 |
| | Texas | San Antonio Missions National Historical Park | 92 Stat. 3636 | 11/10/1978 |
| | Idaho | Frank Church River of No Return Wilderness | 94 Stat. 948 | 7/23/1980 |
| 2020 | American Samoa | National Park of American Samoa | 102 Stat. 2879 | 10/31/1988 |
| | Connecticut | Weir Farm National Historic Site | 104 Stat. 1171 | 10/31/1990 |
| | U.S. Virgin Islands | Salt River Bay National Historical Park and Ecological Preserve | 106 Stat. 33 | 2/24/1992 |
| | Vermont | Marsh-Billings-Rockefeller National Historical Park | 106 Stat. 934 | 8/26/1992 |
| | Kansas | Tallgrass Prairie National Preserve | 110 Stat. 4204 | 11/12/1996 |
| 2021 | Alabama | Tuskegee Airmen National Historic Site | 112 Stat. 3247 | 11/6/1998 |

In Custer, South Dakota, the launch ceremony for the Mount Rushmore quarter features Nick Clifford, the last living worker who helped create the faces on the memorial.

There are no special ceremonies held specifically for the America the Beautiful silver bullion coins, but each of the National Park quarters gets a launch ceremony to celebrate its debut. "When we launched the America the Beautiful Quarters Program, we embarked on a journey to reconnect Americans with our beautiful national parks, forests, wildlife refuges and other sites," said U.S. Mint Director Ed Moy in June 2010. "We hope families across the country will join us on this journey." The launch ceremonies are open to the public and include a coin exchange (visitors can trade their cash for rolls of newly minted quarters bearing the design that honors the featured site). Everyone 18 and younger receives a free new quarter to commemorate the event.

# DESIGN PROCESS FOR THE AMERICA THE BEAUTIFUL SILVER COINS

The obverse of the National Park quarters (and their related America the Beautiful silver coins) features a modern version of the profile portrait of George Washington used on the quarter from 1932 to 1998. The original was designed by New York sculptor John Flanagan, and the later modification was by Mint sculptor-engraver William C. Cousins (formerly director of the Franklin Mint Sculptors' Studio). The legends UNITED STATES OF AMERICA and QUARTER DOLLAR, situated on the reverse of the older coins, were moved to the obverse starting with the State quarters in 1999, to make more room for the changing reverse designs.

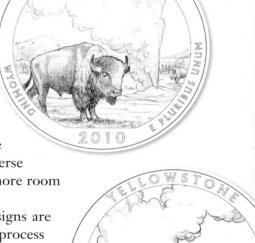

For the National Park quarters, the reverse designs are submitted according to a selection and approval process developed by the secretary of the Treasury. The program's coins are meant to be emblematic of one national site in each host jurisdiction deemed "most appropriate in terms of natural or historic significance."

The Treasury's standards for the coinage designs note the following:

1. Selected sites must be ones that can reasonably be expected to translate into dignified designs of which the citizens of the United States can be proud (for example, must be distinctive and readily recognizable as honoring that site).

2. Selected sites must be ones that can reasonably be expected to translate into designs that are neither frivolous nor inappropriate. Inappropriate designs include, but are not limited to, those bearing logos or depictions of specific commercial, private, educational, civic, religious, sports, or other organizations whose membership or ownership is not universal.

3. Designs must not include any head-and-shoulders portrait or bust of any person, living or dead, nor can designs include a portrait of a living person. Designs must not include an outline or map of a host jurisdiction.

**Three design sketches for the reverse of the Yellowstone National Park coin.**

4. Designs can be based on the same theme as used in the United States Mint's 50 State Quarters Program, or the District of Columbia and U.S. Territories Quarters Program, but cannot be the same design.

The design selection process is broken down into seven steps.

**Step 1.** The U.S. Mint initiates the formal design process for each national site as identified by the order of the official list approved by the secretary of the Treasury. Designs are processed at a rate of five per year.

**Step 2.** The Mint contacts the head of the federal entity responsible for the supervision, management, or conservancy of each national site. The Mint asks this person to appoint a knowledgeable federal official (e.g., a national park superintendent, national forest supervisor, or federal preservation officer) to serve as the liaison for the national site. The liaison assists the Mint by identifying source materials for candidate designs.

**Step 3.** Based on the identified source materials, the Mint produces three to five candidate designs focusing on aesthetic beauty, historical accuracy, authenticity, appropriateness, and coinability.

**Step 4.** The Mint consults with the liaison for the federal entity responsible for the supervision, management, or conservancy of the national site to ensure the historical accuracy, authenticity, and overall composition of each candidate design to ensure it appropriately represents the site.

**Step 5.** Final candidate designs are submitted to the secretary of the Interior, the chief executive of the host jurisdiction, the Commission of Fine Arts (CFA), and the Citizens Coinage Advisory Committee (CCAC) for review and comment. The Mint may make changes to address any concerns or recommendations resulting from this review process.

**Step 6.** The director of the U.S. Mint makes a final recommendation to the secretary of the Treasury, after considering all relevant factors, including the comments and recommendations of the secretary of the Interior, the chief executive, the CFA, the CCAC, and the federal entity responsible for the supervision, management, or conservancy of the national site.

**Step 7.** The secretary of the Treasury makes the final design selection.

# DESIGNERS OF THE AMERICA THE BEAUTIFUL SILVER COINS

Some of the National Park quarters (and their related America the Beautiful silver bullion coins) are designed by members of the U.S. Mint's sculpting and engraving department, based at the Philadelphia Mint. Many others are designed by members of the Artistic Infusion Program, a group of outside artists that was first assembled by the Mint in 2003, with new members added over the years since.

U.S. Mint designers for the coins as of 2015 include Don Everhart, Phebe Hemphill, Joseph Menna, and Charles Vickers. (For their biographies, see chapter 6.) From the roster of AIP designers, those who have worked on the coins so far include Thomas Cleveland, Chris Costello, Barbara Fox, Susan Gamble, Joel Iskowitz, Frank Morris, Ronald Sanders, Donna Weaver, and Gary Whitley. All of these AIP artists except for Sanders have also designed First Spouse gold coins for the Mint, and their biographies are in chapter 6. Sanders is an honors graduate of the Columbus College of Art and Design, and an award-winning fine artist, graphic designer, and teacher.

# PRODUCTION OF THE AMERICA THE BEAUTIFUL SILVER COINS

The basic motifs of the America the Beautiful five-ounce silver coins are the same as for their smaller circulating-coin counterparts. Their designs, however, are cut directly into the die steel on a CNC milling machine, bypassing a hubbing operation. This results in sharper details than are seen on the regular quarters. The fineness and weight are incused on each coin's edge, rather than being part of the obverse or reverse design. The Mint's massive German-made Gräbener press, installed on a specially reinforced foundation at the Philadelphia Mint, strikes 22 coins per minute, with multiple strikes per coin at 450 to 500 metric tons of pressure. (Its full capacity is 40 coins per minute and 1,000 tons of pressure.)

All of the die work and production takes place at the Philadelphia Mint.

The Gräbener press is a marvel of modern machinery. Three workers operate it in a large dedicated room tucked away in the Philadelphia Mint. At any given moment a forklift might be parked just outside the main press paddock, a raised foundation where the Gräbener is situated. The forklift is needed to move trays holding hundreds of five-ounce silver planchets waiting their turn to be transformed into coins. These three-inch rounds of precious metal are purchased by the Mint from large suppliers such as Sunshine Minting, headquartered in Coeur d'Alene, Idaho, and Gold Corporation of Perth, Australia. They arrive in Philadelphia ready for duty—properly annealed, with their rims already "upset" (machined so as to be slightly raised) and their surfaces sonically cleaned to remove any debris. A press operator manually feeds the planchets one by one onto a moving belt, each planchet fitted into a holder that keeps it secure as it moves through the press's conveyor system. Inside the machine a robotic arm swings into action, suction-cups an individual planchet, and moves it onto a shallow "in-place pocket" to be situated for striking. The planchet is moved into position over a stationary "anvil die"—in this case, the die for the obverse of the coin, featuring George Washington's portrait. Surrounding the die is a three-piece collar, one part of which has the edge lettering (.999 FINE SILVER 5.0 OUNCE) that will be stamped incuse into the planchet's smooth edge. A "hammer die," with the design of the coin's reverse, is aligned above the anvil die. After the silver planchet is trapped in the three-part collar, the hammer die plunges downward three times with 450 or more metric tons of hydraulic pressure. (For comparison, minting a quarter dollar requires about 60 tons of pressure, and a silver dollar, about 150 tons.) The silver flows from this forced pressure into the recesses of the hammer and anvil dies (which are machined incuse with the mirror images of what will be the finished coin), and the edge-impression collar die pushes the lettering into the planchet's edge. The planchet—now a fully struck coin—is ejected from the press and slides down a chute into a tray, as another planchet is moved into position for coining. The entire process takes less than three seconds, and it produces a brilliantly mirrored America the Beautiful silver bullion coin.

The Gräbener press is not on the Philadelphia Mint's regular public tour. Earplugs are recommended to muffle the constant repetitive noise of production. Even with earplugs in place, you can hear a rhythmic, almost musical *clink . . . clink . . . clink* as the heavy, freshly struck coins slide out of the press and into the waiting tray.

Details on the 2014 Great Smoky Mountains National Park quarter dollar (left) and its corresponding five-ounce silver bullion coin (right). In the silver coin's design, note the finer detail in the cabin's siding, the grass, the hawk, and other design elements.

# THE GRÄBENER PRESS IN ACTION

This Gräbener press was installed at the Philadelphia Mint in March 2010.

Five-ounce silver planchets awaiting coinage.

The silver planchets are specially prepared, and delivered by their suppliers ready for minting.

A press operator loads planchets into the conveyor.

Freshly struck America the Beautiful silver
coins slide into a tray.

A newly minted 2015 Bombay Hook coin.

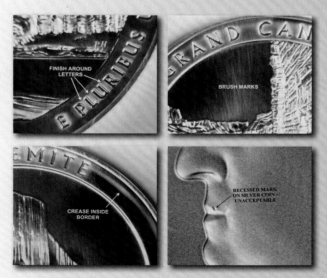

Diagrams instructing Mint workers in potential
problems to look out for during production.

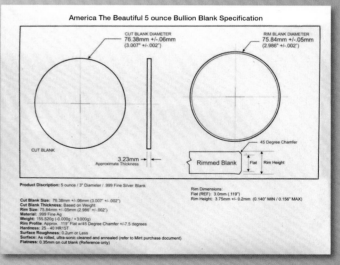

A Mint diagram of the America
the Beautiful planchet specifications.

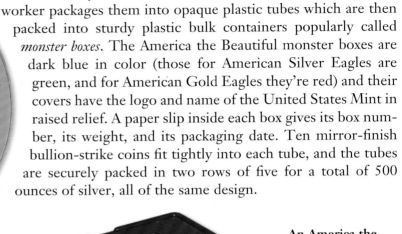

The coins, while impressive in size and artistically significant, in a sense are "merely" bullion. After the bullion strikes are minted a worker packages them into opaque plastic tubes which are then packed into sturdy plastic bulk containers popularly called *monster boxes*. The America the Beautiful monster boxes are dark blue in color (those for American Silver Eagles are green, and for American Gold Eagles they're red) and their covers have the logo and name of the United States Mint in raised relief. A paper slip inside each box gives its box number, its weight, and its packaging date. Ten mirror-finish bullion-strike coins fit tightly into each tube, and the tubes are securely packed in two rows of five for a total of 500 ounces of silver, all of the same design.

Bullion strike, with a mirror finish.

Detail of the incused
edge markings.

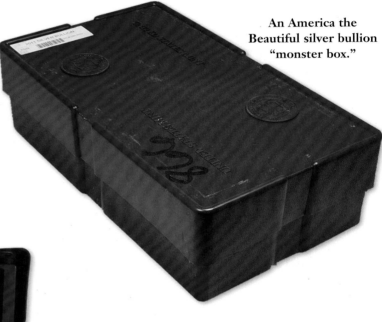

An America the
Beautiful silver bullion
"monster box."

Ten tubes, each containing ten five-ounce silver coins.

The top of a monster-box tube,
imprinted with the logo of the U.S. Mint.

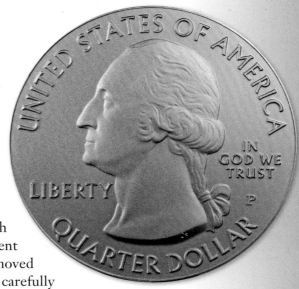

As discussed above, regular bullion strikes of the America the Beautiful silver coins are made with a mirror finish. They bear no mintmark identifying them as products of the Philadelphia Mint. In contrast, the numismatic Specimen strikes (called "Uncirculated" by the Mint) have a soft matte finish, and they feature a P mintmark on the obverse.

The hammer and anvil dies used for the Specimen coins are more highly polished than regular bullion dies. Otherwise, their minting is similar to that of the bullion coins. Each Specimen, however, receives special post-striking treatment that imparts a distinctive finish to its surfaces. The coin is removed from the Gräbener press and taken to another machine to be carefully blasted with a pressure-compressed combination of water vapor and very fine ceramic media. The visual effect is similar to that of a sand-blasted surface.

**Specimen strike, with matte vapor-blasted surfaces.**

Each Specimen coin is ensconced in a plastic capsule and situated in a flocked tray in a cardboard presentation box, along with a certificate of authenticity. The box is slipped into a decorative cardboard sleeve with the logo of the U.S. Mint.

By the summer of 2011, the hobby community had discovered inconsistencies in the surfaces of some Specimen coins. On July 27, the Mint confirmed the existence of these production errors or varieties, and released this statement:

> From photographs we have received, and reports from coin-grading services, it is apparent that several varieties of America the Beautiful five-ounce silver Uncirculated coins exist with differing or missing vapor-blast finishes. We are looking into the cause of the inconsistency in finishes, examining each step in the post-production process when vapor blasting is applied. We are committed to restoring the consistency for which United States Mint products are known worldwide.
>
> While we have ordered new equipment to execute automated vapor-blasting on the America the Beautiful five-ounce silver Uncirculated coins, we are currently using the process originally used for our three-inch medals. That equipment required retro-fitting and readjustment for the process, and has required additional maintenance due to the higher volume and substantially increased wear of this program.
>
> The new equipment will allow us to move from the manual, batch process to more closely integrate the vapor-blasting application into the overall production line for the coin.

**The mintmark on the Specimen coins is on the obverse, to the right of George Washington's hair ribbon.**

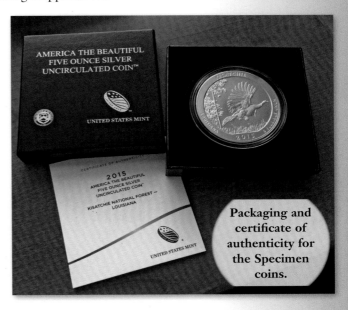

For more information on these errors and varieties, see the individual coin-by-coin listings.

**Packaging and certificate of authenticity for the Specimen coins.**

# DISTRIBUTION OF THE AMERICA THE BEAUTIFUL SILVER COINS

The bullion strikes of the silver America the Beautiful coins are sold in bulk by the U.S. Mint to its network of Authorized Purchasers and their retailers, who in turn sell to individual collectors and investors. This is similar to the distribution of regular-format ("non-numismatic") American Silver Eagles and other bullion coins. The first 11 Authorized Purchasers for the America the Beautiful coins were:

A-Mark Precious Metals (Los Angeles)

Coins 'n Things Inc. (Massachusetts)

Manfra, Tordella & Brookes (New York)

Scotia Mocatta (New York)

American Precious Metals Exchange, Inc. (APMEX) (Oklahoma)

Dillon Gage Incorporated of Dallas (Texas)

Prudential Securities Inc. (New York)

The Gold Center (Illinois)

Commerzbank (New York)

Jack Hunt Coin Broker (New York)

Fidelitrade (Delaware)

In addition to the commercial channels of Authorized Purchasers, the Mint itself sells *numismatic* versions (Specimen coins, struck in a special sandblast-style format and specially packaged, as described above) directly to the public, through mail order and in its gift shops.

The coins' authorizing legislation also granted the director of the National Park Service the right to purchase the numismatic versions in units of at least 1,000 at a time, to resell or repackage at his discretion.

The U.S. Mint under Director Ed Moy overcame significant production challenges to create the massive new America the Beautiful silver coins.

Distribution of the first year's coins was originally slated for late summer 2010. Production was delayed, however—finally starting on September 21—as the Mint wrestled with the technical challenges of striking such a physically large product. Developing, testing, and custom-ordering the oversized silver planchets took time. The diameter of three inches results in a silver coin thinner than the smaller five-ounce pieces struck by other mints, and the congressionally mandated edge lettering also offered challenges.[1] Mint Director Edmund Moy addressed the topic in a February 2010 public forum. "We've got a five-ounce piece of silver," he said, "and we stretch it out to a three-inch diameter. It's paper-thin. And then Congress mandated that we had to edge-letter it. So when you edge-letter a paper-thin coin, you get crumples." The

Mint had to purchase a special $2.2 million press from German firm Gräbener Pressensysteme GmbH & Co. KG, and then install it at its Philadelphia facility. Installation was completed on March 1, 2010.

In an eleventh-hour attempt to alleviate the production challenges, North Carolina congressman Melvin Watt proposed modifications to the coins' authorizing legislation. The Coin Modernization, Oversight, and Continuity Act of 2010 was introduced to the House of Representatives on September 22, passed in a House vote on September 29, then passed in identical form in the Senate on November 30. President Barack Obama signed the act into law on December 14. This removed the requirement of edge lettering, and allowed the coins to be produced as small as 2.5 inches if necessary (the world standard for five-ounce silver coins is 2.75 inches). These solutions arrived too late, however. By that time the Mint had solved the problems and production was already under way. The Mint's original intent had been to strike 100,000 coins of each 2010 design. Philadelphia was able to produce and release 33,000 bullion strikes of each of the five 2010 designs before its scheduled launch of the silver series on December 6.

**Representative Mel Watt of North Carolina sponsored legislation in 2010 to change the coins' specifications and make them easier to produce.**

By then demand for the silver coins was bottled up like a pressure cooker. The delays were creating a sense of urgency, and collectors and investors knew the 2010 mintages would be small. When the exotic silver coins finally debuted, they seemed more like limited-edition collectibles than mass-market bullion pieces. The situation, sadly, was ripe for profiteering. Only hours after sales started Mint officials had to temporarily shut the program down, in a measure taken to protect consumers. Complaints streamed in from collectors who were compelled to pay unreasonable premiums by Authorized Purchasers. These primary distributors were allowed to buy the coins directly from the Mint based on their market value plus a $9.75 markup per coin. Before the coins were officially released on December 6, one of the Authorized Purchasers was taking orders from collectors at a markup of about $130 per coin! The Mint halted the program and sent its Authorized Purchasers a new outline of terms and conditions they had to agree to before the program would be relaunched on December 10. (The Mint reserved the right to change its terms if, in its judgment, "the best interests of the U.S. government and the U.S. bullion coin programs so indicate.") The new terms, aimed at curbing abuses and getting the coins into the hands of as many Americans as possible, were as follows:

1. Authorized Purchasers shall make available for sale to the public all 2010 America the Beautiful Silver Bullion Coins that they acquire. The intention of this condition is to ensure that all 2010 America the Beautiful Silver Bullion Coins minted and issued by the United States Mint are sold to the public.

2. Authorized Purchasers may charge to their customers a price no higher than ten percent above the price at which the Authorized Purchasers acquire 2010 America the Beautiful Silver Bullion Coins from the United States Mint. Authorized Purchasers may charge their customers a reasonable shipping and handling fee; however, Authorized Purchasers may not charge any other fee, premium, or other expense to their

customers to circumvent this ten-percent markup limitation. The intention of this condition is to ensure that members of the public can obtain these coins at a reasonable and affordable purchase price.

3. Authorized Purchasers must establish and enforce an order limit of one coin of each design for each household. A household is defined as all persons of a family, or living as a family, at a single mailing address. The intention of this condition is to ensure the broadest and fairest public accessibility to 2010 America the Beautiful Silver Bullion Coins, which are limited-mintage United States Mint products.

4. Authorized Purchasers may not sell, either directly or indirectly, 2010 America the Beautiful Silver Bullion Coins to their officers or employees. The intention of this condition is to ensure that 2010 America the Beautiful Silver Bullion Coins are available to the public and that Authorized Purchaser officers and employees do not have an unfair advantage over members of the public.

With the new cap on the potential markup, Authorized Purchasers would be able to charge about $170 per coin, or $850 for a five-coin set. Before the Mint temporarily halted the program, one of the Authorized Purchasers had sold 1,000 sets at $1,395 each in less than 24 hours, and some sets were "pre-selling" online (before the coins were even in hand) for $2,500 or more.

The Mint was serious about putting an end to the market shenanigans. For those Authorized Purchasers who agreed to the new terms, the Mint reserved the right "to examine and audit all of the Authorized Purchaser's books, records, documents, and other data to ensure that they have complied with the terms and conditions herein. Violation of any one of the above outlined terms and conditions may be grounds for suspension or permanent removal from the United States Mint's Authorized Purchaser distribution network."

After the 2010 rollout, distribution proceeded more smoothly. Pent-up customer demand was still high, and the Mint was prepared with greater production capacity. This marriage of supply and demand led to nearly quadruple the sales of regular bullion strikes for the first two issues of 2011, compared to those of 2010. Bullion mintages decreased through the rest of the year, with sales in the 30,000 to 40,000 range for most coins 2012 to date (although there were lower-mintage exceptions in 2012). For the special-finish Specimen coins, sales have averaged around 20,000 annually after higher demand the inaugural year.

Bullion-strike mintages at first had no ceiling, being limited only by customer demand. The mintage limits for the Specimen coins (set by the Mint) have varied. For the 2010 issues the limit was 27,000 Specimens of each design; this was increased to 35,000 each for the 2011 issues. In 2015 mintages were set as a total, with a cap of 65,000 coins in both formats for each issue. (See each catalog entry for specifics on mintage limits.)

The 2010 Specimen coins were produced in 2010, but were first offered for sale in early 2011.

Before 2014 the Mint had a subscription program in place as a way for collectors to stay current on series products. On December 23, 2013, it announced a new "Online Subscription Program" that would give a 10 percent discount for several numismatic products, including the America the Beautiful silver bullion coins. Under the old program, after signing up a subscriber would automatically start receiving each new product in the subscription series, with the standard shipping and handling fee of $4.95 added to each order. With the new subscription service introduced in 2014, subscribers would receive a 10 percent discount on their Specimen America the Beautiful silver coins.[2] The discount for a single coin issue-priced at $154.95 would be $15.50, a substantial savings that essentially equated to free shipping and cash back. The promotional discount, introduced on a trial basis, was discontinued on September 30, 2014, the day before the Mint rolled out a newly revamped Web site and ordering system.[3]

# THE FUTURE OF THE AMERICA THE BEAUTIFUL SILVER COINS

As of press time, the America the Beautiful silver bullion coin program is scheduled to end in 2021, which is the year the National Park quarters program wraps up with a single final issue (that of Alabama's Tuskegee Airmen National Historic Site). However, the authorizing legislation—the America's Beautiful National Parks Quarter Dollar Coin Act of 2008—offers an interesting alternative scenario. Section 102 allows for a "second round" at the discretion of the secretary of the Treasury. The secretary has the authority until the end of 2018 to make a decision "to continue the period of issuance until a second national site in each state, the District of Columbia, and each territory . . . has been honored with a design on a quarter dollar." If the secretary decides to continue the program into a second round, he will formalize his decision with a written report to the House Committee on Financial Services and the Senate Committee on Banking, Housing, and Urban Affairs. The second round of the program would then pick up immediately after the issuance of the Tuskegee Airmen quarter. If the secretary of the Treasury invokes this authority, the National Park quarters—and their corresponding five-ounce silver coins—would continue into 2032.

Regardless of when the program ends (in 2021 or in 2032), the obverse of the quarter dollar will eventually revert to the same obverse design it had before the State quarters started in 1999, and the reverse will feature a new image of General George Washington crossing the Delaware River before the Battle of Trenton. These designs are mandated in the program's authorizing legislation.

By Secretary of the Treasury Jack Lew's authority, the America the Beautiful coinage program could be extended in a second round to the year 2032.

The America the Beautiful silver bullion coins have found their niche among coin collectors and silver-bullion investors. The series includes some low-mintage keys and interesting collectible varieties. From an aesthetic viewpoint, the coins are a showcase of the talents of the U.S. Mint's designer-engraver staff and its roster of Artistic Infusion Program designers. From a technical and industrial perspective they highlight the Mint's status as an innovative force in modern minting, with the ability to create impressive products and to overcome complicated mechanical and logistical challenges. In this author's opinion, the secretary of the Treasury is likely to authorize the continuation of the 2010–2021 quarters program, extending the series into 2032. This will give to collectors an even more beautiful panorama of American coins to enjoy, and to investors the most visually stunning 560 ounces of .999 fine silver they could ever hope to sock away.

In a September 18, 2014, article in *Numismatic News*, excerpted here, Connor Falk described the market for the coins and reported the observations of active dealers:

America the Beautiful (ATB) 5-ounce silver coins are big, bold and sought after by collectors and investors alike.

Those loyal to the series will be buying the latest ATB release—Great Sand Dunes.

The 2014 Great Sand Dunes coin shows a father and sun playing in the sand of a creek bed in the national park.

"I'd say about 80 percent are returning buyers," said John Maben, CEO of Modern Coin Mart, Sarasota, Fla. "About 10 percent tend to drop out, but 30 percent are new buyers coming into the series."

Demand was much higher at the start of the series for a number of reasons, he said.

"It started off on a bad note when the Mint was making so few compared to demand at the time," Maben said. "With the economy the way it was then, they could have sold a lot more," he said.

The Mint could have easily made 300,000 of each coin released in 2011 and sold them all. "After that, the demand dropped down quite a bit and the mintages have come down to around 30,000," he said.

Prices for the in-demand 2010 and 2011 coins dropped down as well, he said. "What they sell for today is only 30 percent of what they were selling for back in 2011," he said.

Sales today to collectors are steady, with sales equal between graded bullion coins and the graded collector's version, he said.

Grading services are designating the uncirculated collector's version of the ATB 5-ounce coins with the "P" Philadelphia mintmark with an SP grade.

"When each new coin comes out, we sell about 250 of each. The bullion we sell is graded MS-69 Deep Mirror Proof-Like (DPL) and the vapor-finish coins are graded either SP-69 or SP-70," he said.

Demand is high for high-grade collector's version ATB 5-ounce coins, he said. "The SP-70 graded coins outsell the SP-69 coins 10 to 1," Maben said.

There's a good reason as to why collectors are going after the highest grade for both the collector and the bullion coins. Michael Haynes, CEO of APMEX, Oklahoma City, Okla., said the -70s always draw attention because of the registry sets being created. "These registry sets require the top-grade coins, so there is a big demand for MS-70 and SP-70 ATB 5-ounce coins," he said.

At APMEX, a 2013-P Perry's Victory PCGS-graded SP-69 is priced at $249. The same coin in SP-70 is priced at $349. Both coin's slab labels were also signed by John Mercanti, 12th chief engraver at the U.S. Mint.

The older ATB 5-ounce coins are also in demand, as they are no longer being made, Haynes said.

"The Hawaii Volcanoes and the Mount Rushmore ATB 5-ounce coins are very popular, mainly due to their great designs," he said. The price for an ungraded 2012-P Hawaii Volcanoes ATB 5-ounce coin is $399 at APMEX while an ungraded 2013-P Mount Rushmore ATB 5-ounce coin is $199. "This reflects the popularity of some of these designs, especially when the latest (bullion) issues can be purchased by collectors ungraded for $116," Haynes said.

Maben said that there are key differences between collectors' and investors' views on the America the Beautiful 5-ounce coin program, though.

"Pure bullion buyers who are adding precious metals to their portfolio don't buy the ATB 5-ounce coins," he said. They buy other silver coins, silver bullion bars, or even a 1-ounce gold bar. A 1-ounce gold bar is much easier to store than the equivalent in ATB 5-ounce bullion coins, he said.

"However, a heavy hitter in bullion may go after a monster box of the ATB 5-ounce coins because it is smaller than a monster box of silver American Eagles. They may purchase a box of each new ATB release just to store away," he said.

Diversification is also a factor for investors to consider the series, he said.

"There are bullion investors who want a little bit of everything and will buy some ATB bullion 5-ounce coins," Maben said.

Haynes said some silver buyers seeking to expand their portfolio with the ATB 5-ounce coins become collectors themselves. "It has crossed boundaries when the silver buyers look to buy it for the silver and then begin to collect the series," he said.

Their interest in the series includes both a collector and investor reason for buying the series, he said. "It's a combination of the silver content, where it has a good weight and feel to it, and the designs in the series," he said.

The addition of silver buyers as well as new collectors to the series would lead to a strong market for the coins, he said. "I would say sales are going to go up as more people begin coin collecting and discover that the U.S. Mint created a 5-ounce coin, something they have never heard of. So, they buy one and discover there's a whole series of America the Beautiful 5-ounce silver coins to collect," Haynes said.[4]

The 2012 Hawai'i Volcanoes National Park coin features an explosive design concept.

The popular 2013 Mount Rushmore coin offers collectors a unique perspective of the famous monument.

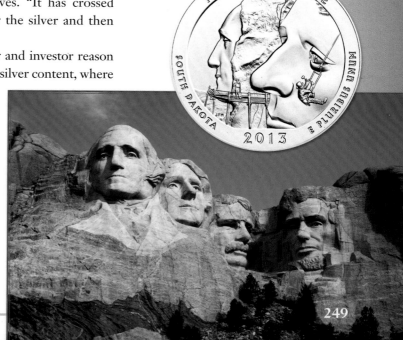

# HOT SPRINGS NATIONAL PARK, ARKANSAS (2010)

***Designer:*** *John Flanagan (obverse); Don Everhart (reverse).* ***Sculptor:*** *Joseph F. Menna (reverse).* ***Composition:*** *.999 silver, .001 copper.* ***Actual Silver Weight:*** *5 ounces.* ***Diameter:*** *76.2 mm.* ***Edge:*** *Lettered.* ***Mint:*** *Philadelphia.* ***Issue Price:*** *variable (bullion); $279.95 (Specimen).* ***Release Date:*** *December 6, 2010 (bullion); April 28, 2011 (Specimen).*

**Bullion strike.**

**Specimen.**

Hot Springs National Park was studied in the 1804 "Grand Expedition" ordered by President Thomas Jefferson as the first scientific exploration into the lower Louisiana Purchase. The three-month journey was led by naturalist William Dunbar and his second-in-command, chemist George Hunter. Hot Springs contains American Indian quarries and 47 springs emerging from the nearby mountain, which led to its name. An active town grew up around the springs and became a destination for health and relaxation. The area was established as a national site on April 20, 1832, to make the water available for drinking and therapy.

The reverse of the silver coin shows the façade of the Hot Springs National Park headquarters building with a thermal spring fountain in the foreground. The headquarters was built during the Great Depression in the Spanish colonial revival style, with construction completed in 1936. The National Park Service emblem is featured to the right of the door.

A small number of the Hot Springs Specimen coins were inadvertently produced in a "Light Finish" or "Light Satin" format—an error in the vapor-blasting process. The Mint was still using a manual process with vapor-blasting equipment designed for its three-inch medals, retro-fitted and adjusted for the America the Beautiful silver coins. The Light Finish coins resulted during the transition to a more customized process. Slabbed SP-68 examples are worth a small premium, with SP-69 Light Finish coins seeing prices of $500 to $1,000. An SP-70 example might fetch $2,000 or more.

**Mintage: 33,000 bullion; 26,788 Specimen**

| Certified Populations and Retail Market Values | | | | | | | | |
|---|---|---|---|---|---|---|---|---|
| | **Raw MS** | **<MS-69** | **MS-69** | **MS-70** | **Raw SP** | **<SP-69** | **SP-69** | **SP-70** |
| **Certified** | — | 3,052 | 5,720 | 0 | — | 157 | 1,317 | 733 |
| **Value\*** | $110 | | $150 | — | $145 | | $165 | $650 |
| *Recent auctions:* $179, MS-69PL, August 2015. $155, SP-69, July 2015. | | | | | | | | |

\* "Raw" value is based on a silver spot price of $16 per ounce, and is for an uncertified bullion-strike or Specimen coin of average quality. This value may vary with the prevailing bullion value.

# YELLOWSTONE NATIONAL PARK, WYOMING (2010)

***Designer:*** *John Flanagan (obverse); Don Everhart (reverse).* ***Sculptor:*** *Don Everhart (reverse).* ***Composition:*** *.999 silver, .001 copper.* ***Actual Silver Weight:*** *5 ounces.* ***Diameter:*** *76.2 mm.* ***Edge:*** *Lettered.* ***Mint:*** *Philadelphia.* ***Issue Price:*** *variable (bullion); $279.95 (Specimen).* ***Release Date:*** *December 6, 2010 (bullion); May 17, 2011 (Specimen).*

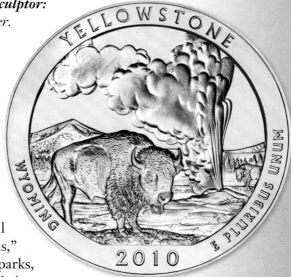

**Bullion strike.**

Established as a national site on March 1, 1872, Yellowstone National Park is home to a large variety of wildlife, including bison, elk, grizzly bears, and wolves. The world's most extraordinary geysers and other geothermal features are found inside its confines.

The reverse of the Yellowstone National Park silver coin features the geyser known as Old Faithful, with a mature bull bison in the foreground. "Through America the Beautiful coins," said Mint Director Ed Moy, "we are transported to national parks, forests, and wildlife refuges, part of a vast public-land legacy belonging to all Americans—natural and cultural treasures protected for our recreation, relaxation, education, inspiration, and transformation."

Buyers quickly bought the 33,000 bullion strikes minted for the Yellowstone issue, and nearly as many (almost 28,000) of the vapor-blasted Specimen coins. The latter went on sale in May of 2011.

On July 25, 2011, the third-party grading firm NGC announced that it had discovered "what may be the first error in the America the Beautiful five-ounce series." The coin was a 2010-P Yellowstone National Park Specimen with the usual matte Specimen finish on the obverse and a brilliant lustrous finish on the reverse. "On this error, only the Washington side was vapor-blasted but the Yellowstone side was untouched," NGC announced. "The Washington side therefore resembles a Specimen while the Yellowstone side appears similar to a bullion issue." An NGC grader discovered the error while grading a bulk submission of Yellowstone five-ounce coins. The firm graded the coin Specimen-69 and appended the description "With Unfinished Reverse" on its label.

**Specimen.**

The coin was classified as an *error*—possibly unique—similar to an off-metal strike (for example, a 1943 cent minted from a bronze planchet, rather than the normal steel) or a coin double-struck or struck off-center. Unlike the "Light Finish" or "Light Satin" coins seen in some other issues of 2010, it was not classified as a *variety*, which would be an anomaly produced across multiple coins struck from a defective die, or multiple coins produced by defective processing (such as a batch misapplication of the vapor-blasting process).

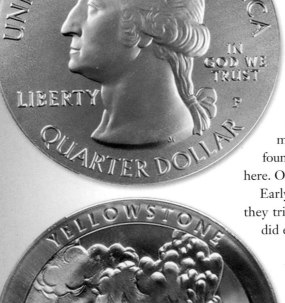

"Unfinished Reverse" error.

Aaron J. McKeon, in *America's Beautiful National Parks: A Handbook for Collecting the New National Park Quarters*, describes Yellowstone:

The Grand Prismatic Spring may be the most visually arresting sight in Yellowstone National Park. Pigmented bacteria living in a hot spring turn the edges of its pool a volcanic red-orange, shifting to yellow and yellow-green. The water in the pool's center is a sapphire blue. The vibrant colors both contrast and complement one another, unlike anything else found in nature. One of the early tourist publications on the park described it as "so dazzling that the eye cannot endure it."

Grand Prismatic is just one of the 10,000 smoking, bubbling thermal features found in Yellowstone. The incredible geysers, more than 300 of them altogether, make up the majority of geysers found on the planet. The tallest in the world, Steamboat, is found here. Old Faithful is known for both its height and its predictability.

Early explorers couldn't believe what they were seeing and, when they tried to tell people back east about the sights here, no one else did either.

When prominent geologist Ferdinand Vandeveer Hayden was planning his famed 1871 expedition to Yellowstone, he made sure to bring along photographer William Henry Jackson and landscape painter Thomas Moran, to ensure a visual record.

Hayden's expedition was more meticulous in its records of the park than previous explorations had been. His report was full of details, photographs, and sketches, and was widely distributed in Washington, building support for the preservation of these natural wonders. . . .

Yellowstone is a national treasure, the crown jewel in the treasure chest of the parks system. And the landscape is only part of Yellowstone's story: the wildlife habitat preserved on its 2.2 million acres is superb and means that visitors frequently get a look at large mammals like wolves, bison, elk, and bears.

More than three million people a year make the journey to northeastern Wyoming. Some hop off a tour bus, get their picture in front of Old Faithful, and hop right back on. Backcountry hikers come for long excursions into the wilderness on the park's 1,100 miles of trail. One of the easier day hikes is the five-mile Fairy Falls Trail that provides views of Fairy Falls and excellent views of Grand Prismatic Spring.[5]

**Mintage: 33,000 bullion; 26,711 Specimen**

| | | | | Certified Populations and Retail Market Values | | | |
|---|---|---|---|---|---|---|---|
| | Raw MS | <MS-69 | MS-69 | MS-70 | Raw SP | <SP-69 | SP-69 | SP-70 |
| Certified | — | 3,147 | 5,617 | 0 | — | 67 | 1,183 | 1,079 |
| Value* | $110 | | $150 | — | $140 | | $165 | $600 |

*Recent auctions:* $172, MS-69PL, August 2015. $475, SP-70, August 2015.

\* "Raw" value is based on a silver spot price of $16 per ounce, and is for an uncertified bullion-strike or Specimen coin of average quality. This value may vary with the prevailing bullion value.

# YOSEMITE NATIONAL PARK, CALIFORNIA (2010)

*Designer: John Flanagan (obverse); Joseph F. Menna (reverse).* **Sculptor:** *Phebe Hemphill (reverse).* **Composition:** *.999 silver, .001 copper.* **Actual Silver Weight:** *5 ounces.* **Diameter:** *76.2 mm.* **Edge:** *Lettered.* **Mint:** *Philadelphia.* **Issue Price:** *variable (bullion); $279.95 (Specimen).* **Release Date:** *December 6, 2010 (bullion); June 9, 2011 (Specimen).*

**Bullion strike.**

Yosemite National Park is one of the oldest wilderness parks in the United States, established as a national site on October 1, 1890. Conservationist John Muir was instrumental in getting Yosemite designated for protection. His descriptions of the land, and his observation of damage being done to it, made the need for preservation clear. Yosemite National Park is best known for its waterfalls, but visitors to its nearly 1,200 square miles also find deep valleys, widespread meadows, ancient giant sequoia trees, and other natural attractions. The image on the reverse of the Yosemite National Park quarter depicts the iconic El Capitan, the largest monolith of granite in the world, which rises more than 3,000 feet above the valley floor. "Yosemite is not only a great valley," says the U.S. Mint's literature, "but also a shrine to human foresight, strength of granite, power of glaciers, the persistence of life, and the tranquility of the High Sierra."

**Specimen.**

"This new quarter is yet another way that Yosemite's legacy will live on by reminding those who take home the Yosemite National Park quarter how special America's national parks are."

—*Yosemite National Park Superintendent Don Neubacher*

"With this quarter, the United States Mint connects America to the wonder, peace, and beauty of one of its most awe-inspiring natural treasures: Yosemite National Park."

—*U.S. Mint Director Ed Moy*

**Mintage: 33,000 bullion; 26,716 Specimen**

| Certified Populations and Retail Market Values | | | | | | | | |
|---|---|---|---|---|---|---|---|---|
| | Raw MS | <MS-69 | MS-69 | MS-70 | Raw SP | <SP-69 | SP-69 | SP-70 |
| Certified | — | 3,386 | 5,266 | 0 | — | 49 | 882 | 1,478 |
| Value* | $110 | | $150 | — | $140 | | $165 | $600 |
| *Recent auctions:* $163, MS-69PL, August 2015. $450, SP-70, August 2015. | | | | | | | | |

\* "Raw" value is based on a silver spot price of $16 per ounce, and is for an uncertified bullion-strike or Specimen coin of average quality. This value may vary with the prevailing bullion value.

# GRAND CANYON NATIONAL PARK, ARIZONA (2010)

*Designer:* John Flanagan *(obverse);* Phebe Hemphill *(reverse).* **Sculptor:** Phebe Hemphill *(reverse).* **Composition:** *.999 silver, .001 copper.* **Actual Silver Weight:** *5 ounces.* **Diameter:** *76.2 mm.* **Edge:** *Lettered.* **Mint:** *Philadelphia.* **Issue Price:** *variable (bullion); $279.95 (Specimen).* **Release Date:** *December 6, 2010 (bullion); June 29, 2011 (Specimen).*

**Bullion strike.**

**Specimen.**

The lands of Grand Canyon National Park have been used by humans for tens of thousands of years, dating back to the Anasazi, Cohonina, Paiutes, Cerbat, and Navajo Indians. More recently, in the late 1800s American tourists traveled to the area by stagecoach, then later by train and by automobile, to have their senses overwhelmed by the Grand Canyon's awe-inspiring landscape—277 miles of river in a canyon up to 18 miles wide and a mile deep. In 1893 the area was protected as a national forest reserve. A luxury hotel welcomed visitors by 1905. Artist Thomas Moran captured the scenery in grand paintings. President Theodore Roosevelt was moved to declare the Grand Canyon a national monument in 1908, and in 1919 it was named a full-fledged national park. That year more than 44,000 visitors were drawn to the Grand Canyon's breathtaking views. Today it hosts nearly 5,000,000 annual guests.

Phebe Hemphill designed and sculpted the reverse of the coin, which features a view of the granaries above the Nankoweap Delta in Marble Canyon near the Colorado River. These granaries were used by native people for storing food and seeds.

The Mint produced and sold almost 26,000 Specimen versions of the Grand Canyon silver coin. They were minted in 2010 but released for sale in July 2011. Collectors soon noticed a few variations in some of the coins' vapor-blasted surfaces. Third-party grading firm NGC confirmed and announced the existence of a distinct variety of the 2010-P Grand Canyon coin on July 20, 2011.

The first variety in the America the Beautiful five-ounce silver coin series has been discovered and will now be recognized by NGC. The variety designated "Light Finish" by NGC is so far seen only on the 2010-P Grand Canyon Specimen issues.

Two distinct surface finishes of the 2010-P Grand Canyon Specimens have been observed: coins with the regular coarse matte finish and coins that have a slightly reflective satin finish. The latter type, designated "Light Finish" by NGC, is distinct from both the bullion version and the standard collector version. This hybrid type is easily identified—it has the same "P" mintmark as the other Specimen issues, but its surfaces are not granular and are more lustrous. The Light Finish coins are also dissimilar from the fully brilliant surfaces of the bullion issue.

It is not known how many of the 27,000 Grand Canyon Specimens struck by the Mint are the Light Finish variety. It is believed that the majority are of the standard matte finish.

Third-party grading firm PCGS also recognizes the variety, calling it "Light Satin."

In *100 Greatest U.S. Modern Coins*, the Light Finish variety is ranked no. 93. Authors Scott Schechter and Jeff Garrett estimate that 15 percent of the mintage of Specimen coins, or about 4,000 pieces, are of the Light Finish variety. "It was easy to distinguish between both types, especially when viewed side by side," they note. "Because of the light finish, handling marks show more readily on these coins, impairing their condition and causing them to grade much lower than their heavy-finish counterparts." In 2014 Schechter and Garrett valued the variety in SP-69 at $750. NGC has graded more than 100 coins as Light Finish, with about two-thirds of them grading SP-65 or lower, and none at SP-70. In July 2015 an SP-63 example sold for $165 in a Heritage auction. In early 2015 SP–67 and 68 coins were selling for between $200 and $300 on eBay. In December 2014 and May 2015 SP-69 examples sold for $1,170 and $811, respectively.

Light Finish (top) and Regular Finish (bottom) varieties of the 2010-P Grand Canyon Specimen coin.

| Certified Populations and Retail Market Values | | | | | | | |
|---|---|---|---|---|---|---|---|
| | Raw MS | <MS-69 | MS-69 | MS-70 | Raw SP | <SP-69 | SP-69 | SP-70 |
| Certified | — | 3,005 | 5,669 | 0 | — | 1,093 | 860 | 1,308 |
| Value* | $110 | | $150 | — | $140 | | $165 | $600 |
| *Recent auctions:* $189, MS-69PL, August 2015. $475, SP-70, August 2015. | | | | | | | | |

* "Raw" value is based on a silver spot price of $16 per ounce, and is for an uncertified bullion-strike or Specimen coin of average quality. This value may vary with the prevailing bullion value.

# MOUNT HOOD NATIONAL FOREST, OREGON (2010)

*Designer: John Flanagan (obverse); Phebe Hemphill (reverse).* **Sculptor:** *Phebe Hemphill (reverse).* **Composition:** *.999 silver, .001 copper.* **Actual Silver Weight:** *5 ounces.* **Diameter:** *76.2 mm.* **Edge:** *Lettered.* **Mint:** *Philadelphia.* **Issue Price:** *variable (bullion); $279.95 (Specimen).* **Release Date:** *December 6, 2010 (bullion); July 28, 2011 (Specimen).*

**Bullion strike.**

**Specimen.**

Mount Hood National Forest, established as a national site in 1893, is situated 20 miles east of Portland, Oregon, and the northern Willamette River Valley. It encompasses more than 1 million acres, including 124,000 acres of wilderness area, more than 150 well-stocked ponds and lakes, and hundreds of miles of hiking trails. The national forest extends south from the Columbia River Gorge across more than 60 miles of forested mountains, lakes, and streams to the Olallie Scenic Area. In the summertime visitors enjoy fishing, boating, camping, and hiking; hunting is a popular attraction in the autumn months; and skiing, snowshoeing, and other outdoor sports beckon in the winter. Enthusiasts frequently mention the Timberline Lodge (a national historic landmark) and the Clackamas Wild and Scenic River.

As with all of the 2010 America the Beautiful silver coins, the Mount Hood issue was minted to the extent of 33,000 bullion strikes (3,000 reserved for each of the 11 original Authorized Purchasers). For the Specimen version, sales were typical of the 2010 issues.

"What a fitting way to memorialize Mount Hood as an American icon. Mount Hood figured very significantly as sacred land for Native Americans and has similar importance for us today. We're honored to have this recognition."

—*Mount Hood Forest Supervisor Gary Larsen*

"Each time Americans see this coin, they will connect with Mount Hood's magnificent beauty, humbling presence, and the spiritual qualities that beckon to us today as they did to early inhabitants."

—*U.S. Mint Deputy Director Andy Brunhart*

**Mintage: 33,000 bullion; 26,637 Specimen**

| | Certified Populations and Retail Market Values | | | | | | | |
|---|---|---|---|---|---|---|---|---|
| | Raw MS | <MS-69 | MS-69 | MS-70 | Raw SP | <SP-69 | SP-69 | SP-70 |
| Certified | — | 3,120 | 5,431 | 0 | — | 60 | 762 | 948 |
| Value* | $110 | | $150 | — | $140 | | $165 | $600 |
| *Recent auctions: $133, MS-68, August 2015. $500, SP-70, August 2015.* | | | | | | | | |

* "Raw" value is based on a silver spot price of $16 per ounce, and is for an uncertified bullion-strike or Specimen coin of average quality. This value may vary with the prevailing bullion value.

# GETTYSBURG NATIONAL MILITARY PARK, PENNSYLVANIA (2011)

*Designer: John Flanagan (obverse); Joel Iskowitz (reverse).* **Sculptor:** *Phebe Hemphill (reverse).* **Composition:** *.999 silver, .001 copper.* **Actual Silver Weight:** *5 ounces.* **Diameter:** *76.2 mm.* **Edge:** *Lettered.* **Mint:** *Philadelphia.* **Issue Price:** *variable (bullion); $279.95 (Specimen).* **Release Date:** *April 25, 2011 (bullion); September 22, 2011 (Specimen).*

**Bullion strike.**

On March 9, 2011, the U.S. Mint announced to its Authorized Purchasers that it was relaxing the December 2010 pricing and distribution restrictions it had established regarding the America the Beautiful bullion coins. With initial mintages of more than 126,000 coins planned for each of 2011's first two issues (Gettysburg National Military Park and Glacier National Park), Mint officials felt that supply would satisfy demand, and price-gouging would no longer be a risk.

The Mint's interest was in seeing the bullion coins distributed as widely and as fairly as possible. On December 1, 2010, a few days before the 2010 coins were first released, it had sent a memo to its Authorized Purchasers—a reminder of their contractual agreement "to maintain buy/sell premiums for the United States gold and silver bullion coins with as narrow a spread between buy and sell prices as prudent business judgment permits. These premiums are to be competitive with those charged for other bullion coins, considering prevailing market conditions." After the Mint heard reports of Authorized Purchasers charging extremely high premiums for the 2010 coins after their December 6 rollout, it put a stop to the profiteering with new rules:

**Specimen.**

> the Authorized Purchasers had to offer for public sale all of the 2010 coins they bought (this would discourage hoarding at the distributor level);
>
> they could charge no more than a 10 percent premium over their cost, plus reasonable shipping and handling (this would keep prices fair);
>
> sales had to be limited to one of each coin design per household (this would ensure broad distribution); and
>
> Authorized Purchasers could not sell the coins to their own employees or officers (this would prevent an unfair advantage over members of the general public).

Starting with the 2011 America the Beautiful silver coins, an Authorized Purchaser would have to first certify that they had sold all of their 2010-dated coins to the public. Then the 2010 restrictions would be lifted, and they would be allowed to return to buying and selling the new coins under their standard agreement. Basically, this would allow them to set their own prices, sell to secondary distributors and coin dealers (instead of only to the public), and sell in whatever quantities they wanted.

The first coin of 2011 was that of the Gettysburg National Military Park in Pennsylvania.

"The Battle of Gettysburg, the Union victory in the summer of 1863 that ended General Robert E. Lee's second and most ambitious invasion of the North, was a turning point in the Civil War. Often referred to as the 'High Water Mark of the Confederacy,' it was among the war's bloodiest battles. Established by concerned citizens in 1864, the Gettysburg Battlefield Memorial Association set out to preserve portions of the battlefield as a memorial to the Union troops that fought in the battle. In 1895, the land was transferred to the federal government and Gettysburg National Military Park was established."[6]

The Gettysburg silver coin features Joel Iskowitz's rendering, engraved by Phebe Hemphill, of the 72nd Pennsylvania Infantry Monument located on the battle line of the Union Army at Cemetery Ridge.

With the Mint's production and distribution straightened out and with customer demand for the new bullion series still at a peak, the first America the Beautiful issue of 2011 saw record sales of 126,700 coins (up from 33,000 for each of the five 2010 issues). That was the quantity struck by the Mint, released to Authorized Purchasers on April 25, and sold out by May 16. Meanwhile, sales of the Specimen format softened a bit, down almost 8 percent compared to the final issue of 2010 (which actually debuted for sale only two months earlier).

Some Gettysburg Specimens are of the Light Finish or Light Satin variety (valued around $500 in SP-68 and $800 in SP-69).

A monument to the 1st Massachusetts Regiment at Gettysburg.

Mintage: 126,700 bullion; 24,625 Specimen

| | | | | | | | | |
|---|---|---|---|---|---|---|---|---|
| **Certified Populations and Retail Market Values** | | | | | | | | |
| | **Raw MS** | **<MS-69** | **MS-69** | **MS-70** | **Raw SP** | **<SP-69** | **SP-69** | **SP-70** |
| **Certified** | — | 1,011 | 3,730 | 0 | — | 23 | 641 | 370 |
| **Value*** | $100 | | $140 | — | $160 | | $185 | $650 |
| *Recent auctions:* $135, MS-69, August 2015. $908, SP-70, March 2015. | | | | | | | | |

* "Raw" value is based on a silver spot price of $16 per ounce, and is for an uncertified bullion-strike or Specimen coin of average quality. This value may vary with the prevailing bullion value.

# GLACIER NATIONAL PARK, MONTANA (2011)

*Designer: John Flanagan (obverse); Barbara Fox (reverse).* **Sculptor:** *Charles L. Vickers (reverse).* **Composition:** *.999 silver, .001 copper.* **Actual Silver Weight:** *5 ounces.* **Diameter:** *76.2 mm.* **Edge:** *Lettered.* **Mint:** *Philadelphia.* **Issue Price:** *variable (bullion); $229.95 (Specimen).* **Release Date:** *April 25, 2011 (bullion); October 25, 2011 (Specimen).*

Bullion strike.

"Glacier National Park is named for its prominent glacier-carved terrain and remnant glaciers descended from the ice age of 10,000 years ago. Glacial forces, ancient seas, geologic faults, and uplifting combined to create some of the most spectacular scenery on earth. Known to the Blackfeet as the 'Backbone of the World,' Glacier National Park preserves more than one million acres of forests, alpine meadows, lakes, rugged peaks, and glacially carved valleys in the Northern Rocky Mountains. These lands were first set aside as a national reserve on February 22, 1897."[7] The park's silver coin shows the northeast slope of Mount Reynolds towering in the distance, with a mountain goat surveying the rocky high-country slopes.

The Glacier National Park coin was the second issue dated 2011, and the bullion versions of both were released to the Mint's Authorized Purchasers on the same day (April 25, 2011). Demand was strong for both issues, and their mintages of 126,700 each were sold out by May 16. Collector interest in the Specimen format continued to decline, however, reaching only 20,805 (compared to 24,625 for the preceding Gettysburg issue, which debuted a month earlier)—despite a price reduction of $50 that reflected silver's drop in the bullion markets. This was a bit more than half of the mintage limit of 35,000 coins.

Specimen.

> "We celebrate the breathtaking landscapes and natural heritage of 'America the Beautiful' by commemorating our country's most treasured places on our currency."
> —*Secretary of the Interior Ken Salazar*

**Mintage: 126,700 bullion; 20,805 Specimen**

| Certified Populations and Retail Market Values | | | | | | | | |
|---|---|---|---|---|---|---|---|---|
|  | Raw MS | <MS-69 | MS-69 | MS-70 | Raw SP | <SP-69 | SP-69 | SP-70 |
| Certified | — | 1,032 | 3,291 | 0 | — | 19 | 569 | 396 |
| Value* | $100 |  | $140 | — | $160 |  | $185 | $650 |
| *Recent auctions:* $127, MS-69PL, August 2015. $710, SP-70, November 2014. | | | | | | | | |

\* "Raw" value is based on a silver spot price of $16 per ounce, and is for an uncertified bullion-strike or Specimen coin of average quality. This value may vary with the prevailing bullion value.

# OLYMPIC NATIONAL PARK, WASHINGTON (2011)

*Designer: John Flanagan (obverse); Susan Gamble (reverse).* **Sculptor:** *Michael Gaudioso (reverse).* **Composition:** *.999 silver, .001 copper.* **Actual Silver Weight:** *5 ounces.* **Diameter:** *76.2 mm.* **Edge:** *Lettered.* **Mint:** *Philadelphia.* **Issue Price:** *variable (bullion); $229.95 (Specimen).* **Release Date:** *May 23, 2011 (bullion); November 29, 2011 (Specimen).*

**Bullion strike.**

**Specimen.**

"The ascent to Blue Glacier is only one of hundreds of adventures beckoning visitors to Olympic National Park. Located on the remote Olympic Peninsula in western Washington State, this park is a smorgasbord of outdoor recreation. In addition to rain forest, lakes, waterfalls, glaciers, and mountain peaks, the park includes long stretches of untamed Pacific coastline."[8] Susan Gamble's design for the Olympic silver coin shows a Roosevelt elk standing on a gravel bar of the Hoh River, with Mount Olympus rising in the background.

Demand for the America the Beautiful silver coins continued to slide downward through 2011, like a snowball gently rolling down Blue Glacier. Sales of the Olympic National Park bullion strikes dipped below 100,000, and the Specimen coins sold fewer than 19,000. Still, combined they accounted for nearly 600,000 ounces of silver—a respectable sum equaling about one ounce of silver sold for every five annual visitors to the park.

"The beauty of Olympic National Park is in its biodiversity: three distinct ecosystems of sub-alpine, coastal, and forest. There is no other national site like it, and the new Olympic National Park quarter will connect America to its natural splendor."
—*U.S. Mint Associate Director for Sales and Marketing B.B. Craig*

**Mintage: 95,600 bullion; 18,345 Specimen**

| Certified Populations and Retail Market Values | | | | | | | | |
|---|---|---|---|---|---|---|---|---|
| | Raw MS | <MS-69 | MS-69 | MS-70 | Raw SP | <SP-69 | SP-69 | SP-70 |
| Certified | — | 104 | 1,277 | 0 | — | 16 | 389 | 331 |
| Value* | $100 | | $140 | — | $160 | | $185 | $650 |
| Recent auctions: $155, MS-69, August 2015. $500, SP-70, March 2015. | | | | | | | | |

* "Raw" value is based on a silver spot price of $16 per ounce, and is for an uncertified bullion-strike or Specimen coin of average quality. This value may vary with the prevailing bullion value.

# VICKSBURG NATIONAL MILITARY PARK, MISSISSIPPI (2011)

*Designer: John Flanagan (obverse); Thomas Cleveland (reverse).* **Sculptor:** *Joseph F. Menna (reverse).* **Composition:** *.999 silver, .001 copper.* **Actual Silver Weight:** *5 ounces.* **Diameter:** *76.2 mm.* **Edge:** *Lettered.* **Mint:** *Philadelphia.* **Issue Price:** *variable (bullion); $204.95 (Specimen).* **Release Date:** *June 20, 2011 (bullion); January 12, 2012 (Specimen).*

**Bullion strike.**

"Vicksburg National Military Park commemorates one of the pivotal battles of the Civil War: the campaign, siege, and defense of Vicksburg, Mississippi. Surrender on July 4, 1863, coupled with the fall of Port Hudson, Louisiana, split the South, giving control of the Mississippi River to the North. The museum exhibits at the park depict the hardships of civilians and soldiers during the 47-day siege of the city. More than 1,350 monuments, a national cemetery, and the restored Union ironclad gunboat USS *Cairo* mark the 16-mile tour road."[9]

The Vicksburg coin's reverse design envisions the *Cairo* on the Yazoo River as it would have looked during the Civil War. This was the first warship sunk by an electrically detonated "torpedo," marking a new age of naval warfare.

Demand for the bullion-strike version of the Vicksburg coin was less than half that of the 2011 Olympic National Park coin. Part of the consumer reluctance may have been from the decreasing value of silver in the bullion market. Specimen coins, made available in January 2012, sold to the tune of nearly the same quantity as for the Olympic National Park issue.

**Specimen.**

"The America the Beautiful quarters are a standing invitation for all Americans to come along on a journey to each national site. Today's launch starts the journey of the Vicksburg National Military Park quarters as they pass from American hand to American hand, connecting America through coins."
—*U.S. Mint Chief of Staff Al Runnels*

**Mintage: 41,200 bullion; 18,528 Specimen**

| Certified Populations and Retail Market Values | | | | | | | | |
|---|---|---|---|---|---|---|---|---|
| | Raw MS | <MS-69 | MS-69 | MS-70 | Raw SP | <SP-69 | SP-69 | SP-70 |
| **Certified** | — | 235 | 1,103 | 0 | — | 2 | 266 | 520 |
| **Value\*** | $110 | | $150 | — | $170 | | $190 | $650 |
| *Recent auctions:* $151, MS-69, August 2015. $453, SP-70, July 2015. | | | | | | | | |

\* "Raw" value is based on a silver spot price of $16 per ounce, and is for an uncertified bullion-strike or Specimen coin of average quality. This value may vary with the prevailing bullion value.

# CHICKASAW NATIONAL RECREATION AREA, OKLAHOMA (2011)

*Designer:* John Flanagan (obverse); Donna Weaver (reverse). *Sculptor:* Jim Licaretz (reverse). *Composition:* .999 silver, .001 copper. *Actual Silver Weight:* 5 ounces. *Diameter:* 76.2 mm. *Edge:* Lettered. *Mint:* Philadelphia. *Issue Price:* variable (bullion); $204.95 (Specimen). *Release Date:* July 18, 2011 (bullion); February 9, 2012 (Specimen).

**Bullion strike.**

The reverse of the Chickasaw National Recreation Area coin features the Lincoln Bridge, a limestone structure dedicated in 1909 to celebrate the centennial of Abraham Lincoln's birth. Albert R. Greene, park superintendent at the time, described the bridge as "not a thing apart—it is as if it had grown there and been made when the rugged banks of the stream and the trees were made." For much of the 1800s the land had been part of the Chickasaw district of the Indian Territory. The Chickasaw Nation sold 640 acres to the federal government for the protection of the local mineral springs in 1902.

Bullion sales declined about 25 percent for this issue, compared to its immediate predecessor, that of Vicksburg National Military Park. Collector-format Specimen versions of these final two 2011-dated coins were minted in that year, as was required by their authorizing legislation, but they went on sale in the early weeks of 2012. The Specimen version of the Chickasaw coin had the lowest sales of the program up to that point, and the bullion strike was the first to dip below the 33,000 level established for the first coins of the series in 2010.

**Specimen.**

"When Americans receive this quarter depicting the Lincoln Bridge in their change, they will hold a piece of our American story in their hands, this one about the beauty and history of a special place conserved for them in Oklahoma."
—*U.S. Mint Associate Director for Sales and Marketing B.B. Craig*

**Mintage: 31,400 bullion; 16,746 Specimen**

| | Certified Populations and Retail Market Values | | | | | | | |
|---|---|---|---|---|---|---|---|---|
| | Raw MS | <MS-69 | MS-69 | MS-70 | Raw SP | <SP-69 | SP-69 | SP-70 |
| **Certified** | — | 221 | 1,259 | 0 | — | 2 | 287 | 515 |
| **Value*** | $120 | | $160 | — | $175 | | $200 | $650 |
| *Recent auctions:* $152, MS-69, August 2015. $561, SP-70, March 2015. | | | | | | | | |

* "Raw" value is based on a silver spot price of $16 per ounce, and is for an uncertified bullion-strike or Specimen coin of average quality. This value may vary with the prevailing bullion value.

# EL YUNQUE NATIONAL FOREST, PUERTO RICO (2012)

**Designer:** *John Flanagan (obverse); Gary Whitley (reverse).* **Sculptor:** *Michael Gaudioso (reverse).* **Composition:** *.999 silver, .001 copper.* **Actual Silver Weight:** *5 ounces.* **Diameter:** *76.2 mm.* **Edge:** *Lettered.* **Mint:** *Philadelphia.* **Issue Price:** *variable (bullion); $204.95 (Specimen).* **Release Date:** *early 2012 (bullion); May 29, 2012 (Specimen).*

**Bullion strike.**

The first America the Beautiful silver coin of 2012 was that of El Yunque National Forest, the only tropical rainforest in the U.S. National Forest System. It is located in the self-governing U.S. territory of Puerto Rico. The coin's reverse design, by Gary Whitley, features a coqui tree frog sitting on a leaf, and a Puerto Rican parrot behind an epiphyte plant with tropical flora in the background.

El Yunque was established as a national site on January 17, 1903. Despite the forest's relatively small 28,000-acre size, it is significant for its immense biodiversity—there are more species of trees in El Yunque than in the rest of the entire U.S. Forest System. More than a million eco-tourists and other visitors every year enjoy the park, its constant tropical climate, and miles of beautifully scenic trails.

Martinez and Martinez, in *Medicinal Herbs From the Caribbean National Forest (El Yunque), Puerto Rico*, note the importance of El Yunque to traditional and modern medicine: "Among the many healing plants found in the forest are the Ortiga brava or stinging nettle (*Urtica urens*), the Yagrumo hembra or weathervane tree (*Cecropia peltata*), and the tabonuco tree (*Dacryoides excelsa*). All are used in the folk medicine on the island. Puerto Rico has over 135 plants with recognized major medicinal uses and an additional 170 with minor therapeutic value. . . . Medicine has a stake in the rain forest, and El Yunque is a national treasure."

**Specimen.**

A tiny coquí llanero, Puerto Rico's smallest tree frog.

263

Demand for the bullion version of the 2012 El Yunque coin tapered by one-third compared to the final issue of 2011 (Chickasaw), which had itself set a record-low mintage for the America the Beautiful silver bullion program. From February through July of 2012 silver's market value dropped steadily, no doubt cooling the interest of investors and speculators.

Collector demand for the Specimen version, meanwhile, increased by several hundred coins compared to its predecessor. The Mint announced on March 11, 2013, that the El Yunque Specimens were sold out. Such announcements don't necessarily mean that a coin's mintage limit (in this case 25,000) has been reached. Rather, it can mean that the Mint's inventory has reached zero and no more of the issue will be produced (either because pre-sellout sales had slowed to a trickle, or because the legislated window for production had passed). The sellout of the El Yunque Specimen coin, coming on the heels of the January sellout of Hawai'i Volcanoes National Park, piqued the interest of collectors and helped boost future sales in the series.

By the time the 2012 America the Beautiful coins were produced, the Mint had long since installed new equipment and mastered the technical intricacies of vapor-blasting for the program's Specimen coins. As a result, no Light Finish or Light Satin varieties have been reported of the 2012-P El Yunque, Chaco Culture, Acadia, Hawai'i, or Denali issues.

**The Puerto Rican parrot: the only remaining native parrot in Puerto Rico—once widespread and abundant, today critically endangered and limited in its habitat.**

"El Yunque National Forest is a perfect selection for the America the Beautiful Quarters Program. As Americans use this new quarter, they will connect to the stories of the endangered Puerto Rican parrot, the magnificent effort you are making to rescue this beautiful bird from extinction, and the biodiverse national treasure that is its home: El Yunque National Forest."
—*Treasurer of the United States Rosie Rios*

**Mintage: 21,900 bullion; 17,314 Specimen**

| | Raw MS | <MS-69 | MS-69 | MS-70 | Raw SP | <SP-69 | SP-69 | SP-70 |
|---|---|---|---|---|---|---|---|---|
| **Certified Populations and Retail Market Values** | | | | | | | | |
| **Certified** | — | 34 | 958 | 0 | — | 9 | 206 | 641 |
| **Value*** | $175 | | $200 | — | $300 | | $400 | $700 |

*Recent auctions: $268, MS-69, August 2015. $549, SP-70, March 2015.*

\* "Raw" value is based on a silver spot price of $16 per ounce, and is for an uncertified bullion-strike or Specimen coin of average quality. This value may vary with the prevailing bullion value.

# CHACO CULTURE NATIONAL HISTORICAL PARK, NEW MEXICO (2012)

*Designer: John Flanagan (obverse); Donna Weaver (reverse). Sculptor: Phebe Hemphill (reverse). Composition: .999 silver, .001 copper. Actual Silver Weight: 5 ounces. Diameter: 76.2 mm. Edge: Lettered. Mint: Philadelphia. Issue Price: variable (bullion); $204.95 (Specimen). Release Date: April 2012 (bullion); July 9, 2012 (Specimen).*

**Bullion strike.**

Donna Weaver's design for the Chaco Cultural National Historical Park silver coin shows a view to the west of two elevated kivas (huge underground ceremonial chambers) that are part of the Chetro Ketl Complex. Also visible are the north walls of Chetro Ketl and of Chaco Canyon. "Chaco Canyon was a major center of Puebloan culture between A.D. 850 and 1250," the Mint noted in an April 2012 press release. "The Chacoan sites are part of the homeland of Pueblo Indian peoples of New Mexico, the Hopi Indians of Arizona, and the Navajo Indians of the Southwest. Chaco is remarkable for its multi-storied public buildings, ceremonial buildings, and distinctive architecture. The Chacoan people combined pre-planned architectural designs, astronomical alignments, geometry, landscaping, and engineering to create an ancient urban center of spectacular public architecture—one that still awes and inspires a thousand years later."

Mintages of both the bullion strike and the Specimen version of the Chaco Cultural National Historical Park silver coin declined compared to its predecessor, that of El Yunque. However, the decline was slight, amounting to only a couple thousand coins' difference in total.

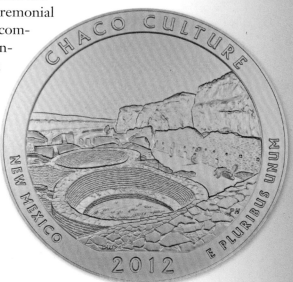

**Specimen.**

> "As Americans use their new quarter, they will connect to the stories of the ancient Chaco inhabitants and the remarkable feats of architecture, engineering, geometry, and landscaping that Chaco Culture National Historical Park represents."
>
> —*U.S. Mint Deputy Director Richard A. Peterson*

**Mintage: 20,000 bullion; 17,146 Specimen**

| Certified Populations and Retail Market Values | | | | | | | | |
|---|---|---|---|---|---|---|---|---|
| | Raw MS | <MS-69 | MS-69 | MS-70 | Raw SP | <SP-69 | SP-69 | SP-70 |
| Certified | — | 22 | 401 | 0 | — | 5 | 171 | 584 |
| Value* | $175 | | $200 | — | $275 | | $375 | $650 |
| *Recent auctions:* $184, MS-69PL, May 2015. $483, SP-70, July 2015. | | | | | | | | |

\* "Raw" value is based on a silver spot price of $16 per ounce, and is for an uncertified bullion-strike or Specimen coin of average quality. This value may vary with the prevailing bullion value.

# ACADIA NATIONAL PARK, MAINE (2012)

***Designer:*** *John Flanagan (obverse); Barbara Fox (reverse).* ***Sculptor:*** *Joseph F. Menna (reverse).* ***Composition:*** *.999 silver, .001 copper.* ***Actual Silver Weight:*** *5 ounces.* ***Diameter:*** *76.2 mm.* ***Edge:*** *Lettered.* ***Mint:*** *Philadelphia.* ***Issue Price:*** *variable (bullion); $204.95 (Specimen).* ***Release Date:*** *July 30, 2012 (bullion); August 6, 2012 (Specimen).*

**Bullion strike.**

**Specimen.**

AIP designer Barbara Fox chose a dramatic view of the Bass Harbor Head Lighthouse and a stretch of rough coastline to depict Acadia National Park—representing nearly 48,000 acres of Maine coast about three hours northeast of Portland. Hikers of all levels of experience can enjoy more than 120 miles of trails in Acadia. They range from gentle slopes to nearly vertical cliffs, with Precipice Trail famously requiring its daring climbers to use iron rungs and ladders secured to the side of Champlain Mountain.

Demand for the bullion version of the Acadia National Park silver coin jumped by more than 25 percent compared to its predecessor. Sales of the Specimen version, in the meantime, dropped by about 15 percent to a new low for the America the Beautiful coinage program. Just under 15,000 Specimens, out of a maximum mintage of 25,000, were bought. The Mint's inventory of Specimen coins sold out in mid-February 2013.

"Awed by its beauty and diversity, early-20th-century visionaries donated land on the rugged Atlantic coast of Maine to create Acadia National Park, the first national park east of the Mississippi River. The new quarter design captures the dramatic sweep from the rocky coastline to the Bass Harbor Head Lighthouse and illustrates the reason Acadia National Park was selected for the America the Beautiful Quarters Program."
—*U.S. Mint Associate Director for Sales and Marketing B.B. Craig*

**Mintage: 25,400 bullion; 14,978 Specimen**

| | Raw MS | <MS-69 | MS-69 | MS-70 | Raw SP | <SP-69 | SP-69 | SP-70 |
|---|---|---|---|---|---|---|---|---|
| **Certified** | — | 33 | 226 | 0 | — | 6 | 281 | 385 |
| **Value*** | $170 | | $200 | — | $350 | | $425 | $725 |
| **Certified Populations and Retail Market Values** | | | | | | | | |

*Recent auctions: $400, MS-69, May 2015. $995, SP-70, May 2015.*

\* "Raw" value is based on a silver spot price of $16 per ounce, and is for an uncertified bullion-strike or Specimen coin of average quality. This value may vary with the prevailing bullion value.

# HAWAI'I VOLCANOES NATIONAL PARK, HAWAII (2012)

**Designer:** *John Flanagan (obverse); Charles L. Vickers (reverse).* **Sculptor:** *Charles L. Vickers (reverse).* **Composition:** *.999 silver, .001 copper.* **Actual Silver Weight:** *5 ounces.* **Diameter:** *76.2 mm.* **Edge:** *Lettered.* **Mint:** *Philadelphia.* **Issue Price:** *variable (bullion); $204.95 (Specimen).* **Release Date:** *fall 2012 (bullion); September 24, 2012 (Specimen).*

**Bullion strike.**

Charles Vickers's dramatic design for the Hawai'i Volcanoes National Park coin shows a magnificent eruption on the east rift of Kilauea Volcano. Visitors can explore the volcano by way of an 11-mile drive around the rim of its crater. Kilauea is 3,980 feet tall, and to the north is the even taller Mauna Loa—the largest volcano in the world, towering 13,600 feet above sea level.

Collectors bought 9,186 of the Specimen coins from their start of sales on September 24 until October 1. This was the strongest opening-week sales of the year—40 percent higher than the debut of the Acadia National Park Specimens. Collectors admired the coin's bold design, and may also have been encouraged by rising silver prices on the bullion market. Ultimately 14,863 coins of the authorized 25,000 mintage limit were bought up by the time the Mint's inventory sold out in mid-January 2013.

> "Beauty, nature's raw power, and the unique Hawaiian culture shaped this place and make Hawai'i Volcanoes National Park a perfect choice for the America the Beautiful Quarters Program."
> —*Denver Mint Plant Manager David Croft*

> "When people come across an 'America the Beautiful' quarter, they will see the word 'Liberty' on one side and a national park, refuge, or forest on the other. They will know that Americans cherish these things dearly and desire to share both the freedom and the beauty of our land with all who likewise cherish them."
> —*Secretary of the Interior Ken Salazar*

**Specimen.**

**Mintage: 20,000 bullion; 14,863 Specimen**

| | Raw MS | <MS-69 | MS-69 | MS-70 | Raw SP | <SP-69 | SP-69 | SP-70 |
|---|---|---|---|---|---|---|---|---|
| **Certified** | — | 27 | 435 | 0 | — | 1 | 190 | 734 |
| **Value*** | $175 | | $210 | — | $360 | | $430 | $735 |

**Certified Populations and Retail Market Values**

*Recent auctions: $306, MS-69, May 2015. $789, SP-70, March 2015.*

* "Raw" value is based on a silver spot price of $16 per ounce, and is for an uncertified bullion-strike or Specimen coin of average quality. This value may vary with the prevailing bullion value.

# DENALI NATIONAL PARK AND PRESERVE, ALASKA (2012)

*Designer:* John Flanagan (obverse); Susan Gamble (reverse). **Sculptor:** Jim Licaretz (reverse). **Composition:** .999 silver, .001 copper. **Actual Silver Weight:** 5 ounces. **Diameter:** 76.2 mm. **Edge:** Lettered. **Mint:** Philadelphia. **Issue Price:** variable (bullion); $229.95 (Specimen). **Release Date:** October 22, 2012 (bullion); November 5, 2012 (Specimen).

Bullion strike.

Susan Gamble's reverse design for the Denali National Park and Preserve coin shows a Dall Sheep walking through the rocky terrain. In the background rises Denali—the mountain formerly known as Mount McKinley, which is the highest peak in North America. "Mount McKinley" was unofficially named by a gold prospector in 1896, and in 1917 the U.S. government made it official to commemorate the recently assassinated President William McKinley. However, Alaskans have long called it *Denali*, from its native Koyukon name meaning "The High One." In August 2015, after 30 years of Alaskan requests, the federal government changed the mountain's official name to Denali.

The national park is larger than the state of Vermont, comprising some 9,400 square miles of Alaskan wilderness.

The U.S. Mint's inventory of Denali Specimen coins sold out on February 26, 2013. Although sales of about 15,000 coins was below the maximum mintage of 25,000, the Mint was limited to producing each coin in its year of issue, and for the 2012 coins that time was past. Denali was the third Specimen issue to sell out in the early months of 2013, sparking interest within the broader hobby community.

Specimen.

"A national site that features Mount McKinley, the tallest mountain in North America, as well as grizzly bears, caribou, Dall sheep, and moose, makes Denali National Park and Preserve a perfect choice for the America the Beautiful Quarters Program."
—*Denver Mint Plant Manager David Croft*

Mintage: 20,000 bullion; 15,225 Specimen

| | Raw MS | <MS-69 | MS-69 | MS-70 | Raw SP | <SP-69 | SP-69 | SP-70 |
|---|---|---|---|---|---|---|---|---|
| **Certified** | — | 34 | 652 | 0 | — | 1 | 197 | 409 |
| **Value*** | $175 | | $210 | — | $340 | | $410 | $675 |

*Certified Populations and Retail Market Values*

*Recent auctions:* $218, MS-69, June 2015. $516, SP-70, August 2015.

\* "Raw" value is based on a silver spot price of $16 per ounce, and is for an uncertified bullion-strike or Specimen coin of average quality. This value may vary with the prevailing bullion value.

# WHITE MOUNTAIN NATIONAL FOREST, NEW HAMPSHIRE (2013)

*Designer: John Flanagan (obverse); Phebe Hemphill (reverse).* **Sculptor:** *Phebe Hemphill (reverse).* **Composition:** *.999 silver, .001 copper.* **Actual Silver Weight:** *5 ounces.* **Diameter:** *76.2 mm.* **Edge:** *Lettered.* **Mint:** *Philadelphia.* **Issue Price:** *variable (bullion); $179.95 (Specimen).* **Release Date:** *May 13, 2013 (bullion); May 16, 2013 (Specimen).*

Phebe Hemphill designed and engraved the first America the Beautiful coin of 2013, commemorating White Mountain National Forest. Her tableau shows Mount Chocorua, the easternmost peak of the Sandwich Range. A lake and pine trees are in the middle of the scene, with a foreground frame of grassland and birch trees. The White Mountain National Forest is one of the most popular destinations in the American national park system, with seven million visitors every year—many of them "leaf peepers" who marvel at the autumn explosion of colorful foliage, and others who go skiing, snowboarding, and mountain biking.

Historian Aaron J. McKeon describes the White Mountain region:

**Bullion strike.**

> Settlers began arriving in the mountains in the 17th and 18th centuries. Farmers cleared and lived on the land for generations, but the terrain was relatively unproductive. By the early 1800s, farmers began abandoning the area and logging interests bought it up. Conservation groups pushed for preservation of the White Mountains, but in the early 1900s there was political resistance to federal spending to preserve scenic areas on the eastern seaboard. In 1911 the Weeks Act authorized federal spending for the conservation of land at the headwaters of major rivers. The White Mountains were among the first lands to be bought up for conservation under the act. The National Forest was established by President Woodrow Wilson in 1918.[10]

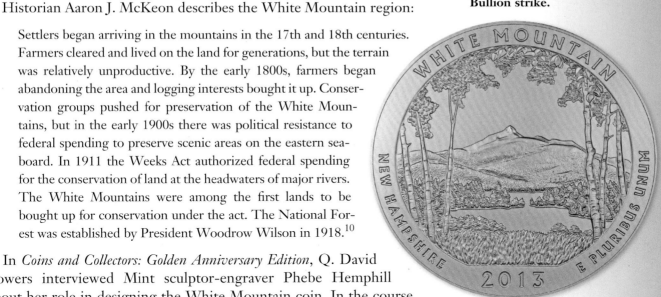

**Specimen.**

In *Coins and Collectors: Golden Anniversary Edition*, Q. David Bowers interviewed Mint sculptor-engraver Phebe Hemphill about her role in designing the White Mountain coin. In the course of the interview, Hemphill describes the artistic process of creating a U.S. coin (excerpted here):

> **Hemphill:** [A clay model is] what I do first. I print out a transparency of my drawing, a piece of film that I can see through. This is used as a guide for creating the low-relief sculpture in clay. For the America the Beautiful quarters I use an eight-inch-diameter coin basin blank which has been machined out of a high-density foam called REN. This is an exact upscale of the coin basin. I sculpt the image in a hard wax-like clay on this surface.
>
> **Bowers:** How long did it take for you to do that?
>
> **Hemphill:** The clay stage takes maybe a week and a half. And then when I get to a point where I can't go any further in the clay, I cast plaster over the top of that and I refine the surface in the negative plaster. Then that gets cast

into a positive plaster, and that gets refined further, and I do that about two times. I cast one negative, one positive, a second negative, and the second positive is usually the final. The process of casting back and forth in plaster facilitates the drafting of the sculpture that is so critical for a successful coin.

**Bowers:** Does anyone critique your work or tell you what to do or not to do?

**Hemphill:** We have an internal review that all of us go through for each design, and then the final plaster model is scanned and converted to a digital sculpture file. At this stage I can make additional changes and further refine the sculpture using 3D software. Rendered images from the 3D digital sculpture are sent down to headquarters [the U.S. Mint office in Washington] and they review the image. So when everything gets the final okay there, that digital sculpture file is converted to tool paths to CNC-cut the master tooling for the quarters. The first reduction is a positive hub, and that is used to create master dies.[11]

The White Mountain bullion-strike coins were distributed in a rationing process to the Mint's Authorized Purchasers starting in mid-May 2013. Investor demand for silver was high that year. Distribution of the 2013 American Silver Eagle (the Mint's main silver-bullion coins) had been temporarily suspended after a sellout in January, and then rationed starting later that month. In total, investors would purchase 35,000 of the White Mountain bullion coins, representing 175,000 ounces of .999 fine silver. This was a 75 percent increase over the quantity sold of the final issue of 2012 (Denali).

For the Specimen version, which also debuted that May, demand was strong from the start. The issue price was $50 less than for Specimens of the Denali type, reflecting silver's declining value in the bullion market. The Mint's inventory sold out by that October. "The sellout notification was posted on the U.S. Mint's Web site on October 9," noted a report at CoinUpdate.com, "meaning that the coins had only been available for sale for less than five months. The cumulative sales figure for the release . . . is well below the stated maximum mintage level [of 25,000 coins]. Last year, the U.S. Mint did not produce these coins to the full extent of their maximum mintages and several early sellouts occurred. Based on the sellout of the White Mountain design, collectors may be in store for a similar situation this year."[12]

From July 26 to September 30, 2013, the U.S. Mint offered free standard shipping and reduced expedited shipping on all domestic online orders. The promotion was designed to attract new customers and to encourage online shopping. That August, the Mint rolled out a redesign of its checkout process, part of its developing state-of-the-art order-management system.

**Scenes from White Mountain National Forest: a Black Cap hiking trail, and Jackson Falls.**

**Mintage: ~35,000 bullion; ~20,530 Specimen**

| | Raw MS | <MS-69 | MS-69 | MS-70 | Raw SP | <SP-69 | SP-69 | SP-70 |
|---|---|---|---|---|---|---|---|---|
| **Certified** | — | 71 | 1,099 | 0 | — | 0 | 292 | 754 |
| **Value*** | $125 | | $135 | — | $160 | | $190 | $230 |

*Recent auctions: $135, MS-69, August 2015. $238, SP-70, July 2015.*

* "Raw" value is based on a silver spot price of $16 per ounce, and is for an uncertified bullion-strike or Specimen coin of average quality. This value may vary with the prevailing bullion value.

# PERRY'S VICTORY AND INTERNATIONAL PEACE MEMORIAL, OHIO (2013)

*Designer: John Flanagan (obverse); Don Everhart (reverse).* *Sculptor: Don Everhart (reverse).* ***Composition:*** *.999 silver, .001 copper.* ***Actual Silver Weight:*** *5 ounces.* ***Diameter:*** *76.2 mm.* ***Edge:*** *Lettered.* ***Mint:*** *Philadelphia.* ***Issue Price:*** *variable (bullion); $179.95 (Specimen).* ***Release Date:*** *June 13, 2013 (bullion); June 6, 2013 (Specimen).*

**Bullion strike.**

Don Everhart captured a dramatic view of the statue of Master Commandant Oliver Hazard Perry in the second America the Beautiful coin of 2013. Perry was the triumphant American commander in the Battle of Lake Erie in September 1813, during the War of 1812. His victory came at great personal risk and against superior British forces and naval technology. After his flagship was destroyed, Perry led four surviving seamen to row over to the USS *Niagara*, from which he reorganized his squadron and turned the battle around. "We have met the enemy," he wrote to Brigadier General William Henry Harrison, "and they are ours." In the background of Everhart's design the International Peace Memorial, built starting in 1912 to celebrate a hundred years of peace since the war, is visible.

Investors bought 13,900 of the Perry's Victory bullion coins in their first nine days of sale in June 2013, and sales would eventually reach 30,000 (an official final audit has not yet been released). Of the vapor-blasted Specimen coins, collectors bought 7,966 in the first five days of sales, and about another 10,000 before the Mint's inventory sold out that November, by which time Mint officials had decided not to order another production run.

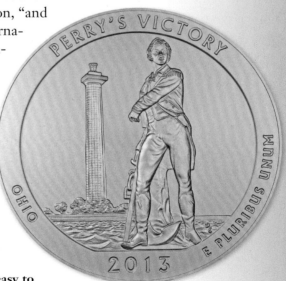

**Specimen.**

"Today we celebrate a national park that is small in acreage but significant in American history, a memorial to those who fought in the Battle of Lake Erie in the War of 1812, a piece of Ohio and American heritage in a setting of extraordinary natural beauty. It is easy to see why the Perry's Victory and International Peace Memorial was chosen to be part of the America the Beautiful Quarters Program."
—*U.S. Mint Acting Associate Director for Sales and Marketing J. Marc Landry*

**Mintage: ~30,000 bullion; ~17,707 Specimen**

| Certified Populations and Retail Market Values | | | | | | | | |
|---|---|---|---|---|---|---|---|---|
| | **Raw MS** | **<MS-69** | **MS-69** | **MS-70** | **Raw SP** | **<SP-69** | **SP-69** | **SP-70** |
| **Certified** | — | 25 | 933 | 0 | — | 2 | 202 | 578 |
| **Value*** | $125 | | $135 | — | $160 | | $190 | $230 |
| *Recent auctions:* $158, MS-69, February 2015. $239, SP-70, July 2015. | | | | | | | | |

\* "Raw" value is based on a silver spot price of $16 per ounce, and is for an uncertified bullion-strike or Specimen coin of average quality. This value may vary with the prevailing bullion value.

# GREAT BASIN NATIONAL PARK, NEVADA (2013)

**Bullion strike.**

*Designer:* John Flanagan (obverse); Ronald D. Sanders (reverse). *Sculptor:* Renata Gordon (reverse). *Composition:* .999 silver, .001 copper. *Actual Silver Weight:* 5 ounces. *Diameter:* 76.2 mm. *Edge:* Lettered. *Mint:* Philadelphia. *Issue Price:* variable (bullion); $154.95 (Specimen). *Release Date:* June 24, 2013 (bullion); July 25, 2013 (Specimen).

Ronald Sanders's design for the Great Basin National Park coin focuses on the intricacies of a Bristlecone pine tree nestled in rocky terrain. These resourceful and hardy plants are well adapted to the harsh, nearly rainless conditions of the Nevada park. They grow very slowly, and very densely, living for hundreds of years but rarely maturing to more than 30 feet tall. One famous Bristlecone pine was determined to be 4,600 years old.

Sales of the Great Basin bullion strikes surged in their first day, with Authorized Purchasers buying 25,500 of the coins—the strongest start of the year.

The Specimen version of the issue debuted at $154.95, a decrease of $25 compared to other recent issues. On November 9 it became the second 2013 issue to be declared sold out (after the White Mountain National Forest coin sold out on October 9). Collectors bought just under 18,000 of the Specimens, about three-quarters of the maximum mintage. The Mint's inventory of the bullion version, meanwhile, sold out on December 10, 2013, and no more were produced after that, capping sales at around 30,000 coins.

**Specimen.**

"There are so many amazing features in this park—mountain peaks, caverns, desert oases, 4,000-year-old trees—it must have been difficult to choose just one for the reverse design of the Great Basin National Park quarter."

—*U.S. Mint Senior Advisor Ron Harrigal*

Mintage: ~30,000 bullion; ~17,792 Specimen

| | Certified Populations and Retail Market Values | | | | | | | |
|---|---|---|---|---|---|---|---|---|
| | Raw MS | <MS-69 | MS-69 | MS-70 | Raw SP | <SP-69 | SP-69 | SP-70 |
| Certified | — | 5 | 1,039 | 0 | — | 2 | 270 | 1,004 |
| Value* | $125 | | $135 | — | $160 | | $190 | $230 |
| Recent auctions: $129, MS-69, July 2015. $256, SP-70, July 2015. | | | | | | | | |

\* "Raw" value is based on a silver spot price of $16 per ounce, and is for an uncertified bullion-strike or Specimen coin of average quality. This value may vary with the prevailing bullion value.

# Fort McHenry National Monument and Historic Shrine, Maryland (2013)

*Designer: John Flanagan (obverse); Joseph F. Menna (reverse). Sculptor: Joseph F. Menna (reverse). Composition: .999 silver, .001 copper. Actual Silver Weight: 5 ounces. Diameter: 76.2 mm. Edge: Lettered. Mint: Philadelphia. Issue Price: variable (bullion); $154.95 (Specimen). Release Date: August 26, 2013 (bullion); August 29, 2013 (Specimen).*

**Bullion strike.**

The Fort McHenry coin was designed and engraved by Joseph Menna. "The reverse design represents the site during the 'Defender's Day' celebration, considered the centerpiece annual event held at Fort McHenry," the Mint announced. "The fireworks symbolize the 'rocket's red glare,' linking the fort to its historic past."

The Mint's Authorized Purchasers bought the last of the remaining inventory of Fort McHenry bullion strikes on November 19, 2013. No more were struck after that, making the final mintage around 30,000 coins. The Mint's final audit is yet to be released.

Sales of the Specimen version were strong from the start, with collectors buying 10,878 of the coins in the first week—the strongest opening of recent years. A rise in silver's spot price may have encouraged sales, as collectors anticipated the Mint would raise its Specimen prices in the near future. The inventory of Specimen coins was depleted on December 3, 2013, after collectors bought nearly 80 percent of their maximum mintage. Mint officials decided not to order another production run, so at that point the Specimen issue was declared sold out.

**Specimen.**

> "The defense of Fort McHenry was the watershed event in the War of 1812, and this new quarter captures the significance of that victory and connects all Americans who use it to Fort McHenry and its honored place in American history."
>
> —*Treasurer of the United States Rosie Rios*

**Mintage: ~30,000 bullion; ~19,802 Specimen**

| Certified Populations and Retail Market Values | | | | | | | | |
|---|---|---|---|---|---|---|---|---|
| | Raw MS | <MS-69 | MS-69 | MS-70 | Raw SP | <SP-69 | SP-69 | SP-70 |
| Certified | — | 11 | 854 | 0 | — | 1 | 250 | 1,108 |
| Value* | $125 | | $135 | — | $160 | | $190 | $230 |
| *Recent auctions:* $151, MS-69, August 2015. $250, SP-70, July 2015. | | | | | | | | |

\* "Raw" value is based on a silver spot price of $16 per ounce, and is for an uncertified bullion-strike or Specimen coin of average quality. This value may vary with the prevailing bullion value.

# MOUNT RUSHMORE NATIONAL MEMORIAL, SOUTH DAKOTA (2013)

**Designer:** *John Flanagan (obverse); Joseph F. Menna (reverse).* **Sculptor:** *Joseph F. Menna (reverse).* **Composition:** *.999 silver, .001 copper.* **Actual Silver Weight:** *5 ounces.* **Diameter:** *76.2 mm.* **Edge:** *Lettered.* **Mint:** *Philadelphia.* **Issue Price:** *variable (bullion); $154.95 (Specimen).* **Release Date:** *November 4, 2013 (bullion); November 7, 2013 (Specimen).*

**Bullion strike.**

**Specimen.**

When the design of South Dakota's America the Beautiful coin was announced in December 2012, the U.S. Mint noted that its subject—Mount Rushmore—had already been featured on four recent coins. A half dollar, silver dollar, and $5 gold coin commemorated the monument in 1991, and it was featured on South Dakota's State quarter in 2006. "This new design is distinctly different," Mint officials observed, "and offers a unique and educational perspective on how Mount Rushmore was created and sculpted." Joseph Menna featured an unusual close-up view of the face of Mount Rushmore, with workers sculpting the portraits of Thomas Jefferson and George Washington.

The Mint anticipated strong demand for a large silver coin featuring such an iconic American landmark. In the first week of sales, Authorized Purchasers bought 14,012 bullion strikes—the most enthusiastic start of the past two years. Bullion-coin sales started on November 4, and the issue was declared sold out before the month ended, with some 35,000 coins purchased.

Collectors were eager for the Specimen version, as well. Nearly 24,000 of the collector coins were bought by the time the Mint declared its inventory sold out on December 12.

> **"This new quarter reflects our continued fascination with the majestic Mount Rushmore National Memorial and the enduring legacies of the four leaders whose faces have become one with the Black Hills."**
> —*U.S. Mint Acting Associate Director for Manufacturing David Croft*

**Mintage: ~35,000 bullion; ~23,547 Specimen**

| | Raw MS | <MS-69 | MS-69 | MS-70 | Raw SP | <SP-69 | SP-69 | SP-70 |
|---|---|---|---|---|---|---|---|---|
| **Certified Populations and Retail Market Values** | | | | | | | | |
| **Certified** | — | 13 | 1,094 | 0 | — | 1 | 456 | 1,234 |
| **Value\*** | $125 | | $165 | — | $160 | | $200 | $250 |
| *Recent auctions:* $198, MS-69, April 2015. $214, SP-69, August 2015. | | | | | | | | |

\* "Raw" value is based on a silver spot price of $16 per ounce, and is for an uncertified bullion-strike or Specimen coin of average quality. This value may vary with the prevailing bullion value.

# GREAT SMOKY MOUNTAINS NATIONAL PARK, TENNESSEE (2014)

*Designer:* John Flanagan *(obverse); Chris Costello (reverse).* **Sculptor:** *Renata Gordon (reverse).* **Composition:** *.999 silver, .001 copper.* **Actual Silver Weight:** *5 ounces.* **Diameter:** *76.2 mm.* **Edge:** *Lettered.* **Mint:** *Philadelphia.* **Issue Price:** *variable (bullion); $154.95 (Specimen).* **Release Date:** *March 17, 2014 (bullion); April 7, 2014 (Specimen).*

**Bullion strike.**

The silver market entered the year 2014 on a gentle upswing, after a general downward trend through much of 2013. In January 2013 the monthly average spot price had been $31.11 per ounce; by January 2014 it was $19.91. It rose above $20 in February and March, lingered in the $19–$20 range for several months, poked slightly above $21 several times in June and July, then started a slow autumn-into-winter decline to $16 in November and December. Sales of the 2014 bullion-strike America the Beautiful coins started strong but declined through much of the year. Investors were wary of the continuing decline, and reluctant to sink cash into a market that didn't yet seem to have reached its bottom.

Chris Costello's design for the year's first coin, that of Great Smoky Mountains National Park in Tennessee, shows a historic log cabin situated within the park, surrounded by forest and with a split-rail fence in the foreground. In the back the

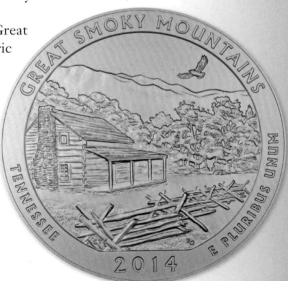

**Specimen.**

**An old cabin is framed by colorful autumn foliage on Roaring Fork Road in Smoky Mountains National Park.**

mountains rise up, leading the viewer's eye to a hawk soaring in the sky. The Smoky Mountains and surrounding lands comprise 814 square miles—one of the largest areas of wild lands in the eastern United States. Some 1,500 black bears call the region home, as do rare and endangered plants, river otters, elk, peregrine falcons, salamanders, and more than 50 species of native trout. Adventurous visitors and sightseers can enjoy more than 800 hiking trails, 2,100 miles of fishing streams, and 384 miles of scenic roadway. The Great Smoky Mountains attract more than nine million visitors per year, making this the most popular of the nation's parks, ahead of the Grand Canyon with about half that number.

Bullion coins went on sale March 17, 2014, and the Mint's Authorized Purchasers bought 12,200 pieces by month's end. By April 15, that quantity was up to 22,400. The Mint's inventory was temporarily sold out in mid-April, and after replenishment the Great Smoky Mountains issue sold 33,000 pieces, for a total of 165,000 ounces of silver.

The Mint established a cap of 25,000 for the Specimen coins, which went on sale April 7. Their issue price was $154.95, or a discounted rate of $139.45 for coins ordered through the Mint's Online Subscription Program. This discount boosted demand for the Specimens, and by April 13 collectors bought 21,415 of the coins—more than 85 percent of their maximum mintage. Sales slowed after this very strong start, but by May 21 nearly 25,000 of the Specimens would leave the Mint, marking a recent high for the program. With sales nearly reaching the maximum Specimen coin mintage, the Mint would raise the ceiling from 25,000 to 30,000 (or more) for subsequent issues. The subscription discount would continue for several more 2014 issues, ending with the Great Sand Dunes coin.

> "We are honored that our park is being commemorated in such a special way by the United States Mint. The collection of cabins protected within Great Smoky Mountains National Park is a resource worthy of national attention, as is the legacy of the memories and feelings they evoke."
> —*Great Smoky Mountains National Park Acting Superintendent Pedro Ramos*

> "This new coin reflects the nation's continuing fascination with the beauty, diversity, and romantic mists of Great Smoky Mountains National Park."
> —*U.S. Mint Acting Associate Director for Manufacturing David Croft*

Scenes from Great Smoky Mountains National Park: fall foliage along Middle Prong, and a view from Newfound Gap Road.

**Mintage: ~33,000 bullion; ~24,710 Specimen**

| | | | Certified Populations and Retail Market Values | | | | | |
|---|---|---|---|---|---|---|---|---|
| | Raw MS | <MS-69 | MS-69 | MS-70 | Raw SP | <SP-69 | SP-69 | SP-70 |
| Certified | — | 5 | 885 | 0 | — | 1 | 118 | 1,461 |
| Value* | $125 | | $165 | — | $160 | | $190 | $220 |

*Recent auctions: $166, MS-69, June 2015. $163, SP-69, July 2015.*

\* "Raw" value is based on a silver spot price of $16 per ounce, and is for an uncertified bullion-strike or Specimen coin of average quality. This value may vary with the prevailing bullion value.

# SHENANDOAH NATIONAL PARK, VIRGINIA (2014)

*Designer: John Flanagan (obverse); Phebe Hemphill (reverse). **Sculptor:** Phebe Hemphill (reverse). **Composition:** .999 silver, .001 copper. **Actual Silver Weight:** 5 ounces. **Diameter:** 76.2 mm. **Edge:** Lettered. **Mint:** Philadelphia. **Issue Price:** variable (bullion); $154.95 (Specimen). **Release Date:** May 5, 2014 (bullion); May 15, 2014 (Specimen).*

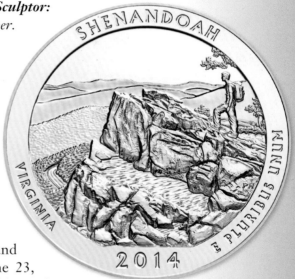

**Bullion strike.**

Shenandoah National Park in Virginia is on the Appalachian Trail, with Skyline Drive running 105 miles through it, reaching heights of 3,500 feet and offering scenic overlooks and breathtaking views. Cabin-camping and 200,000 acres of wilderness and parklands await visitors. Phebe Hemphill's coinage design for Shenandoah shows a hiker with a commanding view from Little Stony Man summit.

The bullion version of the coin went on sale May 5, 2014, and the Mint's inventory of 20,000 pieces was sold out by June 23, prompting another production run. "We will be striking additional coins," the Mint informed its Authorized Purchasers, "and will notify you when they are available for sale." Ultimately a total of approximately 24,400 of the bullion coins would be distributed—a good quantity, but fewer than recent bullion issues.

The limited-edition vapor-blasted Specimen version, interestingly, saw stronger sales. In just four days, between May 15 and May 18, collectors bought an impressive 20,120 of the Shenandoah Specimen coins. The Mint had increased the mintage limit for Shenandoah from 25,000 coins to 30,000, reacting to overall increased demand for silver in early 2014—a smart move, as sales reached beyond 28,000 coins.

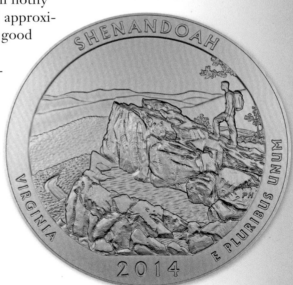

**Specimen.**

> **"I am very happy to be in Front Royal, where my father attended Randolph-Macon Academy, to honor a state with such a rich history and promising future, a state my family and I call home. The Shenandoah National Park coin emphasizes one of my favorite things about Virginia: its natural beauty. Beauty that must be enjoyed and at the same time protected for future generations."**
>
> **—U.S. Mint Deputy Director Richard A. Peterson**

**Mintage: ~24,400 bullion; ~28,276 Specimen**

| Certified Populations and Retail Market Values | | | | | | | | |
|---|---|---|---|---|---|---|---|---|
| | Raw MS | <MS-69 | MS-69 | MS-70 | Raw SP | <SP-69 | SP-69 | SP-70 |
| **Certified** | — | 11 | 667 | 0 | — | 1 | 147 | 1,475 |
| **Value\*** | $125 | | $165 | — | $160 | | $190 | $220 |
| *Recent auctions:* $164, MS-69, August 2015. $208, SP-70, August 2015. | | | | | | | | |

\* "Raw" value is based on a silver spot price of $16 per ounce, and is for an uncertified bullion-strike or Specimen coin of average quality. This value may vary with the prevailing bullion value.

# ARCHES NATIONAL PARK, UTAH (2014)

*Designer: John Flanagan (obverse); Donna Weaver (reverse).* **Sculptor:** *Charles L. Vickers (reverse).* **Composition:** *.999 silver, .001 copper.* **Actual Silver Weight:** *5 ounces.* **Diameter:** *76.2 mm.* **Edge:** *Lettered.* **Mint:** *Philadelphia.* **Issue Price:** *variable (bullion); $154.95 (Specimen).* **Release Date:** *June 9, 2014 (bullion); June 12, 2014 (Specimen).*

**Bullion strike.**

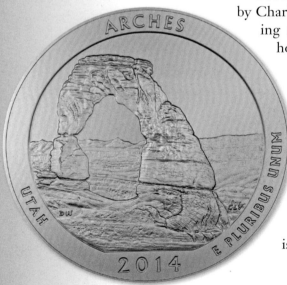

**Specimen.**

"In *Desert Solitaire*, environmentalist/anarchist Edward Abbey describes the scenery at Arches National Park as a 'monstrous and inhuman spectacle of rock and cloud and sky and space.' He goes on to describe his impulse to 'embrace the entire scene intimately.' Abbey's idea of embracing the scene goes well beyond a hike or a climb; he recommends that you 'walk, better yet crawl, on hands and knees, over the sandstone and through the thornbush and cactus.' While not specifically prohibited, the National Park Service would prefer that you keep activity of this sort to the marked trails."[13]

For Arches National Park, Donna Weaver's coinage design, sculpted by Charles Vickers, focuses on Delicate Arch, a 65-foot-tall freestanding natural formation. The La Sal Mountains stretch along the horizon in the distance.

The Mint's Authorized Purchasers bought 5,500 of the bullion-strike coins on the first day of sales. Over time their purchases would reach 22,000. (That quantity is approximate; the Mint's official final audit has yet to be released.) This reflected the year's downward trend in silver bullion sales after a stronger start.

Sales for the Specimen format followed the example set by the Shenandoah National Park coin, which debuted a month earlier. Collectors bought more than 28,000 of the Arches National Park Specimen coins, or 94 percent of the issue's mintage limit.

"Having lived in Utah, I know from firsthand experience that Delicate Arch in Arches National Park is one of the Earth's very special geologic wonders and why it was chosen as the design for Utah's America the Beautiful quarter."
— *U.S. Mint Deputy Director Richard A. Peterson*

Mintage: ~22,000 bullion; ~28,183 Specimen

| Certified Populations and Retail Market Values | | | | | | | | |
|---|---|---|---|---|---|---|---|---|
| | Raw MS | <MS-69 | MS-69 | MS-70 | Raw SP | <SP-69 | SP-69 | SP-70 |
| Certified | — | 5 | 564 | 0 | — | 0 | 152 | 1,484 |
| Value* | $125 | | $165 | — | $160 | | $180 | $200 |
| Recent auctions: $175, MS-69, August 2015. $193, SP-70, August 2015. | | | | | | | | |

\* "Raw" value is based on a silver spot price of $16 per ounce, and is for an uncertified bullion-strike or Specimen coin of average quality. This value may vary with the prevailing bullion value.

# GREAT SAND DUNES NATIONAL PARK AND PRESERVE, COLORADO (2014)

*Designer: John Flanagan (obverse); Don Everhart (reverse).*
*Sculptor: Don Everhart (reverse).* **Composition:** *.999 silver,*
*.001 copper.* **Actual Silver Weight:** *5 ounces.* **Diameter:**
*76.2 mm.* **Edge:** *Lettered.* **Mint:** *Philadelphia.* **Issue**
**Price:** *variable (bullion); $154.95 (Specimen).* **Release Date:**
*August 25, 2014 (bullion); September 15, 2014 (Specimen).*

**Bullion strike.**

"Great Sand Dunes National Park and Preserve has the tallest dunes in North America as the centerpiece of the site's diverse landscape of grasslands, wetlands, conifer and aspen forests, alpine lakes, and tundra," the U.S. Mint noted in its introduction of the park's silver bullion coin. "These can be experienced through hiking, sand sledding, splashing in Medano Creek, and watching wildlife." Since 1932 the park's 30 square miles of dunes have been federally protected from gold-mining and other commercial exploitation, and available for public appreciation and enjoyment.

In Don Everhart's coin for Great Sand Dunes, which he sculpted as well as designed, a father and son play in the sand with a beach-bucket and shovel next to a creek bed. Their backs are turned to the viewer, and they face the mountains and dunes that surround Colorado's San Luis Valley.

The bullion coins were made available to the Mint's Authorized Purchasers in late August 2014. They bought 3,400 in the first day of sales, and some 21,900 over the course of their offering. Collectors scooped up 20,047 of the Great Sand Dunes Specimen coins in their first week of sales, which opened in mid-September. (The 10 percent subscription discount was still in effect.) This early surge represented the bulk of the Specimens' sales; by late October 2015 the mintage would stand at 24,103.

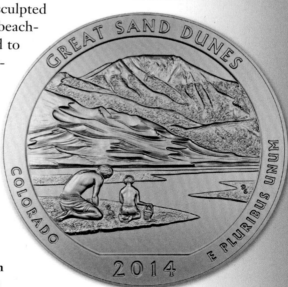

**Specimen.**

**"With its awe-inspiring combination of desert dunes, high mountain peaks, and flowing Medano Creek, I can see why Great Sand Dunes National Park and Preserve was chosen to represent the state of Colorado in the America the Beautiful Quarters Program."**
—*U.S. Mint Associate Director of Manufacturing Dave Croft*

**Mintage: ~21,900 bullion; ~24,103 Specimen**

| | Raw MS | <MS-69 | MS-69 | MS-70 | Raw SP | <SP-69 | SP-69 | SP-70 |
|---|---|---|---|---|---|---|---|---|
| **Certified** | — | 1 | 484 | 0 | — | 0 | 129 | 1,110 |
| **Value\*** | $125 | | $165 | — | $160 | | $180 | $200 |
| | *Recent auctions:* $173, MS-69, August 2015. $203, SP-70, August 2015. | | | | | | | |

*Certified Populations and Retail Market Values*

\* "Raw" value is based on a silver spot price of $16 per ounce, and is for an uncertified bullion-strike or Specimen coin of average quality. This value may vary with the prevailing bullion value.

# EVERGLADES NATIONAL PARK, FLORIDA (2014)

*Designer:* John Flanagan (obverse); Joel Iskowitz (reverse). **Sculptor:** Joseph F. Menna (reverse). **Composition:** .999 silver, .001 copper. **Actual Silver Weight:** 5 ounces. **Diameter:** 76.2 mm. **Edge:** Lettered. **Mint:** Philadelphia. **Issue Price:** variable (bullion); $154.95 (Specimen). **Release Date:** November 3, 2014 (bullion); November 6, 2014 (Specimen).

**Bullion strike.**

**Specimen.**

In her 1947 book *Everglades: River of Grass*, Marjory Stoneman Douglas wrote, "There are no other Everglades in the world. They are, they have always been, one of the unique regions of the earth, remote, never wholly known. Nothing anywhere else is like them: their vast glittering openness, wider than the enormous visible round of the horizon, the racing free saltness and sweetness of their massive winds, under the dazzling blue heights of space."

Joel Iskowitz's vision of the Everglades includes an anhinga (also known as a *snake bird* or *water turkey*) with its wings spread, perched on a willow tree, while a roseate spoonbill stands in the nearby water. A stretch of grass and a lush line of trees round out the design.

The Mint's Authorized Purchasers bought 22,000 of the bullion-strike coins in their first day of sales. The final mintage was 34,000—a notable increase over the America the Beautiful program's other bullion sales for 2014.

The Everglades Specimens, meanwhile, saw the softest sales of the year. The Mint had ended its 10 percent discount for Specimen coins ordered through the online subscription program before the Everglades coins were released. This may have had a chilling effect on sales. Furthermore, in November silver's spot price was in a long downturn (having dropped $5 per ounce since that summer), which made the issue price of $154.95 equal to double the coins' bullion value.

> "A vast mosaic of habitats that protects a thousand plant and bird species, Everglades National Park is the perfect choice to represent Florida in the America the Beautiful Quarters Program."
> —*U.S. Mint Chief Administrative Officer Beverly Ortega Babers*

**Mintage: ~34,000 bullion; ~19,772 Specimen**

| | Certified Populations and Retail Market Values | | | | | | | |
|---|---|---|---|---|---|---|---|---|
| | **Raw MS** | **<MS-69** | **MS-69** | **MS-70** | **Raw SP** | **<SP-69** | **SP-69** | **SP-70** |
| **Certified** | — | 12 | 632 | 0 | — | 0 | 85 | 894 |
| **Value*** | $115 | | $165 | — | $160 | | $180 | $200 |
| | *Recent auctions:* $178, MS-69, August 2015. $257, SP-70, June 2015. | | | | | | | |

\* "Raw" value is based on a silver spot price of $16 per ounce, and is for an uncertified bullion-strike or Specimen coin of average quality. This value may vary with the prevailing bullion value.

# HOMESTEAD NATIONAL MONUMENT OF AMERICA, NEBRASKA (2015)

*Designer: John Flanagan (obverse); Ronald D. Sanders (reverse).*
*Sculptor: Jim Licaretz (reverse).* *Composition: .999 silver,*
*.001 copper.* *Actual Silver Weight: 5 ounces.* *Diameter:*
*76.2 mm.* *Edge: Lettered.* *Mint: Philadelphia.* *Issue*
*Price: variable (bullion); $149.95 (Specimen).* *Release Date:*
*February 17, 2015 (bullion); March 5, 2015 (Specimen).*

**Bullion strike.**

In January 2015, silver's spot price was higher than it had been in late 2014, averaging just over $17 per ounce for the month. It slowly slid below the $16 mark, and then below $15, through the summer of 2015, before weakly rallying late that autumn. Mintages for the America the Beautiful silver coins (bullion and Specimen formats alike) rose in 2015, perhaps because investors finally felt comfortable that the precious metal had reached a solid floor and wouldn't be sliding much below the $15–$16 per ounce range.

The first America the Beautiful coin of 2015 featured a monument that honors much of the nation's hardscrabble pioneer origins. "Established in 1936, Homestead National Monument of America brings the epic homesteading story of early pioneers to life and demonstrates the true scope and importance of the Homestead Act of 1862," the U.S. Mint observed at the release of the coin. "By granting free land, the Homestead Act allowed nearly any man or woman a chance to realize the American dream of owning his or her own land. The uniquely designed Heritage Center was dedicated in 2007 and offers a hilltop vista of the tallgrass prairie much like American pioneers would have seen it."

**Specimen.**

The design of the Homestead coin was developed in consultation with representatives of the national monument. Ronald Sanders's motif, sculpted by Jim Licaretz, assembles the three elements of survival fundamental to all homesteading environments: food (symbolized by corn), shelter (a cabin), and water (a long-handled pump).

New mintage limits were put in place for the America the Beautiful silver coins for 2015. The coins would be limited to 65,000 across both formats (bullion and Specimen). "An announced maximum mintage limit of 30,000 coins has been issued for the America the Beautiful five-ounce Homestead Uncirculated [Specimen] coin," U.S. Mint Deputy Director of Corporate Communications Adam Stump said on March 9. "However, based on demand, the U.S. Mint has the flexibility to mint and issue more than the minimum of 35,000 America the Beautiful five-ounce Homestead silver bullion coins so long as we do not exceed the 65,000 coin limit." In other words, the Mint had the option to produce more bullion coins (beyond its initial production run of 35,000) by "borrowing" from the maximum mintage of 30,000 Specimen coins.

The Mint's Authorized Purchasers bought 14,200 of the Homestead bullion coins on their first day of availability, February 17. They went on to purchase a total of 20,000 that first month. The initial mintage of 35,000 coins was reported sold out on March 31, after six weeks of sales. Silver's steady low prices no doubt encouraged the strong sales. By that time, some 18,198 Specimen coins had also been bought by collectors. The Mint's "Cumulative Numismatic Sales Figures" report put the Specimen sales at 19,887 as of October 25, 2015.

A modern-day garden filled with pumpkins spreads toward a cabin at the 211-acre Homestead National Monument of America. In olden times, to "prove up" a homestead, its owner was required to make improvements including building a home, breaking the soil, and planting a crop for five years.

"This new quarter stands now as a tribute to the strength and the tenacity of the settlers who braved harsh conditions to build the American West."
—*U.S. Mint Associate Director of Manufacturing David Croft*

**Mintage: ~35,000 bullion; ~19,887 Specimen**

| | Raw MS | <MS-69 | MS-69 | MS-70 | Raw SP | <SP-69 | SP-69 | SP-70 |
|---|---|---|---|---|---|---|---|---|
| **Certified Populations and Retail Market Values** | | | | | | | | |
| Certified | — | 6 | 1,331 | 0 | — | 0 | 166 | 1,595 |
| Value* | $110 | | $150 | — | $160 | | $180 | $200 |

*Recent auctions:* $123, MS-69, September 2015. $202, SP-70, August 2015.

* "Raw" value is based on a silver spot price of $16 per ounce, and is for an uncertified bullion-strike or Specimen coin of average quality. This value may vary with the prevailing bullion value.

# KISATCHIE NATIONAL FOREST, LOUISIANA (2015)

**Designer:** *John Flanagan (obverse); Susan Gamble (reverse).*
**Sculptor:** *Joseph F. Menna (reverse).* **Composition:** *.999 silver,
.001 copper.* **Actual Silver Weight:** *5 ounces.* **Diameter:**
*76.2 mm.* **Edge:** *Lettered.* **Mint:** *Philadelphia.* **Issue Price:**
*variable (bullion); $149.95 (Specimen).* **Release Date:**
*April 20, 2015 (bullion); April 28, 2015 (Specimen).*

Kisatchie National Forest (its name derived from that of
the Kichai Indian tribe of the Caddoan Confederacy) is
spread across seven parishes in Louisiana. Divided into five
managed units called ranger districts, it comprises more
than 604,000 acres of public lands. "Hidden in the bayous
underneath the bald cypress groves and old-growth pine lies
a world of natural beauty, excitement, learning, recreation, and
natural and cultural resources," the Mint announced when it
rolled out the Kisatchie coins in 2015.

Susan Gamble's dynamic design for the Kisatchie coin shows a wild
turkey in flight over blue-stem grass in a setting of long-leaf pine trees.

**Bullion strike.**

By the time the Kisatchie Specimen coins went on sale April 28, the
bullion coins had already been available for eight days—and had
sold to the tune of 29,800 pieces (23,000 in their first day alone),
out of 42,000 produced in the Mint's initial press run. As of
November 2, 2015, the Mint reported cumulative sales of
18,383 of the Specimen coins.

"As a Louisiana native, I am especially honored
to be here to introduce the Kisatchie National
Forest quarter to the nation. I know from
firsthand experience that Kisatchie has many
adventures and recreational activities to enjoy,
with all its beauty and all that it has to offer."
—*U.S. Mint Associate Director for Environment,
Safety, and Health B.B. Craig*

"We hope the Kisatchie National Forest
quarter will inspire Louisianans to get
outdoors and explore their national forest."
—*Kisatchie National Forest Public
Affairs, Recreation, Heritage, and
Administration Staff Officer Jim Caldwell*

**Specimen.**

**Mintage: ~42,000 bullion; ~18,383 Specimen**

| Certified Populations and Retail Market Values | | | | | | | | |
|---|---|---|---|---|---|---|---|---|
| | **Raw MS** | **<MS-69** | **MS-69** | **MS-70** | **Raw SP** | **<SP-69** | **SP-69** | **SP-70** |
| **Certified** | — | 0 | 340 | 0 | — | 1 | 98 | 481 |
| **Value*** | $105 | | $145 | — | $155 | | $175 | $195 |
| *Recent auctions:* $138, MS-69, September 2015. $204, SP-70, July 2015. | | | | | | | | |

\* "Raw" value is based on a silver spot price of $16 per ounce, and is for an uncertified bullion-strike
or Specimen coin of average quality. This value may vary with the prevailing bullion value.

# BLUE RIDGE PARKWAY, NORTH CAROLINA (2015)

**Designer:** *John Flanagan (obverse); Frank Morris (reverse).* **Sculptor:** *Joseph F. Menna (reverse).* **Composition:** *.999 silver, .001 copper.* **Actual Silver Weight:** *5 ounces.* **Diameter:** *76.2 mm.* **Edge:** *Lettered.* **Mint:** *Philadelphia.* **Issue Price:** *variable (bullion); $149.95 (Specimen).* **Release Date:** *June 22, 2015 (bullion); July 7, 2015 (Specimen).*

Bullion strike.

Specimen.

Blue Ridge Parkway—a scenic byway with natural attractions—is a unit of the National Park Service with numerous recreational opportunities immersed in a cross-section of Appalachian mountain history. The Mint describes it thus: "Stretching 469 miles along the crest of the Blue Ridge Mountains through North Carolina and Virginia, it encompasses some of the oldest settlements of both pre-historic and early European settlement in the United States." Frank Morris's coinage design shows a curvature of road hugging around the side of a mountain and descending into a pine-surmounted tunnel, with North Carolina's state flower, the blossom of the dogwood tree, in the foreground.

The Mint increased its production of bullion strikes for the Blue Ridge Parkway issue, striking 45,000 coins in total. Its initial inventory sold out temporarily on the day the bullion coins were first made available to Authorized Purchasers, June 22. After another press run they went on sale again on July 13. The entire production of 45,000 bullion coins was sold out by July 29. This was the highest mintage in the series since the issues of 2011.

The Specimen coins went on sale July 7, with first-day sales of 15,295 coins. By November 2, collectors had purchased 17,488 Specimens out of a possible 20,000 mintage.

> "This new coin is a tribute to this national scenic byway—a cross-section of Appalachian mountain history essential to the story of our nation, tying together diverse landscapes and rich history."
> —*U.S. Mint Associate Director of Manufacturing David Croft*

**Mintage: ~45,000 bullion; ~17,488 Specimen**

| | | | Certified Populations and Retail Market Values | | | | |
|---|---|---|---|---|---|---|---|
| | **Raw MS** | **<MS-69** | **MS-69** | **MS-70** | **Raw SP** | **<SP-69** | **SP-69** | **SP-70** |
| **Certified** | — | n/a | n/a | n/a | — | 0 | 54 | 1,033 |
| **Value*** | $105 | | $145 | — | $155 | | $175 | $195 |

*Recent auctions:* $140, MS-69, September 2015. $218, SP-70, September 2015.

\* "Raw" value is based on a silver spot price of $16 per ounce, and is for an uncertified bullion-strike or Specimen coin of average quality. This value may vary with the prevailing bullion value.

# BOMBAY HOOK NATIONAL WILDLIFE REFUGE, DELAWARE (2015)

*Designer: John Flanagan (obverse); Joel Iskowitz (reverse). **Sculptor:** Phebe Hemphill (reverse). **Composition:** .999 silver, .001 copper. **Actual Silver Weight:** 5 ounces. **Diameter:** 76.2 mm. **Edge:** Lettered. **Mint:** Philadelphia. **Issue Price:** variable (bullion); $149.95 (Specimen). **Release Date:** September 28, 2015 (bullion); October 8, 2015 (Specimen).*

Bombay Hook National Wildlife Refuge (from the Dutch *Bompies Hoeck*, for "Little Tree Point"), on the southern shore of Delaware Bay, is 16,000 acres of freshwater pools, swamps, upland forests, agricultural fields, and one of the largest unaltered tidal salt marshes in the Mid-Atlantic region. It gives refuge to hundreds of thousands of migrating ducks, geese, shorebirds, and neo-tropical songbirds in their spring and fall migrations. "Tired and hungry between Canada and the Gulf of Mexico, they seek shelter at Bombay Hook and feast on marsh grasses, fish, and other important foods before continuing their flight."[14]

**Bullion strike.**

Joel Iskowitz's design for the Bombay Hook coin shows two large birds enjoying the refuge's resources: a great blue heron in the foreground and a great egret hunting in the water in the background.

The U.S. Mint produced 45,000 bullion coins and released them for sale to Authorized Purchasers on September 28. On September 29, it was announced that this quantity was sold out. The Specimen coins debuted for sale on October 8; by October 25 the Mint reported that 15,930 of their maximum mintage of 20,000 coins had been purchased.

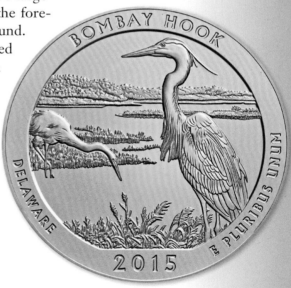

**Specimen.**

> "I'm uniquely excited about this launch because we are making these Bombay Hook quarters 67 miles north of here, at our plant in Philadelphia. Some of the very people in our plant are Delaware residents, so this quarter carries a special meaning to the men and women of the United States Mint."
> —*Philadelphia Mint Plant Manager Marc Landry*

**Mintage: ~45,000 bullion; ~15,930 Specimen**

| Certified Populations and Retail Market Values | | | | | | | | |
|---|---|---|---|---|---|---|---|---|
| | Raw MS | <MS-69 | MS-69 | MS-70 | Raw SP | <SP-69 | SP-69 | SP-70 |
| **Certified** | — | n/a | n/a | n/a | — | n/a | n/a | n/a |
| **Value*** | $105 | | $145 | — | $155 | | $175 | $195 |
| *Recent auctions:* $153, MS-69, October 2015. $199, SP-70, October 2015. | | | | | | | | |

* "Raw" value is based on a silver spot price of $16 per ounce, and is for an uncertified bullion-strike or Specimen coin of average quality. This value may vary with the prevailing bullion value.

# SARATOGA NATIONAL HISTORICAL PARK, NEW YORK (2015)

U.S. Mint sketch.

**Designer:** *John Flanagan (obverse); Barbara Fox (reverse).* **Sculptor:** *Renata Gordon (reverse).* **Composition:** *.999 silver, .001 copper.* **Actual Silver Weight:** *5 ounces.* **Diameter:** *76.2 mm.* **Edge:** *Lettered.* **Mint:** *Philadelphia.* **Issue Price:** *To be announced.* **Release Dates:** *To be announced.*

"At Saratoga in the autumn of 1777, American forces met, defeated, and forced a major British army to surrender. This crucial American victory renewed patriots' hopes for independence, secured essential foreign recognition and support, and forever changed the face of the world. The battlefield, a monument to the fallen, and the restored country house of American general Philip Schuyler make up the three sites of Saratoga National Historical Park. It was established as a national site in 1938." So declared the U.S. Mint in its announcement of the 2015 Saratoga coins.

Barbara Fox's design, engraved by Renata Gordon, shows a close-up view of the moment General John Burgoyne surrendered his sword to General Horatio Gates—a turning point many historians believe marked the beginning of the end of the American Revolutionary War.

As of press time, the release dates, issue prices, and production limits of the bullion and Specimen coins were yet to be announced.

> "U.S. coins are special artifacts that carry within them many opportunities to learn about who we are, where we've come from, and where we are going."
> —*U.S. Mint Education Coordinator Kim Jenkins*

The Saratoga design on the circulating quarter dollar.

A view of the John Neilson Farmhouse: Late-afternoon summer sun brings out the deep red of this one-room home that served as a mid-level headquarters building for the American army during the Battles of Saratoga.

# 2016 AND BEYOND

On July 22, 2015, the U.S. Mint announced the designs of the upcoming 2016 America the Beautiful coins and released their working sketches. Designs for the program's remaining coins, from 2017 to 2021—or to 2032, if the secretary of the Treasury extends the series to a second round—will be announced after each goes through the design review process described in the introduction to this chapter.

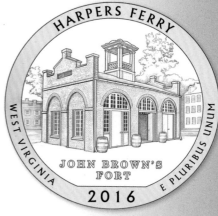

Shawnee National Forest (Illinois). A close view of Camel Rock with natural vegetation in the foreground and a red-tailed hawk soaring in the sky overhead. Designed by Justin Kunz and engraved by Jim Licaretz.

Cumberland Gap National Historical Park (Kentucky). A frontiersman gazing across the mountains to the West. Inscriptions include CUMBERLAND GAP and FIRST DOORWAY TO THE WEST. Designed by Barbara Fox and sculpted by Joseph Menna.

Harpers Ferry National Historical Park (West Virginia). John Brown Fort, the site of John Brown's last stand during his raid on the Harper's Ferry armory. Designed by Artistic Infusion Program artist Thomas Hipschen and sculpted by Phebe Hemphill.

Theodore Roosevelt National Park (North Dakota). Young Theodore Roosevelt on horseback surveying the terrain near the Little Missouri River. Designed by Joel Iskowitz and sculpted by Phebe Hemphill.

Fort Moultrie at Fort Sumter National Monument (South Carolina). Sergeant William Jasper returning the regimental flag to the ramparts while under attack from a British ship. Designed by Richard Scott and sculpted by Joseph Menna.

A model of the 1907 Saint-Gaudens $20 gold piece in the atelier of the Philadelphia Mint's engraving department, July 2015.

# 8

# Special Modern Gold and Silver Coins (2009–2016)

Beyond the ongoing bullion programs described in preceding chapters, the U.S. Mint has introduced several innovative new gold and silver coins in recent years. These coins showcase the Mint's technological and creative abilities in impressive and often surprising ways.

Chapter 31, section 5112, of the United States Code gives the secretary of the Treasury considerable leeway in the specifics of the nation's gold bullion coins. Without needing to get congressional orders or approval, the secretary can change coinage designs, denominations, and other details in coins of that precious metal (similar changes in *silver* bullion coins would require Congress to get involved). The Mint has used this authority to create such modern marvels as the MMIX Ultra High Relief gold double eagle (2009), a gold Kennedy half dollar (2014), and a new American Liberty high-relief gold coin (2015). Authority for 2016 gold coins struck with the designs of the Mercury dime, the Standing Liberty quarter, and the Liberty Walking half dollar, to celebrate the 100th anniversary of their debut, derives from the same legislation.

The U.S. Mint has 40 years of modern experience getting to know what collectors and investors want (and don't want) in terms of gold. Gone are the prohibitions of the 1930s, since gold was made legal to own again in 1974. The minting of the gold National Bicentennial Medals and the Colorado Centennial Medal was followed by the American Arts gold medallions of the early 1980s, which ramped up to the globally popular American Gold Eagles. The American Buffalo and First Spouse programs have found their niches. Now the special coins in this chapter give us a taste of the possibilities of the near future.

The obverse of the 2009 Ultra High Relief gold coin is based on Augustus Saint-Gaudens's original 1907 design of a dramatically striding Miss Liberty, but with 50 stars around the perimeter instead of 46 (the number of states in the Union in 1907). This alteration came from a recommendation of the Citizens Coinage Advisory Committee. Another change (this one advised by the Commission of Fine Arts): the date is rendered as MMIX, in the Roman-numeral style of Saint-Gaudens's original. (shown 2x actual size)

The reverse features the artist's eagle in flight with the sun shining in the background, and the addition of IN GOD WE TRUST, as required by modern law.

# MMIX ULTRA HIGH RELIEF GOLD DOUBLE EAGLE (2009)

*Designer: Augustus Saint-Gaudens. Composition: .9999 gold. Actual Gold Weight: 1 ounce. Diameter: 27 mm. Edge: Lettered. Mint: West Point. Issue Price: $1,189. Release Date: January 22, 2009.*

At the March 13, 2008, meeting of the Citizens Coinage Advisory Committee, U.S. Mint Director Edmund Moy made a historic announcement: the agency planned to produce a modern recreation of the famous 1907 double eagle ($20 gold coin) originally crafted by American sculptor Augustus Saint-Gaudens.

By that time, the Mint had been making American Gold Eagle bullion coins with a version of Saint-Gaudens's design for more than 20 years—but this new coin would be different. Edge lettering, unusual thickness, and remarkably high relief would make the 2009 production much closer in spirit to Saint-Gaudens's original vision of a medallic, visually stunning work of coinage sculpture. It would be truer than even the millions of double eagles struck for circulation from late 1907 through 1933. (In order to mass-produce Saint-Gaudens's design on circulating double eagles, the Mint had been forced to reduce his original high relief to a much flatter style.)

Moy was eager to show off the modern Mint's technology and demonstrate how far the art and science of coinage had come in the past hundred years. "The first decision to be made," he recalls, "was which version [of the Mint's 1907 creations] best represented the artist's purest vision."[1] Mint chief counsel Dan Shaver suggested a conference call with numismatic expert David Tripp, who recommended the pattern coin classified as Judd-1917 in *United States Pattern Coins*, 10th edition. This pattern has a diameter of 27 mm. The diameter of a regular double eagle, in contrast, is 34 mm. Numismatic historian Roger W. Burdette describes the 1907 experimental piece: "The purpose was to determine if a high-relief design could be better struck on a planchet of smaller diameter compensated by greater thickness. In effect, the force of the press was concentrated on a smaller area."[2] Only two of these small, double-thickness test coins from 1907 exist today, permanently housed in the National Numismatic Collection at the Smithsonian. "Once I decided on a 27 mm coin," Moy says, "I sought and received approval to develop the project from Treasury Secretary Hank Paulson." On May 2, 2008, Secretary Paulson's approval was announced. The new coin was authorized under chapter 31, United States Code, section 5112 (i)(4)(c), which allows the secretary of the Treasury to prescribe program procedures and specifications for minting and issuing new gold coins. This provision also gives the secretary the discretion to select each such coin's designs, varieties, quantities, denomination, and inscriptions. For the first time ever, the Mint would be creating a one-ounce 24-karat gold coin in a special ultra-high-relief format.

"Only 2009-dated coins will be minted," spokesman Michael White announced. "The coins will go on sale in early 2009, although sales may continue into 2010 if inventory exists." During its production window, mintage of the new one-year coin would be limited only by customer demand. Everybody who wanted and could afford one would get one.

In *American Gold and Platinum Eagles*, Ed Moy describes the design and technical processes of creating the 2009 coin: scanning and digitally mapping plasters archived at the Smithsonian, using digital technology to transfer the design directly to a working die (bypassing a Janvier lathe or other means of mechanical reduction), creating the edge lettering, and testing and adjusting the coinage results. Ultimately each coin would be struck with two blows of the die at 65 metric tons of pressure.

As the Mint worked on the Ultra High Relief gold coins in 2009, it also continued to produce and distribute other coins in its ongoing gold programs: the 24-karat American Buffalo bullion and Proof coins, the 24-karat First Spouse Proof and Burnished coins, and the 22-karat American Gold Eagles, in Proof and Burnished formats.

**The edge of the 2009 Ultra High Relief coin features the same raised edge-lettering as the 1907 pieces, with E PLURIBUS UNUM and stars in between the letters. It is 4 mm thick.**

Collectors were excited when news broke about the 2009 Ultra High Relief coin. Conversations erupted on the online discussion forums, and *Coin World* and *Numismatic News* ran editorial commentary and letters to the editor. Sales started January 22, 2009, and for some collectors the question was not *whether* to buy the coin, but *how many* to buy. Others expressed frustration at having to rein in the rest of their hobby budget to dedicate money to the Ultra High Relief. The issue price of $1,189 reflected a considerable premium over its melt value (about $950 that summer). Before long that premium would seem like a bargain.

The mintage ended up being large—nearly 115,000 coins—but demand has also stayed high since 2009, resulting in a consistently strong secondary market. Three years after their debut, professional numismatist Ian Russell wrote, "I am still keenly buying these in all grades and services. . . . There is increased demand in PCGS MS-70 and PCGS MS-70 First Strike. Many sales are going overseas, which will help the market in the United States."[3] Coin dealer Jim Sego saw the same robust buy-and-sell activity: "We're still buying these every day."

**The 2009 Ultra High Relief gold coin, and a flat-relief 1907 Saint-Gaudens double eagle (both shown at actual size).**

"No doubt the 2009 Ultra High Relief is a show stopper," says coin dealer and *Guide Book of United States Coins* pricing contributor Troy Thoreson. "Many collectors still have never seen this coin and in my opinion it's one of the most beautiful ever made by the U.S. Mint. Its popularity is strong. This is one of the few modern coins where people don't have a problem paying the extra premium commanded by MS-70 and prooflike examples. The high relief is extreme and gives the coin a modern three-dimensional look."[4] Gold-coin expert Doug Winter says, "It is one of the few issues like this that I think is really beautiful, and a great tribute to the original."

Each coin was encased in a protective clear capsule and mounted in a wood platform housed in a velvet-lined, highly lacquered mahogany box. The box bears inscriptions in a font similar to those used in the early 1900s. An official U.S. Mint companion book (available only with the coin) completed the presentation, chronicling the story of the 2009 Ultra High Relief double eagle by describing the technology and processes used to perfect it.

**The packaging of the 2009 Ultra High Relief coin.**

Collectors today should, if possible, examine these coins before purchasing, to cherrypick for higher-than-average quality. The coins were minted as "business strikes," as the Mint calls them—not with specially polished dies or white-glove handling, although they were plastic-encapsulated and beautifully packaged. Some exhibit light hairline scratches from being struck from polished dies; a connoisseur will wait for an example without such flaws. Professionally certified coins, especially those in MS-70 and those with prooflike surfaces, command substantial premiums over their bullion value. Even the coins that have been kept in their original Mint packaging, in average condition, are worth much more as numismatic collectibles than as little chunks of 24-karat gold.

Mintage: 114,427

| Certified Populations and Retail Market Values | | | | | | | | |
|---|---|---|---|---|---|---|---|---|
| | Raw MS | <MS-68 | MS-68 | MS-68PL | MS-69 | MS-69PL | MS-70 | MS-70PL |
| Certified | — | 84 | 63 | 8 | 6,874 | 971 | 8,916 | 1,037 |
| Value* | $2,000 | $2,100 | $2,125 | $2,150 | $2,250 | $2,300 | $2,600 | $4,000 |
| *Recent auctions:* $1,998, MS-69, June 2015. $3,760, MS-70PL, August 2015. | | | | | | | | |

\* "Raw" value is based on a gold spot price of $1,200 per ounce, and is for an uncertified coin of average quality. This value may vary with the prevailing bullion value.

# NATIONAL BASEBALL HALL OF FAME $5 GOLD COIN (2014)

*Designer: Cassie McFarland (obverse); Don Everhart (reverse).*
*Sculptor: Don Everhart (obverse and reverse). Composition:*
*.900 gold, .100 copper. Actual Gold Weight: .242 ounce.*
*Diameter: 21.6 mm. Edge: Reeded. Mint: West Point. Issue Price:*
*$436.90 (Uncirculated); $441.90 (Proof). Release Date: March 27, 2014.*

Although the United States has issued many gold commemorative coins from 1903 to date, including dozens in the modern era since 1984, the novelty of one in particular warrants its inclusion in this chapter. In 2014 the U.S. Mint released a suite of three commemorative coins—a half dollar, silver dollar, and $5 gold piece—celebrating the 75th anniversary of the National Baseball Hall of Fame in Cooperstown, New York. These coins are unique in that they were the first-ever *curved* coins produced by the Mint. Their obverses are concave, to recreate the cupped curvature of a baseball glove, and their reverses are convex, like the surface of a ball.

"These coins commemorate important aspects of American history and culture," said U.S. Mint Deputy Director Richard A. Peterson. "This is a great way to connect with America's pastime." The nation agreed, with the coins making headlines from coast to coast and collectors buying more than 50,000 in total. In comparison, the Mint sold 25,000 of its 2011 U.S. Army commemorative $5 gold pieces.

On the opening day of sales, March 27, 2014, the Whitman Baltimore Coin & Collectibles Expo and the U.S. Mint Sales Center at Mint headquarters in Washington, DC, were the only two places where collectors could hand over

Uncirculated.

payment and immediately receive the coins. Baseball Hall of Famer and legendary Baltimore Orioles defensive third-baseman Brooks Robinson was on hand at the Whitman Expo to celebrate the coins' launch.

**Mintage: ~17,677 Uncirculated; ~32,427 Proof**

| Certified Populations and Retail Market Values | | | | | | | | |
|---|---|---|---|---|---|---|---|---|
| | Raw MS | <MS-69 | MS-69 | MS-70 | Raw PF | <PF-69 | PF-69 | PF-70 |
| Certified | — | 3 | 441 | 3,757 | — | 0 | 431 | 3,822 |
| Value* | $475 | | $500 | $550 | $500 | | $525 | $640 |
| Recent auctions: $564, MS-70, September 2015. $646, PF-70, September 2015. | | | | | | | | |

\* "Raw" value is based on a gold spot price of $1,200 per ounce, and is for an uncertified Uncirculated or Proof coin of average quality. This value may vary with the prevailing bullion value.

**2014-W Baseball Hall of Fame $5 gold coin, obverse side view.**

**Reverse side view.**

# 50TH ANNIVERSARY GOLD AND SILVER KENNEDY HALF DOLLARS (2014)

*Designer: Gilroy Roberts (obverse); Frank Gasparro (reverse). **Composition:** gold—.9999 gold; silver—.900 silver, .100 copper. **Actual Gold Weight:** .75 ounce. **Actual Silver Weight:** .36169 ounce each. **Diameter:** 30.6 mm. **Edge:** Reeded. **Mint:** gold—West Point; silver—Philadelphia, Denver, San Francisco, and West Point. **Issue Price:** $1,240 (gold half dollar); $99.95 (silver four-coin set). **Release Date:** August 5, 2014 (gold half dollar); October 28, 2014 (silver four-coin set).*

On July 1, 2014, the U.S. Mint announced its release schedule for three new products commemorating the 50th anniversary of the Kennedy half dollar, which debuted in 1964 to honor recently assassinated President John F. Kennedy. This suite of products included, among others, gold and silver coins.

**50th Anniversary Gold Proof Kennedy Half Dollar.** Struck at the West Point Mint, this special Proof half dollar contains three-quarters of a troy ounce of .9999 fine (24-karat) gold. It recreates the original design of the Kennedy half dollar, but with the commemorative dual date 1964–2014. Each coin was packaged in a custom-designed mahogany presentation case with a removable coin well, and came with a certificate of authenticity signed by U.S. Mint Deputy Director Richard A. Peterson. Mintage was limited to 75,000 coins, and the issue price fluctuated with the spot value of gold. Sales opened on August 5, 2014 (online, by phone, and at the Philadelphia, Denver, and Washington, DC, gift shops). The coins were also available starting that day at the 2014 American Numismatic Association World's Fair of Money in Chicago. Excitement for the gold coins was high, not only within the hobby community but also spilling over into mainstream America as they made national headlines.

Disorganized crowds jostled into the ANA convention to wait in line to get the coins available there. *Coin World* editor William Gibbs describes the scene: "The Mint offered limited quantities of the gold coins at the four physical venues, and further, restricted sales to one per person per day. Demand for the

**24-karat gold Proof 1964–2014-W Kennedy half dollar. (1.5x actual size)**

The packaging of the 50th Anniversary gold coin.

coin paired with those restrictions led some prominent dealers to pay people, many of them noncollectors, to stand in line (some for hours) to purchase a coin. These dealers funded the purchase price of the coin, and these buyers agreed to turn over their purchase to the dealers. The dealers then quickly had the coins slabbed with special grading service labels, and immediately offered the specially labeled gold half dollars at prices well above the Mint's issue prices. At the Rosemont ANA show site, the line of potential buyers aiming at the Mint booth began forming in the night before the first day of sales, with the first four people in line traveling all the way from California just to buy the coins."[5] The Mint had planned to offer the coins at its gift shops through August 8, and at the ANA show until the 9th. However, a frenzy at the Denver Mint—with unruly mobs stampeding and people being trampled on August 7—led to an early suspension of all the in-person sales.

This excitement led to exorbitant prices early in the coins' sales period, with some dealers buying at the $1,240 issue price, having the coins slabbed, and flipping them for $3,000 or more to eager buyers. Secondary-market reality prevailed before long, however, and prices soon stabilized. "Late in the year," Gibbs noted, "when the Mint was selling the coins at $1,165, a piece graded Proof-70 Deep Cameo sold for $1,101.10 at auction."

As of September 27, 2015, sales for the 50th Anniversary gold coin amounted to 73,772 pieces. In October 2015 the Mint's inventory was declared sold out.

A tray of freshly struck gold 1964–2014-W Kennedy half dollars at the West Point Mint.

**Mintage: ~75,000**

| Certified Populations and Retail Market Values | | | | | |
|---|---|---|---|---|---|
| | Raw PF | <PF-68 | PF-68 | PF-69 | PF-70 |
| Certified | — | 17 | 56 | 2,301 | 7,558 |
| Value* | $1,000 | | $1,050 | $1,125 | $1,500 |
| *Recent auctions:* $1,105, PF-69, September 2015. $1,602, PF-70, July 2015. | | | | | |

\* "Raw" value is based on a gold spot price of $1,200 per ounce, and is for an uncertified coin of average quality. This value may vary with the prevailing bullion value.

**50th Anniversary Kennedy Half Dollar Silver Coin Collection.** A set of four 90 percent silver 2014 half dollars—one from each of the U.S. Mint's production facilities—was offered by the Mint for $99.95. The set consisted of a Reverse Proof from West Point, a Proof from Philadelphia, an Enhanced Uncirculated from San Francisco, and a Burnished (called *Uncirculated* by the Mint) from Denver. The coins were encapsulated and secured in coin wells within an embossed leatherette folder with a patriotic stars-and-stripes design. The set also included an informative booklet about the design of the 1964 Kennedy half dollar, and a certificate of authenticity. It went on sale October 28, 2014, with a product limit of 225,000 sets.

The Mint had stopped issuing 90 percent silver half dollars for circulation in 1964 (the debut year of the Kennedy half dollar). In 1992 it began producing *Proof* versions of the Kennedy half dollar in silver, at the San Francisco Mint, for inclusion in annually issued Silver Proof sets. This 2014 collection of silver Kennedy half dollars is unique in that the Proof version hails from Philadelphia (not San Francisco), and each of the other three formats is also a "first" for the series.

Describing production of the Enhanced Uncirculated coins from San Francisco, the Mint explained: "This is a special wire-brushing technique. . . . The obverse in the areas of the effigy (portrait), lettering, and border will all receive a heavy laser-frosting treatment. On the reverse, the lettering and border will each receive a heavy laser-frosting treatment. Other elements of the eagle will receive a standard (moderate) laser-frosting treatment to enhance certain artistic details. The stars will receive a laser-polish technique to accentuate them against the field."

**2014-W Reverse Proof.**

As of November 2, 2015, the U.S. Mint reported 217,442 sets sold, with the sets still available at the issue price of $99.95. Collectors have removed some coins from their original Mint packaging for submission to the professional third-party grading firms. Most of them grade MS-70 or PF-70, with smaller numbers grading 69. The secondary market for these individually graded coins is still unsettled. As noted, the four-coin set is still available directly from the Mint for $99.95 and, as of press date, several thousand sets are available, so they carry no premium in their original packaging. Certified four-coin sets in late autumn 2015 were trading for $110 to $150 in -69 grades and for $300 to $330 in -70.

Packaging of the 50th Anniversary Silver Coin Collection.

**2014-P Proof.**

**Mintage: ~217,442**

| | Raw PF | <PF-68 | PF-68 | PF-69 | PF-70 |
|---|---|---|---|---|---|
| **Certified Populations and Retail Market Values** | | | | | |
| **Certified** | — | n/a | n/a | n/a | n/a |
| **Value** | $100 | | | | |

**2014-S Enhanced Uncirculated.**

**2014-D Burnished (Uncirculated).**

**50th Anniversary Uncirculated Kennedy Half Dollar Set.** This $9.95 set included two Uncirculated coins (one from Philadelphia and one from Denver) encapsulated and mounted on a card within a folder. The coins were not silver or gold, but standard-composition copper-nickel, and are mentioned here only for completeness. The set went on sale July 24, 2014, and was limited to production of 200,000, which sold out. (Sets in their original packaging sell for $10 to $15 on the secondary market, while those slabbed and graded SP-67 sell for $30 to $35, and SP-68 for about $100.)

# AMERICAN LIBERTY HIGH RELIEF GOLD COIN (2015)

*Designer: Justin Kunz (obverse); Paul C. Balan (reverse). Sculptor: Phebe Hemphill (obverse); Don Everhart (reverse). Composition: .9999 gold. Actual Gold Weight: 1 ounce. Diameter: 30.6 mm. Edge: Reeded. Mint: West Point. Issue Price: $1,490. Release Date: July 30, 2015.*

As described earlier in this chapter, in 2009 the U.S. Mint fulfilled the artistic vision of sculptor Augustus Saint-Gaudens, bringing his ultra-high-relief 1907 $20 gold designs to a new gold coin—a technological triumph. In the words of the Mint, this closed one era of classic American coin design and ushered in a new one.

The year 2015 brought a new coin to the Mint's High Relief family. "The 2015 American Liberty High Relief gold coin is the latest in the new era, a piece that renders contemporary designs using the latest in modern digital and manufacturing technology."[6] The coin was created under authority granted to the secretary of the Treasury by federal law, in chapter 31, United States Code, section 5112 (i)(4)(c). It was conceptualized by the Mint in mid-2014 after discussions with the Citizens Coinage Advisory Committee. The U.S. Commission of Fine Arts also reviewed designs and made recommendations.

The work of two Artistic Infusion Program artists was chosen for the coin's designs: Justin Kunz created a modern depiction of Miss Liberty for the obverse, "evoking the ideals of liberty, courage, and hope," and Paul C. Balan designed an American eagle rising in flight, "gripping a branch in its talons as an embodiment of freedom."

The American Liberty gold coin's packaging.

Biographies for Kunz and other U.S. Mint coin designers who worked on the First Spouse gold coin program are in chapter 6. Fine artist Paul Cainto Balan, designer of the reverse motif of the American Liberty High Relief coin, is a native of Paete, Laguna, Philippines. He studied fine arts at the University of Santo Tomas in Manila. Many of his religious works, including murals and stained glass, are displayed in churches in the Philippines. Balan moved to the United States in 2001 "with $5 in his pocket," became a U.S. citizen in 2005, and was selected for the Mint's Artistic Infusion Program in 2009.[7]

Balan's flying eagle was praised by the Citizens Coinage Advisory Committee in April 2014, when the CCAC proposed it as a new reverse design for the American Silver Eagle.[8] It was also considered as a potential design for the 2015 U.S. Marshals Service 225th Anniversary gold commemorative coin.

"As an immigrant who became an American citizen," Balan says, "it feels like I've made a full circle to have a role in designing such a historic coin. It's a dream to work with the design management team at the Mint and my fellow AIP artists, who I admire and have great respect for. I'm very grateful for the opportunity to have my work featured in American coins." He describes his style as "clean and simple," and says he hopes Americans "feel a sense of pride, ownership, and belonging" when they see his design.[9]

Obverse detail.

Don Everhart sculpting a plaster model for the reverse design.

Reverse detail.

For the obverse, Justin Kunz was challenged with creating a fresh new interpretation of Miss Liberty, a symbol of America that has appeared on our coins since the 1790s. "The problem we were tasked with solving," he recalls, "to portray Lady Liberty as a modern figure rather than a traditional one, proved a bit more difficult in practice than it sounded in theory. It required a lot of studying, sketching, and meditating about what Lady Liberty represents, what it is that defines our time from past eras, and how these ideas might be distilled down to a simple visual statement that could be expressed in an elegant way." Kunz says he hopes the designs "will be remembered as expressions of faith in this nation's founding ideals, a tribute to our finest accomplishments, and optimism about our potential for the future."

Before the final designs were decided upon, the Mint's technical staff had to answer an important preliminary question: Was production of a high-relief gold coin even viable?

> The development team at the Philadelphia facility started on a test design, or high-relief nonsense design, that would embody the high-relief elements of the yet-to-be-determined designs. Based on several technical factors, the 2009 Ultra High Relief obverse and reverse designs were selected and modified with powerful 3-D sculpting software to the proposed diameter and edge thickness configurations of the 2015 high-relief gold coin.
>
> After the software phase, the team developed gold blank specifications and ordered test blanks. Concurrently, using state-of-the-art technology, the team manufactured research dies directly on computer numerical controlled, or CNC, milling machines. Milling is a machining process that uses a rotating cutting tool to etch the design onto the metal die, which is used to strike the coin. Once the gold test blanks arrived, the coin-development team struck 20 gold coins to test the coining characteristics of this high-relief concept. The strikes were successful, and the resulting coins were used to develop specifications for coin-to-capsule fit so capsule molds could be manufactured well ahead of final coin availability.
>
> Shortly after the team completed research strikes the final 2015 American Liberty High Relief gold design arrived. Once the team finalized the gold sculpts in plaster, they scanned and converted obverse and reverse plaster models into digital 3-D data. The technical staff loaded these data sets into computer-aided design software, where lettering, date, mintmark, and other features were added. The team then adjusted the sculpts for maximum coinability and started the formal master-tooling process.
>
> The team completed the Design Validation (DV), manufactured the dies, worked on DV strikes, conducted coin-to-capsule fit tests, and sent the coins and capsules to Headquarters for acceptance.
>
> Philadelphia sent 100 pairs of W-mintmark gold dies to West Point for production striking.[10]

The American Liberty coins contain one troy ounce of .9999 fine (24-karat) gold and have a nominal face value of $100. Each is struck in what the Mint calls "business strike" format, then encapsulated and packaged in a black velvet presentation case with a certificate of authenticity. Sales opened on July 30, 2015, with mintage capped at 50,000 coins and orders limited to 50 per household.

Note the hairline scratches that are evident on some pieces.

The issue price of $1,490 (which would fluctuate with the weekly prevailing spot price of gold) was about $400 higher than the coin's melt value in the summer of 2015—and $50 higher than the Mint's pricing for American Buffalo 24-karat gold coins. Still, collectors flocked to the innovative new gold pieces with their unique designs.

The U.S. Mint is internationally renowned for the high quality of its coinage. However, for the American Liberty High Relief gold coins, collectors should note that some buyers have reported rim damage (especially on the reverse) and/or hairline scratches on their coins, so cherrypicking for visual appeal is recommended.

**Mintage: ~50,000**

| Certified Populations and Retail Market Values | | | | | |
|---|---|---|---|---|---|
| | **Raw MS** | **<MS-68** | **MS-68** | **MS-69** | **MS-70** |
| **Certified** | — | 0 | 13 | 2,924 | 6,311 |
| **Value\*** | $1,590 | | $1,600 | $1,650 | $1,800 |
| *Recent auctions:* $1,535, MS-69, September 2015. $1,777, MS-70, September 2015. | | | | | |

\* "Raw" value is based on a gold spot price of $1,200 per ounce, and is for an uncertified coin of average quality. This value may vary with the prevailing bullion value.

# 1916 CENTENNIAL GOLD COINS (2016)

On June 17, 2015, the U.S. Mint unveiled mockup images of three 24-karat gold coins that would commemorate the Mercury dime, Standing Liberty quarter, and Liberty Walking half dollar. Each of these classic American silver coins debuted in 1916. The new gold tribute coins would be released in 2016 to mark their 100th anniversary.

The Mint first announced the possibility of the gold coins in September 2014, though that earlier announcement only mentioned the dime and the half dollar. In January 2015 the Mint released expanded plans that would also include the quarter dollar. (Historical information on all three denominations can be found in *A Guide Book of Mercury Dimes, Standing Liberty Quarters, and Liberty Walking Half Dollars*, by Q. David Bowers.)

The June 2015 images show the dime motif as a tenth-ounce gold coin, the quarter as a quarter-ounce, and the half dollar as a half-ounce. Mint officials are considering issuing the coins in the same diameters as their 1916 counterparts. As of this book's press date, details such as the edge reeding, the positioning of the gold fineness and weight, and the coins' thicknesses are yet to be finalized, and the Mint's mockup images are not considered final.

Authority for the coins is granted by chapter 31, United States Code, section 5112 (i)(4)(c). The Mint needs the approval of the secretary of the Treasury to move forward with production of the coins. Some discussion at the Mint has centered around issuing similar commemorative coins in *silver*, but that would require congressional action.

These gold coins represent the modern U.S. Mint's commitment to innovation and its connection to the nation's rich historical past.

**Early U.S. Mint mockups of the 2016 Centennial gold coins, at sizes corresponding to the coins they commemorate. Note the alloy represented as AU 24k on each coin, and the weight as a fraction of an ounce.**

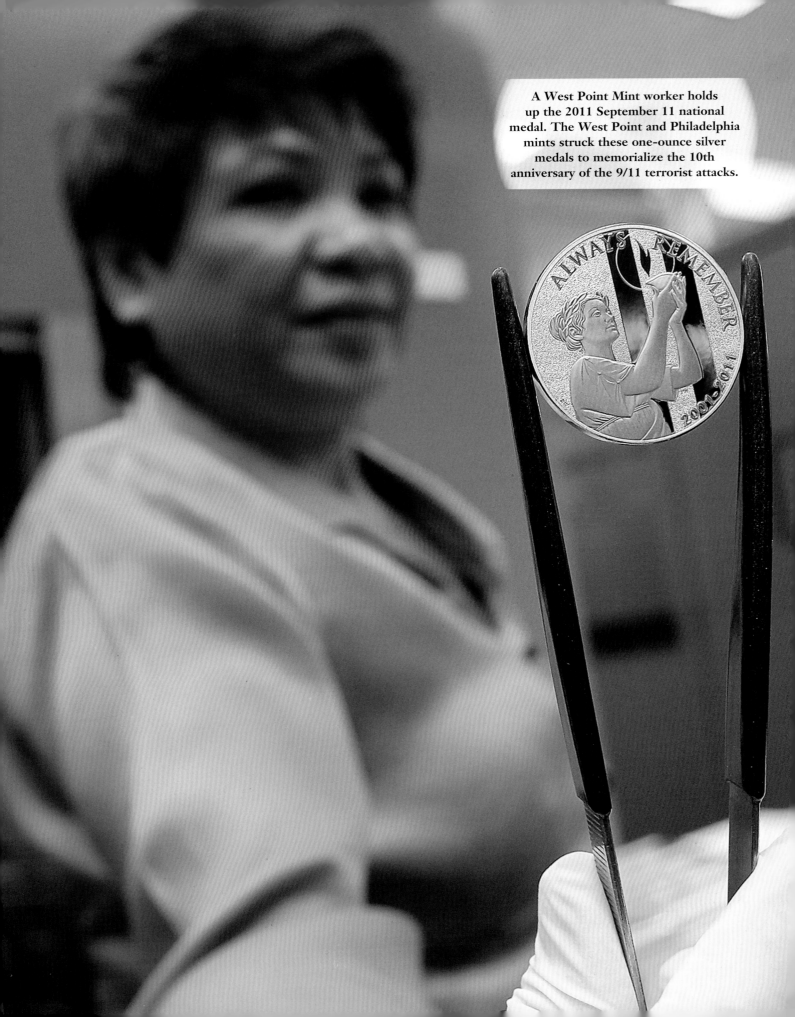

A West Point Mint worker holds up the 2011 September 11 national medal. The West Point and Philadelphia mints struck these one-ounce silver medals to memorialize the 10th anniversary of the 9/11 terrorist attacks.

# 9

# U.S. Mint Gold and Silver Medals
# (Bicentennial to Date)

The mint of the United States has a long history of issuing medals for commemorative and historical purposes, dating back to the early 1800s. Even before that—before there existed a national mint, as far back as during the American Revolution—official medals were authorized to be designed and struck (typically in France) for the fledgling nation.

In 1776 the Continental Congress voted to award the thanks of the Thirteen United Colonies to General George Washington, his officers, and his soldiers, after their victorious bombardment of Boston and the resulting British evacuation. Along with the congressional gratitude a gold medal was presented to General Washington. Medals (separate from military awards and decorations) have been granted to other commanders from the Revolutionary War and the War of 1812 to the present day. Beyond the military, the nation has struck medals to celebrate everything from acts of heroic lifesaving to famous entertainers to wildlife conservation. "The United States Mint produces a variety of national medals to commemorate significant historical events or sites and to honor those whose superior deeds and achievements have enriched U.S. history or the world," the Mint says. "Some of these are bronze duplicates of Congressional Gold Medals authorized by Congress under separate public laws, while others are produced under the secretary of the Treasury's authority to strike national medals."

Numismatic historian Pete Smith, in *Laws of the U.S. Congress Authorizing Medals*, explores the history of these commemorative items:

**U.S. Mint Director Nellie Tayloe Ross standing in her office, August 1, 1945, in front of a cabinet with Presidential medals and a complete series of portrait medals of the secretaries of the Treasury.**

An Act of February 12, 1873, authorized "dies of a national character" for production of medals and prohibited production of private medal dies [by the Mint]. The first medal authorized under that act commemorated the one hundredth anniversary of the first meeting of the Continental Congress and of the Declaration of Independence.

Funding for the Congressional Medals has evolved over more than 220 years. Congress didn't bother to mention costs until 1836 when expenses related to the Daniel Morgan medal were "to be paid out of any money in the Treasury not otherwise appropriated" and that was for a replacement medal. Similar language became common in the 1860s into the 1930s."[1]

Smith notes that since 1956 most such commemorative pieces have been designated as "National Medals." He also observes that their subjects have sometimes stretched the definition of what most Americans would consider nationally significant. "Among topics considered of national importance were the centennial of Scranton, Pennsylvania, the centennial of Ohio Northern University, and the bicentennial of diplomatic relations with the Netherlands. . . . Medals authorized by Congress may, in some cases, represent the very best that is American. In other cases they show nothing more than the final result of a political process requiring a majority vote of members of Congress."

Recipients of congressionally authorized gold medals range from the world-famous, such as poet Robert Frost and actor John Wayne, to people most Americans today would consider obscure. In 1939 a gold medal was authorized for Reverend Francis X. Quinn, pastor of the Church of the Guardian Angel, New York City, "who risked his life by entering a room where an armed desperado held two elderly persons as hostages." Reverend Quinn disarmed the criminals, gallantly saving the two innocent lives and winning himself a gold medal—and a place in the history books (or at least the numismatist history books). In 1949 a sum of $2,500 was appropriated to create a gold medal to present to Vice President of the United States Alben W. Barkley for "recognition of [his] distinguished public service and outstanding contribution to the general welfare." As noted above, some national medals, presented in gold to their honored recipients, are later offered by the Mint for sale to the public in a bronze format. One might imagine that most of Vice President Barkley's bronze medals reside in private collections in rural Kentucky, which claims him as a famous son.

**A plaster for the 1976 National Bicentennial Medal.**

**A master hub for the reverse die of the 2008 Andrew Jackson's Liberty bronze medal.**

In *A Guide Book of United States Tokens and Medals*, Katherine Jaeger describes the Mint's national medals (excerpted here):

Because the new republic had no mint of its own and no engravers of suitable talent, our first national medals—a group of 17 authorized by the revolutionary government in 1776—were struck at the Paris Mint in the 1780s. Called the *Comitia Americana* medals, they honored America's first military heroes, the likes of George Washington, Horatio Gates, Anthony Wayne, and Daniel Morgan. Every court in Europe had its "king's cabinet" of medals, and in 1787 Thomas Jefferson arranged that one of each Comitia Americana medal be given to each sovereign, as well as to each of the major European learning academies. These diplomatic presentations helped gain respect for the new nation as a power capable of upholding long-established political traditions.

The U.S. Mint opened in 1792, and began producing the nation's official medals in 1801. At first private artists sank the dies on commission, but by the mid-19th century Mint staff performed all engraving and striking. In 1861 there were 64 national die pairs in the Mint's possession. Among them were the Indian Peace medals and presidential medals; military and naval medals awarded during the War of 1812, the Mexican War (1846–1848), and the Civil War (1861–1865); and the special lifesaving and heroism awards ordered by Congress. Dies for the Comitia Americana medals were still in France, and the Paris Mint would not relinquish them. For restriking purposes, the U.S. Mint made copy dies, using original medals as models.

It was in the 1860s that the Mint commenced recording events in its own history with medals. New Assay Commission medals were presented annually to members of the commission, and Mint director and superintendent medals were struck for occupants of those posts. Beginning in the 1890s, each new secretary of the Treasury received a specially designed medal. Commercial restrikes of all of these, plus the national medals listed

**Sketches and a clay work-in-progress model of the Congressional Gold Medal for the 65th Infantry Regiment—the "Borinqueneers," from Puerto Rico.**

**Since its founding in 2003, the Citizens Coinage Advisory Committee has reviewed proposed designs for U.S. Mint medals. Here, CCAC member Clifford Northrup takes notes while reviewing the obverse candidate design for the Arnold Palmer Congressional Gold Medal. U.S. Mint headquarters, Washington, DC, October 26, 2010.**

**CCAC member Donald Scarinci discusses candidate designs for the New Frontier Congressional Gold Medal (honoring the astronauts of the *Apollo 11*) during a meeting at U.S. Mint headquarters, October 26, 2010.**

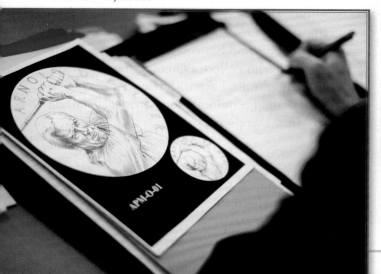

**Silver blanks used to strike the September 11 silver national medal, and a finished product.**

above, were called *list medals* because every year the Mint published a list of which ones were available for purchase. The Mint still sells bronze replicas of its medals to the public, and the list of available pieces can now be found on its Web site, usmint.gov.

From the 1870s through the 1910s, restrikes of certain U.S. Mint medals were surreptitiously made by members of the staff, and sold "out the back door" through several Philadelphia medals dealers, William Idler and John Haseltine being the most prominent. For the most part, these were *not* the national medals, but rather those produced on the order of private citizens, employing the facilities of the Mint's medals department. The practice of the Mint taking commercial orders for medals ended in 1910, and commercial medal production ceased altogether in the 1940s.

In the 20th century, Mint engravers designed special congressional medals for specific recipients, such as George Morgan's 1909 plaquette honoring Orville and Wilbur Wright for their successful powered flight and Gilroy Roberts's 1955 medal to Dr. Jonas Salk for his development of a successful polio vaccine.[2]

Pete Smith classifies the medals authorized by Congress as: medals granted for military victories; campaign medals; lifesaving medals; medals for achievement; exposition medals; commemorative medals; national medals; list medals; medals and decorations; and the Congressional Medal of Honor.

John T. Dean, who continues the award-winning research of Howard Turner published in articles in *The Numismatist* from the late 1960s to the late 1980s, regards the U.S. Mint's medals of 1954 to 1982 as being the nation's "fill-gap" for its terminated commemorative half dollar program. Congress had authorized commemorative silver and gold coins since 1892, but an era of abuse started in the 1930s with self-serving promoters pushing for coins intended mainly to line their own pockets with collectors' hard-earned cash. Earlier coins had commemorated truly national and significant people, places, and events, such as the Marquis de Lafayette (French hero of the American Revolution), the Lewis and Clark expedition, and the 150th anniversary of American independence. In contrast, one of the Mint's silver half dollars in the pork-barrel era honored the centennial of Bridgeport, Connecticut (1930s population, about 147,000). Another 1936 coin celebrated Cincinnati as, dubiously, "A Music Center of America." These and other boondoggles led Congress to stop the nation's commemorative coinage program after 1954. It would eventually start up again in 1982, and has continued to date. In the 28-year interim collectors itching for commemoratives might not have had new *coins* to collect, but they could acquire national medals from the U.S. Mint. Dean writes:

**A West Point Mint worker inspects a freshly struck September 11 medal, May 18, 2012.**

Many of these medals are much rarer than their commemorative coin counterparts and yet can still be obtained at a fraction of the cost. Many of these are amazingly rare United States Mint products, yet almost undiscovered by the numismatic collecting community.

These are referred to as National Medals, based upon legislation being introduced, which is normally referred to the committee on banking and currency. Upon favorable recommendation by this committee, a bill is passed, afterwards being signed into law by the president of the United States. A Public Law was thus required for each of these medals to be struck by the United States Mint, thus a national medal.[3]

Congressional medals of a personal nature, struck in gold for presentation to deserving individuals and groups, obviously are not considered readily "collectible." Most reside permanently in family collections or are donated to public institutions for posterity. Their bronze versions, however, are very much collectible, and many still are available directly from the Mint or on the secondary market from coin dealers. Some recent awardees of Congressional Gold Medals, bronze versions of which can be purchased from the Mint, include:

The Monuments Men

American fighter aces

The Doolittle Tokyo Raiders

Jack Nicklaus

Dr. Martin Luther King Jr. and Coretta Scott King

Native American Code Talkers of World War II

The 16th Street Baptist Church bombing victims

Professor Muhammad Yunus

Daw Aung San Suu Kyi

Arnold Palmer

Constantino Brumidi

The Montford Point Marines

The Nisei Soldiers of World War II

The Women Airforce Service pilots

Senator Edward William Brooke III

Dr. Michael E. DeBakey

The Dalai Lama

Dr. Norman Borlaug

Byron Nelson

The Tuskegee Airmen

National medals make up a rich and fascinating area of numismatics. This chapter covers the gold and silver U.S. Mint medals issued since around the time gold was made legal for everyday Americans to own again, in the early 1970s.[4] A good place to begin is the Bicentennial of the American Revolution.

**A tray of newly minted Jacqueline Kennedy bronze medals at the Philadelphia Mint, July 13, 2015.**

# AMERICAN REVOLUTION BICENTENNIAL MEDALS (1972–1976)

## Annual Historical Medals

**Patrick Henry and Samuel Adams, silver, 1973.**

**John Adams, silver, 1974.**

The federal American Revolution Bicentennial logo appears on bronze, silver, and gold medals made by the U.S. Mint.

On the national level, plans to encourage, develop, and coordinate the celebration of the 200th anniversary of the American Revolution started with the formation of a federal commission in 1966. Related to the commission a Coins and Medals Advisory Panel was set up, and it included numismatists such as Eric P. Newman, John J. Pittman, Don Taxay, Herbert Bergen (president of the American Numismatic Association), U.S. Mint Director Mary Brooks, Clifford Mishler (president of Krause Publications, publisher of *Numismatic News*), and Margo Russell (editor of *Coin World*).

Public Law 92-228 was passed on February 15, 1972, to provide for the striking of Bicentennial medals. It ordered a national medal to commemorate the year 1776 and its significance to American independence, plus up to 13 medals of different designs celebrating "historical events of great importance, recognized nationally as milestones in the continuing progress of the United States of America toward life, liberty, and the pursuit of happiness."

In December 1973 the American Revolution Bicentennial Administration (ARBA) was established and put in charge of, among other things, the preparation, distribution, exhibition, and sale of Bicentennial commemorative medals. It also collaborated with the U.S. Postal Service to issue annual Philatelic-Numismatic Combinations (PNCs), which were packages of a bronze Bicentennial medal with related postage stamps in a postmarked first-day cover.

The first official U.S. Mint–produced Bicentennial medal was struck in 1972 (under the 1966 federal commission, not the ARBA) and made only in bronze. Designed by artist Ralph J. Menconi, it features a profile portrait of George Washington reminiscent of Jean-Antoine Houdon's famous bust, and a depiction of the Liberty Tree in Boston, a rallying point for anti-British protest in the 1760s and early 1770s. Medals from 1973 to 1976 were issued in sterling (.925 fine) silver, priced at $10, as well as bronze, at $3.50. Medals distributed in postmarked PNCs bear no dates, but those issued individually (in plush blue boxes) feature the year date of their issue.

The silver Bicentennial medals include:

**Patrick Henry and Samuel Adams (1973).** Honoring the famous patriots, and the Committees of Correspondence, a network of communications for America's revolutionary colonists. Designed by Richard C. Layton.

**John Adams (1974).** Honoring the coauthor of the Declaration of Independence, as well as the Continental Congress, to which Adams was a delegate. Designed by Robert A. Weinman.

**Paul Revere (1975).** Honoring the patriot whose famous midnight ride alerted others to the approach of British troops, and featuring a Minuteman with a rifle before the Battles of Lexington and Concord. Designed by Margaret Grigor.

**Thomas Jefferson (1976).** Honoring the principal author of the Declaration of Independence, along with a view of the document and Independence Hall in Philadelphia. Designed by Michael Lantz.

Numismatist Michael B. Costanzo, writing in *The Numismatist* in July 2015, observes that when it comes to mintages and units sold of each of the Bicentennial medals, official data can be confusing and contradictory, that poor record-keeping by the ARBA includes discrepancies, that many medals were given away by ARBA officials without being accounted for, and that surplus gold and silver medals of unknown quantity were melted by the government in or after May 1981. John T. Dean, *National Commemorative Medals of the United States Mint*, also notes that mintage data for these medals vary by source.[5] The following chart is based on research by Costanzo and Dean:

Paul Revere, silver, 1975.

| 1972–1976 American Revolution Bicentennial Medals | | | | | |
|---|---|---|---|---|---|
| Year | Item† | Composition | Size | Units Sold* | Current Value |
| 1972 (undated) | PNC | (bronze medal) | | 791,000 | $6 |
| 1972 | medal | bronze | 1.5-inch (38.1 mm) | 672,200 | $4 |
| 1973 (undated) | PNC | (bronze medal) | | 475,812 | $6 |
| 1973 | medal | bronze | 1.5-inch (38.1 mm) | 237,790 | $4 |
| 1973 | medal | .925 silver | 1.5-inch (38.1 mm) | 208,120 | $25 |
| 1974 (undated) | PNC | (bronze medal) | | 511,428 | $6 |
| 1974 | medal | bronze | 1.5-inch (38.1 mm) | 188,308 | $4 |
| 1974 | medal | .925 silver | 1.5-inch (38.1 mm) | 150,428 | $25 |
| 1975 (undated) | PNC | (bronze medal) | | 668,419 | $6 |
| 1975 | medal | bronze | 1.5-inch (38.1 mm) | 327,677 | $4 |
| 1975 | medal | .925 silver | 1.5-inch (38.1 mm) | 212,542 | $25 |
| 1976 (undated) | PNC | (bronze medal) | | 446,939 | $6 |
| 1976 | medal | bronze | 1.5-inch (38.1 mm) | 98,408 | $4 |
| 1976 | medal | .925 silver | 1.5-inch (38.1 mm) | 98,677 | $25 |

Thomas Jefferson, silver, 1976.

* "*Note:* The figures represent units sold. Some of these numbers differ greatly from stated mintages given in the *Annual Report of the Director of the Mint (1976)*. For example, the [mintage] figures for the 1976 bronze medals are given as 153,300, while the silver medals are listed at 146,213. As for the 1974 medals, the 1974 PNC is listed at about 530,000, while the silver medal is 156,000."[6] † PNC = Philatelic-Numismatic Combination (medal, stamp, and first-day cover).

# The National Bicentennial Medal

**National Bicentennial Medal, gold, 76.2 mm variety, 1976. (actual size)**

There was some congressional discussion in the early 1970s about whether the United States should strike commemorative gold *coins* (legal tender, not medals) bearing the official federal logo of the American Revolution Bicentennial. Representative Philip Crane of Illinois and Senator Mark Hatfield of Oregon in particular promoted the issuance of up to 60 million gold coins for the Bicentennial.[7] In September 1975 Mint Director Mary Brooks made the Carter Administration's position clear. She stated that the Mint opposed issuing commemorative gold coins, and that Americans who wanted to acquire U.S. gold from the Treasury's reserves would have that opportunity in 1976, with the planned debut of a new gold National Bicentennial Medal.

The bronze 1972 medal and the 1973–1976 bronze and sterling silver medals were produced as the "maximum of thirteen medals each of a different design" authorized by Public Law 92-228 in 1972. As noted above, this law also ordered the striking of a national medal "commemorating the year 1776 and its significance to American independence." The National Bicentennial Medal was released on January 1, 1976.

The obverse of the National Bicentennial Medal, designed by U.S. Mint Chief Engraver Frank Gasparro, features the Statue of Liberty with the legend LIFE, LIBERTY, AND THE PURSUIT OF HAPPINESS, and dual dates 1776–1976. The reverse, by sculptor-engraver Edgar Z. Steever, is a heraldic American eagle derived from the Great Seal of the United States, with the legends AMERICAN REVOLUTION BICENTENNIAL and WE THE PEOPLE.

This official medal was offered in seven different versions (including gold and silver) and four sizes. The medals proved to be very popular—so popular, in fact, that customer demand led to delivery delays at the Mint. On December 7, 1976, Director Brooks stated in a press release, "The Mint's ability to respond to this huge demand for special coins and medals was not achieved without some unforeseen difficulties. We have experienced delays in the delivery of sets to some of our customers. And we appreciate their patience in waiting for their orders to be filled." The release further noted that "orders for the . . . national gold medals produced for the American Revolution Bicentennial Administration surpassed all expectations. . . . However, the Mint expects to receive the balance of the required gold blanks by the middle of January and intends to complete the striking of the . . . national gold medals by the end of January 1977."

Some of the silver and gold Bicentennial medals were melted by their owners during the bullion-market skyrocket of the late 1970s and early 1980s. Add to that the record-keeping discrepancies noted above, and we can presume that existing field populations are considerably lower than the government's mintage and sales figures would suggest. The National Bicentennial Medals in gold and silver command numismatic premiums well above their melt value.

As noted above, the government's record-keeping for sales and distribution of the Bicentennial medals included errors and discrepancies. This chart is based on the research of Costanzo and Dean:

| 1976 National Bicentennial Medals | | | | | | | | |
|---|---|---|---|---|---|---|---|---|
| Size | Composition | ASW/AGW* | Finish | Packaging | Mintage | Units Sold† | Issue Price | Current Value |
| 1.5-inch (38.1 mm) | bronze | — | Unc. | box | 426,459 | 438,971 | $5.00 | $5 |
| 1.5-inch (38.1 mm) | .925 silver | .99 oz. | Proof | box | 209,885 | 211,772 | $25.00 | $25 |
| 1.5-inch (38.1 mm) | gold-plated bronze | — | Unc. | box | 47,150 | 45,163 | $15.00 | $10 |
| 3-inch (76.2 mm) | .925 silver | 7.94 oz. | matte/ antiqued | box | 9,425 | 8,824 | $150.00 | $325 |
| .906-inch (23.01 mm) | .900 gold | 0.37 oz. | Proof | velvet-lined birch box | 30,239 | 29,468 | $100.00 | $600 |
| 1-5/16-inch (33.34 mm) | .900 gold | 1.167 oz. | Proof | velvet-lined cherrywood box | 5,383 | 5,396 | $400.00 | $2,000 |
| 3-inch (76.2 mm) | .900 gold | 13.18 oz. | Unc. | velvet-lined cherrywood box | 424 | 423 | $4,000.00 | $26,000 |

\* ASW = Actual silver weight; AGW = Actual gold weight. † *Note:* Some of these numbers differ greatly from stated mintages given in the *Annual Report of the Director of the Mint (1976).*[8]

# COLORADO STATEHOOD CENTENNIAL MEDAL (1976)

Colorado was the only state to join the Union in 1876 (before it, Nebraska had joined in 1867; after it, the Dakotas, Montana, and Washington would join in 1889). Because of its unique status, celebrating its 100th anniversary during the nation's Bicentennial year, Congress on December 29, 1973, authorized the Colorado Statehood Centennial national medal. Similar to the 1972–1976 American Revolution Bicentennial medals, it was issued in bronze, gold-plated bronze, silver, and gold. Naturally it was produced at the Denver Mint—the first commemorative medal made there.

The medal shows a bearded nineteenth-century Colorado pioneer on horseback, gazing across a forested and mountainous vista of "The Land of Promise." The reverse features the official emblem of the 1876–1976 centennial. Designed by Colorado artist Sue C. Hughey (obverse) and art educator Randy Moyle (reverse), the medal was sculpted by Edgar Z. Steever of the U.S. Mint. (Chief Engraver Frank Gasparro's initials also appear on the obverse.) The bronze versions have more sentimental value than retail value in today's market. While the silver medal has increased in dollar value, it hasn't kept pace with inflation. The gold version—scarce in the first place, and likely scarcer today due to attrition from melting during the bullion spike of 1979 and 1980—has performed very well and is worth a large premium over its melt value.

Colorado Statehood Centennial medal, gold, 1976.

| 1976 Colorado Statehood Centennial Medal | | | | | | |
|---|---|---|---|---|---|---|
| Composition | Size | Weight | ASW/AGW* | Mintage | Issue Price | Current Value |
| bronze** | 1.3-inch (33.3 mm) | 18.4 g | — | 41,000 | $5.00 | $6 |
| gilt bronze | 1.3-inch (33.3 mm) | 18.5 g | — | 5,000 | $15.00 | $8 |
| .900 silver | 1.3-inch (33.3 mm) | 19.7 g | ~0.57 oz. | 20,200 | $18.76 | $32 |
| .900 gold*** | 1.3-inch (33.3 mm) | 40.4 g | ~1.17 oz. | 100 | $500.00 | $5,200 |
| three-piece set† | | | | 1,876 | $40.00 | $45 |

\* ASW = Actual silver weight; AGW = Actual gold weight. \*\* A variety exists with the standard 1876–1976 centennial logo reverse muled to a United States Mint, Denver Colorado, obverse (showing the mint building in Denver). It is fairly common and worth about the same as the regular variety. \*\*\* The remaining .100 was .06 silver, .04 copper. Presented to individuals and groups who donated $500 or more to the State Bicentennial Commission. † Issued by the Colorado Centennial–Bicentennial Commission in a hard plastic case, containing one each of the bronze, gilt bronze, and silver medals.

# VALLEY FORGE MEDAL (1978)

The United States Capitol Historical Society, founded in 1962, is chartered by Congress to educate the public on the history and heritage of the U.S. Capitol, its institutions, and the people who have served therein. From 1978 to 1991 the Society issued 14 annual medals commemorating, in order: Valley Forge; John Paul Jones; James Madison; the surrender of Cornwallis; George Washington; the Treaty of Paris; the 350th anniversary of Maryland; women of the American Revolution; Benjamin Franklin; the signing of the Constitution; the ratification of the Constitution; the bicentennial of the U.S. Congress; the U.S. judicial system; and the Bill of Rights.

Of these medals, the first was authorized by Public Law 95-229 (February 14, 1978). It was designed by the U.S. Mint's chief engraver, Frank Gasparro, and produced at the Philadelphia Mint. The obverse shows George Washington in a standing portrait at a Valley Forge campfire with two soldiers and a snow-covered cabin in the distance. A wind-flapped cape drapes Washington's frame; his hands rest on his sword and his demeanor is contemplative. Thirteen stars representing the original colonies surround him like a constellation in the night sky. The reverse features Old Glory and a remarkably detailed view of the York County (Pennsylvania) Courthouse, where the Continental Congress met after being forced to flee Philadelphia during the American Revolution. Legends mark the 200th anniversary of the Articles of Confederation and the adoption of the American flag.

**Valley Forge medal, silver, 76.2 mm variety, 1978. (actual size)**

The U.S. Capitol Historical Society's other medals were struck privately, and therefore fall outside the scope of this book.

The Valley Forge medal was issued in small quantities in several formats.

| Composition | Size | Weight | ASW/AGW* | Mintage | Issue Price | Current Value |
|---|---|---|---|---|---|---|
| bronze | 3-inch (76.2 mm) | 7.1 oz. | — | ~2,500 | $25.00 | $45 |
| gilt bronze | 1.5-inch (38.1 mm) | 0.82 oz. | — | ~5,000 | $7.00 | $15 |
| .925 silver | 1.5-inch (38.1 mm) | 1.00 oz. | ~0.93 oz. | ~1,999 | $30.00 | $50 |
| .925 silver | 3-inch (76.2 mm) | 8.5 oz. | ~7.90 oz. | ~1,000 | $145.00 | $600 |
| .900 gold | 1.31-inch (33.0 mm) | 1.30 oz. | ~1.20 oz. | ~339 | $450.00 | $5,000 |

**1978 Valley Forge Medal**

* ASW = Actual silver weight; AGW = Actual gold weight.

# AMERICAN ARTS GOLD MEDALLIONS (1980–1984)

From 1980 to 1984 the U.S. Mint struck .900 fine gold medallions in half-ounce and one-ounce formats at the West Point Bullion Depository. These congressionally mandated bullion pieces were intended to compete with South Africa's Krugerrand, the Canadian Maple Leaf, and other gold coins that American investors were purchasing since the metal had become legal for them to own again in 1974. The medals honored two American artists per year, from the fields of literature, the performing and fine arts, music, and architecture. They were designed and sculpted by the Philadelphia Mint's sculptor-engravers including Frank Gasparro, Matthew Peloso, Sherl Joseph Winter, John Mercanti, Edgar Steever, Philip Fowler, and Michael Iacocca. The medals were sold to the general public at a competitive price equal to the free-market value of the gold they contained plus the cost of manufacture, including labor, materials, dies, use of machinery, and overhead expenses.

Despite creative efforts by the Treasury Department and private retailers to market and sell the American Arts gold medallions, the five-year program brought sluggish sales. Two years later the Mint would introduce a much more popular series of gold bullion *coins*, the American Eagles, leaving the American Arts medallions behind as an interesting chapter in U.S. minting history.

The program is explored in full detail in chapter 3 of this book.

The 1982 Louis Armstrong American Arts gold medallion, one of 10 designs in the series.

**Young Astronauts bronze medal, 1988.**

# YOUNG ASTRONAUTS MEDALS (1988)

The nonprofit Young Astronaut Council was created by the White House Office of Private Sector Initiatives in 1984 to encourage greater American proficiency and interest in science, math, and technology, using space as its underlying theme. "The sky's not the limit," President Ronald Reagan said at the launching of the Young Astronaut Program in October 1984, "because the opportunities of space are unlimited." Thousands of local chapters of the YA program, privately funded by membership fees, were set up nationwide in schools, libraries, science centers, and in home-school groups, with individual memberships also available.

Senator Jake Garn of Utah (the first member of Congress to fly in space) and Representative Frank Annunzio of Illinois sponsored the Young Astronaut Program Medal Act of 1985, which was approved in May 1986. The medals struck under this act honored the program and its educational objectives. They were sold by the Young Astronaut Council, headquartered on Connecticut Avenue in Washington, DC, and 10 percent of the proceeds went to the Council to support its mission.

The reverse common to all the medals was designed by artist Robert Ahlcrona and engraved by U.S. Mint sculptor-engraver John Mercanti. It shows a right-facing eagle surmounting the YA logo with stars in the field. The three obverse designs were chosen from among 17,000 submitted by American youngsters in a national competition, and were executed by sculptor-engravers on the Mint's staff:

The **bronze medal** was designed by 15-year-old Erac Priester of St. Augustine, Florida, and engraved by Edgar Z. Steever. It shows the Space Shuttle atop the Stars and Stripes.

The **silver medal** was designed by 11-year-old Essan Ni of San Diego, California, and engraved by Jim Licaretz. It shows an astronaut saluting on the moon with the American flag.

The **gold medal** was designed by 12-year-old Brian Kachel of Jersey City, New Jersey, and engraved by Chester Y. Martin. It shows the Space Shuttle in flight on a clear field.

Priester, Ni, and Kachel were honored for their designs at a ceremony at Cape Canaveral.

All three medals were struck at the Philadelphia Mint and bear its P mintmark. They have a more coin-like appearance than many national medals, thanks to the legends UNITED STATES OF AMERICA and LIBERTY arced around the perimeters, and the standardized appearance of the mintmark and year date.

Space-themed medals are a popular topical niche within numismatics. All of the Young Astronauts medals today are worth more than their issue prices (a distinction not every national medal can boast), with the gold and silver medals commanding substantial premiums.

**Young Astronauts silver medal, 1988.**

| 1988 Young Astronauts Medals | | | | | | | | |
|---|---|---|---|---|---|---|---|---|
| Composition | Size | Weight | ASW/AGW* | Format | Mintage | Issue Price | Current Value |
| bronze | 1.5-inch (38.1 mm) | 26 g | — | Unc. | 28,700 | $8.00 | $10 |
| bronze | 1.5-inch (38.1 mm) | 26 g | — | Proof | 17,250 | $11.50 | $15 |
| .900 silver | 1.5-inch (38.1 mm) | 0.86 oz. | 0.77 oz. | Unc. | 15,400 | $28.00 | $45 |
| .900 silver | 1.5-inch (38.1 mm) | 0.86 oz. | 0.77 oz. | Proof | 33,250 | $34.00 | $50 |
| .999 silver | 3-inch (76.2 mm) | 6 oz. | 5.99 oz. | Unc. | 1,075 | $225.00 | $350 |
| .999 silver | 3-inch (76.2 mm) | 12 oz. | 11.99 oz. | Unc. | 3,700 | $325.00 | $600 |
| .900 gold | .875-inch (22.2 mm) | 0.27 oz. | 0.24 oz. | Unc. | 13,000 | $290.00 | $600 |
| .900 gold | .875-inch (22.2 mm) | 0.27 oz. | 0.24 oz. | Proof | 3,400 | $325.00 | $700 |
| .900 gold | 3-inch (76.2 mm) | 12 oz. | 10.8 oz. | Unc. | 38 | $8,950.00 | $20,500 |
| Unc. three-medal set** | | | | | | $315.00 | $650 |

**Young Astronauts gold medal, 1988.**

\* ASW = Actual silver weight; AGW = Actual gold weight. \*\* The Uncirculated three-medal set consisted of the bronze, small silver, and small gold medals in Uncirculated format in a blue box. Other two- and three-medal sets were issued as well, varying in their packaging and which medals were included. Each is worth about the combined retail value of the medals it contains.

# BENJAMIN FRANKLIN FIREFIGHTERS MEDAL (1993)

Public Law 102-406, October 12, 1992, was the Benjamin Franklin National Memorial Commemorative Medal and Fire Service Bill of Rights Act. It authorized up to 1.5 million one-ounce silver medals to be struck to commemorate Franklin's contributions to the American Fire Service (he formed the country's first organized fire company in Philadelphia in 1736). The medal was designed by Mint sculptor-engravers Thomas D. Rogers (obverse) and T. James Ferrell (reverse). It was struck on silver planchets used for American Silver Eagles—with a fineness of .999 silver, and slightly larger than a silver dollar.

Sales started on July 1, 1993, and concluded on June 30, 1994. During an introductory period the Proof was priced at $33 and the Uncirculated at $29. Prices were increased by $3 for the regular sales period. A surcharge of $15 per medal was split among the Benjamin Franklin National Memorial and various firefighting councils, foundations, institutes, and associations. President George Bush signed the act into law at Springfield Township (Pennsylvania) Fire Co. No. 44, on October 12, 1992. "For your bravery and for your unfailing dedication," he said, speaking to the nation's million and a half emergency responders, "I say this from the bottom of my heart: Thank you on behalf of all Americans."

**Benjamin Franklin Firefighters medal, 1993.**

If the Franklin medal had been congressionally authorized as a *coin*, it likely would have enjoyed sales in the hundreds of thousands—as did the commemorative silver dollars of the early 1990s—instead of the tens of thousands. "The Ben Franklin Firefighter medal is an interesting item of historical significance," says coin dealer and longtime Red Book pricing contributor Harry Miller, of Miller's Mint, "but it lacks the credibility of bearing a monetary unit. Such items almost always have a poor track record for value." Coin dealer Julian Leidman, another Red Book contributor, says, "The Ben Franklin and later Mint medals are marketable, but not terribly liquid. Since numismatics is a luxury, coin dealers are at the mercy of the collecting public." However, he notes, "If they gain in popularity, they will go up in value."

| 1993 Benjamin Franklin Firefighters Medal | | | | | | |
|---|---|---|---|---|---|---|
| Composition | Size | Actual Silver Weight | Format | Mintage | Issue Price | Current Value |
| .999 silver | 1.6-inch (40.6 mm) | 1 oz. | Unc. | 26,011 | $32.00 | $38 |
| .999 silver | 1.6-inch (40.6 mm) | 1 oz. | Proof | 89,311 | $36.00 | $43 |

# PHILADELPHIA MINT COINAGE BICENTENNIAL MEDAL (1993)

"A truly unique collector's item. Presenting THE PHILADELPHIA SET. Commemorating U.S. Mint history." Thus did the Mint advertise a new numismatic package in 1993, part of which was a unique silver medal. "Specially created for 1993 is The Philadelphia Set. It includes the one-half, one-quarter, and one-tenth ounce American Eagle Proof gold coins; the one-ounce silver coin; and a special silver medal commemorating the 200th anniversary of the first official U.S. coins at the Philadelphia Mint—all bearing the 'P' mint mark. We plan to offer this unique collection only in 1993, the first year the silver one-ounce coin is being minted in Philadelphia. Next year, the minting of the gold fractional coins will move from the Philadelphia Mint to the West Point Mint. You won't want to miss this special numismatic opportunity."

Nearly 13,000 collectors took the Mint up on its offer. Packaged in a green velvet box with a certificate of authenticity, the set was issue-priced at $499. Today the silver medal alone is worth a good portion of that original cost, and the entire set sells for nearly $2,000.

The Philadelphia Mint Bicentennial silver medal was struck on a .900 fine planchet the size of a silver dollar. The obverse shows a rendering of the famous John Ward Dunsmore painting of Martha Washington inspecting the first coins from the Mint. (For the full story of this painting, see the award-winning *Secret History of the First U.S. Mint: How Frank H. Stewart Destroyed—and Then Saved—a National Treasure*, by Joel Orosz and Leonard Augsburger.) The reverse features a spiraling montage of U.S. coins dating from the 1790s to the 1990s.

Many of the silver medals (and the accompanying American Silver Eagle) have toned over the years from exposure to the heavy green cardboard of the set's packaging. The resulting coloration can be dramatic and visually appealing—of course with beauty being in the eye of the coin holder.

Philadelphia Mint Coinage Bicentennial medal, 1993.

| 1993 Philadelphia Mint Coinage Bicentennial Medal | | | | | | |
|---|---|---|---|---|---|---|
| Composition | Size | Actual Silver Weight | Format | Mintage | Issue Price | Current Value |
| .900 silver | 1.5-inch (38.1 mm) | 0.76 oz. | Proof | 12,869 | (a) | $125 |

a. The medal was available only as part of the 1993 Philadelphia Set, which was available from the Mint for $499.

# NATIONAL WILDLIFE REFUGE SYSTEM CENTENNIAL MEDALS (2003)

In 2003 the U.S. Mint released what it described as its first-ever *series* of silver national medals, to celebrate the 100th anniversary of the National Wildlife Refuge System. Sales of the medals started on July 24 with the Bald Eagle variety, available in bronze and silver formats. The Salmon, Elk, and Canvasback Duck varieties were released successively every few weeks after that. (Production and distribution delays pushed delivery of some of the issues into 2004, though all were dated 2003.) The bronze Bald Eagle had no mintage limit; the silver Bald Eagle was limited to 35,000 medals; and each of the other silver medals was limited to 25,000.

"The silver medals . . . are finished in a similar fashion to that of Proof coins, which feature distinctive matte-finish artwork on a mirror-finish background," Mint spokesman Michael White said on July 11. "The medals will be the first United States Mint products to use laser technology." Some early strikes of the silver medals were not as heavily frosted as later issues, with less pronounced cameo contrast between the fields and the design devices. This transition was caused by the Mint experimenting with its laser technology (as opposed to traditional sandblasting) for texturing the dies. The laser technique would later be used in the Mint's annual Proof sets and various commemorative coins.

The medals are plain-edged (not reeded). The obverse common to all varieties was designed by Mint sculptor-engraver Norman E. Nemeth. It shows a standing portrait of President Theodore Roosevelt, the founder of the National Wildlife Refuge System, who designated Florida's Pelican Island as the first wildlife refuge in March 1903. Since then the system of public lands and waters set aside to conserve fish, animals, and plants has grown to more than 560 units, plus 38 wetland management districts of more than 150 million acres. The animals on the medals (bald eagle designed by Donna Weaver; salmon designed by John Mercanti; elk designed by Al Maletsky; and canvasback duck designed by T. James Ferrell) represent the biological diversity of the national refuge system. "These designs celebrate the priceless natural treasures of our nation," said U.S. Mint Director Henrietta Holsman Fore, "and the legacy of a pioneering, visionary president who a century ago recognized the value of conserving this nation's precious resources."

A portion of the proceeds from the sale of the medals—10 percent of each silver medal and 5 percent of each bronze—benefited the National Fish and Wildlife Foundation and its conservation efforts.

**National Wildlife Refuge System Centennial medal, 2003. (common obverse)**

**Bald Eagle reverse.**

**Salmon reverse.**

**Elk reverse.**

**Canvasback Duck reverse.**

The Mint offered a subscription program for the silver medals (excluding the bronze), so collectors could receive them automatically as they became available. The medals were struck at the Philadelphia Mint without a mint-mark. Silver strikes were encapsulated in plastic and packaged in presentation cases; bronze strikes in Mylar® pouches. They came with a certificate of authenticity from the director of the Mint.

Interest was very high for these medals, with collectors excitedly discussing them online and in the hobby newspapers, and eagerly awaiting their purchases to arrive from the Mint. In the late-2003 and early-2004 aftermarket the silver medals were selling for multiples of their $29.50 issue price, sometimes for more than $100 apiece. Some sellers who had orders confirmed by the Mint offered them for resale even before the medals were in hand. All of the designs sold out within several months of their issue.

In the *2003 United States Mint Annual Report*, Director Fore reported that the National Wildlife Refuge System Centennial Medal Series "sold out in record-setting time." As of September 30, 2004, the National Fish and Wildlife Foundation received $304,000 from the sale of the medals.

The Mint made the bronze Eagle medal available in its product catalog for years. It was included in the 2008 Bald Eagle Coin and Medal set (along with a 2008 Bald Eagle Recovery and National Emblem commemorative silver dollar, Uncirculated), and in the 2013 Theodore Roosevelt Coin and Chronicles Set.

The secondary market cooled with time as the medals filtered into the hobby community and settled into their long-term homes. Today, more than a decade after their release, the Wildlife Refuge silver medals can be collected for close to (or sometimes even below) their original issue prices. Coin dealer Troy Thoreson, a bullion specialist who contributes pricing to the *Guide Book of United States Coins*, says, "Of all the medals produced by the U.S. Mint in recent decades, the 2003 National Wildlife Refuge System Centennial silver medals stand out in my opinion as some of the most beautiful, especially the Canvasback Duck and Elk medals. The attention to detail and quality is very impressive and rarely seen. These medals remain very affordable in today's market, even with low mintages."

| 2003 National Wildlife Refuge System Centennial Medals | | | | | | | |
|---|---|---|---|---|---|---|---|
| Type | Composition | Size | Actual Silver Weight | Format | Mintage | Issue Price | Current Value |
| Bald Eagle | bronze | 1.5-inch (38.1 mm) | — | Unc. | (a) | $4.50 | $5 |
| Bald Eagle | .900 silver | 1.5-inch (38.1 mm) | 0.76 oz. | prooflike | 35,000 | $29.50 | $27 |
| Salmon | .900 silver | 1.5-inch (38.1 mm) | 0.76 oz. | prooflike | 25,000 | $29.50 | $29 |
| Elk | .900 silver | 1.5-inch (38.1 mm) | 0.76 oz. | prooflike | 25,000 | $29.50 | $28.50 |
| Canvasback Duck | .900 silver | 1.5-inch (38.1 mm) | 0.76 oz. | prooflike | 25,000 | $29.50 | $28 |

a. The Mint established no production limit for the bronze medal. Mintage was ongoing into the early 2010s. At least 22,000 were distributed as part of the Mint's 2008 Bald Eagle Coin and Medal Set, and at least 15,000 in the 2013 Theodore Roosevelt Coin and Chronicles Set.

# U.S. Mint Rittenhouse Medal for Excellence (2008 to Date)

The Rittenhouse Medal for Excellence, begun in 2008, is an internal award named for the first director of the U.S. Mint, David Rittenhouse, a leading American scientist who was appointed by President George Washington. Rittenhouse served as director for the critical first three years of the Mint's existence. During his tenure he set a high standard of excellence that today's Mint workers aspire to achieve. The bureau's goal is to be recognized as the finest mint organization in the world through excellence in its people, products, customer service, and workplace. The Rittenhouse Medal for Excellence recognizes employees across the organization who have significantly furthered and ultimately improved Mint programs, operations, and services. Through the Rittenhouse Medal awards program the Mint honors the legacy of its famous first director.

Each year an award may be given to Mint employees (individuals or teams) in any or all of these categories, for "sustained superior performance": customer service; safety; innovation; sustainability; craftsmanship; security and law enforcement; and supervisory leadership. Rittenhouse Medal for Excellence recognition is also given in the categories of the Emerging Leader Award; Excellent Contributions by a New Employee; and the Model Employee Award.

Award ceremonies usually take place at Mint headquarters in Washington, DC, with the Mint's director (or acting director or principal deputy director) acting as master of ceremonies, and with remarks by the treasurer of the United States and other dignitaries. Plant managers (in the past called *superintendents*), field chiefs, and team leaders from the different mints typically present the awards.

Examples of recent Rittenhouse Medal awardees include:

Sergeant **Jackson S. Chan**, of the Office of Protection, San Francisco Mint. Sergeant Chan's professionalism and dedication were key to the San Francisco Mint Police achieving a first-time personnel qualification rate of 100 percent during the transition to the Smith & Wesson M&P .45-caliber pistol and Colt M4 rifle, while incurring zero unintended discharges or weapons or other safety violations or concerns. He researched best practices for training and further supported the transition by becoming a certified armorer, allowing immediate corrective maintenance and repair on site. He exemplified U.S. Mint Strategic Goal #4: "Foster a safe, engaged, and innovative workforce." Chan was awarded the 2012 Rittenhouse Medal for Excellence in Security and Law Enforcement on June 12, 2013.

**Thomas Jurkowsky**, director of the Office of Corporate Communications. Jurkowsky planned the Public Tour Upgrade Project for the Philadelphia Mint and was a key supervisor and facilitator throughout its three-year, $3.9 million (on time and within budget) creative design, fabrication, and installation. The Mint's public tour now provides a fresh, interactive, educational, and engaging experience to some 250,000 visitors annually. Other Mint employees awarded the Rittenhouse Medal for Excellence for this project included **Dean Bidle**, Finance Department, Washington; **Albert Croce**, Plant Engineering Division, Philadelphia Mint; **Raymond Dibble**, Procurement and Support Services Division, Washington; **Robert Goler**, Sales and Marketing Department, Washington; **Timothy Grant**, Exhibits Division, Philadelphia Mint; **Mary Lhotsky**, Sales and Marketing Department, Washington; **Anthony**

The annually awarded
Rittenhouse Medal
for Excellence.

**Mallamaci**, Plant Engineering Division, Philadelphia Mint; **Michael Smith**, Procurement and Support Services Division, Washington; and **April Stafford**, Office of Design and Engraving, Washington. All received the 2012 Rittenhouse Medal for Excellence in Customer Service on June 12, 2013.

**Joe Vasquez** of the Manufacturing Department, San Francisco Mint. Vasquez was instrumental in helping the facility develop a Visual Coin Alignment Tool (V-CAT) to quickly and easily measure coin alignment within +/-1 degree. This reduced the measuring time by 80 percent—from 2.5 minutes per coin to 30 seconds or less. Vasquez was awarded the 2012 Rittenhouse Medal for Excellence in Innovation on June 12, 2013. Two years later he would be awarded the 2014 medal for Excellence in Sustainability as part of the San Francisco Water Conservation and Blank Process Improvement Team, which reduced the Mint's water consumption by 126,785 gallons per month.

**Terry D. Michel** of the Manufacturing Department, Denver Mint. Michel was awarded the 2014 Rittenhouse Medal for Excellence in Craftsmanship for improving preventive maintenance at the Denver Mint, resulting in equipment down-time of less than 5 percent and an 81 percent coin press Overall Equipment Efficiency rating. "He embodies the Mint's priorities of safety, quality, delivery, and cost," said Principal Deputy Director Matthew R. Jeppson at the June 30, 2015, awards presentation.

**Dennis Flaherty** of the Manufacturing Department, West Point Mint. Flaherty's expertise in Proof coin polishing techniques resulted in improved appearance of the Baseball Hall of Fame commemoratives. He also developed a new technique of using custom-cut laser tape to protect die art during polishing, which dramatically streamlined the polishing process, saving man-hours and cutting the die scrap rate by more than half. He was awarded the 2014 Rittenhouse Medal for Excellence in Craftsmanship on June 30, 2015.

The Fort Knox Bullion Depository maintenance team, including **Thomas Trigg**, **Stanley King**, **Eric Dean**, **Michael Rothman**, and **John Iacono**, all of the Fort Knox Protection Department. They developed a self-sufficient approach to preventive maintenance checks and services that reduced reliance on outside contractors and resources. The team received the 2014 Rittenhouse Medal for Excellence in Innovation on June 30, 2015.

The Rittenhouse Medal is struck from one-ounce American Silver Eagle planchets on a Gräbener GMP 360 press at the Philadelphia Mint (the same press used to strike commemorative silver dollars). The medals are struck in Proof format with cameo contrast. Their dies are thinly chrome-plated and feature sandblasted devices and inscriptions against mirror-polished fields. Each planchet receives three strikes at 202 metric tons of pressure. The medal's obverse and reverse are both based on William Barber's circa-1871 designs for the Medal Series of the U.S. Mint (likely first sold by the Mint to collectors starting in 1874). The obverse shows a profile portrait of Rittenhouse with the start and end years of his service as director of the Mint (1792–1795). The reverse features a quote, "He belonged to the whole human race," along with his birth year of 1732 and death year of 1796.

Because these medals are of a personal nature, most if not all reside in permanent family collections and they will rarely if ever be seen on the secondary market, at least for several generations. For that reason the Rittenhouse Medal for Excellence can be considered non-collectible and priceless.

| U.S. Mint Rittenhouse Medal for Excellence | | | | | | |
|---|---|---|---|---|---|---|
| Composition | Size | Actual Silver Weight | Format | Mintage | Issue Price | Current Value |
| .999 silver | 1.6-inch (40.6 mm) | 1 oz. | Proof | ~300 | n/a | — |

# SEPTEMBER 11, 2011, NATIONAL MEDAL (2011)

On September 11, 2001, nearly 3,000 people were killed in terrorist attacks at three sites in the United States. Most died in and around the World Trade Center in lower Manhattan, from the suicide collisions of two airplanes into the Twin Towers; some perished from a plane crashing into the Pentagon in Arlington, Virginia, across the Potomac River from the nation's capital; and others in a thwarted attack and subsequent plane crash in a rural field in Shanksville, Pennsylvania. Hundreds of courageous first responders risked their lives to save others, many of them perishing in the performance of their sworn duties.

On June 20, 2011, the U.S. Mint started accepting orders for a new silver national medal to mark the 10th anniversary of the September 11, 2011, terror attacks. With Public Law 111-221, President Barack Obama had authorized the "National September 11 Memorial & Museum Commemorative Medal Act of 2010," allowing the minting and issuance of up to two million one-ounce silver medals in commemoration of the establishment of the National September 11 Memorial & Museum at the World Trade Center site.

The medal was designed by U.S. Mint Artistic Infusion Program Master Designer Donna Weaver (obverse and reverse) and sculpted by medallic sculptors Phebe Hemphill (obverse) and Joseph Menna (reverse). It was struck in Proof format. On the obverse, Lady Liberty holds the Lamp of Remembrance, while behind her are two towers of light stretching into the sky. These elements "symbolize not only the immeasurable loss on that fateful day, but also the resiliency and triumph of those who persevered," the Mint announced. The obverse legends are ALWAYS REMEMBER and the dual dates of 2001–2011. On the reverse is an eagle, symbolizing the strength of the survivors, their families, emergency responders, and the nation as a whole, against a backdrop of cascading water. The flowing water represents peace, serenity, healing, and the continuity of life. The reverse legends are HONOR and HOPE.

The Mint announced that approximately half of the medals would be struck at the West Point Mint (featuring the W mintmark) and half at the Philadelphia Mint (with the P mintmark), with customers able to purchase one or both options. No household order limit was established. Sales concluded on December 17, 2012.

A $10 surcharge collected from the sale of each medal was paid to the National September 11 Memorial & Museum, a private not-for-profit organization overseeing the design and funding of the memorial and museum at the World Trade Center site. The funds supported the museum's operations and, once it was completed, its maintenance. "This medal's design is intended

September 11, 2011, national medal.

to exalt the memory of those who sacrificed their lives or were injured," said United States Treasurer Rosie Rios at a launch ceremony at the 9/11 Memorial Preview Site on June 20, "and the families who continue to show dignity and strength in the face of terrible loss."

| 2011 September 11, 2011, National Medal | | | | | | | |
|---|---|---|---|---|---|---|---|
| Mint | Composition | Size | Actual Silver Weight | Format | Mintage | Issue Price | Current Value |
| Philadelphia | .999 silver | 1.6-inch (40.6 mm) | 1 oz. | Proof | ~67,928 (a) | $66.95* | $60 |
| West Point | .999 silver | 1.6-inch (40.6 mm) | 1 oz. | Proof | ~109,365 (b) | $66.95* | $55 |

* An introductory sales price of $56.95 was in effect from June 20 to August 18, 2011. After 5 p.m. Eastern Time on August 18 a new price of $66.95 went into effect. **a.** The Philadelphia Mint struck 95,072 medals as of September 30, 2012 (source: "Commemorative Coin Reform Act Report to Congress, Fiscal Year 2011 Third Quarter–Fiscal Year 2012 Fourth Quarter [April 1, 2011–September 30, 2012]"). Some were rejected and some were unsold. The mintage figure here represents coins sold by the end of sales in December 2012. **b.** The West Point Mint struck 141,602 medals as of September 30, 2012. Some were rejected and some were unsold. The mintage figure here represents coins sold by the end of sales in December 2012.

# THEODORE ROOSEVELT SILVER PRESIDENTIAL MEDAL (2013)

On December 17, 2013, the U.S. Mint released a Coin and Chronicles Set honoring President Theodore Roosevelt. It included a 2013-S Proof Roosevelt Presidential dollar; a 2003 National Wildlife Refuge System Centennial bronze medal; a 4 x 6–inch print honoring the president's military service; a booklet with educational information about his life and legacy; and a .999 fine one-ounce silver Presidential medal.

This marked the first time the Mint struck a Presidential medal in .999 fine silver. The medal's planchets were the same as those used for American Silver Eagle bullion coins. The obverse fea-

**2013 Theodore Roosevelt Presidential medal.**

tures Roosevelt's portrait facing left, in pince-nez glasses, by U.S. Mint Chief Engraver Charles E. Barber. The reverse, by Assistant Engraver George T. Morgan, shows Columbia with her right hand resting on a column bearing a cinerary urn. The fasces on the column symbolizes the authority of the federal government. The U.S. Capitol is visible in the background, and the legends give the dates of Roosevelt's presidential service.

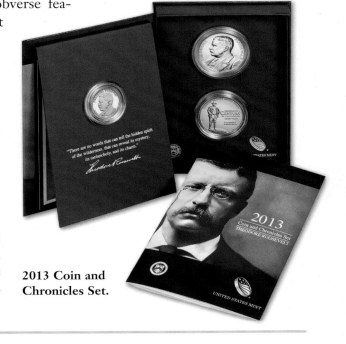

**2013 Coin and Chronicles Set.**

| 2013 Theodore Roosevelt Silver Presidential Medal | | | | | | |
|---|---|---|---|---|---|---|
| Composition | Size | Actual Silver Weight | Format | Mintage | Issue Price | Current Value |
| .999 silver | 1.6-inch (40.6 mm) | 1 oz. | Unc.* | ~15,144 | (a) | $50 |

\* A regular strike, not Burnished or Proof. **a.** The medal was available only as part of the 2013 Coin and Chronicles Set, which was available from the Mint for $57.95.

# FRANKLIN D. ROOSEVELT SILVER PRESIDENTIAL MEDAL (2014)

"FDR fan?" the U.S. Mint asked collectors when it rolled out its 2014 Coin and Chronicles Set on December 22 of that year. The year's set included a rich variety of Franklin Roosevelt memorabilia "perfect for the coin collector, history buff, or as a special gift." It included a Proof 2014-S Roosevelt Presidential dollar; a Proof 2014-S Roosevelt dime; four postage stamps (showing Hyde Park, Little White House, the White House, and Norman Rockwell's "Four Freedoms"); a bronze 1-5/16–inch bronze Presidential medal; and a .999 fine silver Presidential medal. It also came with a companion booklet with images from FDR's life and presidency.

**2014 Coin and Chronicles Set.**

The 2014 Roosevelt silver Presidential medal recreates a memorial piece designed by U.S. Mint Chief Engraver John R. Sinnock in 1945. The fields are artfully textured. On the obverse is Sinnock's strong profile portrait of President Roosevelt. On the reverse, a seated woman draped in robes, symbolizing the nation in mourning, drops a memorial wreath into the ocean. On the left is a sailing ship in departure, representing the late president, who died before he could see the Allies triumph in World War II. To the right is a field of graveyard crosses. The legends are FOR COUNTRY AND HUMANITY and IN MEMORIAM, along with Roosevelt's inaugural and death dates.

There was a production limit of 20,000 sets.

**2014 Franklin D. Roosevelt Presidential medal.**

| 2014 Franklin D. Roosevelt Silver Presidential Medal | | | | | | |
|---|---|---|---|---|---|---|
| Composition | Size | Actual Silver Weight | Format | Mintage | Issue Price | Current Value |
| .999 silver | 1.6-inch (40.6 mm) | 1 oz. | Unc.* | ~20,000 | (a) | $45 |

\* A regular strike, not Burnished or Proof. a. The medal was available only as part of the 2014 Coin and Chronicles Set, which was available from the Mint for $57.95.

# HARRY S. TRUMAN SILVER PRESIDENTIAL MEDAL (2015)

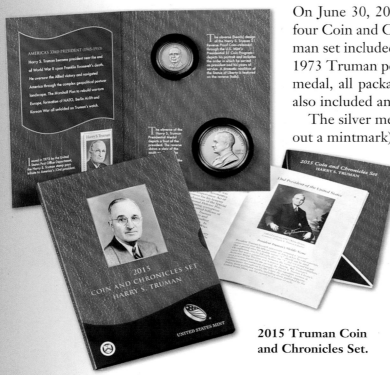

**2015 Truman Coin and Chronicles Set.**

On June 30, 2015, the U.S. Mint opened sales of the first of four Coin and Chronicles sets for that year. The Harry S. Truman set included a 2015-P Reverse Proof Presidential dollar, a 1973 Truman postage stamp, and a .999 fine silver Presidential medal, all packaged in a textured soft-touch display folder. It also included an informative booklet about the president's life.

The silver medal was struck at the Philadelphia Mint (without a mintmark) from planchets of the type used for American Silver Eagles. Maximum production was lower than for the previous year's Coin and Chronicles Set—17,000 units instead of 20,000—and the Mint established a sales limit of five sets per household. The Mint based its production limit on the sales track record of the preceding Coin and Chronicles sets. However, the Truman set had a built-in element of much higher demand: it was the only way collectors could acquire the Reverse Proof Presidential dollar. As 12 noon on June 30 approached and the clock ticked down, collectors nationwide hovered their fingers over the "Place Order" button on the Mint's Web site. "Give 'Em Hell Harry" lived up to his name as thousands of orders quickly flooded in, but the Mint's computer servers and ordering system survived the tide. The inventory of 16,780 sets sold out within 15 minutes of the opening of sales. (The rest were kept on hand to fulfill any exchanges.)

The obverse of the silver Presidential medal features U.S. Mint Chief Engraver John R. Sinnock's bust portrait of Harry S. Truman. The reverse shows a view of the south portico of the White House after reconstruction, surmounted by the Presidential Seal, with Truman's inaugural dates below.

**2015 Harry S. Truman Presidential medal.**

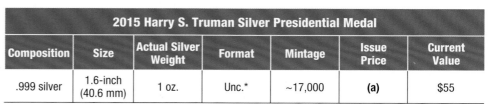

| 2015 Harry S. Truman Silver Presidential Medal | | | | | | |
|---|---|---|---|---|---|---|
| Composition | Size | Actual Silver Weight | Format | Mintage | Issue Price | Current Value |
| .999 silver | 1.6-inch (40.6 mm) | 1 oz. | Unc.* | ~17,000 | (a) | $55 |

* A regular strike, not Burnished or Proof. **a.** The medal was available only as part of the 2015 Truman Coin and Chronicles Set, which was available from the Mint for $57.95.

# DWIGHT D. EISENHOWER SILVER PRESIDENTIAL MEDAL (2015)

The second of four 2015 Coin and Chronicles sets went on sale August 11. Honoring President Dwight David Eisenhower, this package included a 2015-P Reverse Proof Presidential dollar (available only within the set), a 1969 commemorative postage stamp, a booklet with a history of Eisenhower's life and presidency, and a .999 fine silver Presidential medal.

Production of the Eisenhower set was capped at 17,000, the same as for the earlier-issued Harry S. Truman set. The latter had sold out within 15 minutes, due to collector demand for the Reverse Proof dollar, which was available exclusively in that set. In a move to guarantee broad distribution of the Eisenhower set, the Mint lowered the ordering limit from five per household to two. Its inventory sold out within minutes of the start of sales at 12 noon Eastern Time on August 11.

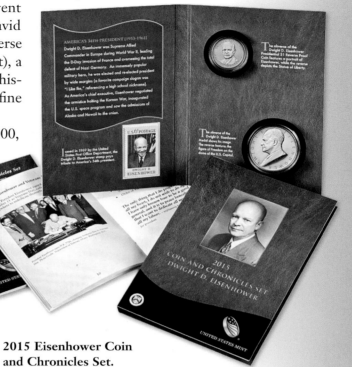

The Eisenhower silver medals were struck on planchets used for American Silver Eagle bullion coins, slightly larger than a silver dollar and of finer silver. They were produced at the Philadelphia Mint.

**2015 Eisenhower Coin and Chronicles Set.**

The obverse features U.S. Mint Chief Engraver Gilroy Roberts's 1954 profile portrait of President Eisenhower. The reverse shows Frank Gasparro's rendering of the statue *Freedom*, which stands atop the dome of the U.S. Capitol, with Western pioneers, a farmer and horses, and a city skyline in the background.

| 2015 Dwight D. Eisenhower Silver Presidential Medal | | | | | | |
|---|---|---|---|---|---|---|
| Composition | Size | Actual Silver Weight | Format | Mintage | Issue Price | Current Value |
| .999 silver | 1.6-inch (40.6 mm) | 1 oz. | Unc.* | ~17,000 | (a) | $55 |

\* A regular strike, not Burnished or Proof. **a.** The medal was available only as part of the 2015 Eisenhower Coin and Chronicles Set, which was available from the Mint for $57.95.

**2015 Dwight D. Eisenhower Presidential medal.**

# JOHN F. KENNEDY SILVER PRESIDENTIAL MEDAL (2015)

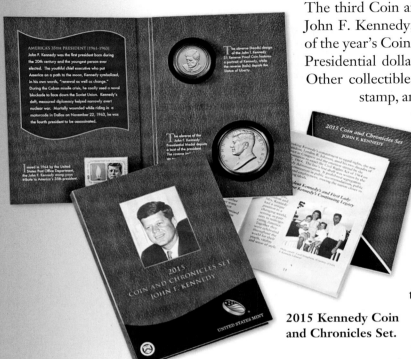

The third Coin and Chronicles set of 2015 was that of President John F. Kennedy, released for sale on September 16. As with all of the year's Coin and Chronicles sets, it included a Reverse Proof Presidential dollar that was available exclusively in this product. Other collectibles in the Kennedy set included a 1964 postage stamp, an informative booklet, and a .999 silver Presidential medal.

**2015 Kennedy Coin and Chronicles Set.**

Production of the Kennedy set was limited to 50,000—an increase over the 17,000 of the year's Truman and Eisenhower sets. The Mint had adjusted its mintage plans after the earlier sets completely sold out within minutes of being offered for sale. Orders were again limited to two per household, to encourage broad distribution. By September 20 the Mint's inventory was close to a sellout, with 48,462 sets recorded as sold.

The silver Kennedy medals were struck on American Silver Eagle planchets, 40.6 mm in diameter and containing a full troy ounce of silver. They were minted in Philadelphia without a P mintmark. On the obverse is U.S. Mint Chief Engraver Gilroy Roberts's profile portrait of President Kennedy, which Roberts finished after showing Kennedy early models and getting his feedback. (After the president's assassination Roberts would base his design for the Kennedy half dollar on this portrait.) The medal's reverse, by Frank Gasparro, depicts the Presidential Seal with burning torches and a quote from Kennedy's inaugural address: "We shall pay any price, bear any burden, meet any hardship, support any friend, oppose any foe to assure the survival of liberty."

**2015 John F. Kennedy Presidential medal.**

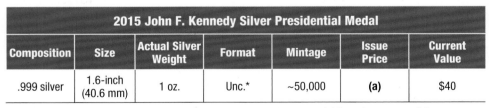

| 2015 John F. Kennedy Silver Presidential Medal | | | | | | |
|---|---|---|---|---|---|---|
| Composition | Size | Actual Silver Weight | Format | Mintage | Issue Price | Current Value |
| .999 silver | 1.6-inch (40.6 mm) | 1 oz. | Unc.* | ~50,000 | (a) | $40 |

\* A regular strike, not Burnished or Proof. **a.** The medal was available only as part of the 2015 Kennedy Coin and Chronicles Set, which was available from the Mint for $57.95.

# LYNDON B. JOHNSON SILVER PRESIDENTIAL MEDAL (2015)

The fourth and final Coin and Chronicles set of 2015 was that of President Lyndon B. Johnson, which debuted on October 27. As with the year's three earlier Coin and Chronicles products, it included a Reverse Proof Presidential dollar that was available exclusively within the set. Other collectibles in the Johnson set included a 1973 commemorative postage stamp, an illustrated historical booklet, and a .999 silver Presidential medal.

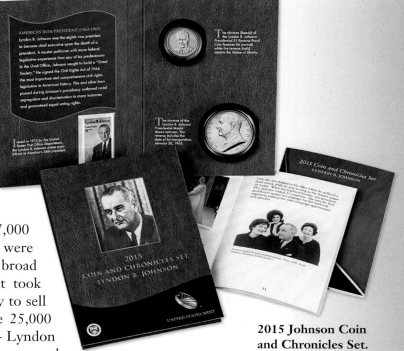

The Mint limited production of the Johnson set to 25,000 units—half that of the Kennedy set, but an increase over the 17,000 of the Truman and Eisenhower sets. Orders were limited to two per household, to help ensure broad distribution among interested collectors. It took less than four hours for the Mint's inventory to sell out. "The United States Mint has sold the 25,000 units of the 2015 Coin and Chronicles Set – Lyndon B. Johnson," the Mint announced. "All accepted orders will be processed and fulfilled on a first-in, first-served basis according to existing United States Mint policies. The product inventory is at the fulfillment center for immediate shipment to customers. No additional inventory will be produced. Product shipments, returns, and exchanges will be monitored daily over the next few weeks."

The silver Johnson medals were struck on American Silver Eagle planchets, slightly larger than a silver dollar in diameter and containing a full troy ounce of precious metal. They were produced at the Philadelphia Mint without a P mintmark. On the obverse is U.S. Mint Chief Engraver Gilroy Roberts's first-term profile portrait of President Johnson. The medal's reverse, by Frank Gasparro, shows the Presidential Seal and a quote: "We will serve all the nation; a united people with a united purpose."

**2015 Johnson Coin and Chronicles Set.**

**2015 Lyndon B. Johnson Presidential medal.**

| 2015 Lyndon B. Johnson Silver Presidential Medal | | | | | | |
|---|---|---|---|---|---|---|
| Composition | Size | Actual Silver Weight | Format | Mintage | Issue Price | Current Value |
| .999 silver | 1.6-inch (40.6 mm) | 1 oz. | Unc.* | ~25,000 | (a) | $40 |

\* A regular strike, not Burnished or Proof. **a.** The medal was available only as part of the 2015 Johnson Coin and Chronicles Set, which was available from the Mint for $57.95.

# A
# Investing in Gold and Silver

Silver and gold can be intelligent choices for a diversified portfolio of investments. As with any investment, there is a level of risk involved in buying, holding, and selling precious metals. General caveats that apply to all investing naturally apply to the bullion and rare-coin markets, along with some warnings unique to these fields. The advice in this appendix is derived from guidelines recommended by the Securities and Exchange Commission, the Commodity Futures Exchange Commission, and other federal and state regulatory agencies, as well as the insight and experience of professional coin dealers and numismatists. This advice is addressed mainly toward the investor in *gold*, but it applies to silver, platinum, palladium, and other precious metals as well.

## SOME GUIDELINES FOR PRECIOUS-METAL INVESTORS

**Keep a healthy level of skepticism.** It's the oldest advice in the investment world: If something appears too good to be true, it probably is. If an insider had access to a fail-safe investment, or an incredible bargain, or a guaranteed profit, why would he offer it to anyone else? Carefully investigate any claims of "secret," "new," or unusual ways of extracting or mining gold. Beware sensationalistic hard-sell tactics that rely on fear, e.g., threats of the federal government seizing privately owned gold, or the imminent collapse of civilization leading to the U.S. dollar losing all value.

**Use common sense.** Just as you would be suspicious of a door-to-door sales-man who appeared on your front step offering expensive investments, you should be wary of unsolicited mail, email, or telephone offers to sell you bullion or gold-investment products (such as rare coins or certificates or stock in gold mines). Take common-sense steps to avoid identity theft (for example, never giving your Social Security number, bank-account information, or other financial details over the phone to unknown parties).

**Deal with people and firms you trust.** Deal only with professional sellers you feel comfortable with, and whom you've vetted for trustworthiness. Get neutral, third-party advice from a knowledgeable and trusted friend or associate. Investigate a seller's membership in business organizations such as the Professional Numismatists Guild (www.PNGdealers.com). Are they registered with the SEC or a state securities agency? Has the Better Business Bureau logged any complaints about them? If you search for their name on the Internet plus the word *lawsuit*, do you find anything disturbing?

**Learn as much as you can.** Don't give in to pressure to make an immediate buying decision, or to make a decision with information missing. Take your time and learn before you buy ("Investigate before you invest"). Almost any "opportunity" offered today will still be available next week, and the same opportunity may be offered at a lower price elsewhere. If possible, ascertain the seller's profit margin (how much they buy gold for, versus their selling price). Verify claims made by the seller through your own research, and if you have questions, ask for clarification.

**Look for guarantees of quality.** Most gold bullion coins bear marks of their fineness and weight, as do many bars, ingots, rounds, and similar non–legal-tender gold instruments. Ask potential sellers if they guarantee the fineness and weight of their products.

**Understand the terms and details of your investment.** Some sellers add hidden fees and expenses to the base cost of the gold bullion and coins they sell. Refining and assay charges, shipping and handling fees, storage fees, insurance fees, and sales commissions are some ways a seller might increase your expense. Study all terms of sale and understand delivery and other details.

**Be mindful of taxes and reporting.** Your state might charge a sales tax or a use tax on gold bullion purchases. Also be aware that the IRS has reporting requirements for large sales of precious metals (more than 20 ounces). A tax professional will be able to guide you on current laws and how they apply to your situation. Some bullion coins can be included in Individual Retirement Accounts; others are not eligible.

**Know your own comfort level with risk.** Analyze whether you can afford to invest in a tangible asset such as gold, and to risk a reasonable potential loss. The price of precious metals has risen in some periods and has fallen in others.

**Look for a two-way market.** Modern bullion coins such as those produced by the U.S. Mint are readily *sold* as well as being easily *bought*. Other forms of gold, such as privately minted medallions, or scrap gold, might be harder to sell after you buy them, or might be sold easily only for a discount. If a non-standard form of gold needs to be assayed before you can sell it, the expense will eat into any profits.

**Always take possession.** Some firms will offer to sell you gold and then securely store it for you. While this might seem like a good idea, most professional coin dealers encourage taking physical possession of your gold and storing it yourself, in a bank safe deposit box or other secure place under your personal control. This allows you to avoid fraud—in the case of a seller who oversells his actual inventory—and gives you more immediate access to your gold in emergencies. Insurance for safe deposit boxes is inexpensive.

**Make sure your precious metals are secure.** A safe deposit box is very secure, can hold a large bullion investment in a small space, and is affordable. If you store your gold or silver at home, take common-sense security precautions: install an alarm system and strong locks, secure your doors and windows, invest in a good fireproof safe, and don't let people know that you keep coins or bullion at home.

**Know the pros and cons of different forms of precious metal.** Some of these are discussed in chapter 3. Modern bullion coins—legal-tender gold or silver pieces minted by a government and guaranteed as to weight and fineness—often are bought, sold, and traded much more easily than ingots, bars, medals, jewelry, nuggets, and the like. Larger gold *bars* will sometimes require an independent assay for resale, to authenticate their gold content. Smaller bars, weighing one ounce or up to five ounces, can have higher liquidity, especially those manufactured by a recognized refiner such as Credit Suisse or Engelhard. Older foreign gold coins often trade similarly to bullion, with a buy-sell spread based on their gold content (with no additional numismatic value despite their age).

**Purchase strategically.** If you invest in the stock market through a mutual fund or other means, you're probably familiar with the concept of dollar cost-averaging. This is a strategy that reduces the impact of volatility on large purchases by dividing the total sum of your investment into smaller amounts put into the market at regular intervals. Taking a steady, long-term approach to bullion purchases won't always maximize profits, but it helps reduce downside risk. For example, if you invest a lump sum of $12,000 to buy 10 ounces of gold at $1,200 per ounce, you risk the metal's spot value slowly declining to, say, $900 per ounce over the course of 12 months. This brings a costly downside when you sell a year later. However, if you invest $1,000 per month for 12 months, you'll be buying along with the market, and by the end of the same period your $1,000 will purchase more than one ounce of gold. You'll lose less money when selling than you would have with the single investment of $12,000 at the market's peak.

# SCHEMES TO LOOK OUT FOR

The Securities and Exchange Commission has warned investors about scams involving gold since the metal was made legal to buy again in the early 1970s. "The areas which are fraught with the greatest potential for fraud are representations concerning the existence, amount, and purity of gold, accuracy of assays and geological surveys, and secret refining processes," the SEC reported in December 1974. The following are some schemes that it described at that time, some of which still are concerns today.

> **False mining claims** were used to inflate a company's financial position and to tout its investment merit. Bogus or speculative geological surveys by a purported expert or misleading ore samples were used by the company as the basis for unwarranted high estimates of mineral value.

> Purportedly large quantities of gold located outside of the United States and obtained from underdeveloped countries were being offered in the form of **certificates of ownership** through offshore banks.

> An unscrupulous assayer conspired with a seller to certify that **bars of almost pure lead** were pure gold.

> Gold coins of **low purity** were issued by small foreign entities.

> **Secret processes** were promoted as promising to extract gold from ore previously labeled as worthless. Investors were induced to finance the construction of the secret-process machinery necessary for the production of the gold.

The SEC recommends that victims of fraud consult an attorney to assert and protect their rights if possible, and to report at the federal level to the SEC (which regulates public interstate offerings of and trading in securities related to gold), the Federal Trade Commission (which enforces laws prohibiting unfair or deceptive acts in interstate commerce), the Commodity Futures Trading Commission, the U.S. Postal Service (for mail fraud), and the Department of Justice. On the state and local level, fraud victims can contact the Consumer Protection Division of their state Attorney General's Office, the state Securities Commissioner, and the local Better Business Bureau. Although these agencies cannot intervene in your behalf or offer legal representation to obtain redress of your individual rights, your complaint may prevent others from being defrauded.

# INVESTING IN GOLD AND SILVER COLLECTOR COINS

As the coin-by-coin discussions throughout this book illustrate, the U.S. Mint's modern bullion coins often have a kind of "split personality" in the marketplace and within the hobby community. This can lead to pitfalls for uneducated buyers.

Coins struck purely as *bullion* (not in a limited-edition numismatic format) are intended to be sold for their precious-metal content, as investments, hedges against inflation, a store of value, etc. The U.S. Mint will produce as many bullion coins as the public demands. In essence they should be regarded as commodities, each individual bullion coin being as valuable as every other—no more valuable, no less—just as one bushel of wheat or one barrel of oil is comparable to every other. However, sometimes hobbyists collect these bullion coins more like rare coins: they assemble them into one-per-year or one-of-each-variety coin collections, the way they might collect old Morgan silver dollars or Buffalo nickels; and they seek the finest grades they can find. Third-party grading firms like NGC, PCGS, and ANACS grade and slab the bullion coins just as they do old Liberty Head and Saint-Gaudens double eagles—this despite the fact that the modern coins are struck by the tens or hundreds of thousands (or millions), their quality from coin to coin is nearly perfect and nearly identical, and they're distributed as commodities rather than collectibles.

At the same time, collectors and investors often discuss the Mint's *numismatic* coins—limited-edition Burnished pieces, Proofs, and the like—as if they were bullion. The coins often trade at close to their precious-metal value, sometimes despite having very low mintages. When they're first released, the Mint prices them according to sliding scales based on the market value of their precious metal (a premium is added, but the basis is their spot value). And collectors often perceive the coins' numismatic values more closely in relation to their current bullion values than they would an old Mint State silver dollar or rare-date gold coin.

This blurry kinship between the bullion value and the numismatic value of the Mint's modern silver and gold coins requires you, as a buyer, to be savvy to the modern marketplace. The following caveats are made by professional numismatists:

"**Buy the coin, and not the slab.**" Professional third-party grading firms sometimes release autographed holders, special labels, and slabs that signify a coin was issued at a particular coin convention or other venue, or is an "early strike" or has some other seemingly exotic feature. This kind of special packaging has limited premium value over the long run, in the secondary marketplace. A slab autographed by a coin designer or other famous person might have personal sentimental value, but ask yourself if other collectors will pay a premium for it in the future, and let your own buying be guided by the answer. Usually coin collectors consider only the alphanumeric certified grade (MS-69, PF-70, and the like) and pay little or no premium for extra adjectives.

**Shop around.** Sellers who advertise in non-numismatic media—for example, in full-page mainstream newspaper ads, or on television shopping programs—sometimes have overhead expenses that result in higher retail prices. (In one instance in 2015, a television offer of $700 for a modern U.S. Mint item was five times the price the same item could be bought for on eBay!) Even among numismatic sellers, coin prices can vary. Shop around for competitive pricing; get offers from your local coin shop and from professional coin dealers who advertise in *The Numismatist* (www. money.org/the-numismatist), *Coin World* (www.coinworld.com), *Numismatic News* (www.numismaticnews.net), and other hobby publications.

**Don't overvalue high-grade coins.** The U.S. Mint's modern products, on the whole, enjoy very high production quality. The difference between an MS-69 and MS-70 coin, each professionally graded by a third-party firm, can be visually indistinguishable for the average collector. If you pay a huge premium for the one graded 70, are you getting real value for your money, or are you buying into a fragile bubble that will burst? Older coins struck for circulation, before the mid-1900s, can be very expensive and rare in grades such as MS–68, 69, or 70. Many modern U.S. Mint products such as commemoratives coins and numismatic versions of bullion coins are extremely common in such grades. Be aware of the difference between modern and old.

**Be mindful of collecting vs. investing.** You can collect coins for pleasure, to enjoy their artistry, history, and educational and cultural significance. If you do, as the *Guide Book of United States Coins* advises, "A secondary consideration is that of investment, the profits from which are usually realized over the long term based on careful purchases." In other words, enjoy the hobby and don't expect or worry too much about profiting financially (although it's normal to think about such things).

If, on the other hand, you consider yourself solely to be an *investor* in modern bullion coins: Keep an open mind, learn about the coins you're investing in, and spend some time studying their designs. You might get bitten by the "coin bug" and become a *collector* as well!

# BERNARD BARUCH AND THE 10 RULES OF INVESTING

American financier, stock investor, philanthropist, and statesman Bernard Baruch, in his two-volume 1957 memoir, *My Own Story*, admitted he was hesitant to lay down any magisterial "rules" on investing. However, he did list some points of advice for investing and speculating wisely and with self-discipline:

1. Don't speculate unless you can make it a full-time job.

2. Beware of barbers, beauticians, waiters—or anyone—bringing gifts of "inside" information or "tips."

3. Before you buy a security, find out everything you can about the company, its management and competitors, its earnings and possibilities for growth.

4. Don't try to buy at the bottom and sell at the top. This can't be done—except by liars.

5. Learn how to take your losses quickly and cleanly. Don't expect to be right all the time. If you have made a mistake, cut your losses as quickly as possible.

6. Don't buy too many different securities. Better have only a few investments which can be watched.

7. Make a periodic reappraisal of all your investments to see whether changing developments have altered their prospects.

8. Study your tax position to know when you can sell to greatest advantage.

9. Always keep a good part of your capital in a cash reserve. Never invest all your funds.

10. Don't try to be a jack of all investments. Stick to the field you know best.

Baruch encapsulated this advice in two lessons that experience had taught him: "getting the facts of a situation before acting is of crucial importance," and "getting these facts is a continuous job which requires eternal vigilance."

Today's coin collectors and investors in gold and silver will profit from this shared wisdom.

# B
# The U.S. Assay Commission

A special annual assembly of government officials (and, later, invited citizens) started in the late 1790s, not long after the first U.S. Mint was established in Philadelphia. These dignitaries comprised the United States Assay Commission. Their charge was to review silver and gold coins selected at random from the previous year's mintage. Their goal: to confirm that the nation's coins were of full weight and fineness, conforming with established laws.

The tradition of formally testing coins for purity dates back to medieval England and the "Trial of the Pyx," named for the locked chest that held the sample coins picked each year for adjudication. In those days the risk of a minter illicitly tampering with the nation's coins—debasing their alloy, for example, or reducing their dimensions—was a legitimate threat to the Crown and its treasury. Public confidence rode on the strength of the coin of the realm. In Britain today the jury of the Trial of the Pyx is made up of at least six assayers of the Goldsmiths' Company, operating under the Coinage Act of 1971. Its annual assignment is more symbolic than truly protective—a respectful nod, in this machine age, to an ancient custom.

In the United States the tradition lasted nearly 200 years. The Assay Commission was mandated by the Coinage Act of April 2, 1792; the first Commission gathered on March 20, 1797. Former Commission member David L. Ganz, writing for *The E-Sylum* in 2005, noted that in 1792 the commission was "deemed so essential to the confidence of the public in the national money that section 18 of the legislation directed that the original inspectors were to include the Chief Justice of the United States, the Secretary and Comptroller of the Currency, the Secretary of the Department of State, and the

Attorney General of the United States." The last public meeting was in 1976, and for four more years the ceremony was played out by government employees alone. (Citizen commission members continued to be named, but took no part in those final meetings.) The gatherings ended completely in 1980.

Today there exist tangible and collectible mementoes of this obscure and largely forgotten ceremony. Starting in 1860, the U.S. Mint struck special presentation medals for those attending the annual assay—federal officials, dignitaries, and the public, as well as members of the commission. The artistry of Chief Engraver James B. Longacre was featured on the first medal, which featured his French Liberty Head design from a pattern half dollar of 1859.

By its centennial in 1897 the assay was already a quixotic salute to the olden times, and the custom of issuing annual medals had faded to a shadow of its heyday. For years, the Mint had struck medals in silver, copper, bronze, and aluminum, occasionally in white metal or nickel, sometimes with strange and anachronistic die combinations, and sometimes offered for private sale to collectors. By the early 1900s, most assays were memorialized by a single variety. At no point were the medals mass-produced; for most years about a dozen specimens, perhaps two dozen, are known. By the Roaring Twenties the medals had devolved to brass. The final issue, from 1977, was pewter.

Kenneth Bressett, senior editor of the *Guide Book of United States Coins*, who has been active in numismatic research since the 1940s, recalls his participation as a member of the U.S. Assay Commission:

> Early in 1966 I was quoted as saying "United States coins are as good as gold." This statement was hardly profound. Our nation's coinage had been solid and trustworthy since its inception in 1792. Throughout the years all gold and silver coins minted for commercial use had been faithfully monitored to guarantee their purity and value. To assure this consistency President George Washington established a citizens committee to be appointed each year to test and affirm the validity of our national coinage.
>
> The United States Assay Commission met and tested current coinage production nearly every year thereafter for almost 200 years. It was my good fortune to be one of the presidential appointees in 1966, and to travel to the U.S. Mint in Philadelphia that year to test the coins. It was a unique time in numismatic history because our task was to test not only the nation's final production of silver coins, but also the first copper-nickel clad coins. Unfortunately, the commission was disbanded in 1980 and the tradition no longer exists.
>
> My odyssey began in the last days of January 1966 when I received a call from Director of the Mint Eva Adams, informing me that I had been appointed by President Lyndon B. Johnson to serve on the 1966 Assay Commission. The meeting convened on February 9. During the formalities Ambassador R. Henry Norweb was selected as chairman. He then appointed others to serve on the Counting, Weighing, and Assaying committees. I served on the latter, which I found to be the most interesting. Our involvement was mainly one of observing dedicated Mint staff workers performing their routine testing of sample coins that had been periodically saved from quarterly batches of coinage production from each of the three mint facilities during 1965.

At the conclusion of the ceremony our group of 22 commissioners received a specially minted silver medal and a certificate for our participation. We were then treated to a spectacular tour of the Philadelphia Mint and dinner at a local restaurant. It was a day I shall never forget.

The U.S. Assay Commission medals as a type were voted no. 28 in *100 Greatest American Medals and Tokens*, by Katherine Jaeger and Q. David Bowers (2007). "Although all are scarce," Jaeger and Bowers note, "most often seen are 19th-century issues in copper. Those in silver or aluminum are rarer and more valuable, as are rare die varieties and combinations in all metals. Many 20th-century strikings are in brass, typically selling for the same rate." No Assay Commission medals were issued from 1862 through 1866; the 1936 medal was actually a Roosevelt presidential medal obverse with a Washington medal reverse; and none were issued in 1954. Collectors eagerly await their appearance at auction or in private sales, as they represent a colorful and historic part of U.S. coinage history.

# A GALLERY OF SELECT U.S. ASSAY COMMISSION MEDALS

1860. "French Liberty Head" by Longacre.

1867. "French Liberty Head" by Longacre.

1868. Peace Victorious Over War.

1869. Liberty Seated, With Stars.

1869. Liberty Seated, No Stars.

1869. Peace Victorious Over War.

# A GALLERY OF SELECT U.S.
# ASSAY COMMISSION MEDALS *(continued)*

1870. Goddess Juno Moneta.

1871. Mathematician Archimedes.

1873. Mathematician Archimedes.

1876. President George Washington.

1879. Mint Director H.R. Linderman.

1880. President Rutherford B. Hayes.

1882. President James A. Garfield.

1884. President Chester A. Arthur.

1886. President Grover Cleveland.

# A GALLERY OF SELECT U.S.
## ASSAY COMMISSION MEDALS (continued)

1890. President Benjamin Harrison.        1891. Treasury Secretary William Windom.

1892. President Benjamin Harrison.        1893. President Benjamin Harrison.

1894. President Grover Cleveland.

1897. President Grover Cleveland.        1898. President William McKinley.

1899. President William McKinley.        1900. President William McKinley.

# A GALLERY OF SELECT U.S. ASSAY COMMISSION MEDALS *(continued)*

1901. President William McKinley.

1902. First Meeting in the New Mint.

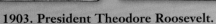

1903. President Theodore Roosevelt.

1904. President Theodore Roosevelt.

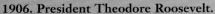

1906. President Theodore Roosevelt.

1909. Treasury Secretary George B. Cortelyou.

# A GALLERY OF SELECT U.S. ASSAY COMMISSION MEDALS *(continued)*

**1911. President
William H. Taft.**

**1914. President
Woodrow Wilson.**

**1916. Treasury Seal.**

**1918. Treasury Secretary
William Gibbs McAdoo.**

**1919. President
Woodrow Wilson.**

**1920. President
Woodrow Wilson.**

# A Gallery of Select U.S.
## Assay Commission Medals (continued)

**1921. President Woodrow Wilson.**        **1922. Treasury Secretary Andrew W. Mellon.**

**1923. President**               **1924. President**          **1925. Presidet**
**Warren G. Harding.**            **Calvin Coolidge.**          **Calvin Coolidge.**

# A GALLERY OF SELECT U.S. ASSAY COMMISSION MEDALS *(continued)*

**1926. President
Calvin Coolidge.**

**1927. President
Calvin Coolidge.**

**1935. President
Franklin D. Roosevelt.**

**1937. President
Thomas Jefferson.**

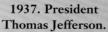

# A GALLERY OF SELECT U.S. ASSAY COMMISSION MEDALS *(continued)*

1938. Benjamin Franklin.

1940. President Franklin D. Roosevelt.

1942. President Franklin D. Roosevelt.

1944. Mint Director David Rittenhouse.

# A GALLERY OF SELECT U.S. ASSAY COMMISSION MEDALS *(continued)*

1953. Mercury.

1966. Treasury Secretary
Henry H. Fowler.

1977. Martha
Washington.

# C

# Authorizing Legislation

his appendix provides the text (in some cases extracted or annotated, as indicated) of selected legislation relevant to coins and medals made by the U.S. Mint since 1972.

## COINAGE ACT OF 1873

**Chapter CXXXI.**—An Act revising and amending the Laws relative to the Mints, Assay-offices, and Coinage of the United States.

*Be it enacted by the Senate and House of Representatives of the United States of America in Congress assembled*, That the mint of the United States is hereby established as a bureau of the Treasury Department, embracing in its organization and under its control all mints for the manufacture of coin, and all assay offices for the stamping of bars, which are now, or which may be hereafter, authorized by law. The chief officer of the said bureau shall be denominated the director of the mint, and shall be under the general direction of the Secretary of the Treasury. He shall be appointed by the President, by and with the advice and consent of the Senate, and shall hold his office for the term of five years, unless sooner removed by the President, upon reasons to be communicated by him to the Senate.

**[Section 52 is reproduced here, as relevant to the production of national medals.]**

**SEC. 52.** That dies of a national character may be executed by the engraver, and national and other medals struck by the coiner of the mint at Philadelphia, under such regulations as the superintendent, with the approval of the director of the mint, may prescribe: *Provided*, That such work shall not interfere with the regular coinage operations, and that no private medal dies shall be prepared at said mint, or the machinery or apparatus thereof be used for that purpose.

Approved, February 12, 1873.

## PUBLIC LAW 92-228 (AMERICAN REVOLUTION BICENTENNIAL MEDALS), 1972

"An Act to provide for the striking of medals in commemoration of the bicentennial of the American Revolution."

*Be it enacted by the Senate and House of Representatives of the United States of America in Congress assembled*, That in commemoration of the bicentennial of the birth of the United States and the historic events preceding and associated with the American Revolution, the Secretary of the Treasury (hereafter referred to as the "Secretary") is authorized and directed to strike medals of suitable sizes and metals, each with suitable emblems, devices, and inscriptions to be determined by the American Revolution Bicentennial Commission (hereafter referred to as the "Commission") subject to the approval of the Secretary.

**SEC. 2.** A national medal shall be struck commemorating the year 1776 and its significance to American independence. In addition to the national medal, a maximum of thirteen medals each of a different design may be struck to commemorate sp ecific historical events of great importance, recognized nationally as milestones in the continuing progress of the United States of America toward life, liberty, and the pursuit of happiness.

**SEC. 3.** The Secretary shall strike and furnish to the Commission such quantities of medals as may be necessary, with a minimum order of two thousand medals of each design or size. They shall be made and delivered at such times as may be required by the Commission, but no medals may be made after December 31, 1983.

**SEC. 4.** The medals authorized under this Act are national medals within the meaning of section 3851 of the Revised Statutes (31 U.S.C. 368).

**SEC. 5.** The medals shall be furnished by the Secretary at a price equal to the cost of the manufacture, including labor, materials, dies, use of machinery, and overhead expenses.

Approved February 15, 1972.

# PUBLIC LAW 95-630 (AMERICAN ARTS GOLD MEDALLIONS), 1979

### Title IV—American Arts Gold Medallions

**SEC. 401.** This title may be cited as the "American Arts Gold Medallion Act."

**SEC. 402.** The Secretary of the Treasury (hereinafter referred to as the "Secretary") shall, during each of the first five calendar years beginning after the date of enactment of this title, strike and sell to the general public, as provided by this title, gold medallions (hereinafter referred to as "medallions") containing, in the aggregate, not less than one million troy ounces of fine gold, and commemorating outstanding individuals in the American arts.

**SEC. 403.**

(a) Medallions struck under authority of this title shall be minted in two sizes containing, respectively, one troy ounce and one-half troy ounce of fine gold. During the first year in which such medallions are struck, at least five hundred thousand troy ounces of fine gold shall be struck in each size of medallions authorized by this subsection. In succeeding years, the proportion of gold devoted to each size of medallions shall be determined by the Secretary on the basis of expected demand.

(b) Medallions struck under authority of this title shall be of such fineness that, of one thousand parts by weight, nine hundred shall be of fine gold and one hundred of alloy. Medallions shall not be struck from ingots which deviate from the standard of this subsection by more than one part per thousand.

(c) Medallions struck under the authority of this title shall bear such designs and inscriptions as the Secretary may approve subject to the following—

(1) during the first calendar year beginning after the date of enactment of this title, one-ounce medallions shall be struck with a picture of Grant Wood on the obverse side and one-half ounce medallions shall be struck with a picture of Marian Anderson on the obverse side;

(2) during the second calendar year beginning after the date of enactment of this title, one-ounce medallions shall be struck with a picture of Mark Twain on the obverse side and one-half ounce medallions shall be struck with a picture of Willa Cather on the obverse side;

(3) during the third calendar year beginning after the date of enactment of this title, one-ounce medallions shall be struck with a picture of Louis Armstrong on the obverse side and one-half ounce medallions shall be struck with a picture of Frank Lloyd Wright on the obverse side;

(4) during the fourth calendar year beginning after the date of enactment of this title, one-ounce medallions shall be struck with a picture of Robert Frost on the obverse side and one-half ounce medallions shall be struck with a picture of Alexander Calder on the obverse side; and

(5) during the fifth calendar year beginning after the date of enactment of this title, one-ounce medallions shall be struck with a picture of Helen Hayes on the obverse side and one-half ounce medallions shall be struck with a picture of John Steinbeck on the obverse side.

The reverse side of each medallion shall be of different design, shall be representative of the artistic achievements of the individual on the obverse side, and shall include the inscription "American Arts Commemorative Series."

**SEC. 404.** Dies for use in striking the medallions authorized by this title may be executed by the engraver, and the medallions struck by the Superintendent of coining department of the mint at Philadelphia, under such regulations as the Superintendent, with the approval of the Director of the Mint, may prescribe. In order to carry out this title, the Secretary may enter into contracts: *Provided* That suitable precautions are maintained to secure against counterfeiting and against unauthorized issuance of medallions struck under authority of this title.

**SEC. 405.** For purposes of section 485 of title 18 of the United States Code, a coin of a denomination of higher than 5 cents shall be deemed to include any medallion struck under the authority of this title.

**SEC. 406.**

(a) Medallions struck under authority of this title shall be sold to the general public at a competitive price equal to the free market value of the gold contained therein plus the cost of manufacture, including labor, materials, dies, use of machinery, and overhead expenses including marketing costs. In order to carry out the purposes of this section, the Secretary shall enter into such arrangements with the Administrator of General Services (hereinafter referred to as the "Administrator") as may be appropriate.

(b) The Administrator shall make such arrangements for the sale of medallions as will encourage broad public participation and will not preclude purchases of single pieces.

(c) The Administrator may, after consultation with the Secretary, issue rules and regulations to carry out this section.

**SEC. 407.** This title shall take effect on October 1, 1979.

# PUBLIC LAW 99-185 (GOLD BULLION COIN ACT OF 1985), 1985

"An Act to authorize the minting of gold bullion coins."

*Be it enacted by the Senate and House of Representatives of the United States of America in Congress assembled,*

**SECTION 1.** This Act may be cited as the "Gold Bullion Coin Act of 1985."

## MINTING GOLD BULLION COINS:

**SEC. 2.**

(a) Section 5112(a) of title 31, United States Code, is adding at the end thereof the following new amended by paragraphs:

"(7) A fifty dollar gold coin that is 32.7 millimeters in diameter, weighs 33.931 grams, and contains one troy ounce of fine gold.

"(8) A twenty-five dollar gold coin that is 27.0 millimeters in diameter, weighs 16.966 grams, and contains one-half troy ounce of fine gold.

"(9) A ten-dollar gold coin that is 22.0 millimeters in diameter, weighs 8.483 grams, and contains one-fourth troy ounce of fine gold.

"(10) A five-dollar gold coin that is 16.5 millimeters in diameter, weighs 3.393 grams, and contains one-tenth troy ounce of fine gold."

(b) Section 5112 of title 31, United States Code, is amended by adding at the end thereof the following new subsection:

"(i)(l) Notwithstanding section 5111(a)(1) of this title, the Secretary shall mint and issue the gold coins described in paragraphs (7), (8), (9), and (10) of subsection (a) of this section, in quantities sufficient to meet public demand, and such gold coins shall—

"(A) have a design determined by the Secretary, except that the fifty-dollar gold coin shall have—

"(i) on the obverse side, a design symbolic of Liberty; and

"(ii) on the reverse side, a design representing a family of eagles, with the male carrying an olive branch and flying above a nest containing a female eagle and hatchlings;

"(B) have inscriptions of the denomination, the weight of the fine gold content, the year of minting or issuance, and the words 'Liberty,''In God We Trust,''United States of America,' and 'E Pluribus Unum'; and

"(C) have reeded edges.

"(2)(A) The Secretary shall sell the coins minted under this subsection to the public at a price equal to the market value of the bullion at the time of sale, plus the cost of minting, marketing, and distributing such coins (including labor, materials, dies, use of machinery, and promotional and overhead expenses).

"(B) The Secretary shall make bulk sales of the coins minted under this subsection at a reasonable discount.

"(3) For purposes of section 5132(a)(1) of this title, all coins minted under this subsection shall be considered to be numismatic items.".

(c) Section 5116(a) of title 31, United States Code, is amended by adding at the end thereof the following:

"(3) The Secretary shall acquire gold for the coins issued under section 5112(i) of this title by purchase of gold mined from natural deposits in the United States, or in a territory or possession of the United States, within one year after the month in which the ore from which it is derived was mined. The Secretary shall pay not more than the average world price for the gold. In the absence of available supplies of such gold at the average world price, the Secretary may use gold from reserves held by the United States to mint the coins issued under section 5112(i) of this title. The Secretary shall issue such regulations as may be necessary to carry out this paragraph.".

(d) Section 5118(b) of title 31, United States Code, is amended—

(1) in the first sentence, by striking out "or deliver"; and

(2) in the second sentence, by inserting "(other than gold and silver coins)" before "that may be lawfully held".

(e) The third sentence of section 5132(a)(1) of title 31, United States Code, is amended by striking out "minted under section 5112(a) of this title" and inserting in lieu thereof "minted under paragraphs (1) through (6) of section 5112(a) of this title".

(f) Notwithstanding any other provision of law, an amount equal to the amount by which the proceeds from the sale of the coins issued under section 5112(i) of title 31, United States Code, exceed the sum of—

(1) the cost of minting, marketing, and distributing such coins, and

(2) the value of gold certificates (not exceeding forty-two and two-ninths dollars a fine troy ounce) retired from the use of gold contained in such coins, shall be deposited in the general fund of the Treasury and shall be used for the sole purpose of reducing the national debt.

(g) The Secretary shall take all actions necessary to ensure that the issuance of the coins minted under section 5112(i) of title 31, United States Code, shall result in no net cost to the United States Government.

**SEC. 3.** This Act shall take effect on October 1, 1985, except that no coins may be issued or sold under section 5112(i) of title 31, United States Code, before October 1, 1986.

Approved December 17, 1985.

# PUBLIC LAW 109-145 (PRESIDENTIAL $1 COIN ACT OF 2005), 2005

"An Act to require the Secretary of the Treasury to mint coins in commemoration of each of the Nation's past Presidents and their spouses, respectively, to improve circulation of the $1 coin, to create a new bullion coin, and for other purposes."

*Be it enacted by the Senate and House of Representatives of the United States of America in Congress assembled,*

SECTION 1. Short Title. This Act may be cited as the "Presidential $1 Coin Act of 2005."

**Title I—Presidential $1 Coins**

**[Section 101, "Findings," and Section 102, "Presidential $1 Coin Program," are here deleted.]**

**SEC. 103.** FIRST SPOUSE BULLION COIN PROGRAM. Section 5112 of title 31, United States Code, as amended by section 102, is amended by adding at the end the following:

"(o) FIRST SPOUSE BULLION COIN PROGRAM.—

"(1) IN GENERAL.—During the same period described in subsection (n), the Secretary shall issue bullion coins under this subsection that are emblematic of the spouse of each such President.

"(2) SPECIFICATIONS.—The coins issued under this subsection shall—

"(A) have the same diameter as the $1 coins described in subsection (n);

"(B) weigh 0.5 ounce; and

"(C) contain 99.99 percent pure gold.

"(3) DESIGN REQUIREMENTS.—

"(A) COIN OBVERSE.—The design on the obverse of each coin issued under this subsection shall contain—

"(i) the name and likeness of a person who was a spouse of a President during the President's period of service;

"(ii) an inscription of the years during which such person was the spouse of a President during the President's period of service; and

"(iii) a number indicating the order of the period of service in which such President served.

"(B) COIN REVERSE.—The design on the reverse of each coin issued under this subsection shall bear—

"(i) images emblematic of the life and work of the First Spouse whose image is borne on the obverse; and

"(ii) the inscription 'United States of America'.

"(C) DESIGNATED DENOMINATION.— Each coin issued under this subsection shall bear, on the reverse, an inscription of the nominal denomination of the coin which shall be '$10'.

"(D) DESIGN IN CASE OF NO FIRST SPOUSE.—In the case of any President who served without a spouse—

"(i) the image on the obverse of the bullion coin corresponding to the $1 coin relating to such President shall be an image emblematic of the concept of 'Liberty'—

"(I) as represented on a United States coin issued during the period of service of such President; or

"(II) as represented, in the case of President Chester Alan Arthur, by a design incorporating the name and likeness of Alice Paul, a leading strategist in the suffrage movement, who was instrumental in gaining women the right to vote upon the adoption of the 19th amendment and thus the ability to participate in the election of future Presidents, and who was born on January 11, 1885, during the term of President Arthur; and

"(ii) the reverse of such bullion coin shall be of a design representative of themes of such President, except that in the case of the bullion coin referred to in clause (i)(II) the reverse of such coin shall be representative of the suffrage movement.

"(E) DESIGN AND COIN FOR EACH SPOUSE.—A separate coin shall be designed and issued under this section for each person who was the spouse of a President during any portion of a term of office of such President.

"(F) INSCRIPTIONS.—Each bullion coin issued under this subsection shall bear the inscription of the year of minting or issuance of the coin and such other inscriptions as the Secretary may determine to be appropriate.

"(4) SALE OF BULLION COINS.—Each bullion coin issued under this subsection shall be sold by the Secretary at a price that is equal to or greater than the sum of—

"(A) the face value of the coins; and

"(B) the cost of designing and issuing the coins (including labor, materials, dies, use of machinery, overhead expenses, marketing, and shipping).

"(5) ISSUANCE OF COINS COMMEMORATING FIRST SPOUSES.—

"(A) IN GENERAL.—The bullion coins issued under this subsection with respect to any spouse of a President shall be issued on the same schedule as the $1 coin issued under subsection (n) with respect to each such President.

"(B) MAXIMUM NUMBER OF BULLION COINS FOR EACH DESIGN.—The Secretary shall—

"(i) prescribe, on the basis of such factors as the Secretary determines to be appropriate, the maximum number of bullion coins that shall be issued with each of the designs selected under this subsection; and

"(ii) announce, before the issuance of the bullion coins of each such design, the maximum number of bullion coins of that design that will be issued.

"(C) TERMINATION OF PROGRAM.—No bullion coin may be issued under this subsection after the termination, in accordance with subsection (n)(8), of the $1 coin program established under subsection (n).

"(6) QUALITY OF COINS.—The bullion coins minted under this Act shall be issued in both proof and uncirculated qualities.

"(7) SOURCE OF GOLD BULLION.—

"(A) IN GENERAL.—The Secretary shall acquire gold for the coins issued under this subsection by purchase of gold mined from natural deposits in the United States, or in a territory or possession of the United States, within 1 year after the month in which the ore from which it is derived was mined.

"(B) PRICE OF GOLD.—The Secretary shall pay not more than the average world price for the gold mined under subparagraph (A).

"(8) BRONZE MEDALS.—The Secretary may strike and sell bronze medals that bear the likeness of the bullion coins authorized under this subsection, at a price, size, and weight, and with such inscriptions, as the Secretary determines to be appropriate.

"(9) LEGAL TENDER.—The coins minted under this title shall be legal tender, as provided in section 5103.

"(10) TREATMENT AS NUMISMATIC ITEMS.— For purposes of section 5134 and 5136, all coins minted under this subsection shall be considered to be numismatic items.".

[Section 104, "Removal of Barriers to Circulation," and Section 105, "Sense of the Congress," are here deleted.]

## Title II—Buffalo Gold Bullion Coins

SEC. 201. GOLD BULLION COINS. Section 5112 of title 31, United States Code, is amended—

(1) in subsection (a), by adding at the end the following: "(11) A $50 gold coin that is of an appropriate size and thickness, as determined by the Secretary, weighs 1 ounce, and contains 99.99 percent pure gold."; and

(2) by adding at the end, the following:

"(q) GOLD BULLION COINS.—

"(1) IN GENERAL.—Not later than 6 months after the date of enactment of the Presidential $1 Coin Act of 2005, the Secretary shall commence striking and issuing for sale such number of $50 gold bullion and proof coins as the Secretary may determine to be appropriate, in such quantities, as the Secretary, in the Secretary's discretion, may prescribe.

"(2) INITIAL DESIGN.—

"(A) IN GENERAL.—Except as provided under subparagraph (B), the obverse and reverse of the gold bullion coins struck under this subsection during the first year of issuance shall bear the original designs by James Earle Fraser, which appear on the 5-cent coin commonly referred to as the 'Buffalo nickel' or the '1913 Type 1'.

"(B) VARIATIONS.—The coins referred to in subparagraph (A) shall—

"(i) have inscriptions of the weight of the coin and the nominal denomination of the coin incused in that portion of the design on the reverse of the coin commonly known as the 'grassy mound'; and

"(ii) bear such other inscriptions as the Secretary determines to be appropriate.

"(3) SUBSEQUENT DESIGNS.—After the 1-year period described to in paragraph (2), the Secretary may—

"(A) after consulting with the Commission of Fine Arts, and subject to the review of the Citizens Coinage Advisory Committee, change the design on the obverse or reverse of gold bullion coins struck under this subsection; and

"(B) change the maximum number of coins issued in any year.

"(4) SOURCE OF GOLD BULLION.—

"(A) IN GENERAL.—The Secretary shall acquire gold for the coins issued under this subsection by purchase of gold mined from natural deposits in the United States, or in a territory or possession of the United States, within 1 year after the month in which the ore from which it is derived was mined.

"(B) PRICE OF GOLD.—The Secretary shall pay not more than the average world price for the gold mined under subparagraph (A).

"(5) SALE OF COINS.—Each gold bullion coin issued under this subsection shall be sold for an amount the Secretary determines to be appropriate, but not less than the sum of—

"(A) the market value of the bullion at the time of sale; and

"(B) the cost of designing and issuing the coins, including labor, materials, dies, use of machinery, overhead expenses, marketing, and shipping.

"(6) LEGAL TENDER.—The coins minted under this title shall be legal tender, as provided in section 5103.

"(7) TREATMENT AS NUMISMATIC ITEMS.—For purposes of section 5134 and 5136, all coins minted under this subsection shall be considered to be numismatic items.

"(8) PROTECTIVE COVERING.—

"(A) IN GENERAL.—Each bullion coin having a metallic content as described in subsection (a) (11) and a design specified in paragraph (2) shall be sold in an inexpensive covering that will protect the coin from damage due to ordinary handling or storage.

"(B) DESIGN.—The protective covering required under subparagraph (A) shall be readily distinguishable from any coin packaging that may be used to protect proof coins minted and issued under this subsection.".

[Title III, "Abraham Lincoln Bicentennial 1-Cent Coin Redesign," is here deleted.]

Approved December 22, 2005.

# PUBLIC LAW 110-456 (AMERICA'S BEAUTIFUL NATIONAL PARKS QUARTER DOLLAR COIN ACT OF 2008), 2008

"An Act to provide for a program for circulating quarter dollar coins that are emblematic of a national park or other national site in each State, the District of Columbia, and each territory of the United States, and for other purposes."

*Be it enacted by the Senate and House of Representatives of the United States of America in Congress assembled,*

SECTION 1. Short Title. This Act may be cited as the "America's Beautiful National Parks Quarter Dollar Coin Act of 2008".

## Title I—National Site Quarter Dollars

SEC. 101. Findings. The Congress finds as follows:

(1) Yellowstone National Park was established by an Act signed by President Ulysses S. Grant on March 1, 1872, as the Nation's first national park.

(2) The summer and autumn of 1890 saw the establishment of a number of national sites:

(A) August 19: Chickamauga and Chattanooga established as national military parks in Georgia and Tennessee.

(B) August 30: Antietam established as a national battlefield site in Maryland.

(C) September 25: Sequoia National Park established in California.

(D) September 27: Rock Creek Park established in the District of Columbia.

(E) October 1: General Grant National Park established in California (and subsequently incorporated in Kings Canyon National Park).

(F) October 1: Yosemite National Park established in California.

(3) Theodore Roosevelt was this nation's 26th President and is considered by many to be our "Conservationist President".

(4) As a frequent visitor to the West, Theodore Roosevelt witnessed the virtual destruction of some big game species and the overgrazing that destroyed the grasslands and with them the habitats for small mammals and songbirds and conservation increasingly became one of his major concerns.

(5) When he became President in 1901, Roosevelt pursued this interest in conservation by establishing the first 51 Bird Reserves, 4 Game Preserves, and 150 National Forests.

(6) He also established the United States Forest Service, signed into law the creation of 5 National Parks, and signed the Act for the Preservation of American Antiquities in 1906 under which he proclaimed 18 national monuments.

(7) Approximately 230,000,000 acres of area within the United States was placed under public protection by Theodore Roosevelt.

(8) Theodore Roosevelt said that nothing short of defending this country in wartime "compares in importance with the great central task of leaving this land even a better land for our descendants than it is for us".

(9) The National Park Service was created by an Act signed by President Woodrow Wilson on August 25, 1916.

(10) The National Park System comprises 391 areas covering more than 84,000,000 acres in every State (except Delaware), the District of Columbia, American Samoa, Guam, Puerto Rico, and the Virgin Islands.

(11) The sites or areas within the National Park System vary widely in size and type from vast natural wilderness to birthplaces of Presidents to world heritage archaeology sites to an African burial ground memorial in Manhattan and include national parks, monuments, battlefields, military parks, historical parks, historic sites, lakeshores, seashores, recreation areas, scenic rivers and trails, and the White House.

(12) In addition to the sites within the National Park System, the United States has placed numerous other types of sites under various forms of conservancy, such as the national forests and sites within the National Wildlife Refuge System and on the National Register of Historic Places.

**[Section 102, "Issuance of Redesigned Quarter Dollars Emblematic of National Parks or Other National Sites in Each State, the District of Columbia, and Each Territory," is here deleted.]**

## Title II—Bullion Investment Products

**SEC. 201.** Silver Bullion Coin.

Section 5112 of title 31, United States Code, is amended by inserting after subsection (t) (as added by title I of this Act) the following new subsection:

"(u) Silver Bullion Investment Product.—

"(1) In general.—The Secretary shall strike and make available for sale such number of bullion coins as the Secretary determines to be appropriate that are exact duplicates of the quarter dollars issued under subsection (t), each of which shall—

"(A) have a diameter of 3.0 inches and weigh 5.0 ounces;

"(B) contain .999 fine silver;

"(C) have incused into the edge the fineness and weight of the bullion coin;

"(D) bear an inscription of the denomination of such coin, which shall be 'quarter dollar'; and

"(E) not be minted or issued by the United States Mint as so-called 'fractional' bullion coins or in any size other than the size described in paragraph (A).

"(2) Availability for sale.—Bullion coins minted under paragraph (1)—

"(A) shall become available for sale no sooner than the first day of the calendar year in which the circulating quarter dollar of which such bullion coin is a duplicate is issued; and

"(B) may only be available for sale during the year in which such circulating quarter dollar is issued.

"(3) Distribution.—

"(A) In general.—In addition to the authorized dealers utilized by the Secretary in distributing bullion coins and solely for purposes of distributing bullion coins issued under this subsection, the Director of the National Park Service, or the designee of the Director, may purchase numismatic items issued under this subsection, but only in units of no fewer than 1,000 at a time, and the Director, or the Director's designee, may resell or repackage such numismatic items as the Director determines to be appropriate.

"(B) Resale.—The Director of the National Park Service, or the designee of the Director, may resell, at cost and without repackaging, numismatic items acquired by the Director or such designee under subparagraph (A) to any party affiliated with any national site honored by a quarter dollar under subsection (t) for repackaging and resale by such party in the same manner and to the same extent as such party would be authorized to engage in such activities under subparagraph (A) if the party were acting as the designee of the Director under such subparagraph.".

Approved December 23, 2008.

# CHAPTER 31, UNITED STATES CODE, SECTION 5112 (I)(4)

(A) Notwithstanding any other provision of law and subject to subparagraph (B), the Secretary of the Treasury may change the diameter, weight, or design of any coin minted under this subsection or the fineness of the gold in the alloy of any such coin if the Secretary determines that the specific diameter, weight, design, or fineness of gold which differs from that otherwise required by law is appropriate for such coin.

(B) The Secretary may not mint any coin with respect to which a determination has been made by the Secretary under subparagraph (A) before the end of the 30-day period beginning on the date a notice of such determination is published in the Federal Register.

(C) The Secretary may continue to mint and issue coins in accordance with the specifications contained in paragraphs (7), (8), (9), and (10) of subsection (a) and paragraph (1)(A) of this subsection at the same time the Secretary is minting and issuing other bullion and proof gold coins under this subsection in accordance with such program procedures and coin specifications, designs, varieties, quantities, denominations, and inscriptions as the Secretary, in the Secretary's discretion, may prescribe from time to time.

# Notes

## Preface

1. Schechter, Scott, and Jeff Garrett. *100 Greatest U.S. Modern Coins*, third edition. Atlanta, GA, 2014.

## Chapter 1

1. Derived from data courtesy of Key to Metals AG, a privately owned Swiss company, from its *Total Materia* comprehensive materials database.

2. Based upon "Commodities and Statistics: Production of Silver, Mine," 2013, with the permission of the British Geological Survey, sponsored by the Natural Environment Research Council, the leading funder of independent research, training, and innovation in environmental science in the United Kingdom.

3. Based upon "Commodities and Statistics: Production of Silver, Gold," 2013, with the permission of the British Geological Survey.

## Chapter 2

1. Wright, Robert E. *The First Wall Street: Chestnut Street, Philadelphia, and the Birth of American Finance*, 2005.

2. Correspondence with the author, May 9, 2014.

3. Macy, Jesse. *Our Government, How it Grew, What it Does, and How it Does It*, 1890.

4. Peffer, William Alfred. *The Farmer's Side: His Troubles and Their Remedy*, 1891.

5. Bowers, Q. David. "The Coin Market, Early Times to 1857," *The Expert's Guide to Collecting and Investing in Rare Coins*, 2006.

6. Haxby, James A. *A Guide Book of Canadian Coins and Tokens*, p. 10.

7. *Ibid.*

8. Barnhart, David K., and Allan A. Metcalf. *America in So Many Words: Words That Have Shaped America*, Houghton Mifflin Company, 1997.

9. Bressett, Kenneth. *Milestone Coins: A Pageant of the World's Most Significant and Popular Money*, Whitman Publishing, 2007.

10. In his 1844 essay "Politics," Ralph Waldo Emerson would observe that gold was good for buying iron, and that iron (the materiel of war) was good for acquiring gold—a neat and circular equation of international statecraft. ("Gold and iron are good / To buy iron and gold.")

11. Doty, Richard. "The Thirteen Colonies and Their Monies," *America's Money, America's Story*, Whitman Publishing, 2008.

12. Interesting theories of this sort are researched and ruminated upon by members of the nonprofit Colonial Coin Collectors Club (online at www.colonialcoins.org) in publications like their *C4 Newsletter*. Early American Coppers (www.eacs.org), another nonprofit hobby organization, also is devoted to the study of colonial and early American tokens and coins. EAC publishes an excellent quarterly journal, *Penny-Wise*.

13. Reflecting on the flexible value of money, Unitarian minister and American historian Charles Fletcher Dole, in his 1892 book *The American Citizen*, wrote, "Governments coin money, but the commerce of the world fixes its value. For commerce, in her great markets, like London, where the business of the world meets and is settled, asks of all commodities, and the coins of every nation also, What is their real worth? A government may put a false mark on a coin or mix alloy with the metal, but commerce weighs and tests the coin, and will not give more for it than it really is worth."

14. Correspondence with the author, May 9, 2014.

15. Kenneth Bressett, in May 2014 correspondence with the author, noted, "This custom [of using whatever coins and tokens are handy to even out transactions, regardless of their real value] is still in vogue in countries where small-denomination coins are being phased out or are of such low value that they use a 'take a penny or leave a penny' system. In some cases, things as odd as wrapped candy or gum have bridged the gap." Robert D. Leonard discusses this phenomenon in chapter 3 of *Curious Currency: The Story of Money From the Stone Age to the Internet Age*. An example: "In 1975, a bus driver in Lima, Peru, tendered a handful of caramels in change for a five-sol note. The same day, another drive refused a stick of gum and a one-sol coin in payment, only to back down when outraged passengers brandished the caramels and chewing gum they had received in change." Another example: "Italy experienced a persistent coin shortage in the mid-1970s, forcing shoppers to accept change in gumdrops, toffee candy, or mints" (Leonard, p. 40).

16. "Credit is a thing so very common here, that there is not one person in a hundred who pays the ready money, for the goods he takes up, to a store." Thus wrote David Wardrobe, a gentleman in Westmoreland County, Virginia, to his friend Archibald Provan in Glasgow, Scotland (June 30, 1774). (From *American Archives, Documents of the American Revolution, 1774–1776*.)

17. Doty, Richard. "An Age of Revolution, 1776–1914," *Money of the World: Coins That Made History*.

18. For additional discussion of the paper money of the Continental Congress, see Bowers, *Obsolete Paper Money Issued by Banks in the United States, 1782–1866*.

19. William Cobbett (1763–1835), English farmer, pamphleteer, and journalist, spoke for many hard-money proponents on both sides of the Atlantic when he lamented: "Oh! accursed

paper-money! Has Hell a torment surpassing the wickedness of thy inventor?" (Quoted by William Forsyth in *Essays Critical and Narrative*, 1874.)

20. Correspondence with the author, May 9, 2014. Q. David Bowers, in correspondence of May 11, 2015, differs: "They were probably not made as petition coins but for commercial circulation."

21. These imitation British "coins" bear close study by numismatists, who classify them in various groups, as noted in the *Guide Book of United States Coins* (see pages 66 and 67 of the 70th edition) and other references. Kenneth Bressett notes, "Only group III pieces can positively be attributed to Machin. Group II pieces were made by Brasher and Bailey. They should not all be lumped together as Machin's, even though most collectors do" (correspondence, May 9, 2014).

22. Quoted by R.S. Yeoman in *A Guide Book of United States Coins*, 70th edition. Atlanta, GA, 2016.

23. Q. David Bowers has related, in correspondence with the author, how bank tellers would be instructed by their superiors to inform inquiring customers that they had no gold and silver coins to pay out—even as their vaults were heavy with them. When the precious-metal value of U.S. coins was greater than their face value, banks would reserve them for bullion speculators and foreign agents who could afford to buy them in bulk at a premium and still make a profit selling them as bullion. The bankers and the speculators benefited from this arrangement, leaving regular Americans to make do with paper notes, smaller silver coins, foreign coins, copper, tokens, and other money.

24. The feasibility of this scenario has been questioned by some numismatic historians, including Bowers.

25. Of the $4,525,166,503 face value of regular-issue U.S. gold coins struck from 1795 to 1933, roughly 78 percent ($3,482,112,120) was in the form of double eagles. (Source: *A Guide Book of Double Eagle Gold Coins*, Bowers, derived from the 1934 *Annual Report of the Director of the Mint*.)

26. Gordon, John Steele. "The High Cost of War," *Barron's Online*, April 9, 2011.

27. Carothers, Neil. *Fractional Money*, p. 187.

28. Q. David Bowers notes, however, that even for a time after passage of the Coinage Act of April 22, 1864, "the private minting of tokens was nearly universally continued. In Milwaukee the private coiners Mossin & Marr announced that because of the act they would no longer mint Civil War tokens. Then a few months later they continued on their merry way!" (Correspondence with the author, May 29, 2015)

29. Not all gold had to be turned in to the Federal Reserve. Every citizen was allowed to hold up to $100 face value in gold coins and certificates; dentists, artists, and others with a professional or industrial need could keep a reasonable supply of gold on hand; and numismatic collectibles ("gold coins having a recognized special value to collectors of rare and unusual coins") were exempt from the executive order.

# Chapter 3

1. Many of the direct quotes in this chapter are from the Congressional record, "Treasury Sales of U.S. Gold and the Gold Medallion Act of 1978: Hearing Before the Committee on Banking, Housing, and Urban Affairs—Ninety-Fifth Congress, Second Session, on S. 2483 . . . To Provide for the Issuance of Gold Medallions, and for Other Purposes, August 25, 1978."

2. The Gold Medallion Act of 1978 used curiously worded language to define the purity of the proposed medals. Section 2.a.1. ordered that the medals "shall contain one ounce [or one-half ounce] of .999 fine gold but shall be manufactured from .900 fine gold." Representative George Hansen of Idaho disagreed with Senator Helms on this particular provision. "Most of the United States gold stock," he noted, "is, in fact, 90% pure. Why the Helms bill doesn't just say 'fine gold' [defined as at least 99.9% pure] and instead imports this matter of minimum-purity fine gold is a puzzle to me. Indeed, why this subject of pure gold is mentioned at all confuses me. Read strictly, it might require that the Treasury refine our 90% gold to 99.9% purity, then add the alloy back in to make the blanks for striking. There would be no point in this exercise and I cannot imagine that this is what is being aimed at. It is surely sufficient for us to direct, in law, that each piece be 90% gold. How the bars are alloyed is of no importance. All we have to do is direct that there be certain standard weights and a standard fineness, and certain allowable deviations from these standards in each piece or group of pieces."

3. Mistakenly identified as Morris Cannon in the Congressional record.

4. Dr. Roosa had been vice president of research for the Federal Reserve Bank of New York before joining the Treasury Department in 1961. One of his tasks at the Treasury was to address the United States' balance of payments. Roosa felt that the international economy should be referenced on the U.S. dollar, and he developed a system of bonds that foreign investors could purchase with dollars (and later cash out in Swiss francs) as an alternative to acquiring American gold.

5. American economist, statesman, and author Elgin Groseclose, formerly treasurer-general of Persia during World War II, submitted a supportive statement at the request of Senator Helms. He took a philosophical (and sharp-tongued) approach to what he called "the sophistry of a gold-defined dollar." The Treasury's objection on the grounds that producing gold medallions would be contrary to the policy of reducing gold's monetary role was "sheer nonsense," he stated. "If the Treasury really means to reduce the monetary role of gold it should ask for legislation removing the official

definition of the dollar as the equivalent of so many grains of gold [first established by the Coinage Act of April 2, 1792]. No secretary of the Treasury, no administration, has dared go so far, so we may take their protestations of reducing the monetary role of gold as hypocrisy of the most blatant sort. The fact is that until the government has become so totalitarian as to control the thoughts of the citizens, it cannot control what they will use as money. The government may deny its citizens good [i.e., intrinsic-value] coinage, it may declare worthless pieces of paper as valid for so much in the payment of taxes and debits denominated in official terms, but it will not succeed in making the citizens hoard these pieces of paper in a jar as security for old age, nor will it be able to compel Arab sheiks or German businessmen to accept them as equivalent to the number of grains of gold which the law declares them to be. If one-ounce and one-half-ounce gold pieces are struck they may well become, under the law as it now stands [as of 1977, when gold was again allowed to be used to settle contracts], the subject of contract and a substitute for the official legal tender. This would be a good thing. It has happened before in history—the existence of a gold currency beside a debased and depreciated coin or paper currency. It happened during and following the Civil War. If the market finds these pieces a convenience, and as more stable in the international markets than the paper dollar, then so much the better. The result will be to encourage rather than deter trade."

6. Mexico had a long tradition of minting gold dating back to its days as a colony of the Spanish Empire, and its modern gold coins were popular in the market. (See Bailey and Bailey, *Whitman Encyclopedia of Mexican Money.*) Canada was in the process of developing its own bullion-coin program. Its legal-tender .999 fine gold Canadian Maple Leaf would debut in 1979. (See Haxby, *A Guide Book of Canadian Coins and Tokens.*)

7. Mistakenly referred to as Alfred Goldman in some places within the Congressional record.

8. Concerning the fineness of the Treasury's gold stockpile, Chairman Proxmire asked Assistant Secretary Bergsten, "Is it true that the gold bars now being auctioned off by Treasury are composed largely of melted-down gold coins from the U.S. citizens in the 1930s?" Bergsten replied, "No. In fact, none of the bars we are selling now come from that source. The gold being sold is a very high degree of fineness. It's industrial quality. That's one reason it has sold effectively. The gold that was taken in the 1930s was melted into a lower quality of bar, all of which is still part of the stock."

9. The Krugerrand accounted for 90 percent of the world gold-coin market by 1980, according to economic journalist Tom Bethell ("Crazy as a Gold Bug," *New York Magazine*, February 4, 1980).

10. Bernstein had been a U.S. Treasury official in the early 1940s, and was instrumental in the Bretton Woods international monetary conference of July 1944. This conference, attended by U.S. Treasury Secretary Henry Morgenthau Jr., British economist John Maynard Keynes, and other leading economists, was convened to plan for postwar reconstruction. It established a global fixed exchange-rate program that pegged currencies to the U.S. dollar, and resulted in the founding of the World Bank and the International Monetary Fund. Bernstein would serve as the first director of research at the IMF, from 1946 to 1958. At Bretton Woods he was credited with convincing Keynes that the United States would not fall into an economic depression after World War II ended. "His reasoning was that the United States had given up the gold standard in 1933 and would no longer allow gold reserves to regulate the money supply's growth" (*New York Times*, June 10, 1996, "Edward Bernstein, Economics Expert, Is Dead at 91").

11. From an October 6, 1978, marketing-plan proposal for U.S. gold medallions, presented by Goulding to the Senate Committee on Banking, Housing, and Urban Affairs.

12. The Franklin Mint was a well-known private mint founded in Pennsylvania in 1964. Its numismatic product line began with the design, manufacture, and marketing of gold and silver commemorative rounds and medallions, and in the 1970s it branched out into coinage contracts with various foreign nations. For a detailed historical overview, see chapter 13 of *A Guide Book of United States Tokens and Medals* (Jaeger).

13. Today the American Numismatic Association's national headquarters (including the Dwight N. Manley Numismatic Library and the Edward C. Rochette Money Museum) is located in Colorado Springs, Colorado. The association's Web site is at www.money.org.

14. U.S. Representative George Hansen of Idaho testified before the Senate committee as well, describing a House bill that he had introduced, H.R. 13309. Like Leach's American Arts Gold Medallion Act, Hansen's bill and various others were very similar to Helms's Gold Medallion Act, differing in their wording and in some provisions (e.g., defining the medals' purity, or explicitly prohibiting counterfeiting). All the proposed legislation agreed in that the gold pieces should not be legal tender, and that they should be small enough for the average American family to afford.

15. The House of Representatives portrait of Leach pictured in this chapter dates from later in his long and influential career, about 20 years after the American Arts gold medallion program ended. The House Office of Art & Archives provides this description: "One of the most striking portraits in the House's collection is that of Financial Services Committee Chairman Jim Leach. Artist Michael Roberts evokes fellow Iowa artist

Grant Wood's Midwestern realism, matte palette, and studied naiveté, but there are bigger surprises than the unusual style. The artist has scratched the words 'Iowa City,' 'working,' and 'hands' into the surface. The frame, carved by Connie Roberts, captures elements of Leach's life: a wrestler, cornstalks, landmark legislation, and even Huck Finn rafting down the Mississippi, which forms the eastern border of Leach's congressional district."

16. These costs, defined in section 406(a) of title IV of the omnibus bill, included manufacturing expenses "including labor, materials, dies, use of machinery, and overhead expenses including marketing costs."

17. As described in the GSA marketing plan submitted to the Senate Committee on Banking, Housing, and Urban Affairs, October 6, 1978, this would have been an "over-the-counter" sale through local banks on a consignment basis. "Under this method, an advertising program would be conducted to obtain the broadest practical coverage of notification to prospective buyers for the sale of the medallions. The medallions would be produced at the Philadelphia Mint and shipped to Federal Reserve Banks upon their request. Individual buyers would be able to go to their local banks and order any number of medallions at the current day's gold market price plus a surcharge of approximately $4.41 to cover the Government's manufacturing and distribution costs. Banks receiving requests from customers would then order the medallions from their local Federal Reserve Banks as they currently do with national coinage. Banks would be allowed to add a small prescribed surcharge to cover their costs. In addition, banks wanting to maintain an inventory of medallions could order them in advance from a Federal Reserve Bank. Medallions would always be sold to individuals or dealers at the current day's market price for gold."

18. The surcharge itself would also change from time to time; for example, in 1980 it was $12 per ounce, and in 1981 it was $14. According to the March 31, 1982, *Report to Congress of the Commission on the Role of Gold in the Domestic and International Monetary Systems*, submitted by Treasury Secretary Donald T. Regan, this surcharge averaged less than 3 percent of the gold bullion price.

19. This particular version of the Associated Press article was published in the Lakeland, Florida, *Ledger*.

20. The Gold Commission (officially the Commission on the Role of Gold in the Domestic and International Monetary Systems) was appointed on June 22, 1981. Its goals, pursuant to section 10(b) of Public Law 96-389 (94 Stat. 1555), were to "conduct a study to assess and make recommendations with regard to the policy of the U.S. Government concerning the role of gold in domestic and international monetary systems" and to report its findings to Congress.

21. From the *Fort Scott* (Kansas) *Tribune*, June 26, 1984.

22. Other recent coverage of the American Arts medallions: Noted numismatic researcher David T. Alexander discussed them in his addendum chapter in the 2007 update of Dr. Cornelius Vermeule's classic work, *Numismatic Art in America: Aesthetics of the United States Coinage*. The series has also been summarized by John M. Mercanti and Edmund C. Moy in their respective books on the American Eagle silver, gold, and platinum bullion-coinage programs.

23. This commentary and other unreferenced quotes in this section are from personal correspondence with the author, 2014 and 2015.

24. "A New Registry Set for Modern U.S. Gold," PCGS *U.S. and World Coin News*, June 17, 2014.

25. "Before the Gold Eagles: 1980 Medal Series Often Forgotten," *Coin World*, May 11, 2015.

26. Bowers, Q. David. *A Guide Book of Washington and State Quarters*, p. 223.

27. The Art Institute of Chicago. "About This Artwork: *American Gothic*," *Essential Guide*, p. 56.

28. "Mint Offers Marian Anderson National Medal," U.S. Mint press release, October 26, 1978.

29. Gasparro's recollections were sent to Q. David Bowers on March 20, 1991, for publication in his *Commemorative Coins of the United States: A Complete Encyclopedia* (appendix III).

30. This Styrofoam packaging has been described by numismatic historian David T. Alexander as "thoroughly ugly" (*Numismatic Art in America*, second edition, p. 212). It's certainly a far cry from the beautiful boxes and holders of the U.S. Mint's later high-value issues.

31. United States Mint, Gold Medallion Data Sheet, May 1983.

32. The American Arts gold medallions are still sometimes referred to colloquially (e.g., in advertisements, auction-lot descriptions, etc.) as "postal medallions," "Post Office gold medals," "postal gold coins," or similar—nicknames they picked up from their sale and distribution through U.S. post offices.

33. Eskey, Kenneth. "U.S. Mint Offers Buyers 'Golden' Coin Opportunity," *Pittsburgh Press*, July 22, 1980 (syndicated by Scripps-Howard News Service).

34. *1980 Report of the Secretary of the Treasury*, p. 192.

35. Egan, Jack. "Less Gold for Less: The New Krugerrands," *New York Magazine*, October 20, 1980, pp. 14–16.

36. Heller, Patrick. "Rare Gold Medallions Going Cheap," Numismaster.com, March 20, 2012.

37. *Writers at Work: The Paris Review Interviews*, Malcolm Cowley, editor (New York, 1959), p. 137.

38. "Mark Twain Bids Winter Defiance: Resplendent in a White Flannel

Suit, Author Creates a Sensation in the National Capital," *The New York Herald*, December 8, 1906. The *Herald*, the *Times*, the *Tribune*, and other New York papers reported gleefully on Twain's nose-tweaking of polite society's sartorial rules.

39. Numismatic historian and medallic-art specialist Dick Johnson describes galvanos in volume 8, number 9, of *The E-Sylum* (February 7, 2005, article 9, "Collecting and Conserving Galvanos"): "Galvanos are a necessary intermediate step between an artist's bas-relief model and the die to strike a coin or medal. An artist prepares his oversize model in clay, wax, plaster, wood, plastilene (a modeling compound)—any media he is comfortable with. However, none of these are sturdy enough as a pattern to place on the die-engraving pantograph, commonly called a 'reducing machine'. . . . A galvano is an electrolytic cast. The artist's model, which now becomes the pattern, is coated with a metal powder as a release agent. Often this pattern is plaster. . . . The metal powder covers the surface of the pattern and must conduct electricity. The pattern is wired from this coated surface to connect to a bar overhead.

This wired pattern is immersed in the electrolyte solution. A direct current is turned on. It travels from a rectifier to bars alongside the tank to copper (or silver or gold) anodes in the solution, through this to the surface of the pattern, up the wires to the overhead bar, back to the rectifier to complete the circuit.

The electric current carries away ions of metal from the anodes (they wear away like a bar of soap) and deposit on the surface of the pattern. The ions are microns thick but deposit immediately and rapidly. It takes about three days' time, however, to build up, say, an eighth of an inch of deposited metal. The metal galvano is pried apart from the pattern.

While galvanos are pure copper metal, with time they can become brittle. Its molecular structure is such that it is not like rolled or cast metal. Care must be taken in handling a galvano."

40. "Mint Will Take Orders for 2 Gold Medallions," *Chicago Tribune*, July 14, 1981, p. 8.

41. Bergreen, Laurence. *Louis Armstrong: An Extravagant Life*. New York: Broadway Books, 1997, p. 6.

42. *Report to the Congress of the Commission on the Role of Gold in the Domestic and International Monetary Systems*, March 1982, p. 5.

43. United States Mint, Gold Medallion Data Sheet, May 1983.

44. In a 1987 court case, *U.S. Gold & Silver Investments, Inc., an Oregon corporation, Plaintiff, v. Director, United States Mint, and J. Aron & Company, a New York partnership, Defendants*, the plaintiff firm claimed that J. Aron infringed its trademark by using the phrase "U.S. Gold" in its marketing. The case was dismissed.

45. Farnsworth, Clyde H. "Gold Coin Sales Go Private," *The New York Times*, April 13, 1983.

46. Goeller, David. "U.S. Coins Miss the Gold Rush," Associated Press, June 27, 1984 (quoted as published in the *Lawrence Journal-World*, Lawrence, Kansas).

47. Heller, Patrick. "Rare Gold Medallions Going Cheap," Numismaster.com, March 20, 2012.

48. Goeller, David. "U.S. Coins Miss the Gold Rush," Associated Press, June 27, 1984.

49. Correspondence with the author, June 4, 2015.

## Chapter 5

1. The U.S. Mint's Web site, which includes a product schedule as well as a full catalog and online ordering options, is at www.USMint.gov. The Mint's Customer Service phone number is 1-800-USA-MINT (872-6468), with representatives available seven days a week from 8:00 a.m. to 12:00 midnight Eastern Time. Hearing- and speech-impaired customers with TTY equipment can reach the Mint Monday through Friday from 8:30 a.m. to 5:00 p.m. Eastern Time. Product-related inquiries can be mailed to United States Mint, 1201 Elm Street, Suite 400, Dallas, TX 75270. The email address is usmint-support@catalog.usmint.gov.

2. U.S. Mint, "Procedures to Qualify for Bulk Purchase of Gold and Platinum Bullion Coins," p. 2.

3. The National Numismatic Collection went through a major renovation that was capped in July 2015 when the Smithsonian's expanded new exhibit gallery opened on the first floor of the Museum of American History. Visitors to Washington, DC, are heartily encouraged to spend some time exploring the amazing treasures displayed in this new gallery. To visit the NNC online, go to americanhistory.si.edu/numismatics.

4. Moy, Edmund C. *American Gold and Platinum Eagles*, p. 158.

5. Correspondence with the U.S. Mint Office of Corporate Communications, August 31, 2015.

6. "Gold Buffalo interest at limits?" *Numismatic News*, March 30, 2011.

7. "Reverse Proof gold $50 coins in production: West Point Mint saves 'first strike' American Buffalo," *Coin World*, June 10, 2013.

8. "Gold Buffalo Brightens ANA Future," *Numismatic News*, "The Buzz With Dave Harper," August 19, 2013.

9. "Current sales of Proof 2015-W American Buffalo $50 coins half of 2014 final totals," *Coin World*, June 17, 2015.

## Chapter 6

1. In addition to authorizing the Presidential dollars and their companion gold bullion coins, the Presidential $1 Coin Act of 2005 also gave the secretary of the Treasury authority to strike and sell bronze medals bearing the same general designs as the First Spouse bullion pieces. Furthermore, it created the American Buffalo gold bullion coin program (see chapter 5); directed the 2009 redesign of the Lincoln cent for

the bicentennial of Abraham Lincoln's birth; and also ordered the cent's 2010 redesign with an emblem of Lincoln's preservation of the United States.

2. Mercanti, John M. *American Silver Eagles: A Guide to the U.S. Bullion Coin Program*, second edition, p. 41.

3. This included "identifying, analyzing, and overcoming barriers to the robust circulation of $1 coins . . . including the use of demand prediction, improved methods of distribution and circulation, and improved public education and awareness campaigns."

4. Moy, Edmund C. *American Gold and Platinum Eagles*, p. 149.

5. Information on the NGC Registry can be found online at www.collectors-society.com/AboutRegistry.aspx. According to the firm: "The NGC Registry is a community where collectors can showcase their coins and compete for the best sets. . . . Coins are ranked based on relative rarity and grade, and collectors receive points accordingly. It's a great way to participate in the Registry, as it offers friendly competition and establishes collecting goals. It's also easy to compare collections and see some outstanding sets."

Information on the PCGS Set Registry is online at www.pcgs.com/SetRegistry. The firm says, "Building collections of United States coins can be rewarding and very pleasurable. Participating in the PCGS Set Registry program can also be a lot of fun," noting the enjoyment of comparing your coins to the greatest sets of all time; gaining peer recognition; and establishing a collection pedigree.

6. The U.S. Mint established the Artistic Infusion Program (AIP) in 2003 to enrich and invigorate the nation's coin and medal designs by contracting with "a pool of talented professional American artists representing diverse backgrounds and a variety of interests." These artists, in conjunction with sculptor-engravers on the Mint staff, create and submit new designs for U.S. coins and medals.

7. "What went wrong with the Jefferson first spouse coin?" Collectors Universe "U.S. Coins" forum, November 5, 2007. Herndon's observations were in response to a question posted by Young Numismatist Samuel Ernst: "I know a lot of people here thought they were going to be killer. I talked to a couple dealers here locally who thought the same thing. So what happened? Why didn't it increase in value, or is it going to but it's more of a tortoise instead of a hare kind of thing? Curious YN minds like to know."

8. *Massachusetts Ploughman and New England Journal of Agriculture*, volume 8, no. 7, November 18, 1848, p. 2.

9. The Numismatic Bibliomania Society, online at www.coinbooks.org, "is an educational organization founded in 1979 to support and promote the use and collecting of numismatic literature. Numismatic literature includes books, periodicals, catalogs, and other written or printed material relating to coins, medals, tokens, or paper money, ancient or modern, U.S. or worldwide. Membership is open to any individual or organization interested in the study of numismatics and the study and collecting of numismatic literature." The group's Web site features an archive search function for *The E-Sylum* (its award-winning weekly electronic newsletter), a Community Resources wiki that allows members to easily contribute content to the site, and a photo gallery.

10. *Top 50 Most Popular Modern Coins*, p. 37.

11. Turner, Justin G., and Linda Leavitt Turner, editors. *Letters of Mary Todd Lincoln*, p. 179.

12. "First Spouse Julia Grant Available on 6/23/2011," Collectors Universe "U.S. Coins" forum, June 22, 2011.

13. Paul Gilkes of *Coin World* described the problem: "Finning is a production problem often encountered with circulation coins, which is usually rectified with the excess metal rising from the rims being separated from the coins as the coins repeatedly

collide with one another, according to the Mint. Finning occurs when the striking pressure on the coinage press is set higher than normal. The coin metal is forced up between the collar and the edge of the coin dies, resulting in a sharp, wire rim. U.S. Mint officials define 'bottle capping' as 'high finning along the edge of the coin causes the coin to resemble a bottle cap.'" ("Striking problems plague First Spouse coins," *Coin World*, September 30, 2013)

14. "Mint delays help keep First Spouse gold series 'forgotten'," *Coin World*, October 30, 2013.

15. "Edith's Gold Coin," *Theodore Roosevelt Association Journal*, Fall 2013, pp. 23–29.

16. Zielinski, Michael. "Helen Taft First Spouse Gold Coin," mintnewsblog.com, December 2, 2013.

17. "Last six designs for First Spouse Series gold coins reviewed by CCAC," *Coin World*, September 29, 2014.

# Chapter 7

1. Australia, Canada, China, France, Mexico, and Poland are among the other world mints that have struck five-ounce silver bullion coins.

2. In addition to America the Beautiful silver bullion coins, the new subscription program discounted Proof sets, Silver Proof sets, Proof and Burnished (Uncirculated) American Silver Eagles, Presidential dollar Proof and Uncirculated sets, America the Beautiful (ATB) quarters Proof sets, ATB quarters Silver Proof sets, ATB quarters Circulation Coin sets, ATB three-coin sets, and American Presidency $1 Coin Covers.

3. Although the discount was ended, collectors can still subscribe and get the convenience of automatic shipments through the U.S. Mint "Product Enrollment Program." According to the Mint: "This program is structured much like a magazine subscription. Sign up once and we will send your chosen Product Enrollment to you as it becomes available. After you

sign up, you will receive the next product released in the series, and continue to receive products until you cancel. You can cancel at any time with no penalty, and even pause your enrollment if you would like to skip products." More information is online at catalog.usmint.gov/shop/product-enrollments.

4. Falk, Connor. "Loyal buyers buoy 5-ounce silver coin series," *Numismatic News*, September 18, 2014.

5. McKeon, Aaron J. *America's Beautiful National Parks: A Handbook for Collecting the New National Park Quarters*, p. 12.

6. U.S. Mint, press release of January 25, 2011.

7. U.S. Mint, press release of October 20, 2011.

8. McKeon, Aaron J. *America's Beautiful National Parks*, p. 24.

9. U.S. Mint, press release of August 30, 2011.

10. McKeon, Aaron J. *America's Beautiful National Parks*, p. 40.

11. Bowers, Q. David. *Coins and Collectors: Golden Anniversary Edition*, pp. 317–318. Note that Hemphill's description is for the creation of hubs and dies for a quarter dollar. The process to create the larger America the Beautiful silver coins is different (with the design being CNC-cut directly into the die steel, without a hub).

12. "US Mint Sales Report: White Mountains Five Ounce Silver Coins Sold Out," CoinUpdate.com, October 15, 2013.

13. McKeon, Aaron J. *America's Beautiful National Parks*, p. 54.

14. U.S. Mint, "Bombay Hook National Wildlife Refuge."

## Chapter 8

1. Moy, Edmund C. *American Gold and Platinum Eagles*, p. 193. Four versions of the Saint-Gaudens $20 gold piece were created in 1907. The first was the size of a standard double eagle, 34 mm in diameter, struck in ultra-high relief with the date in Roman numerals. An estimated 16 to 22 of these coins were produced before it was determined that the minting process was too strenuous for mass production. Today most of the Ultra High Relief coins are in private collections. A second version with similar design elements and ultra-high relief was minted on a gold blank of 27 mm diameter, about twice as thick as a $10 gold piece. Two of these are still known to exist, in the Smithsonian's National Numismatic Collection. The third version returned to the standard diameter of 34 mm. The design remained similar but was executed in high relief, rather than ultra-high relief. Some 12,000 of these coins were minted and issued into circulation. The fourth and final version, which began mintage at the end of 1907, had an even more lowered relief, and the Roman numerals (MCMVII) were replaced with Arabic numerals (1907). These low-relief coins were produced in mass quantities for circulation from late 1907 through 1933.

2. Quoted in Judd, *United States Pattern Coins*, 10th edition, p. 267.

3. "Temperature Check: 2009 Ultra High Reliefs (UHR)," Collectors Universe Message Board, February 19, 2012.

4. Correspondence with the author.

5. "Gold 50th Anniversary 2014 Kennedy half dollars draw crowds: Top 10 Stories of 2014," *Coin World*, December 31, 2014.

6. U.S. Mint press release, "United States Mint Set to Release American Liberty High Relief Gold Coin on July 30," July 16, 2015.

7. Dunn, Catherine. "Heroes of the Fortune 500," *Fortune*, 2014.

9. U.S. Mint press release, "2015 American Liberty High Relief Gold Coin: The Artists Behind the Designs," July 15, 2015.

10. U.S. Mint press release, "Mint Technical Staff Aids Development of 2015 American Liberty High Relief Gold Coin," July 22, 2015.

## Chapter 9

1. Smith, Pete. *Laws of the U.S. Congress Authorizing Medals*, p. 1.

2. Jaeger, Katherine. *A Guide Book of United States Tokens and Medals*, p. 124.

3. Dean, John T. *National Commemorative Medals of the United States: An Illustrated Catalog*, p. viii.

4. The Mint created many interesting bronze medals, as well, but only the gold and silver pieces fall within the scope of this book.

5. Dean, pp. 61–62.

6. Costanzo, Michael B. "American Revolution Bicentennial Medals," *The Numismatist*, July 2015, pp. 30–43.

7. Ganz, David L. "Right to own gold due to Phil Crane," *Numismatic News*, November 20, 2014.

8. Costanzo.

# Glossary

**alloy**—A combination of two or more metals.

**blank**—The formed piece of metal on which a coin or medal design will be stamped.

**bullion**—Uncoined gold or silver in the form of bars, ingots, or plate. Also, a term to describe precious-metal coins or medals created for investment rather than as numismatic collectibles.

**certified coin**—A coin that has been graded, authenticated, and encapsulated by a professional independent (neither buyer nor seller) grading service.

**cherrypick**—To search through an inventory of coins or medals to find uncommon varieties, or to find higher-than-average-quality pieces, that are available for regular price.

**circulation strike**—A coin intended to eventually be used in commerce, as opposed to a numismatic collectible such as a Proof or Burnished specimen.

**Citizens Coinage Advisory Committee**—An 11-member body established by Congress in 2003 to advise the secretary of the Treasury on the themes and designs of all U.S. coins and medals. The CCAC meets several times per year, sometimes at U.S. Mint headquarters in Washington, DC, and often in public venues such as the annual American Numismatic Association World's Fair of Money. It serves as an informed, experienced, and impartial resource to the Treasury secretary and represents the interests of American citizens and collectors.

**collar**—The outer ring, or die chamber, that holds a planchet in place in the coinage press while the planchet is impressed by the obverse and reverse dies, creating a coin or medal.

**Commission of Fine Arts**—An independent federal agency established by Congress in 1910 and charged with giving expert advice to the president, Congress, and the federal and District of Columbia governments on matters of design and aesthetics regarding federal interests and the dignity of the nation's capital. The commission's seven members are presidentially appointed experts in art, architecture, and urban design. The CFA reviews designs proposed for memorials, coins, medals, and new or renovated government buildings, as well as privately owned properties in certain areas of Washington.

**designer**—The artist who creates a coin's or medal's design. The designer might or might not also be its engraver.

**die**—A piece of metal, usually of specially prepared steel, engraved with the incuse mirror image of a coinage design and used for stamping coins or medals.

**double eagle**—The U.S. $20 gold coin.

**eagle**—The U.S. $10 gold coin. Also refers to the U.S. silver and gold bullion coins made from 1986 to date, and platinum bullion coins made from 1997 to date.

**edge**—The periphery of a coin or medal, often bearing reeding, lettering, or other decoration.

**encapsulated coin**—A coin that has been authenticated, graded, and sealed in plastic ("slabbed") by a professional grading service.

**engraver**—The person who engraves or sculpts a model for use in translating a design to a coinage die.

**sculptor**—Another term for *engraver*.

**exergue**—The portion of a coin or medal beneath its main design, often separated from it by a line, and typically bearing the date.

**field**—The background portion of a coin or medal's surface not used for a design or inscription.

**fineness**—The purity of gold, silver, or any other precious metal, expressed in terms of one thousand parts. A coin of 90 percent pure silver is expressed as .900 fine.

**hub**—A positive-image punch used to impress a coin's design, incuse and in reverse, into a die for coinage.

**incuse**—Impressed below a surface.

**inscription**—A legend or lettering on a coin or medal.

**intrinsic value**—The bullion or "melt" value of a precious-metal coin or medal.

**legal tender**—Money that is officially issued and recognized for redemption by an authorized agency or government.

**legend**—The principal inscription on a coin or medal.

**mintmark**—A small letter or other particular mark on a coin or medal, indicating the mint at which it was struck.

**mule**—A coin or medal struck from two dies not originally intended to be used together.

**obverse**—The front or face side of a coin or medal.

**pattern**—An experimental or trial coin, generally struck to test a new design, denomination, planchet size, or alloy.

**planchet**—The blank piece of metal upon which a coin or medal is stamped.

**Proof**—A coin or medal created by a method of manufacture that uses specially polished dies and planchets, high-pressure stamping, and, often, multiple impressions of the die.

**Red Book**—The popular nickname of the *Guide Book of United States Coins*, published since 1946 and so called because of its traditionally red cover.

**reeded edge**—The edge of a coin or medal with grooved lines that run vertically around its perimeter.

**registry set**—A collection of coins or medals assembled in competition with other collectors who seek to have the most complete and finest collection of the same type. Registry sets are sponsored by the major third-party grading firms, NGC and PCGS.

**relief**—Any part of a coin's or medal's design that is raised above its field.

**reverse**—The back side of a coin.

**slab**—A hard plastic case containing a coin or medal that has been authenticated, graded, and encapsulated by a professional third-party grading firm.

**spot price**—The daily quoted market value of a precious metal in bullion form.

**third-party**—An adjective describing a professional grading firm that is neither the buyer nor the seller of the item being graded. The firm's independence removes any conflict of interest in determining the grade.

**Uncirculated**—The U.S. Mint's designation for numismatic (collectible) coins and medals struck from specially burnished planchets. Called *Burnished* in this book and other Whitman Publishing references in order to distinguish the term from "Uncirculated" in the grading sense (meaning Mint State).

# Selected Bibliography

Bowers, Q. David. *Coins and Collectors: Golden Anniversary Edition*, Whitman Publishing, Atlanta, Georgia, 2014.

———. *Commemorative Coins of the United States: A Complete Encyclopedia*, Bowers and Merena Galleries, Wolfeboro, New Hampshire, 1991.

———. *The Expert's Guide to Collecting and Investing in Rare Coins*, Whitman Publishing, Atlanta, Georgia, 2006.

———. *A Guide Book of Double Eagle Gold Coins*, Whitman Publishing, Atlanta, Georgia, 2006.

———. *A Guide Book of Mercury Dimes, Standing Liberty Quarters, and Liberty Walking Half Dollars*, Whitman Publishing, Atlanta, Georgia, 2015.

———. *Obsolete Paper Money Issued by Banks in the United States, 1782 to 1866*, Whitman Publishing, Atlanta, Georgia, 2006.

Bressett, Kenneth. *Milestone Coins: A Pageant of the World's Most Significant and Popular Money*, Whitman Publishing, Atlanta, Georgia, 2007.

Carothers, Neil. *Fractional Money*, J. Wiley & Sons, New York, 1930.

Crosby, Sylvester. *The Early Coins of America, and the Laws Governing Their Issue*, published by the author, Boston, 1875.

Dean, John T. *National Commemorative Medals of the United States Mint*, second edition, 2012.

Dole, Charles Fletcher. *The American Citizen*, D.C. Heath & Co., Boston, 1892.

Doty, Richard. *America's Money, America's Story*, Whitman Publishing, Atlanta, Georgia, 2008.

Forsyth, William. *Essays Critical and Narrative*, Longmans, Green, and Co., London, 1874.

Goldberg, Ira, and Lawrence Goldberg, editors. *Money of the World: Coins That Made History*, Whitman Publishing, Atlanta, Georgia, 2007.

Guth, Ron. *100 Greatest Women on Coins*, Whitman Publishing, Atlanta, Georgia, 2015.

Haxby, James A. *A Guide Book of Canadian Coins and Tokens*, Whitman Publishing, Atlanta, Georgia, 2012.

Jaeger, Katherine. *A Guide Book of United States Tokens and Medals*, Whitman Publishing, Atlanta, Georgia, 2008.

Jordan, Eric, and John Maben. *Top 50 Most Popular Modern Coins*, Krause Publications, Iola, Wisconsin, 2012.

Judd, J. Hewitt. *United States Pattern Coins*, 10th edition, Whitman Publishing, Atlanta, Georgia, 2009.

Julian, R.W. *Medals of the United States Mint: The First Century, 1792–1892*, Token and Medal Society, El Cajon, California, 1977.

Leonard, Robert D. *Curious Currency: The Story of Money From the Stone Age to the Internet Age*, Whitman Publishing, Atlanta, Georgia, 2010.

Loubat, J.F. *The Medallic History of the United States of America, 1776–1876*, published by the author, New York, 1878.

Macy, Jesse. *Our Government, How it Grew, What it Does, and How it Does It*, Ginn and Company, Boston, 1890.

McKeon, Aaron J. *America's Beautiful National Parks: A Handbook for Collecting the New National Park Quarters*, Whitman Publishing, Atlanta, Georgia, 2011.

Mercanti, John, with Michael Standish. *American Silver Eagles: A Guide to the U.S. Bullion Coin Program*, Whitman Publishing, Atlanta, Georgia, 2013.

Moy, Edmund C. *American Gold and Platinum Eagles: A Guide to the U.S. Bullion Coin Programs*, Whitman Publishing, Atlanta, Georgia, 2013.

Newman, Eric P. *Early Paper Money of America*, fifth edition, Krause Publications, Iola, Wisconsin, 2008.

Orosz, Joel J., and Leonard D. Augsburger. *The Secret History of the First U.S. Mint: How Frank H. Stewart Destroyed—And Then Saved—A National Treasure*, Whitman Publishing, Atlanta, Georgia, 2011.

Peffer, William Alfred. *The Farmer's Side: His Troubles and Their Remedy*, D. Appleton and Co., New York, 1891.

Phillips, Henry. *Historical Sketches of the Paper Currency of the American Colonies, Prior to the Adoption of the Federal Constitution*, W.E. Woodward, Roxbury, Massachusetts, 1865.

Schechter, Scott, and Jeff Garrett. *100 Greatest U.S. Modern Coins*, third edition, Whitman Publishing, Atlanta, Georgia, 2013.

Smith, Pete. *Laws of the U.S. Congress Authorizing Medals*, 1998.

Sumner, William Graham. *A History of American Currency, with Chapters on the English Bank Restriction and Austrian Paper Money, to which is appended "The Bullion Report,"* Henry Holt and Company, New York, 1878.

Vermeule, Cornelius. *Numismatic Art in America*, second edition, Whitman Publishing, Atlanta, Georgia, 2007.

Wright, Robert E. *The First Wall Street: Chestnut Street, Philadelphia, and the Birth of American Finance*, University of Chicago Press, Chicago, 2005.

# Credits and Acknowledgments

A book of this scope doesn't happen overnight and it can't make the long journey from early concepts to press without the help of many people and organizations. In alphabetical order I'd like to gratefully thank the following—and apologize for the oversight if anyone was accidentally left out.

At the **American Numismatic Association**, **Barbara Gregory** and **Jerri C. Raitz** (Editor-in-Chief and Senior Editor of *The Numismatist*, monthly magazine of the ANA), along with **Rob Kelley** (ANA Museum Specialist and Photography Director), helped with photograph research and provided historical images, while **Susan McMillan**, Education Project Manager, coordinated ANA presentations that allowed me to meet with other collectors and researchers.

The Honorable **Stephen T. Ayers**, Architect of the U.S. Capitol, assisted with historical images. **Allegra K. Boverman** provided photographs of White Mountain National Forest. Coin dealer **Andrew Bowers** shared insight into the modern bullion market. Numismatic historian **Q. David Bowers** reviewed the manuscript, was a constant source of guidance and inspiration, and graciously wrote this book's foreword. **Kenneth Bressett**, senior editor of the *Guide Book of United States Coins*, provided vital review and feedback on chapters 1, 2, and 3 in particular, and shared recollections of the U.S. Assay Commission and other information. The **British Geological Survey** was a source of data relating to worldwide silver- and gold-mining production. Numismatic historian **Tom DeLorey** shared insight and recollections of the American Arts gold medallion program, and provided photographs. **Connor Falk** shared information from his work in *Numismatic News*. Coin dealer and current ANA president **Jeff Garrett** advised on the modern coin market. Numismatic columnist **Louis Golino** provided encouragement and information. The Honorable **Karen L. Haas**, Clerk of the U.S. House of Representatives, provided an image. **Dave Harper**, editor of *Numismatic News*, gave permission to extract from the newspaper. Coin dealer and bullion specialist **Patrick Heller** shared insight on the American Arts gold medallions. **Heritage Auction Galleries** shared historical and coin images. **Wayne Homren**, *The E-Sylum*, facilitated research. **Joel Iskowitz** discussed his First Spouse coinage designs. **Charla S. Kucko**, Simon Business School, University of Rochester, assisted with research and provided an image. The **Library of Congress** provided numerous historical images. **Littleton Coin Company** provided various photographs. Coin dealer **Harry Miller** shared reflections on the modern coin market. Numismatist **Michael Moran** contributed observations on various topics. **Edmund C. Moy**, 38th director of the U.S. Mint, shared memories and behind-the-scenes insight into the modern Mint. Certain images, of various coins previously published in Whitman books, are by numismatic photographer **Tom Mulvaney**. Coin dealer **Richard Nachbar** shared insight on the American Bicentennial gold medals. **Numismatic Guaranty Corporation of America (NGC)** opened its image archives and also provided certified-population data. **John Pack**, Executive Director of Consignments at Stack's Bowers Galleries, shared his knowledge of the coin market. **Professional Coin Grading Service (PCGS)** provided information and data. The **Peterson Institute for International Economics**, Washington, DC, offered assistance. Treasurer of the United States **Rosie Rios** facilitated research. **Alexander R. Santos** provided invaluable support and encouragement. The **Securities and Exchange Commission** shared advice on investment in silver and gold. **Jeff Shevlin** discussed national medals struck by the Philadelphia Mint. Numismatic historian **Pete Smith** shared research on the national medals of the U.S. Mint. **Max Spiegel**, vice president of sales and marketing for NGC, assisted with information and coin images. **Stack's Bowers Galleries** provided some images. **David Sundman** of Littleton Coin Company shared insight on various aspects of numismatics. American popular-culture historian **Gerry Szymanski** reviewed various sections of the manuscript. Numismatist **Troy Thoreson** advised on the secondary market for gold and silver bullion coins. Officers, staff, and employees of the **United States Mint** (see below for a detailed listing) shared information and resources including historical photographs, coin images, data, personal knowledge, and perspective. Coin dealer **Rodger Virtue** contributed images of the American Arts gold medallion packaging. Coin dealer **Fred Weinberg** shared insight on the American Arts medallions. **Stephanie Westover** assisted with certain images.

At the Washington, DC, headquarters of the U.S. Mint, the following people and their teams were very helpful: **Dave Croft**, Associate Director for Manufacturing; **Judy Dixon**, Office of the Director; **Carolyn Fields**, Corporate Communications; **Abby Gilbert**, Assistant Historian; **Robert Goler**, Curator; **Maria Goodwin**, Historian; **Rhett Jeppson**, Principal Deputy Director; **Tom Jurkowsky**, Director, Office of Corporate Communications; **Mary Lhotsky**, Deputy Associate Director, Numismatics and Bullion; **William Norton Jr.**, Director, Legislative and Intergovernmental Affairs; **Dennis O'Connor**, Headquarters Chief of U.S. Mint Police; **Richard A. Peterson**, Deputy Director; **Heather Sabharwal**, Corporate Communications; **Tracy Scelzo**, Corporate Communications; **Lateefah Simms**, Corporate Communications; **April Stafford**, Division Manager, Design Management; **Adam Stump**, Deputy Director, Corporate Communications; **Greg Weinman**, Senior Legal Counsel; and **Michael White**, Corporate Communications.

At the Philadelphia Mint: thanks to **Don Everhart**, Sculptor-Engraver; **Michael Gaudioso**, Medallic Sculptor; **Renata Gordon**, Medallic Sculptor; **Tim Grant**, Exhibits Division; **Phebe Hemphill**, Medallic Sculptor; **Steve Kunderewicz**, Deputy Plant Manager (now retired); **Marc Landry**, Plant Manager; **Jim Licaretz**, Medallic Sculptor; **Joseph F. Menna**, Medallic Sculptor; and **Charles L. Vickers**, Sculptor-Engraver. Thanks to the Philadelphia Mint Design and Engraving Division (**Stacy Kelley**, Division Chief; **Steve Antonucci**, **John McGraw**, **Eric Custer**,

Jay Kushwara, and **Jerry Burdsall** [retired]); the Die Manufacturing Division (**Dave Puglia**, Division Chief; **Brian Cassidy**, **Thomas Larizzio**, **Dallas Williams**, **Doug Wiggins**, and **Gwenevere Holiman**); the Numismatics Division (**Paul Zwizanski**, **Stan Ostaszewski**, **Chris Luberski**, **Larry Hoffman**, **Chrystal Jones**, and **Joyce Williams**); the Coin Manufacturing Division (**Joe Falls**, **Frank Perkins Jr.**, and **Matt McComb**); the Protection Division (**Robert Bankhead**, **Tanya Washington**, and **Nancy Filoon**); and to **Anthony Mallamaci**, Facility Management Division.

At the West Point Mint: thanks to **Jennifer Butkus**, Production Manager; **Luigi DiCocco**, Chief Engineer; **Tom DiNardi**, Deputy Plant Manager; **William Giraud**, Acting Division Chief, Plant Engineering; Jeanette Grogan, Assayer/Chemist; and **Ellen McCullom**, Plant Manager.

At the Denver Mint, thanks to **Rebecca Barnstein**, Public Affairs; **Patrick H. Brown**, Visual Information Specialist; **Jennifer H. DeBroekert**, Public Affairs; **Tom Fesing**, Public Affairs; **Gary Hall**, Chief of Die Manufacturing; **Laurie Johnson**, Acting Deputy Plant Manager; and **Randy Johnson**, Plant Manager.

At the San Francisco Mint, thanks to **Monica Barnes**, Coining Division; **Lynn Black**, Office of the Plant Manager; **Loretta** Dickerson, Quality Assurance Division; **Carlos Dumpit**, Manufacturing Department; **Larry Eckerman**, Plant Manager (now retired); **Ralph Hodge**, Coining Division; **Dawn Hoef**, Office of the Plant Manager; **Dave Jacobs**, Plant Manager; **Tonya Jones**, Packaging Division; **Michael Levin**, Inventory Manager (and de facto historian); **Paul Lewis**, Industrial Manager; **Lynn Lobb**, Coining Division; **Don Penning**, Packaging Division; and **Joe Vasquez**, Manufacturing Department.

The writings of **Richard G. Doty**, **Robert Wilson Hoge**, **Ana Lonngi de Vagi**, **Bruce Lorich**, **Michael J. Shubin**, and **David L. Vagi** were particularly helpful in understanding the global significance of silver and gold, especially in coinage but also in relationship to mercantilism, war, and trade, going back to Antiquity and covering ancient Greece and Rome, the Middle Ages, the Age of Reason, the New World from the 1500s to the formative years of the United States, and to the end of World War I.

In chapter 2, parts of the discussion of American money in the Civil War are adapted from "Look Closer—That's Not a Cent: Civil War Tokens Tell the Story of America in the 1860s," by Q. David Bowers and Dennis Tucker, *COINage* Magazine, April 2014.

# Image Credits and Notations

The frontispiece portrait of Mark Twain, original copyright A.F. Bradley, New York (1907), is courtesy of the **Library of Congress**. On page vi, the photograph of White Mountain National Forest is by **Allegra K. Boverman**.

In chapter 1, the chapter-opener image of Charlie Chaplin's *Gold Rush* is courtesy of **Heritage Auctions**. On page 2, the images of Ionian electrum coins are from **Kenneth Bressett**'s *Milestone Coins: A Pageant of the World's Most Significant and Popular Money*. On page 3, the photograph of the treasure of the SS *Central America* is by **Henry Groskinsky**, from the LIFE Images Collection, courtesy of Getty Images. On pages 4 and 5, the photographs of natural gold and silver are courtesy of **Stack's Bowers Galleries**. On page 5, the photograph of the Georgia State Capitol "Gold Dome" is by **Brent Cook**. On page 7, the Waltham gold pocket watch is courtesy of **Heritage Auctions**. On page 10, the stained-glass panel is from the numismatic display of the **Museo Nazionale Romano**, Palazzo Massimo alle Terme, in Rome, Italy. On page 11, the portrait of Kaiser Wilhelm II is by **Reichard & Lindner, Berlin**, from the author's collection. On page 13, the image of devils pouring gold coins from a man's hat into a woman's apron and a boy's hat is courtesy of the **Library of Congress Prints and Photographs Division** (original copyright Warren, Johnson & Co. Designers, Engravers and Printers, Buffalo, circa 1870).

In chapter 2, the chapter-opener image is courtesy of **Heritage Auctions**. On page 17, the oil painting *Embarkation of the Pilgrims*, by Robert Walter Weir, 1857, is from the American Art Collection of the **Brooklyn Museum**, A. Augustus Healy Fund and Healy Purchase Fund B. On page 18, the wampum beads are from the collection of the **American Numismatic Association**; the *Puck* illustration "Christmas Marketing Before the Days of 'The High Cost of Living'" (original copyright 1913 Keppler & Schwarz-

mann) is courtesy of the **Library of Congress**. On page 20, the 1885 photograph of Chah is by Ben Wittick, courtesy of the **Library of Congress**. On page 25, the engraving of the celebrated Ceylonese/Dutch performing elephant Hansken (1630–1655) is part of a larger engraving that resides in the **Rijksprentenkabinet**, Amsterdam, the Netherlands. On page 25, the painted engraving of a rose is by **Pierre-Joseph Redouté**, 1824, originally published in *Les Roses*; it is not actually an American rose, but a French one. On page 30, the image of Revolutionary War soldiers is from a painting by Henry Alexander Ogden, first published by the **Office of the U.S. Army Quartermaster General**, 1890. On page 36, Allyn Cox's *The Constitutional Convention, 1787*, a mural depicting Alexander Hamilton, James Wilson, James Madison, and Benjamin Franklin meeting in Franklin's garden, is courtesy of the **Architect of the Capitol**. On page 37, Howard Chandler Christy's *Signing of the Constitution*, which is displayed in the east grand stairway of the House wing of the U.S. Capitol, is courtesy of the Architect of the Capitol; the portrait of Thomas Jefferson is from the **Bureau of Engraving and Printing**; and *George Washington—The Constable/Hamilton Portrait*, 1797, hangs in the **Crystal Bridges Museum of American Art**. On page 51, the photograph of a Kentucky coin shop is courtesy of **Jeff Garrett**.

In chapter 3, the chapter-opener portrait of Helen Hayes is by **Clarence Sinclair Bull** for Metro-Goldwyn-Mayer. On page 55, **John Ruberry** gave permission to use the 1970 photograph of Adlai Stevenson III, from his father's collection; the uncropped original shows Stevenson with longtime Cook County assessor Patrick J. Cullerton in the Bismarck Hotel's Walnut Room, when Stevenson was running for U.S. Senate. On page 55, the portrait of Richard Lugar is courtesy of the **Universidad de Alcalá, Biblioteca, Colecciones Especiales**. On page 56, the 1955 portrait of Arthur Burns as economic advisor to President Dwight Eisenhower is courtesy of the **United States Army**. On page 58, the circa-1981 portrait of Jesse Helms, which reposes in the Special Collections Research Center at North Carolina State University Libraries, is courtesy of **NCSU Libraries' Digital Collections: Rare and Unique Materials**. On page 60, the portrait of William E. Simon is courtesy of the **Simon Business School, University of Rochester**. On page 62, artist **Everett Raymond Kinstler** granted permission to reproduce his oil-painting portrait of Treasury Secretary Michael Blumenthal; the photograph is courtesy of the **U.S. Mint**. On page 63, the portrait of S.I. Hayakawa is from the **Hayakawa Family Archives**. On page 69, the anti-apartheid pamphlet cover is from the **American Committee on Africa**. On page 73, the painting *James Albert Smith Leach*, oil on panel, by Michael D. Roberts (2002), is from the **Collection of the U.S. House of Representatives**. On pages 84 and 92, the photograph portraits of Marian Anderson and Willa Cather are from the **Library of Congress**, Prints and Photographs Division, Van Vechten Collection. On page 87, the portrait of Stella Hackel Sims is courtesy of the **Office of the Secretary of State, Vermont**, from the *Vermont Legislative Directory and State Manual, 1975 to 1976*. On page 88, the photograph of the U.S. Mint engraving staff is courtesy of **John M. Mercanti**. On page 93, the portrait of Willa Cather as a girl is from the Judith Kaplan Women's History Collection, courtesy of **Heritage Auctions**. On page 97, the portrait of Louis Armstrong is from the *New York World-Telegram and Sun*, courtesy of the Library of Congress; the photograph of the Selmer trumpet, which resides in the Satchmo Collection of the Louis Armstrong House Museum, Queens, New York, is credited to **Joe Mabel**. On page 98, the portrait of Frank Lloyd Wright, by *New York World-Telegram and Sun* staff photographer **Al Ravenna**, is from the Library of Congress, Prints and Photographs Division. On page 99, the exterior photograph of Fallingwater is by **Daderot**. On page 105, the 85th-birthday portrait of Robert Frost is by **Walter Albertin**, photographer for the *New York World-Telegram and Sun*; courtesy of the Library of Congress; the Karsh print is courtesy of **Heritage Auctions**. On page 106, the portrait of Alexander Calder is courtesy of the **Calder Foundation** (www.calder.org). On page 110, the portrait of Helen Hayes is from the Library of Congress, **George Grantham Bain Collection**. On page 116, the September 28, 1966, portrait of Arthur Miller is by **Eric Koch**, courtesy of the **Dutch National Archives, The Hague, Fotocollectie Algemeen Nederlands Persbureau**; the November 1946 portrait of Ella Fitzgerald is by **William P. Gottlieb**, courtesy of the Library of Congress; the portrait of George Gershwin is by the **Bain News Service**, courtesy of the Library of Congress; the September 7, 1962, portrait of Aaron Copland is from the **CBS Television Network**, for "Opening Night at Lincoln Center"; the portrait of Thomas Hart Benton in the north lobby of the Harry S. Truman Library, Independence, Missouri, circa 1957, is by **Paul Renshaw**, *Independence Examiner*, courtesy of the **Harry S. Truman Library & Museum**; the circa-1900 portrait of Charles Marion Russell, from the Charles Scribner's Sons Art Reference Department Records, is courtesy of the **Archives of American Art**. On page 117, the 1950 portrait of Georgia O'Keeffe is by **Carl Van Vechten**; the portrait of I.M. Pei, circa 1967, is originally from **I.M. Pei and Partners**; the portrait of

Ernest Hemingway is courtesy of the **National Portrait Gallery**; the White House copy of John Syme's 1826 painting of John James Audubon is courtesy of the **White House Historical Association**; the portrait of Bix Beiderbecke is courtesy of the **National Portrait Gallery**; the June 18, 1856, daguerreotype of Henry David Thoreau, by **Benjamin D. Maxham**, is courtesy of the **National Portrait Gallery**; the 1926 portrait of Paul Robeson is originally from the **Otto Bettmann** archive.

In chapter 4, the chapter-opener photograph of an American bald eagle is by **Ferenc Cegledi**.

In chapter 5, the chapter-opener photograph of an American bison is by **Ricardo Reitmeyer**. On page 128, the photographs of assay gold and Reverse Proof coins are by **Scott Eells / Bloomberg**, via Getty Images.

In chapter 6, the chapter-opener photograph, taken in the East Room of the White House, November 19, 2007, is by **Chip Somodevilla**, courtesy of Getty Images. Most of the chapter's portraits of the First Ladies are from the Library of Congress and the Whitman Publishing image archives. On page 159, the photograph of Joel Iskowitz and Carolyn Maloney is by **Tom Williams**, courtesy of Getty Images. On page 170, the portrait of Dolley Madison, 1804, by **Gilbert Stuart**, is courtesy of the **White House Historical Association** (gift of the Walter H. and Phyllis J. Shorenstein Foundation in memory of Phyllis J. Shorenstein, 1994). On pages 203, the portrait of Caroline Harrison, by **Lawrence Williams**, is courtesy of **Heritage Auctions**. On page 226, the portrait of Lady Bird Johnson is by **Aaron Shikler**, courtesy of the **National Archives and Records Administration**.

In chapter 7, the chapter-opener photograph of a ram in the Grand Canyon is by **James Marvin Phelps**. On pages 233, 234, 235, and 236, the photographs of State quarter launch ceremonies are courtesy of the **U.S. Mint**. On page 248, the photograph of the Great Sand Dunes is by **Daniel Gross**. On page 249, the photographs of Hawai'i Volcanoes National Park and Mount Rushmore are by **S. Geiger** (National Park Service) and **Dean Franklin**, respectively. On page 258, the photograph of the 1st Massachusetts Monument at Gettysburg is by **Steven C. Berger**. On pages 263 and 264, the photographs of a coquí llanero and a Puerto Rican parrot are courtesy of the **U.S. Fish and Wildlife Service**. On page 270, the photographs of White Mountain National Forest are by **Allegra K. Boverman**. On page 275, the photograph of Great Smoky Mountains National Park is by **Dean Fikar**. On page 276, 282, and 286, the park photographs are courtesy of the **National Park Service**.

In chapter 8, the chapter-opener photograph is from the author's collection.

In chapter 9, the chapter-opener photograph is by **Justin Sullivan**, taken May 18, 2012, courtesy of Getty Images. On page 302, the photograph of Nellie Tayloe Ross is by **Marie Hansen**, from the LIFE Picture Collection, courtesy of Getty Images. On page 303, the photographs of Clifford Northrup and Donald Scarinci are by **Andrew Harrer**, Bloomberg, via Getty Images. On page 304, the photographs of production of the September 11 medals are by **Justin Sullivan**, courtesy of Getty Images.

In appendix B, the photographs of U.S. Assay Commission medals are courtesy of **Stack's Bowers Galleries**.

# About the Author

Dennis Tucker is an award-winning numismatic researcher who has written and lectured nationwide on coins, medals, and other antiques and collectibles. A collector since the age of seven, he is a Life Member of the American Numismatic Association and a past governor of the Token and Medal Society. His writing has appeared in *The Numismatist*; *Coin World*; *Numismatic News*; *COINage*; *Coins Magazine*; *Postcard World*; the journals of the Token and Medal Society, the Civil War Token Society, the Barber Coin Collectors Society, and the Numismatic Bibliomania Society; and other hobby periodicals. He has earned the Extraordinary Merit Award from the Numismatic Literary Guild; the Forrest Daniel Award for Literary Excellence from the Society of Paper Money Collectors; the silver medal of the Original Hobo Nickel Society; and the Gloria Peters Literary Award from Women in Numismatics.

As publisher at Whitman Publishing he specializes in books on numismatics (the study of money), banking and financial history, the American presidency, U.S. political and military history, and other nonfiction topics.

Tucker grew up in Phoenix, New York, earned a degree in political science from the University of Rochester, and started his career in corporate and nonprofit communications and publishing in that city. He moved to Georgia in 2002 and now lives with his family in Atlanta. He was honored in January 2015 by Governor Nathan Deal for his career in book publishing and his promotion of the state's history.

# Index